The Only

BABY NAME BOOK

You'll Ever Need

The Only
BABY
NAME
BOOK
You'll Ever Need

6,000 names for your soon-to-be-famous child

Heidi Overhill
Illustrations by Anthony Jenkins

KEY PORTER BOOKS

Cataloguing in Publication Data

Overhill, Heidi
    The only baby name book you'll ever need : 6,000 names for your soon-to-be-famous child

ISBN 1-55013-754-9

1. Names – Personal – Dictionaries.   I. Title.

CS2377.084   1996   929.4'4 03   C96-930922-8

The publisher gratefully acknowledges the assistance of the Canada Council and the Ontario Arts Council.

Key Porter Books Limited
70 The Esplanade
Toronto, Ontario
Canada M5E 1R2

Design: Leah Gryfe
Electronic Formatting: Heidi Palfrey

Printed and bound in Canada

96 97 98 99 6 5 4 3 2 1

To my husband, Alan Rosenthal,
who had the seminal concept for this book,
and for the baby.

How I Came to Write a Baby-Name Book

Phase 1: Denial

In 1989, just back from a business trip to India, I started to feel tired—*really* tired, with strange stomach gurglings.

"Starting to get old," I told myself. My exercise regimen of lying on the sofa reading novels and eating snacks was starting to show at last. Not in fat, but in this alarming lassitude beyond the reach of the strongest espresso.

I set the alarm clock, struggled out of bed and into a pair of polyester shorts left over from high school, and set off across the park towards the tennis courts at a moderate clip. It almost killed me. I clung to the wire as black spots closed my vision. This was not just passing thirty. I could barely stand up. Something was seriously wrong.

My doctor agreed, and sent me straight to a tropical-disease centre to test for intestinal parasites. I was still testing two weeks later when I stepped out of the shower into my husband's field of vision. He stopped brushing his teeth and eyed me critically.

"Heidi, you're pregnant," he announced.

Phase 2: Anger (or is that mirth?)

Not me! I couldn't be pregnant! I wasn't the pregnant *kind!* I'm not a *mum*, I'm a *professional*. I'm an industrial designer. I own steel-toed boots. And besides, I'm too thin.

The news created a great stir among our relatives. There had been no baby on either side of the family in sixteen years. Grandparents and aunties began rubbing their hands. Photo albums were dusted off, old toys unearthed.

Our friends were more sympathetic. One veteran mum offered a valuable hint on impending motherhood: "When you get home from the hospital, take the baby, stand in front of the mirror looking at yourself holding it, and say out loud, 'I am a MOTHER, I AM a mother.' This will help you get used to the idea so you won't twitch as much when people mention it."

My sister mailed me a *Far Side* cartoon greeting card showing two dogs sitting watching a third dog run through heavy traffic. The caption read: "Hey, Rusty! You've joined the club!"

Phase 3: Bargaining

"How about 'Sascha'?"

"No. My first wife had a cat named Sascha."

"'Sarah'?"

"No. You have an aunt Sarah, remember?"

"So?"

"So it's bad luck to name the baby after someone living."

"No it's not. It's flattery."

"No it isn't! It's an insult!"

"Well, then, that's perfect. My aunt Sarah is bonkers."

"No."

"Of course, she might not realize it's an insult, she might be flattered."

"No. Besides, Mark's daughter Heather says that half of her grade six class is called Sarah. It's too popular."

"Oh, all right. 'Carmen.'"

"My mother had a fit when I suggested 'Carmen.'"

"Why?"

"I don't know. She just went ballistic."

"Hmm. Maybe it's the castanets. You know, the opera *Carmen*."

"Ha ha."

"Well, I give up then. Your turn."

"Hand me that list."

Phase 4: Depression

Typed into the computer, the list of names printed out into a scroll that trailed all the way out of the office, down the stairs, and into the living-room. Not one name was usable.

The problem was they weren't just names. They were brand-names. Liz was not Liza. Liz had violet eyes to die for, while Liza fluttered her green fingernails on her way to the cabaret. Winston, Spike, Dizzy, Clytemnestra—they were all package deals of astonishing precision, capsule predictions of the future destiny of our child.

Everyone could name his or her own famous namesake without hesitation. "Daphne du Maurier," said my mother promptly, "the novelist. *Jamaica Inn*—there's a movie." Aha! Now I knew why my mother, in her wanton bohemian youth, had smoked *du Maurier* brand cigarettes.

There's no escaping a famous namesake. Even if you don't remember, someone else does. When Andy Warhol predicted that everyone would be famous for fifteen minutes, he didn't realize that someone else would remember that moment, and archive it for future generations.

Fame has become a social taste-test. Verbal pop quizzes weed out imposters. Quick, what's the difference between Ginger and Mary Ann on *Gilligan's Island*? What's your favourite of the early Spike Lee films? Is Cal Ripken's batting average up or down? Is Dieter Rams the god of industrial design for Braun or Olivetti? Can you distinguish a Barnett Newman stripe painting from a Guido Molinari stripe painting?

To name our baby, we had to know every pitfall. Consider "Roberto." You take the RO from Roma, the BER from Berlin, and the TO from Tokyo, and there you go: ROBERTO. We could name our baby after the fascist Axis Alliance.

We had to anticipate, too. If little Frank grew up tall, he'd end up racing down the street pursued by packs of classmates shouting "Frank-enstein! Frank-enstein!" In 1954, my friend Charles's parents had thought "Manson" was a perfectly reasonable middle name.

Where was the baby name that admitted we didn't know what we were doing? Where was the name that left something to the imagination?

Trying to name the baby was as painful as getting dressed in the morning—and I couldn't reach my feet anymore without grunting. I still wasn't plump, though. My skinny arms and legs stuck out as usual from behind a vast brand-new belly. I looked like someone trying to shoplift a medicine ball. It was a remarkable effect. Every morning without fail, I came down the stairs and did a double-take in the hall mirror.

"So, what *are* you going to name the baby?" asked a dinner guest. We were plying our visitors with wine and urging them to add to our baby-name list.

I lifted my face out of my jumbo bowl of ice cream and smiled cautiously. "If it's a boy, Noah; if it's a girl, Nora."

"Ah," said the guest, and offered no further comment.

Good.

Phase 5: Acceptance

The baby was born and immediately began to grow. It was like watching the sand blow away from the Sphinx, revealing something that had been there all along. It didn't matter what we'd called her, she was always going to be herself.

I went back to work and it was awful. Then it got worse; I was laid off.

The baby was so patently smug about my being home that I began to suspect she'd had a hand in arranging things; crawling to the phone in her diaper and negotiating to have my contract chosen for downsizing. The truth was, she was better company than my former co-workers: cuter, funnier, and *way* more intelligent.

Baby asleep, laundry drying, and sun flooding the newspapers in the kitchen, I found myself abstractedly jotting down a really good baby name we'd somehow overlooked. Furtively, late at night, I transcribed the new entries into the database. Baby names seemed to be filling the space in my life previously occupied by interoffice memos and five-year budget projections. It was the intellectual equivalent of needle-point, but I was hooked.

How many famous people could there be? Surely there must be an end? I had 4,000 entries, but the list continued to grow, even with only one example for each name. John Lennon? No, John Bunyan. I bought a biographical dictionary, and started reading at page one, cruising history with a pair of nail scissors, on the lookout for baby facts. It was perfect reading for motherhood, because it didn't matter that I got interrupted every three minutes. Each entry was only two minutes long.

It was also soothing. It put my life into perspective. Everything I might do, someone else had already done, bigger and better. I gave money to a beggar at the corner store; Francis of Assisi got stigmata. I ate a box of chocolate raisins; Orson Welles told an interviewer, "Gluttony is not a secret vice." I told a tasteless joke; Nell Gwyn, mistress to Charles II, told a rioting crowd of anti-Catholic protesters, "Pray good people, be civil. I am the Protestant whore."

Somewhere, some time, someone had become famous for everything. Florence Nightingale was famous for nursing the sick, and Lou Gehrig for being sick. Jane Goodall watched chimpanzees, Ronald Reagan hugged Bonzo. Cruising the dictionary, I discovered whole lives spent translating Mesopotamian poets, negotiating Balkan boundaries, introducing modern dance to China. In nineteenth century France, Le Pétomane became rich and famous with a novelty farting act, until the First World War made his grand-finale military gun barrage suddenly seem less amusing.

And then one day a publisher told me—over lunch, fulfilling my every expectation of the world of publishing—that they wanted to publish my œuvre. "We think the baby-name market is stale," they said. "It's ready for something different."

Of course, they didn't want the full 15,000 entries, with *all* of the Greek gods and *everyone* from the Bible merged with Third World dictators, American B-movie stars, and Renaissance architects into a stunning legion of some of the dullest famous people you could possibly imagine. "Paper is so expensive," said the editor tactfully.

I rushed home and phoned my mother to tell her the news.

"Someone's giving you money for the baby names?" said my mother. "Gosh, well, that just goes to show you should never criticize anyone for doing anything."

Aage Aage Bohr *(1922–)*
Danish physicist, winner of the 1975 Nobel Prize for physics. He was born the year that his father, Niels Bohr, also won the Nobel Prize for physics.

Aaron Aaron Burr *(1756–1836)*
American politician. While serving as vice-president in 1804, he fought a regrettably successful duel with Alexander Hamilton.

Abas Abas *trans. lizard*
Mythical son of Greek King Celeus. The goddess Demeter turned him into a lizard for commenting rudely on her slurping.

Abbie Abbie (Abbott) Hoffman *(1936–1989)*
American founding Yippie (Youth International Party member) and one of the "Chicago Seven."

Abby "Dear Abby" *(1956–)*
American newspaper column, written by "Abigail van Buren," real name Mrs. Morton "Popo" Phillips, née Pauline Esther Friedman *(1918–)*.

Abel Abel Bonnard *(1883–1968)*
French poet. He was sentenced to death for being minister of education in the Vichy government, then merely banished.

Abelard Peter Abelard *(1079–1142)*
French theologian castrated by irate relatives of his wife, Éloïse. (The relatives did not know that Abelard and Éloïse had been secretly married.)

Abigail Abigail Adams, *née Smith (1744–1818)*
American political worker, wife of one president and mother of another. She is author of *Remember the Ladies*, a plea written to her husband, John Adams, while he was composing the American Declaration of Independence.
"All Men would be tyrants if they could."

ABRAHAM LINCOLN

Abner *L'il Abner (1934–1977)*
American cartoon strip by Al Capp *(1909–1979)*.

Abraham Abraham Lincoln *(1809–1865)*
American politician and 19th president, "Honest Abe."
"God must have loved the plain people; he made so many of them."

Abram Abram Hoffer *(20th century)*
Canadian psychologist. He coined the word "psychedelic" to describe the effects of LSD.

Absalom Absalom *trans. father of peace, 2 Sam. 114: 25 (c. 11th century B.C.)*
Old Testament handsome son of King David: "From the sole of his foot to the crown of his head there was no blemish in him." His thick hair was his undoing when he led a revolt against his father, as it caught in a bush and left him dangling for soldiers to finish off.

Absolutely Absolutely Nobody *(formerly David Powers) (1956–1993)*
American politician. He changed his name to run for lieutenant-governor, with a campaign pledge to eliminate the position of lieutenant-governor. His slogan was "Hi, I'm Absolutely Nobody. Vote for me." He got 7% of the vote.

Ace *Ace Ventura: Pet Detective (1993)*
American movie starring "postmodern doofus" Jim Carrey.
"Until Ace Ventura, no actor had considered talking through his ass."

Achille Achille Castiglioni *(20th century)*
Italian furniture designer.

Achilles Achilles *trans. lipless*
Legendary Greek warrior, the greatest fighter of the Greeks attacking Troy, who was killed with an arrow in his one vulnerable heel. His mother had given him a magic dip in water to make him invulnerable, but had held on to one heel. The "Achilles tendon" is named after him.

Acker Acker Bilk *(originally Bernard Bilk) (1929–)*
British jazz clarinettist.

Actaeon Actaeon *trans. shore-dweller*
Mythical Greek son of Aristaeus. When he accidentally saw the goddess Artemis naked, she turned him into a stag and had him torn to pieces by his own dogs.

Acton Acton Bell *(pen-name of Anne Brontë)* *(1820–1849)*
English poet and novelist. Her sisters, Emily Jane (*Wuthering Heights*, 1847) and Charlotte (*Jane Eyre*, 1847), wrote under the pen-names Ellis Bell and Currer Bell, respectively.

Ada Ada, Countess of Lovelace, *née Augusta Ada Byron (1815–1852)*
English writer and self-taught mathematician, daughter of the poet Lord Byron, and author of *Sketch of the Analytical Engine* (1843) about Charles Babbage's mechanical computer. A computer language is named "ADA" in her honour.
> *"The Analytical Machine weaves algebraical patterns just as the Jacquard loom weaves flowers and leaves."*

Adah Adah Isaacs Menken, *née Adah Bertha Theodore (c. 1835–1868)*
American actress. Clad in a scanty yellow slip, she rode a stallion up a cardboard mountain on stage in *Mazeppa* (1861). Charles Dickens was among her many admirers.

Adalaide Adalaide Bunker, *née Yates (married 1843)*
American wife of "Siamese twin" Eng Bunker. They had twelve children.

Adam Adam Smith *(1723–1790)*
British philosopher, author of *An Inquiry into the Nature and Causes of the Wealth of Nations* (1776).
> *"People of the same trade seldom meet together, even for merriment and diversion, but the conversation ends in a conspiracy against the public or some contrivance to raise prices."*

Adamnan St. Adamnan *(c. 625–704)*
Irish abbot. He was the first to propose that women and children should not be killed or imprisoned in war, a principle now known as "Adamnan's Law."

Addison Addison Mizner *(1872–1933)*
American architect and New York bon vivant.
> *"Absinthe makes the heart grow fonder."*

Adelaide St. Adelaide *(in German, Adelheid)* *(931–999)*
Holy Roman Empress. Following the death of her husband, Otto the Great, she remained as regent to her son, and then grandson, before retiring to found a convent.

Adele Adele Astaire *(1897–1981)*
American dancer, sister and partner of Fred Astaire.

Adelene Adelene Teo *(20th century)*
Australian ex-wife of Canadian diplomat Edward Cashelman. In 1995, he invoked diplomatic immunity to avoid paying her alimony. He was recalled.

Adelina Adelina Patti *(1843–1919)*
Italian-born British singer, the original "Sweet Adeline."

Adeline Adeline Van Buren *(1894–1949)*
American motorist. In 1916, she and her sister Augusta were the first women to cross the United States on motorcyles, as an unsuccessful publicity stunt to gain acceptance for women in the military during the First World War.

Adelle Adelle Davis *(1904–1974)*
American nutrition writer.

Adeodatus St. Adeodatus I *(or Deusdedit)* *(d. 618)*
Roman-born pope, the first to use lead seals (or "bullae") on papal documents, now known as "bulls."

Adlai Adlai Stevenson *(Adlai Ewing Stevenson)* *(1900–1965)*
American politican and presidential candidate, twice defeated by Dwight David Eisenhower.
> *"An editor is one who separates the wheat from the chaff and publishes the chaff."*

Admetus King Admetus of Crete *trans. untamed*
Legendary Cretan Argonaut. His friend Apollo saved his life once by getting the Three Fates too drunk to remember it was time for his death.

Adnan Adnan Khashoggi *(20th century)*
Apolitical international arms dealer.

Adolf Adolf Hitler *(1889–1945)*
German politician, the 1938 Man of the Year in *Time* magazine.
> *"Anyone who sees and paints a sky green and pastures blue ought to be sterilized."*

Adolfo Adolfo Besciana *(known as Dino Bravo)*
(1949–1993)
Canadian pro wrestler, "the world's strongest
man." He was shot.

Adolph Adolph Eugen Fick *(1829–1901)*
German physiologist. "Fick's Law" of liquids
states that the mass of solute diffusing a unit
area per second is proportional to the concentration gradient.

Adolphe Adolphe Sax *(originally Antoine-Joseph Sax)*
(1814–1894)
Belgian musician and inventor. In 1845, he and
his father patented a valved brass "sax-horn,"
now known as the "saxophone."

Adonis Adonis *trans. lord*
Mythical Greek mortal, the beautiful son of the
incestuous Smyrna. Both Aphrodite and
Persephone vied for his favour until he was
killed by the jealous Ares. The flower anemone
sprang from his blood.

Adrian Adrian Mole *(aged 13¾)*
British hero of Sue Townsend's book *The Secret
Diary of Adrian Mole Aged 13¾* (1982).

Adriana Adriana Caselotti *(20th century)*
American actress. She was the voice of Walt
Disney's Snow White.

Adrienne Adrienne Vittadini *(20th century)*
Budapest-born Italian fashion designer.

Aelius Aelius Donatus *(4th century A.D.)*
Roman grammarian. His books were such standard texts in the Middle Ages that "Donat"
became slang for any book of grammar.

Aeneas Aeneas *trans. praise-worthy*
Legendary Greek hero, son of the
goddess Aphrodite and the
mortal Anchises. He escaped
the fall of Troy and made it to
Rome, breaking Dido's heart
in Carthage along the way.

Aeronwy Aeronwy Thomas-Ellis
(20th century)
British daughter of Dylan
Thomas and his wife, Caitlin.

Aesop Aesop *(working 550 B.C.)*
Greek fable writer.

ADOLF HITLER

"Do not count your chickens before they are
hatched."

Aetna Aetna
Greek nymph. The volcano is named after her.

Afrika Afrika Bambaata *(1958–)*
American dee-jay, a co-creator of hip-hop.

Agamemnon King Agamemnon of Argos and
Mycenae *trans. very resolute*
Legendary Greek commander-in-chief at the
Trojan War. He was murdered by his wife,
Clytemnestra, because he had killed their
daughter Iphigeneia as a sacrifice to the goddess
Artemis.

Agassou Agassou
Dahomey royal panther god.

Agatha Agatha Christie *(Dame Agatha Mary Clarissa
Christie), née Miller, later Lady Mallowan
(1890–1976)*
British queen of the mystery novel, creator of
the intrepid Miss Marple. In 1994, the royalties
on her estate averaged about US$4.25 million.
"I like living. . . just to be alive is a grand thing."

Aglaus Aglaus *trans. splendid*
Legendary poorest man in Arcadia. An oracle
pronounced him happier than his ruler, King
Gyges.

Agnes Agnes De Mille *(1905–1993)*
American dancer, choreographer, and writer,
author of the autobiography *Dance to the Piper*
(1952).
*"The truest expression of a people is in its dances
and its music. . . . Bodies never lie."*

Agnetha Agnetha Fältskog *(1950–)*
Swedish pop singer with the group Abba.

Agnieszka Agnieszka Holland *(1948–)*
Polish-born film director of *The Secret Garden*
(1993).

Agnolo Agnolo di Cosimo di Mariano *(known as Il
Bronzino) (1503–1572)*
Italian Mannerist painter.

Agostino Agostino Ramelli *(c. 1531–c. 1610)*
Italian military engineer, author of *The Various
and Ingenious Machines of Agostino Ramelli*
(1588). None of these machines was ever built.

Agrippina Agrippina the Younger *(c. 15–59)*
Roman schemer. During her third marriage to
her uncle the Emperor Claudius, she persuaded
him to adopt her son Nero as heir, and proceeded
to poison all of Nero's rivals, including finally
Claudius. Then, the new Emperor Nero had her
put to death.

Ahab King Ahab of Israel *trans. father's brother, I
Kings 16: 32 (ruled 874–853 B.C.)*
Old Testament ruler. During his long rule he
consolidated the dynasty and cooperated with
neighbours, but he was the husband of Jezebel,
who promoted worship of her Phoenician gods
Baal and Astarte, greatly alarming the prophet
Elijah.

Ahmad Ahmad Jamal *(1930–)*
American pianist, a "master of jazz," according
to the American National Endowment for the
Arts.

Ahmes Ahmes *(c. 1650 B.C.)*
Egyptian mathematical scribe. His "Rhind
papyris" contain the earliest-known version of
the riddle "As I was going to St. Ives, I met a
man with seven wives. Each wife had seven
sacks, each sack had seven cats, each cat had
seven kits. Kits, cats, sacks and wives, how
many were going to St. Ives?"

Ahmet Ahmet Ertegun *(1924–)*
Turkish-born American record producer, a co-
founder of Atlantic Records and of the
Rock'n'Roll Hall of Fame.

Aïda *Aïda (1871)*
Italian opera by Giuseppe Verdi (1813–1901),
about an Egyptian slave who is really the
daughter of the King of Ethiopia.

Aiken Aiken Drum
Trickster hero of Julian May's novel *The Many-
Coloured Land*.

Ailbhe St. Ailbhe *(or Albeus) (d. c. 526)*
Irish preacher. He was raised by wolves.

Aileen Aileen Riggin *(1906–)*
American swimmer and diver, winner of two
1924 Olympic medals.

Aimable Aimable-Jean-Jacques Pélissier, Duc de
Malakoff *(1794–1864)*
French soldier remembered for suffocating 500
Arabs in caves of the Dahna.

Aimée Aimée Semple McPherson, *née Kennedy
(1890–1944)*
Canadian-born American Pentecostal religious
worker, the self-promoted "World's Most
Pulchritudinous Evangelist." Widowed in
China, she returned to found the International
Church of the Foursquare Gospel in Los
Angeles, with its own temple, radio station,
Bible school, magazine, and social workers.

Aino Aino Marsio *(20th century)*
Finnish wife and partner of architect Alvar
Aalto. "Aino" is a Finnish mythic heroine in the
Kalevala epic.

Aislin Aislin *(pen-name of Terry Mosher) (1942–)*
Canadian editorial cartoonist.

Aissa Aissa Wayne *(1955–)*
American celebrity daughter, author of *John
Wayne, My Father* (1991).

Ajax Ajax *(or Aias) trans. of the earth*
Mythical Greek warrior. Next to Achilles, he was
the bravest of all the Greeks who fought at Troy.

Akhenaton Akhenaton *(originally Amenhotep IV)
(ruled 1353–1335 B.C.)*
Heretic pharaoh of Egypt, husband of Nefertiti
and father-in-law of Tut'ankhamen.

Akio Akio Morita *(1920–)*
Japanese founder of Sony and author of the
autobiography *Made in Japan* (1986).

Akira Akira Kurosawa *(1910–1993)*
Japanese film director, creator of *The Seven
Samurai* (1955), which was remade in America
as *The Magnificent Seven*.

Al Al Jolson *(originally Asa Yoelson) (1886–1950)*
Russian-born American singer, star of the first
talking film, *The Jazz Singer* (July 1929).
"You ain't heard nothin' yet, folks."

Alain Alain LeRoy Locke *(1886–1954)*
American educator, the first black Rhodes
Scholar, author of *The New Negro* (1925), and a
leader of the Harlem Renaissance.

Alak Alak Krishnan *(20th century)*
British unlucky traveller. He lost his luggage nearly every trip until 1995, when he was discovered nesting empty suitcases inside each other at a luggage carousel, and was charged with fraud.

Alan Alan Watts *(1915–1973)*
American philosopher, author of *The Taboo Against Knowing Who You Are.*

Alanis Alanis Obamsawin *(20th century)*
Canadian Mohawk filmmaker whose *Kanesatake: 270 Years of Resistance* (1993) documented the 1990 stand-off between the Canadian army and militant Mohawk forces at Oka, Quebec.

Alannah Alannah Currie *(1959–)*
New Zealand–born rock singer with the group the Thompson Twins.

Alaric Alaric I *(c. 370–410)*
King of the Visigoths. In 410, his troops sacked Rome, with instructions to spare the churches and not rape anyone.

Alastair Alastair Sim *(1900–1976)*
Scottish-born character actor, noted for his film portrayal of the title character in *Scrooge* (1951).

Alban Alban Berg *(1885–1935)*
Austrian composer.

Albert Albert Einstein *(1879–1955)*
Bavarian-born American physicist.
> *"If I would be a young man again and had to decide how to make my living, I would not try to become a scientist or scholar or teacher. I would rather choose to be a plumber."*

Alberta Alberta Hunter *(1895–1984)*
American blues singer.
> *"Blues means what milk does to a baby."*

Albertine *Albertine disparue (1925)*
Immortal French novel by Marcel Proust.

Alberto Alberto Giacometti *(1901–1966)*
Swiss sculptor of elegant "thin man" bronzes.

Albertus St. Albertus Magnus *(Albert the Great)* *(c. 1206–1280)*
German intellectual, known as "the Universal Doctor" for his vast knowledge of the sciences and theology.

Albie Albie Sachs *(1935–)*
South African judge, author of *The Jail Diary of Albie Sachs* describing his 168-day solitary confinement.
> *"All constitutions are based on extreme optimism on the one hand, and total distrust on the other."*

Albrecht Albrecht Dürer *(1471–1528)*
German painter and engraver. He was the first to use acid-etching of metal to make paper prints, after it had been developed as a technique for decorating armour.
> *"If a man devotes himself to art, much evil is avoided that happens otherwise if one is idle."*

Alcestis *Alcestis (438 B.C.)*
Greek play by Euripedes. Alcestis volunteers to go to Hades in place of her selfish husband, King Admetus of Thessaly. A servant remarks, "The King will not know his loss until he suffers it."

Alcibiades Alcibiades *(c. 450–404 B.C.)*
Athenian politician. He spent his life in constant motion, causing trouble between the Athenians, the Spartans, and the Persians. Plutarch said about him: "One colour, indeed, they say the chameleon cannot assume: it cannot itself appear white; but Alcibiades, whether with good men or bad, could adapt himself to his company."

Alcindo Alcindo Pereira *(c. 1955–)*
Brazilian beach bum–entrepreneur, inventor of the "filo dento" ("dental floss") bikini, and founder of the chain of Bum Bum bikini stores.
> *"I don't even want to be associated with the dental-floss bikini any more. It's vulgar."*

Alcyoneus Alcyoneus *trans. mighty ass*
Greek Titan, leader of the giants' revolt against the Olympian gods. His breath was so bad that Heracles had to breathe through a sweet herb while killing him.

Alden Alden C. Flagg *(20th century)*
American citizen. In 1917, his number (258) was the first to be drawn in the national lottery for drafting civilians into the military. In 1940, his son Alden C. Flagg, Jr., held the first number drawn in that national military lottery (158).

Aldo Aldo Manuzio *(or Aldus Manutius, or Manucci)* *(c. 1450–1515)*
Italian printer, the inventor of *italic* type. The sign on the door of his office read:
"Talk of nothing but business, and dispatch that business quickly."

Aldous Aldous Huxley *(Aldous Leonard Huxley)* *(1894–1963)*
British novelist, author of *Brave New World* (1932).

Alec Sir Alec Guinness *(1914–)*
English actor, winner of an Academy Award for *The Bridge on the River Kwai* (1957).

Alecto Alecto *trans. unnameable*
One of the Three Greek Erinnyes, or Avenging Furies. They are usually referred to as "the Eumenides," or "Kindly Ones," since it is considered unwise to mention their real names.

Aleister Aleister Crowley *(originally Edward Alexander Crowley)* *(1875–1947)*
English satanic provocateur. He called himself "Beast 666" in reference to Revelation 13: 8 about the "number of the beast."

Aleksandr Aleksandr Isayevich Solzhenitsyn *(1918–)*
Russian-born writer, author of *One Day in the Life of Ivan Denisovich* (1962), winner of the 1970 Nobel Prize for literature.

Alene Alene B. Duerk *(1920–)*
American sailor, the first female American admiral.

Alessandra Alessandra Mussolini *(20th century)*
Italian film actress and politician, the niece of Sophia Loren and the granddaughter of Benito Mussolini.

Alessandro Alessandro Volta *(Count Alessandro Giuseppe Anastasio Volta)* *(1745–1827)*
Italian physicist, inventor of the electric battery. The unit of measurement of electric potential, the "volt," is named after him.

Alex Alex Haley *(1922–1992)*
American author. He wrote the inspirational autobiographical family saga *Roots* (1977), which, alas, has proved to be largely fictional.

Alexander Alexander the Great *(356–323 B.C.)*
Macedonian imperialist genius, student of Aristotle, and conqueror of the entire known world.
"I am dying with the help of too many physicians."

Alexandr Alexandr Romanovich Luria *(1902–1977)*
Russian pioneer of neuropsychology, author of *The Man with a Shattered World* (trans. 1972).

Alexandra Alexandra David-Neel *(1868–1969)*
French-born scholar and traveller, author of *My Journey to Lhasa* (1927).

Alexandre Alexandre Dumas *(Alexandre Dumas Davy de la Pailleterie)* *(1802–1870)*
French novelist, author of *The Three Musketeers* (1845).
"Nothing succeeds like success."

Alexina Alexina Louie *(Alexina Diane Louie)* *(1949–)*
Canadian composer. Her music has been sent to outer space.

Alexine Alexine Tinne *(1840–1870)*
Dutch heiress and explorer. She was killed by bandits outside Tripoli, while setting off in search of Timbuktu.

Alexis Alexis Soyer *(1809–1858)*
French chef. He tried to help the Irish famine, and wrote a military food text called *Culinary Campaign in the Crimea* (1857).

Alfalfa Carl "Alfalfa" Switzer *(1926–1959)*
American child actor, from 1935 to 1942 one of *Our Gang*.

Alfatin Alfatin
Moorish hero. With his green horse, he sleeps beneath the Sierra de Agner mountains.

Alferd Alferd G. Pacher *(1847–1907)*
American tour-group leader. He robbed and murdered a group of prospectors in midwinter, and cut up their bodies to eat.
"I threw away the strips of flesh I had left, and I confess I did so reluctantly, as I had grown fond of human flesh, especially that portion around the breast."

Alfons Alfons Maria Mucha *(known as Alphonse Mucha)* *(1860–1939)*
Czechoslovakian-born Art Nouveau graphic designer.

Alfred Alfred Nobel *(1833–1896)*
Swedish inventor of the manageable form of nitroglycerine called "dynamite." He endowed the Nobel prizes.

Alger Alger Hiss *(1904–)*
American bureaucrat jailed for perjury. It took two tries by the congressional House Un-American Activities Committee to convict him; he was released the first time.

Algernon Algernon Charles Swinburne *(1837–1909)*
Extravagant English Victorian poet. He spent most of his life living in semi-seclusion at the home of a friend.
"A broken blossom; a ruined rhyme."

Ali Ali MacGraw *(1939–)*
American sweetheart. She played the heroine in the film *Love Story*.

Alice Alice Liddell *(b. 1852)*
British daughter of the dean of Christ Church, Oxford. After an afternoon boat trip with Alice and her sisters, Lorina and Edith, the mathematician Charles Dodgson was inspired to write *Alice's Adventures in Wonderland* (1865) under the pseudonym Lewis Carroll.

Alick Alick Isaacs *(1921–1967)*
British virologist. He developed the anti-virus drug interferon.

Aline Aline Kilmer *(1888–1944)*
American poet, wife of poet Joyce Kilmer, author of "For the Birthday of a Middle-Aged Child":
"I'm sorry you are wiser,
I'm sorry you are taller,
I liked you better foolish,
And I liked you better smaller."

Alison Alison Hargreaves *(1962–1995)*
British mountaineer, the first woman to climb Mount Everest without oxygen. She died near the summit of K2.
"One day as a tiger is better than a thousand as a sheep."

Alistair Alistair "Mouse" Grahame *(1900–1920)*
Ne'er-do-well English son of Kenneth Grahame, author of *The Wind in the Willows* (1908). He committed suicide.

Alix Alix Grès *(originally Germaine Krebs, known as Madame Grès) (1903–1993)*
Parisian haute-couture designer. She created the original shop with little gilt chairs on which clients sat to view clothes.

Alla Alla Nazimova *(originally Alla Leventon) (1878–1945)*
Russian-born American actress. She had her own theatre, the Nazimova, in New York.

Allan Allan Pinkerton *(1819–1884)*
Scottish-born American detective, founder of Pinkerton's Detective Agency. He foiled an assassination attempt on Abraham Lincoln on the train going to his inauguration.

Allegra Allegra Shelley *(d. 1822)*
Short-lived illegitimate daughter of Percy Bysshe Shelley by his wife, Mary's, half-sister Jane "Claire" Clairmont. Her father died the same year that she did, in a boating accident.

Allen Allen Ginsberg *(1926–)*
American Beat poet, author of *Howl and Other Poems* (1956). He took his first LSD trip in 1959 in government-sponsored experiments at Stanford University.
"I saw the best minds of my generation destroyed by madness, starving hysterical naked."

Almeida Almeida Lima *(20th century)*
Portuguese surgeon. In 1936, he and Antonio Egas Moniz invented the lobotomy operation.

Alois Alois Alzheimer *(1864–1915)*
German neuropathologist, the first person to describe "Alzheimer's disease."

Aloysia Aloysia Weber *(18th century)*
German singer. Wolfgang Amadeus Mozart fell in love with her briefly, then later married her sister Constanze.

Aloysius St. Aloysius *(originally Luigi Gonzaga) (1568–1591)*
Short-lived but well-intentioned Spanish Jesuit, who died tending plague victims. He is the patron saint of youth.

Alpheius Alpheius *trans. whiteish*
Greek river god. He fell in love with Artemis, but she daubed herself with mud to escape his attentions.

Alphonse Alphonse Daudet *(1840–1897)*
French writer and cultural luminary.

Althea Althea Gibson *(1927–)*
American tennis player, the first successful black woman in the sport.

> *"I didn't think about the racial issue or anything. All I thought about was how am I going to play this game and win?"*

Alton Alton Glenn Miller *(known as Glenn Miller) (1904–1944)*
American swing band-leader, composer of "In the Mood" (1939).

Alun Alun Lewis *(1915–1944)*
Welsh soldier-poet, author of *Ha! Ha! Among the Trumpets* (1945).

Alva Alva Myrdal, *née Reimer (1902–1986)*
Swedish sociologist and politician, winner of the 1982 Nobel Peace Prize.

Alvar Alvar Aalto *(Hugo Henrik Alvar Aalto) (1898–1976)*
Finnish Modernist architect and designer, a pioneer of curved laminated plywood furniture.

Alvin Alvin Toffler *(1928–)*
American writer.

> *"Parenthood remains the greatest single preserve of the amateur."*

Alwitha Alwitha *(c. 901)*
English wife of Alfred the Great. Virtually nothing is known about her.

Alzina Alzina Parsons Stevens *(1849–1900)*
American printer and trade-union activist, the first president of the Working Woman's Union Number 1.

Amadou Amadou Toure *(d. 1983)*
Senegal-born French pop musician with the group Toure Kunda.

Amalia Amalia Freud, *née Nathansohn (married 1855–1930)*
Viennese third wife of Jacob Freud and mother of Sigmund Freud.

Amaltheia Amaltheia *(or Adamanthaea) trans. tender*
Greek goat nymph, the nursemaid of baby Zeus. One of her horns was called "cornucopia." Her image is set in the stars as Capricorn.

Amanda Amanda McKittrick Ros *(1860–1939)*
Irish novelist and poet.

Amber *Forever Amber (1944)*
American hot historical fiction by Kathleen Winsor.

Ambroise Ambroise Paré *(c. 1510–1590)*
French surgeon, the "father of modern surgery" for learning to tie off arteries after amputations. Previously, stumps were cauterized with a red-hot iron.

Ambrose Ambrose Bierce *(Ambrose Gwinnett Bierce) (1842–c. 1914)*
American journalist and misanthrope who vanished without trace in Mexico; author of *The Devil's Dictionary*.

> *"Bore: a person who talks when you wish him to listen."*

Amédée Amédée Ozenfant *(1886–1966)*
French artist, co-author with Le Corbusier of the Purist Manifesto.

> *"What we wished to express in art was the Universal and Permanent and to throw to the dogs the Vacillating and the Fashionable."*

Amedeo Amedeo Modigliani *(1884–1920)*
Italian painter and sculptor, famed for his elegant attenuated nudes.

Amelia Amelia Bloomer, *née Jenks (1818–1894)*
American temperance worker. In 1849 she founded the feminist paper *Lily*, which popularized a new fashion style of Turkish pantaloons under a short skirt, later known as "bloomers."

Amelita Amelita Galli-Curci *(1889–1963)*
American operatic soprano.

> *"Nobody really sings in an opera—they just make loud noises."*

Amerigo Amerigo Vespucci *(1454–1512)*
Italian-born Spanish contractor who outfitted one of Christopher Columbus's expeditions. Published forged letters using his name became so popular that German cartographer Martin Waldseemüller wrote "Americus" on a map he drew of the new continents.

Amiens Amiens
Cheerful lord in William Shakespeare's play *As You Like It* (1623). He sings the song "Under the Greenwood Tree."

Amor Amor de Cosmos *(originally William Smith) (1825–1897)*
Canadian publisher and politician. He persuaded British Columbia to join Canada, then retired to an insane asylum.

Amos "Amos 'n' Andy" *(b. March 19, 1928)*
American radio program brought to television in 1951.

Amr Amr ibn al-As *(d. 664)*
Arab conqueror of Egypt. Author Alan L. Mackay wrote, "As Amr lay on his death-bed a friend said to him: 'You have often remarked that you would like to find an intelligent man at the point of death, and to ask him what his feelings were. Now I ask you that question.' Amr replied, 'I feel as if heaven lay close upon the earth and I between the two, breathing through the eye of a needle.'"

Amy Amy Tan *(1952–)*
American novelist, author of *The Joy Luck Club* (1989; film 1993).

Amyas Sir Amyas Paulet *(or Amyas Poulet) (c. 1536–1588)*
English courtier, the jailer of Mary, Queen of Scots.

Ana Ana Castillo *(20th century)*
American novelist, author of *Massacre of the Dreamers*, describing "Xicanisma" feminism for "brown women in a black-and-white country."

Anacreon Anacreon *(563–478 B.C.)*
Greek lyric poet.
> ". . . *shining with desire and gleaming with unguents . . .*"

Anaïs Anaïs Nin *(1903–1977)*
Parisian-born American writer. Seven volumes of her *Diary* were published between 1966 and 1980.
> "*Life shrinks or expands in proportion to one's courage.*"

Anastasia Grand Duchess Anastasiya Nikolayevna Romanov *(b. 1901)*
Last of the Russian princesses. New evidence proves that she did not die in 1918 in the cellar with the rest of her family, after all.

Anastasio Anastasio Somoza *(1896–1956)*
Nicaraguan president. Franklin D. Roosevelt said, "He may be a son of a bitch, but he's our son of a bitch."

Anatole Anatole France *(pseudonym of Jacques Anatole François Thibault) (1844–1924)*
French novelist and critic, winner of the 1921 Nobel Prize for literature.
> "*I do not know any reading more easy, more fascinating, more delightful than a catalogue.*"

Anatoly Anatoly Yevgenyevich Karpov *(1951–)*
Soviet chess player; world champion 1975–85.

Anchises Anchises *trans. living with Isis*
Mythical handsome Greek prince who had a night of passion with the goddess Aphrodite. When he unwisely boasted about this, Zeus sent a thunderbolt to kill him, but Aphrodite protected him so that he was merely crippled.

Anders Anders Celsius *(1701–1744)*
Swedish astronomer. He devised the Celsius scale for measuring temperature, in which water freezes at a convenient 0 degrees, and boils at 100 degrees.

Anderson Anderson Hatfield *(also known as Preacher Hatfield, or Devil Anse) (19th century)*
American older brother of 1882 murder victim Ellison Hatfield. He seized and executed the three sons of Ran'l McCoy in retaliation, setting off the famous backhills feud of the Hatfields and the McCoys.

Andie Andie MacDowell *(1958–)*
American actress and model.
> "*It's human nature that people want to criticize models because it looks like things have been given to them and they make so much money.*"

Andoche Andoche Junot, Duc d'Abrantès *(1771–1813)*
French noble. When asked about his ancestry, he replied: "I know nothing about it; I am my own ancestor."

André André-Gustave Citroën *(1878–1935)*
French automobile manufacturer.

Andrea Andrea Dworkin *(1946–)*
American feminist, author of the explicit semi-autobiographical *Ice and Fire* (1986).

Andrea Andrea Palladio *(originally Andrea di Pietro della Gondola) (1508–1580)* Italian architect and author of the influential *I quattro libri dell'architettura* (1570). His classical "Palladian" style, modelled on Roman examples, is still widely copied.

ANDY WARHOL

Andreas Andreas Baader *(1943–1977)*
West-German anarchist, co-founder of the Red Army Faction or "Baader-Meinhof Gang." He committed suicide in prison.

Andrei Andrei Sakharov *(Andrei Dmitrievich Sakharov) (1921–1989)*
Soviet dissident physicist, winner of the Nobel Peace Prize. Freed from internal exile by Mikhail Gorbachev, he was promptly elected to Congress.

Andrés Andrés Segovia, Marquis of Salobrena *(1894–1987)*
Spanish guitarist. His self-taught technique used both fingertips and nails to increase the range of tones.

Andrew Andrew Mellon *(1855–1937)*
American tycoon. As his brother Richard lay dying in 1933, he beckoned Andrew closer, touched his arm, whispered "last tag," and died.

Andromeda Andromeda *trans. ruler of men*
Legendary Ethiopian princess, rescued from a monster by Perseus. Athena immortalized her as a constellation.

Andronichus Andronichus of Cyrrhus *(c. 100 B.C.)*
Greek astronomer. His "tower of the winds" in Athens is the oldest observatory building still standing.

Andy Andy Warhol *(Andrew Warhola) (1927–1987)*
American pop artist.
"In the future, everyone will be world-famous for fifteen minutes."

Aneurin Aneurin Bevan *(1897–1960)*
Welsh Labour politician.
"No amount of cajolery, and no attempts at ethical and social seduction, can eradicate from my heart a deep burning hatred for the Tory party . . . so far as I am concerned, they are lower than vermin."

Angel Angel Cordero *(1942–)*
Puerto Rican jockey.

Angela Angela Davis *(1944–)*
American political activist.
"When white people are indiscriminately viewed as the enemy, it is virtually impossible to develop a political solution."

Angelico Fra Angelico *(originally Guido di Pietro) (1387–1455)*
Italian monk and painter.

Angie Angie Dickinson *(1932–)*
American actress.

Angus Angus *(or Mac Og the "Young God")*
Celtic god of love, son of Dagda and Boann.

Anita Anita Loos *(1893–1981)*
American screenplay writer, author of *Gentlemen Prefer Blondes*.
"Fate keeps on happening."

Anjelica Anjelica Huston *(1951–)*
American actress, daughter of director John Huston and granddaughter of actor Walter Huston.

Ann Ann Lee *(originally Ann Lees) (1736–1784)*
English-born American religious leader, "Mother Ann," founder of the United Society of Believers in Christ's Second Appearing, or the "Shakers." Her followers believed that the second coming of Christ would be as a woman since he first appeared as a man.

Ann-Margret Ann-Margret *(Ann-Margaret Olsson) (1941–)*
American sex kitten.

Anna Anna M. Jarvis *(1864–1948)*
American inventor of Mother's Day. She spent eight years working to get official recognition

for the event, achieved it in 1915, and then spent the rest of her life trying to stop its commercialization.

Annabella Annabella Drummond *(c. 1350–1402)*
Scottish queen, wife of Robert III.

Annabelle Dame Annabelle Jane Mary Rankin *(1908–1986)*
Australian politician, the first female whip in the British Commonwealth.

Annalisa Annalisa Wray *(1974–)*
Irish screamer. She set a Guinness record of 119.4 decibels in 1992 at the 7th International Rally.

Anne Anne Frank *(1929–1945)*
German diarist. She died in the Belsen concentration camp.

Annette Annette Funicello *(1942–)*
American actress, a Mickey-Mouseketeer and star of the film *Beach Blanket Bingo*.

Annibale Annibale Carracci *(1560–1609)*
Italian painter, a forefather of the Baroque style. He once described critics as "that gang of spiteful rascals that are always baiting us as if we had committed murder."

Annie Annie Oakley *(originally Phoebe Anne Oakley Moses) (1860–1926)*
American sharp-shooter. She toured with the Buffalo Bill Wild West Show, and inspired the Irving Berlin musical *Annie Get Your Gun* (1946). She met her husband when he lost a shooting match to her.

Anonymous Anonymous *(20th century)*
American author of the bestselling *Primary Colours* (1995), an unflattering exposé of the 1992 Bill Clinton primary. It is copyrighted by "Machiavelliana Inc." and dedicated "To my spouse, living proof that flamboyance and discretion are not mutually exclusive."

Ansel Ansel Adams *(Ansel Easton Adams) (1902–1984)*
American photographer, best remembered for his scenic views of the Yosemite Valley.

Anson Anson Dyer *(originally Ernest Anson-Dyer) (1876–1962)*
English animator, "Britain's answer to Walt Disney."

Anthelme Anthelme Brillat–Savarin *(1755–1826)*
French politician, gastronome, and writer.
"Tell me what you eat, and I will tell you what you are."

Anthony Anthony Trollope *(1815–1882)*
English novelist.
"He argued that the principal duty which a parent owed to a child was to make him happy."

Antiphanes Antiphanes *(c. 388–c. 311 B.C.)*
Greek comic playwright.
"The writer of tragedy is a lucky fellow! The audience always knows the plot as soon as his play begins. All the poet has to do is give a jog to their memories. He just says 'Oedipus': they all know the rest."

Antoine Antoine-Marie-Roger de Saint-Exupéry *(1900–1944)*
French aviator, author of *Le Petit Prince* (1943).

Antoinette Antoinette Brown, *née Blackwell (1825–1921)*
American scholar, author of *The Sexes Throughout Nature* (1875) criticizing Charles Darwin's limited male perspective.

Anton Anton Pavlovich Chekhov *(1860–1904)*
Russian short-story writer and playwright, author of *The Cherry Orchard* (1904).
"Love, friendship, respect, do not unite people as much as common hatred for something."

Antonia Lady Antonia Fraser *née Pakenham (1932–)*
English biographer, wife of playwright Harold Pinter, author of *My Oxford*.
"Once there was a Drag Hunt Ball just outside Oxford, to which I had unaccountably failed to be asked. I asked God to do something about it, and God recklessly killed poor King George VI, as a result of which the Hunt Ball was cancelled."

ANNE FRANK

Antonín Antonín Dvořák *(1841–1904)*
Czech composer.

Antonina Antonina Ivanovna Miliukova *(married 1877)*
Russian bride of composer Piotr Tchaikovsky. He abandoned her after one month, and later committed suicide following a "court of honour" concerning his close relationship with a young male aristocrat.

Antonio Antonio Carlos "Tom" Jobim *(1927–1994)*
Brazilian musician, inventor of the bossa nova, and composer of the song "The Girl from Ipanema."

Antony St. Antony *(251–356)*
Egyptian hermit. The group of ascetics gathered outside his isolated fort became the first monastery.

Anu Anu
Babylonian sky god, chief of the great triad of gods.

Anubis Anubis
Egyptian jackal-headed god. He conducted souls to the Underworld.

Anwar Anwar Sadat *(Mohamed Anwar el-Sadat) (1918–1981)*
Egyptian politician, winner of the 1978 Nobel Peace Prize.

Aphra Aphra Behn, *née Johnson (1640–1689)*
English wit, traveller, spy, and the first female playwright to support herself by writing. Virginia Woolf said, "All women together ought to let flowers fall on the tomb of Aphra Behn . . . for it was she who earned them the right to speak their minds."

Aphrodite Aphrodite *trans. foam born*
Greek goddess of Venus and love. She rose naked from the foam of the sea and rode to land on a scallop shell. She was notoriously unfaithful to her ugly husband, Hephaestus, who adored her anyway.

Arabella Arabella Churchill *(1648–1730)*
English aristocrat, the mistress of James II.

ARETHA FRANKLIN

Arachne Princess Arachne of Colophon *trans. spider*
Lydian weaver, so skilful that the goddess Athene tore up her work in jealousy. Fearful, Arachne hung herself from the rafters, and Athene turned her into a spider.

Aragorn King Aragorn
Warrior of Middle Earth in J.R.R. (John Ronald Reuel) Tolkien's English fantasy triology *The Lord of the Rings* (1954–55).

Archibald Archibald Belaney *(better known as Grey Owl) (1888–1938)*
English-born Canadian writer, a self-styled "Apache half-breed." He wrote popular books about beavers, with whom he shared his well-chewed wooden home.

Archie Archie Williams *(1915–1993)*
American engineer, an Olympic gold-medallist in the 1936 Munich Olympics. Being black, he helped to spoil Adolf Hitler's Aryan showcase, but back home could find work only digging ditches.

Archimedes Archimedes *(287–212 B.C.)*
Greek mathematician and engineer.
"Give me a firm place to stand and I will move the earth."

archy archy and mehitabel *(1927)*
American collected love poems by Don Marquis, recording the passion of archy the cockroach for aging louche mehitabel the alley cat. Because he wrote by bouncing on the keys of a mechanical typewriter, archy was unable to operate the shift key for capital letters.
*"dance mehitabel dance
caper and shake a leg
what little blood is left
will fizz like wine in a keg"*

Arctic Arctic Elvis *(or Nunavuk Elvis, real name Jimmy Ekho) (1970–)*
Canadian Inuit musician. He has never, ever, performed an Elvis song, mainly because the lyrics don't make sense after they've been translated into Inuktituk.
"No matter what I do, people keep calling me that. It drives me nuts sometimes."

Ares Ares *trans. male warrior*
Greek god of war, straight-limbed, impetuous, drunken, and quarrelsome. Dogs and vultures were his favourite animals, because they scavenge battlefields.

Aretha Aretha Franklin *(1942–)*
American singer and pianist, "Lady Soul," the first woman inducted into the Rock 'n' Roll Hall of Fame.

Arethusa Arethusa *trans. the waterer*
Greek wood nymph. Artemis changed her into a stream so that she could escape the lust of the river god Alpheus.

Ariadne Princess Ariadne of Crete *trans. most pure*
Legendary daughter of King Minos who slipped Theseus a sword to kill the Minotaur in the maze. Her second husband was the god Dionysus.

Arianna Arianna Stassinopoulos-Huffington *(c. 1946–)*
Greek-born American social climber, wife of failed $20-million Senate candidate Michael Huffington, "the most upwardly mobile Greek since Icarus."

Ariel Ariel
"Airy spirit" of William Shakespeare's play *The Tempest* (1611–12). She sings the song "Full Fathom Five."

Aristide Aristide Briand *(1862–1932)*
French politician, winner of the Nobel Peace Prize.

Aristophanes Aristophanes *(446–380 B.C.)*
Much-admired Greek playwright.
> *"Master, shall I begin with the usual jokes*
> *That the audience always laugh at?"*
He also wrote: *"I laugh'd till I cried."*

Aristos Aristos *(active c. 309 B.C.)*
Greek orchestra leader. He led the earliest recorded strike in history, over a dispute about meal breaks.

Aristotle Aristotle *(384–322 B.C.)*
Greek philosopher, a student of Plato, and the teacher of Alexander the Great.
> *"The whole is more than the sum of its parts."*

Arizona Arizona Donnie Clark Barker *(better known as Ma Barker) (1872–1935)*
American gang leader who organized her four sons into a crack team of bank robbers. She was never arrested, but died in a gun battle with the FBI.

Arlene Arlene Smith *(1941–)*
American rock singer with the group The Chantels.

Arlette Arlette Rafferty Schweitzer *(1948–)*
American grandmother. When her daughter Christa proved unable to bear children, Arlette served as surrogate mother, and in 1991 gave birth to her own grandchildren.

ARNOLD SCHWARZENEGGE[R]

Arletty Arletty *(originally Léonie Bathiat) (1898–1992)*
Parisian actress, known for the film *Les Enfants de Paradis* (1945). Marlon Brando said that, on his first visit to Paris, "I asked to see Arletty . . . What a disillusionment! She was a tough article!"

Arlo Arlo Guthrie *(1947–)*
American folk-singer. He sang the theme song in the film *Alice's Restaurant* (1969).

Armand Armand Bombardier *(1907–)*
Canadian inventor of the snowmobile.

Armando Armando "Buddy" Greco *(1926–)*
American nightclub pianist and singer. His big hit was "The Lady Is a Tramp" (1962).

Arnaut Arnaut Daniel *(active 1180–1200)*
Provençal poet, troubadour to Richard Coeur de Lion.

Arne Arne Jacobsen *(1902–1971)*
Danish Modernist architect, designer of the "Egg" chair.

Arnold Arnold Schwarzenegger *(1947–)*
Austrian-born American body-builder and film star.

Árpád Árpád *(d. 907)*
Magyar chieftain, a national hero of Hungary.

Arron Arron Gaskarth *(1990–)*
British baby. He and his twin sister, Laura, are the most premature twins ever to survive, born 107 days before term. He weighed 1 lb 11 oz.

Arsenio Arsenio Hall *(1959–)*
American actor and talk-show host.

Arshile Arshile Gorky *(originally Vosdanig Manoog Adoian) (1905–1948)*
Armenian-born American Action painter.

Art Art Linkletter *(1912–)*
Canadian-born American TV personality.
"The four stages of man are infancy, childhood, adolescence, and obsolescence."

Artem Artem Ivanovich Mikoyan *(1905–1970)*
Armenian-born Soviet aircraft engineer. His name gave the "Mi" to the name of the "MiG" fighters he designed with Mikhail Iosifovich Gurevich.

Artemis Artemis *trans. high source of water*
Ancient Greek moon goddess, patroness of childbirth and little children.

Artemisia Artemisia Gentileschi *(1593–c. 1652)*
Italian painter. Her rape by the less-talented painter Agostino Tassi was the subject of a 1992 Canadian short film by Adrienne Clarkson.

Artemus Artemus Ward *(pseudonym of Charles Farrar Browne) (1834–1867)*
American humorist, author of *Artemus Ward, His Panorama* (1865).
"The ground flew up and hit me in the head."

Arthur Arthur Scammell *(1913–1995)*
Canadian songwriter. He wrote the classic "Squid-Jiggin' Ground" at age fifteen, for a school assignment.

Artie Artie Shaw *(Arthur Jacob Arshawsky) (1910–)*
American swing band-leader.

Artin Artin Cavoukian *(1915–1995)*
Armenian-born Canadian photographer, father of children's entertainer Raffi.

Artur Artur Rubinstein *(1887–1982)*
American pianist. He made his début at age twelve. His daugher Eva said, "I absolutely adored going to my father's concerts because then I saw his real face and heard his real self."

Arturo Arturo Toscanini *(1867–1957)*
Italian cellist and conductor. He first conducted in public at a performance of *Aïda* in Brazil, after the audience booed the original conductor off the stand.

Arun Arun Gandhi *(20th century)*
Indian grandson of Mahatma Gandhi. He quotes his grandfather on the seven "blunders" of humanity:
1. *wealth without work*
2. *pleasure without conscience*
3. *knowledge without character*
4. *commerce without morality*
5. *science without humanity*
6. *worship without sacrifice*
7. *politics without principles.*

Arundell Arundell Clarke *(20th century)*
English interior decorator.

Asa Asa Philip Randolph *(1889–1979)*
American labour activist, founder of the Brotherhood of Sleeping Car Porters. He organized the great Washington march of 1963, at which Martin Luther King told 200,000 people, "I have a dream."

Ascanio Ascanio Sobrero *(1812–1888)*
Italian chemist, the discoverer of nitrogylcerine.

Ashleigh Ashleigh Brilliant *(1920–)*
English-born Californian epigram maker, author of *Be a Good Neighbour and Leave Me Alone* (1991).
"I may not be totally perfect, but parts of me are excellent."

Ashley Ashley Montagu *(originally Montague Francis Ashley Montague) (1905–)*
English-born American anthropologist. He wrote *The Natural Superiority of Women* (1953).

Ashtar Ashtar *(or Ashtaroth, or Ashtoreth)*
Palestinian child-god who temporarily occupied the throne of heaven while Baal was detained. At rites in his honour, a young goat was seethed (boiled) in its mother's milk, as later prohibited in the Bible (Exodus 23: 19).

Ashurnasirpal Ashurnasirpal II *(ruled 883–859 B.C.)*
Assyrian king. His tomb is beneath the palace at Ashur.

Asmundur Asmundur Sveinsson *(1893–1982)*
Icelandic sculptor. He built a spherical workshop for himself in Reykjavik, now a museum.

Asta Asta Neilsen *(d. c. 1972)*
Danish-born silent-film actress, author of the memoir *The Silent Muse* (1946).

Aston Sir Aston Webb *(1849–1930)*
British architect of the east façade of Buckingham Palace.

Astrea Astrea *(or Astraea)*
Roman goddess of justice during the Golden Age. The wickedness of humanity during the following Bronze and Iron ages drove her to leave the planet for heaven, and become the constellation Virgo.

Astrid Astrid Lindgren *(1907–)*
Swedish author of *Pippi Longstocking* (1945).

Astrolabe Astrolabe Abelard *(b. c. 1116)*
French son of famous lovers Abelard and Éloïse.

Atalanta *Atalanta in Calydon (1865)*
Lyric English drama by Algernon Swinburne. Atalanta of Arcadia raced her suitors, killing the losers, until she was defeated and married by Hippomenes.

Athene Athene *(or Athena)*
Greek goddess of wisdom and skill, who won control of Athens from Poseidon. She is said to have sprung full grown from Zeus's forehead, but this story is just a revisionist male attempt to cover up her true pre-Greek matriarchal origins.

Athol Athol Fugard *(pseudonym of Harold Lanigan) (1932–)*
South African playwright and actor.

Atlas Atlas
Greek Titan of the moon. He lost a battle against Zeus, and was sentenced to carry the world on his shoulders as punishment. In 1585 the world's first published book of maps, by Gerardus Mercator, was illustrated with a drawing of Atlas holding the globe, which is why such books are now known as "atlases."

Atreus Atreus *trans. fearless*
Mythical Greek father of Agamemnon and Menelaus. Eight of the thirty-three surviving Greek tragedies concern his doomed family.

Atsuko Atsuko Yamano *(20th century)*
Japanese punk-rock drummer, one of the girl trio Shonen Knife.
> "He is a cat but he's very very fat. He is not just a standard cat. He is a cat but he's still very fat. American calico cat."

Atticus Atticus Finch
Moral American attorney, hero of *To Kill a Mockingbird* (1960) by Harper Lee.

Attila Attila the Hun *(c. 406–453)*
Asian military genius.

Auberon Auberon Waugh *(originally Alexander Waugh) (1939–)*
British diarist and satirist, the son of Evelyn Waugh.

Aubrey Aubrey Beardsley *(Aubrey Vincent Beardsley) (1872–1898)*
English Decadent illustrator. He died young of tuberculosis.
> "Really I believe I'm so affected, even my lungs are affected."

Audie Audie Murphy *(1924–1971)*
American actor, previously the most highly decorated American soldier of the Second World War. He joined the army at sixteen by lying about his age.

Audrey Audrey Hepburn *(originally Edda van Heemstra Hepburn-Ruston) (1929–1993)*
Belgian-born actress and UNICEF worker. She won an Academy Award for *Roman Holiday* (1953).

Augeias King Augeias of Elis *trans. bright ray*
Legendary Greek owner of the Augean stables, which Heracles cleaned as his sixth labour. The stables contained 3,000 cattle and hadn't been cleaned for thirty years. Heracles diverted a small river through them.

August August Ferdinand Möbius *(1790–1868)*
German mathematician, creator of the Möbius
strip. A strip of paper *half*-twisted, and then
joined to the other end with tape will allow a
single pencil line to draw around to meet itself,
because now the paper only has one side.

Augusta Augusta Main *(arrested 1897)*
American farmer, a foe of trespassers.
> *"I never sees men or dogs but what [I] aches to
> kill them."*

Augustin Augustin Jean Fresnel *(1788–1827)*
French physicist and lighthouse expert, the
inventor of the flat "Fresnel" lens.

Augustine St. Augustine of Hippo *(Aurelius
Augustinus) (354–430)*
Leader of the Latin Christian Church, "Doctor
of Grace."
> *"Give me chastity and continence, but not yet."*

Augustus Augustus Owsley Stanley III *(20th century)*
American LSD chemist, manufacturer of the
popular 1960s "Owsley Acid."

Aurel Sir Aurel Stein *(originally Mark Aurel Stein)
(1862–1943)*
Hungarian-born British archaeologist, the first
person to enter the Cave of a Thousand
Buddhas near Tan Huang, China, for the first
time since it was sealed in the 11th century.

Aurora *Aurora Leigh (1856)*
English poem by Elizabeth Barrett Browning.
> *"The devil's most devilish when
> respectable."*

Austen Sir Austen Henry Layard
(1817–1894)
French-born English
archaeologist and ambas-
sador. He excavated the
palace of Ashurnasirpal II
at Tell Nimrud and the
palace of Sennacherib at
Nineveh.

Ava Ava Gardner *(originally
Lucy Johnson)
(1922–1990)*
American actress. While
filming *On the Beach*

AXL ROSE

(1958) she remarked "Melbourne is the perfect
place for a film about the end of the world."

Avisa "Avisa" *(full title: "Willobie his Avisa, the True
Picture of a Modest Maid and of a Chast and
Constant Wife") (1594)*
English poem by Henry Willoughby about his
wife, Avisa. She may have been the mysterious
"Dark Lady" of William Shakespeare's love son-
nets.

Avril Avril Phaedra Douglas Campbell *(known as
Kim Campbell) (1948–)*
Canadian politician, the short-term first female
prime minister.

Axel Axel Munthe *(1857–1949)*
Swedish physician, author of the enduring best-
seller *The Story of San Michele* (1929). The profits
from this book help fund a bird sanctuary in
Capri.

Axl Axl Rose *(1962–)*
American lead singer with the band Guns 'n'
Roses.

Ayako Ayako Takeda Tsuchihashi *(20th century)*
Japanese mother in 1978 of the world's heaviest
quadruplets. The girls totalled 22 lbs 13 oz at
birth.

Ayesha Ayesha *or Aishah (c. 613–678)*
Favourite wife of the prophet Muhammad.

Aylwin *Aylwin (1898)*
English gypsy novel by Walter Watts-Dunton.
(It was Dunton who cared for ageing poet
Algernon Swinburne in his home for thirty
years.)

Ayn Ayn Rand *(originally Alice Rosenbaum)
(1905–1982)*
Russian-born American novelist and cult leader.

Aynsley Aynsley Dunbar *(1946–)*
English-born American pop star with the band
Journey.

Ayrton Ayrton Senna *(1960–1994)*
Brazilian Formula One racing-car driver killed
in a controversial crash at the San Marino
Grand Prix.

Azzo Azzo d'Este *(1205–1264)*
Italian ruler of Ferrara.

Baal Baal

Phoenician moon god. Baal-worship was the court religion of King Ahab.

Babe Babe Ruth *(George Herman Ruth) (1895–1948)*

American baseball hero of the Yankees, the "Sultan of Swat," possibly the best baseball player of all time. Told he earned more money than President Herbert Hoover, Ruth replied, "I had a better year than he did."

Baby Baby LeRoy *(b. 1933)*

American child actor. He starred with Maurice Chevalier in *A Bedtime Story* (1933) at three months old. Baby LeRoy was too young to sign a contract, and so was his sixteen-year-old mother; his grandfather signed the contracts.

Bacchus Bacchus

Roman god of wine.

Bache Sir Bache Cunard *(20th century)*

British husband of Emerald Cunard. When his daughter Nancy questioned him about whether he was really her father, he replied, "Oh my Lord! Never ask your mother that. . . . I wish I could think so, Nancy. . . . But I fear not, I fear not."

Balder Balder *(or Baldur)*

Mythic Nordic son of Odin and Frigga. He was the most beautiful of all the Aesir.

Baldur Baldur von Schirach *(1907–1974)*

German founder of the Hitler Youth.

Balkrishna Balkrishna Vithaldas Doshi *(1927–)*

Indian Modernist architect, an associate of Le Corbusier. He designed Toronto's new City Hall (1958).

Balloon James "Balloon" Tytler *(c. 1747–1804)*

Scottish journalist and scientist, the first Briton to fly (1784). He used a homemade balloon.

Balso *The Dream Life of Balso Snel (1931)*

Avant-garde American novel by Nathanael West. *"I must laugh at myself."*

BABE RUTH

Baltasar Baltasar y Morales Gracián *(1601–1658)*

Spanish writer and philosopher.

"Great things, when short, are twice as good."

Baltazarini Baltazarini di Belgioioso *(or Beaujoyeux) (d. 1587)*

Italian musician. Catherine de Médici commissioned him to create the *Ballet comique de la reine* in 1581; the first "ballet" combining dance with song.

Balto Balto *(active 1925)*

Alaskan half-breed malamute dog, leader of a dog team driven 655 miles in six days by Gunnar Kaasen to bring diphtheria antitoxen to a remote community to halt an epidemic. A statue of Balto stands in the zoo in New York City.

Bambi *Bambi (1923)*

Austrian animal story by Felix Salten, later a Walt Disney movie.

Ban Ban Johnson *(Byron Bancroft Johnson) (1864–1931)*

American baseball executive, creator of the new American League. He had a nasty temper, and once told pitcher Jack Quinn, "I made you, and by God I'll break you!"

Banana Banana Yoshimoto *(1974–)*

Japanese novelist, author of *Kitchen*.

Banjo Banjo *(originally Andrew Barton Paterson) (1864–1941)*

Australian journalist and poet. He wrote the words to the song "Waltzing Matilda."

Barabbas Barabbas *trans. teacher, Matthew 27 (active c. A.D. 30)*

Jewish bandit. He was in jail at the same time as Jesus, and when Pilate tried to wiggle out of condemning Jesus by giving him the traditional Passover pardon, the crowd demanded the release of Barabbas instead.

Barbara Barbara Cartland *(Mary Barbara Hamilton Cartland) (1901–)*

English popular novelist, the step-grandmother of Diana, Princess of Wales. She set a Guinness record by writing twenty-six books in 1983.

"I didn't have any idea how babies were born until I was 19, and yet, you see, I came out unscathed with a perfect marriage. That tells you something, doesn't it?"

Barbarella *Barbarella (1968)*
American film starring a scantily clad Jane Fonda.

Barbarossa Barbarossa
Legendary Teutonic king, possibly based on the real Frederick I of Germany. He is said to sleep in a cavern under the Kyffhauser Mountains, awaiting the recall to arms.

Barbie Barbie Doll *(full name Barbie Millicent Roberts) (1959–)*
Enduring mid-American stereotype, named for Barbie Handler, the daughter of Mattel Toy founders Elliot and Ruth Handler.

Barbra Barbra Streisand *(originally Barbara Joan Streisand) (1942–)*
American Broadway artiste and film director.
"A man is forceful—a woman is pushy. . . . He's assertive—she's aggressive. He strategizes—she manipulates."

Barnard Barnard Elliott Bee *(1824–1861)*
American soldier, the first person to refer to General Thomas Jackson as a "stone wall."

Barnes Sir Barnes Wallis *(Barnes Neville Wallis) (1887–1979)*
English engineer. He helped to develop the R100 airship, and the "bouncing bombs" of the Second World War.

Barnett Barnett Newman *(1905–1970)*
American artist. He painted a large striped *Voice of Fire* bought by the National Gallery of Canada.

Barney "Barney" *(20th century)*
American children's TV show starring a life-size giggling purple dinosaur puppet.
"I love you, you love me. We're a perfect family."

Barrett Barrett Cocks *(1907–)*
British journalist.
"A committee is a cul-de-sac down which ideas are lured and then quietly strangled."

Barrington Barrington Nevitt *(1911–1995)*
Canadian engineer and philosopher, an associate of Marshall McLuhan's.

Barry Barry *(1800–1814)*
Swiss dog, the original canine hero of the mountain Hospice of St. Bernard.

Bart Bart Simpson
Childish anti-hero of the American animated-cartoon TV series "The Simpsons."
"Cool, man."

Bartholomew Bartholomew Cubbins
Hero of the American children's book *The 500 Hats of Bartholomew Cubbins* (1938) by "Dr." Theodor Seuss.

Bartimaeus Bartimaeus *trans. son of Timaeus, Mark 10: 46*
Jericho roadside beggar healed of blindness by Jesus.

Bartolommeo Bartolommeo Eustachio *(1520–1574)*
Italian anatomist. The Eustachian tube in the ear is named after him.

Baruch Baruch Spinoza *(or Benedictus de Spinoza) (1632–1677)*
Dutch philosopher.
"Nature abhors a vacuum."

Bashir Bashir Gemayal *(1947–1982)*
Lebanese politician. He died in a bomb assassination.

Basil Basil Rathbone *(Philip St. John Basil Rathbone) (1892–1967)*
British actor. He played the black-and-white film version of Sherlock Holmes.

Bast Bast *(or Bastet)*
Egyptian fire goddess. She is the "Little Cat," and her sister Sehkmet is the "Great Cat."

Bathsheba Bathsheba Bowers *(c. 1672–1718)*
American Quaker preacher.

Bathsua Bathsua Makin, *née Pell (c. 1612–c. 1674)*
English Restoration educational reformer, tutor to Charles II's daughter Elizabeth.

Battista Battista "Pinin" Farina *(1893–1966)*
Italian car designer, founder of the firm Pininfarina which has designed Ferraris, Alfa Romeos, and the Hyundai Pony.

Batty Batty Langley *(1696–1751)*
English Neogothic designer, author of *Ancient Architecture Restored* (1742).

Baucis Baucis *trans. overly modest*
Mythical Phrygian peasant. After he and his wife, Philemon, generously entertained the gods Zeus and Hermes disguised as beggars, the gods rewarded them by turning their humble cottage into a palace.

Bayard Bayard Taylor *(James Bayard Taylor) (1825–1878)*
American poet, travel-writer, and ambassador.
> *"Learn to live, and live to learn,*
> *Ignorance like a fire doth burn,*
> *Little tasks make large return."*

Bea Bea Arthur *(1926–)*
American actress, star of the TV series "Maude" *(1972–78)*.

Beaky Beaky John Dymond *(1944–)*
British pop musician with the group Dave Dee, Dozy, Beaky, Mitch and Tich ('DDDBM&T').

Beat Beat Takeshi *(20th century)*
Japanese comic, voted one of the two most trusted people in the country in a 1994 poll. He appeared in the American film *Johnny Mnemonic* (1995).

Beatrice Beatrice Portinari *(c. 1265–1290)*
Italian love of the poet Dante Alighieri.

Beatrix Beatrix Potter *(Helen Beatrix Potter) (1866–1943)*
Reclusive British author and illustrator, creator of *The Tale of Peter Rabbit* (1900).
> *"Don't go into Mr. McGregor's garden: your Father had an accident there; he was put in a pie by Mrs. McGregor."*

Beau Beau Brummell *(originally George Bryan Brummell) (1778–1840)*
English dandy.
> *"Who's your fat friend?"* (It was the Prince of Wales, and he knew it.)

Beauclerc Beauclerc *(or Henry I) (1068–1135)*
English ruler who set a British royal record of twenty-four offspring. By the time of his death only one legal heir survived: Matilda.

Beautiful Beautiful Joe *(1893)*
Canadian children's novel by Marshall Saunders (Margaret Marshall Saunders) based on a real abused dog from Meaford, Ontario. The author

Top 10 Military Baby Names

Alden • Alene • Alexander • Ares • Boadicea • Colin • Genghis • Hannibal • Pyrrhus • Vortigern

changed her name to disguise herself as a man and changed the Canadian setting to Maine, to improve sales potential.
> *"My name is Beautiful Joe and I am a brown dog of medium size."*

Bebe Bebe Shopp *(20th century)*
American model, Miss America 1948.

Becky Becky Thatcher
Pigtailed girlfriend of the hero in Mark Twain's novel *Tom Sawyer* (1876).

Bede St. Bede the Venerable *(or The Venerable Bede) (c. 673–735)*
Anglo-Saxon scholar and saint, the best early source for English history from his *Historia ecclesiastica gentis anglorum* (731). He was the first person to date events as "anno Domini" or "A.D."

Bedivere Sir Bedivere
Legendary Knight of the Round Table. He tended the dying King Arthur.

Beefheart Captain Beefheart *(Don Van Vliet) (1941–)*
American surreal musician, composer of *Trout Mask Replica* (1969). He went to high school with Frank Zappa.

Beerbohm Sir Herbert Beerbohm Tree *(1853–1917)*
British actor and director.
> *"Ladies, just a little more virginity, if you don't mind."*

Beilby Beilby Porteus *(1731–1808)*
English poet.
> *"One murder made a villain,*
> *Millions, a hero."*

Bela Bela Lugosi (originally Béla Ferenc Denzso) (1884–1956)
Hungarian-born character actor. He was buried in his Dracula cape.

Belacqua Belacqua Shuah
Hero of Samuel Beckett's *Dream of Fair to Middling Women* (1932). He is named after the lazy lute player found in purgatory by Dante Alighieri.

Belinda Belinda
Heroine of Alexander Pope's epic drama *The Rape of the Lock* (1712), which was based on a real-life feud over a lock of hair from Arabella "Belinda" Fermor.

Belle Belle Starr (originally Myra Belle Shirley) (1848–1889)
American horse thief, the "Petticoat Terror of the Plains."

Bellerophon Bellerophon *trans. bearing darts*
Greek master of winged Pegasus. He rode Pegasus to kill the Chimaera.

Belva Belva Ann Bennett McNall Lockwood (1830–1917)
American lawyer. She ran for president on a platform of universal peace, and won Indiana.
    "We shall never have rights until we take them."

Ben Ben Jonson (c. 1573–1637)
English dramatist. His bar-room disciples were known as "the sons o' Ben."
    "Fortune, that favours fools."

Benazir Benazir Bhutto (1953–)
Pakistani politician, the successor to her father, Zulfikar Ali Bhutto, who had been hanged by his political opponents.

Bendigo William "Bendigo" Thompson (1811–1880)
British bareknuckles heavyweight boxing champion. He wore a fur cap called a "bendigo," and retired to become a preacher.

Benedict Benedict Arnold (1741–1801)
American soldier; a British patriot.

Bengt Bengt Norberg (1951–)
Swedish car driver. He set a Guinness record by driving 192.872 miles non-stop while balanced on two side wheels of his car (a Mitsubishi Colt).

Benigno Benigno Aquino (1932–1983)
Filipino politician, whose assassination led to the overthrow of Ferdinand Marcos. In 1954, he once dated the future Imelda Marcos.

Benito Benito Mussolini (1883–1945)
Italian politician, "Il Duce."
    "The history of saints is mainly the history of insane people."

Benjamin Dr. Benjamin Spock (Benjamin McLane Spock) (1903–)
American baby doctor, author of *The Common Sense Book of Baby and Child Care* (1946), which was the first book to advocate feeding your children when they were hungry, rather than on a schedule. In 1924, he won an Olympic gold medal as a member of the Yale rowing team.

Bennett Bennett Cerf (1898–1971)
American editor of Eugene O'Neill. The manuscript of *Long Day's Journey into Night* was locked in his safe, to be kept for twenty-five years until the family died, but on O'Neill's wife's insistence, it was published in 1956.

Bennetta Bennetta Washington (1918–1991)
American teacher, first leader of the Job Corps training program.

Benny Benny Hill (originally Alfred Hawthorne Hill) (1925–1992)
English TV comedian, a master of tacky innuendo, "King Leer."

Benoit Benoit Mandelbrot (1924–)
Polish-born French mathematician, author of *The Fractal Geometry of Nature* (1982).

Benso Camillo Benso di Cavour (1810–1861)
Italian politician.
    "I have discovered the art of fooling diplomats; I speak the truth and they never believe me."

Benvenuto Benvenuto Cellini (1500–1571)
Italian Mannerist goldsmith, the egotistical author of the *Memoirs of Benvenuto Cellini* (c. 1558).

Beowulf Beowulf
Anglo-Saxon epic tale, first translated by Icelandic scholar Thorkelin in 1807.

Berengaria Berengaria of Navarre *(married 1191)*
French wife of Richard I, Coeur de Lion. She never came to England, but Richard never spent a full year in England, and may not have spoken English.

Bernabe Bernabe "El Dynamitero" Ferreyra *(1909–1972)*
Argentinian soccer star.

Bernadette St. Bernadette of Lourdes *(originally Marie Bernarde Soubirous) (1844–1879)*
French miller's daughter who saw a vision of the Virgin Mary in a cave on the riverbank every day between February 18 and March 4, 1858. "Bernadette" was her childhood pet-name.

Bernard Bernard Berenson *(1865–1959)*
Lithuanian-born American art critic and double-dealer.

Bernardine Bernardine *(or Barnardine)*
Dissolute prisoner in William Shakespeare's play *Measure for Measure* (1604–1605). She is beheaded in Act IV.

Bernardino Bernardino Ramazzini *(1633–1714)*
Italian doctor, the first to link work with illness, observing factors such as potters' exposure to lead.

Bernardo Bernardo Bertolucci *(1940–)*
Italian film director.

Bernice Bernice *trans. victorious, Acts 25: 13*
Roman great-granddaughter of Herod the Great, wife of King Ptolemy of Sicily, and mistress of the Emperor Titus.

Bernie Bernie Taupin *(1950–)*
British lyricist for pop star Elton John. They met through a newspaper ad.

Bert Bert Sutcliffe *(1923–)*
New Zealand cricketer.

Bertha Bertha Krupp von Bohlen und Halbach *(1886–1957)*
German factory owner, manufacturer of the massive gun known as "Big Bertha" used to bombard Paris during the war.

Berthe Berthe Marie Pauline Morisot *(1841–1895)*
French Impressionist painter.

Berthold Berthold Schwarz *(originally Konstantin Anklitzen) (14th century)*
German Franciscan monk and alchemist, inventor in 1320 of the first guns. He gained the name "schwarz," or "black," because of his interest in gunpowder.

Bertolt Bertolt Brecht *(originally Eugen Berthold Friedrich Brecht) (1898–1956)*
Austrian poet and playwright, author of *The Threepenny Opera* (1928).
  "Fodder comes first, then morality."

Bertram Bertram Brockhouse *(c. 1930–)*
Canadian physicist, winner of a 1994 Nobel Prize.

BENITO MUSSOLINI

Bertrand Bertrand Russell *(Bertrand Arthur William, 3rd Earl Russell) (1872–1970)*
Prolific Welsh philosopher and mathematician, winner of the 1950 Nobel Prize for literature, author of the essay "Why I Am Not a Christian" (1957).
  "Boredom is a vital problem for the moralist, since at least half the sins of mankind are caused by the fear of it."

Beryl Beryl Bainbridge *(1933–)*
English novelist.
  "As a child she had been taught it was rude to say no unless she didn't mean it. If she was offered another piece of cake and she wanted it she was obliged to refuse out of politeness. And if she didn't want it she had to say yes, even if it choked her."

Bess Bess Truman *(20th century)*
American political worker, wife of President Harry S. Truman.

Bessica Bessica Raiche *(1874–1932)*
American pilot, the first woman in the United States to fly solo. She wore breeches after a near-fatal accident when her long skirt tangled in the controls.

Bessie Bessie Smith *(Elizabeth Smith) (1894–1937)*
American singer, "Empress of the Blues."
"No time to marry, no time to settle down; I'm a young woman, and I ain't done runnin' around."

Bessy Bessy Throckmorton *(married 1592)*
English maid-of-honour to Queen Elizabeth. Sir Walter Raleigh was thrown in the Tower of London for having an affair with her. They married after his release.

Bethenia Bethenia Owens *(1840–1926)*
American milliner who retrained to become one of the first female doctors.
"I was not prepared for the storm of opposition that followed."

Betsy Betsy Ross *née Elizabeth Griscom (1752–1836)*
American seamstress. Her grandson started the story that she designed the first American flag; changing the six-pointed stars to five to make them easier to cut out.

Bette Bette Davis *(originally Ruth Elizabeth "Betty" Davis) (1908–1989)*
American actress, winner of an Academy Award for *Jezebel* (1938), author of *The Lonely Life* (1962).
"I have eyes like a bullfrog, a neck like an ostrich and long limp hair."

Bettina Bettina Graziana *(20th century)*
Parisian fashion model. Hubert Givenchy created the 1952 "Bettina Blouse" for her, made of shirting material with an open neck and ruffled sleeves with broderie anglaise.

Betty Betty Friedan, *née Elizabeth Goldstein (1921–)*
American feminist, author of *The Feminine Mystique* (1963), and co-founder of the National Organization for Women (NOW) in 1966.

BETTE DAVIS

Beulah Beulah Bondi *(1892–1981)*
American character actress. She specialized in portraying old ladies.

Bevan Bevan Ernest Congdon *(1938–)*
New Zealand cricket player.

Beverley Beverley "Bubbles" Sills *(originally Belle Miriam Silverman) (1929–)*
American coloratura soprano.
"You may be disappointed if you fail, but you are doomed if you don't try."

Bevil Sir Bevil Grenville *(1596–1643)*
English royalist soldier. He inspired Robert Hawker's ballad "Song of the Western Men."

Bezaleel Bezaleel *trans. in the Lord's shadow, Exodus 31: 2 (13th century)*
Old Testament interior designer of the Tabernacle, the Ark, and furniture and fittings in gold, silver, and embroidery. The Lord told Moses, "I have filled him with the Spirit of God, with ability and intelligence, with knowledge and all craftmanship."

Bhagwat Bhagwat Subramanya Chandrasekhar *(1945–)*
Indian cricket player, the "freak bowler," because he achieved his success after childhood polio.

Bianca Bianca Jagger, *née Bianca Peres Morena de Macias (20th century)*
Nicaraguan-born ex-wife of Mick Jagger.

Bibi Bibi Andersson *(Birgitta Andersson) (1935–)*
Swedish actress.

Bigas Bigas Luna *(20th century)*
Spanish director of the film *La teta y la luna (The Breast and the Moon)* (1995).

Bil Bil
Minor Nordic goddess. Bil and Hjuki were returning from a spring with a pail of water when they were seized by the moon god Mani, so she may be the original "Jill" of the children's rhyme "Jack and Jill."

Bilbo Bilbo Baggins
Intrepid hobbit hero of J.R.R. (John Ronald Reuel) Tolkien's novel *The Hobbit* (1937).

Bilhah Bilhah *trans. cheerfulness, Genesis 29: 29 (16th century B.C.)*
Old Testament maidservant to Jacob's wife Rachel. Childless Rachel suggested that Jacob have children with Bilhah so she could share them.

Bill Bill Cosby *(originally William Henry Cosby) (1937–)*
American comedian. In fiscal year 1987–88 the world's best-paid entertainer with an income of US$92 million.
> *"Always end the name of your child with a vowel, so that when you yell, the name will carry."*

Billie Billie Holiday *(originally Eleanora Fagan) (1915–1959)*
Tragic American jazz singer, "Lady Day."
> *"Without drugs, life wouldn't be worth living."*

Billy Billy the Kid *(William H. Bonney, Jr.) (1859–1881)*
American bandit, a killer from the age of fourteen, dead before the age of twenty-two.

Bing Bing Crosby *(originally Harry Lillis Crosby) (1904–1977)*
American velvet crooner. He won an Academy Award for *Going My Way* (1944).

Bird Charlie "Bird" Parker *(originally Charles Christopher Parker) (1920–1955)*
American jazz alto-saxophonist, composer of "Ornithology."

Birgit Birgit Nilsson *(Märta Birgit Nilsson) (1922–)*
Swedish operatic soprano.

Birgitta St. Birgitta *(or Bridget) (1303–1373)*
Patron saint of Sweden.

Biruté Dr. Biruté Goldikas *(1946–)*
Lithuanian-born Canadian anthropologist, mentor of the orangutans of Borneo. With Dian Fossey (gorillas) and Jane Goodall (chimpanzees), she forms the trio of primate experts "appointed" by Louis Leakey.

Bix Bix Beiderbecke *(originally Leon Bismarck Beiderbecke) (1903–1931)*
American jazz cornet player.

Biz Raleigh "Biz" Mackey *(1897–1959)*
American baseball centrefielder in the Negro Leagues, an All-Star.

Björn Björn Rune Borg *(1956–)*
Swedish tennis player. He set a modern record by winning five consecutive Wimbledon titles (1976–80).

Black Black Bart *(originally Charles E. Bolton) (b. c. 1820)*
American stagecoach robber. He took up robbery at age sixty, and left this poem in his first emptied safe-box:
> *"I've laboured long and hard for bread,*
> *For honor and for riches.*
> *But on my corns too long you've tred,*
> *You fine-haired sons-of-bitches."*

Blaine Blaine Trump *(20th century)*
American socialite.

Blair Blair Brown *(1948–)*
American actress, star of the TV series "The Days and Nights of Molly Dodd" (1987–88).

Blaise Blaise Pascal *(1623–1662)*
French philosopher and mathematician. His father did not want him to start school "too early," but at age eleven young Blaise was discovered to have worked out by himself the first twenty-three of Euclid's propositions.
> *"I have made this letter longer than usual, only because I have not had the time to make it shorter."*

Blake Blake Edwards *(originally William Blake McEdwards) (1922–)*
American film director of *The Pink Panther* (1963).

Blanche Blanche Dubois
American belle of Tennessee Williams's play *A Streetcar Named Desire* (1948).
> *"I have always depended on the kindness of strangers."*

Bliss Bliss Carman *(1861–1929)*
Canadian poet.
> *"Have little care that life is brief*
> *And less that life is long*
> *Success is in the silences*
> *Though fame is in the song."*

BILL COSBY

Blondel Blondel de Nesle *(12th century)*
French troubadour who followed Richard Coeur de Lion to Palestine. His story is told in Walter Scott's *The Talisman* (1825).

Blondie "Blondie" *(1930–)*
American cartoon strip created by Chic Young. Blondie's maiden name before her marriage to Dagwood (during the Great Depression) was "Boopadoop."

Bloody Bloody Mary *(Queen Mary I) (1516–1558)*
English daughter of Henry VIII, successor to her half-brother Edward VI. She executed about three hundred opponents during her efforts to re-establish Roman Catholicism in England.

Blower Blower Brown *(19th century)*
British walking champion. In 1879 he lost the coveted Astley Belt competition to American Edward Weston.

Bluebeard "Bluebeard" *(1697)*
French fairy-tale, one of the eight *Histoires ou Contes du temps passé* written by Charles Perrault, which also included "Sleeping Beauty" and "Red Riding Hood."

Bo Bo Diddley *(originally Ellias Bates) (1928–)*
American rock and blues songwriter.

Boadicea Queen Boadicea *(also called Boudicca) (d. 62 A.D.)*
English warrior, leader of the Iceni tribe of East Anglia. After the Romans publicly whipped her and raped her daughters, she ravaged Colchester, killing 7,000 Romans. However, two Roman legions then killed 8,000 of her tribesmen, and Boadicea took poison.

Bob Bob Marley *(1945–1981)*
Jamaican reggae star.

Bobbie Bobbie Gentry *(originally Roberta Lee Street) (1944–)*
American country singer and songwriter of "Ode to Billie Joe" (1967).

Bobby Bobby Seale *(1937–)*
American co-founder of the Black Panther Party, also one of the Chicago Eight charged with disrupting the 1968 Democratic National Convention.
  "Seize the time!"

Bobo Margaret "Bobo" Macdonald *(d. 1993)*
British royal employee for sixty-seven years, the nursemaid to Queen Elizabeth II. "Bobo" may have been baby Elizabeth's first word.

Bobs Bobs *(Frederick Sleigh Roberts, 1st Earl Roberts) (1832–1914)*
English field marshal, awarded the Victoria Cross during the Mutiny in India. "Bobs bahadu" means "hero" in Hindustani, and the Irish Guards are now called "Bob's Own."

Boctou Boctou *(c. 6th century)*
Legendary inhabitant of Mali. Her well became a caravan stop known as "place of Boctou," or "Tomboctou," now Timbuktu.

Bogomilla Bogomilla Welsh *(20th century)*
Canadian art historian, author of *Charles Pachter* (1993).

Boies Boies Penrose *(1860–1921)*
American senator. During the 1923 presidency campaign of Warren Harding, he advised, "Keep Warren at home. Don't let him make any speeches. If he goes on tour, somebody's sure to ask him a question, and Warren's just the sort of damn fool that'll try to answer them."

Bojangles Bill "Bojangles" Robinson *(originally Luther Robinson) (1878–1949)*
American tap dancer and film co-star with Shirley Temple.

Bombardier Billy "Bombardier" Wells *(1888–1967)*
British heavyweight boxing champion, author of *Physical Energy: Showing How Physical and Mental Energy May Be Developed by Means of the Practice of Boxing* (1924).
  "We are all born to a vocation, but many of us fail to discover what it is until it is too late. Without desiring for a moment to compare my own modest career with that of the great names mentioned here, I would like to point out that my youthful talent for boxing was determined to find expression in the same way as the boy Mozart's genius for music or young Murillo's for painting."

Bomber Bomber Harris *(Sir Arthur Travers Harris Bt.)* *(1892–1984)*
English Air Force marshal, inventor of the plan to bomb German cities during the Second World War, including Dresden, a baroque architectural jewel of no military significance.

Bonnie Bonnie Parker *(1911–1934)*
American waitress and bank robber, half of the team of "Bonnie and Clyde." She predicted their deaths in her poem "The Story of Suicide Sal":
"Now Sal was a girl of rare beauty,
Though her features were somewhat tough . . ."

Bonnie Bonnie Prince Charlie *(Prince Charles Edward Louis Philip Casimir Stuart) (1722–1788)*
Scottish claimant to the English throne, the "Young Pretender." He became an expatriate drunk.

Bono Bono Vox *(originally Paul Hewson) (1960–)*
Irish rock singer with the band U2. His nickname was taken from a hearing-aid store called Bono Vox, which almost translates into "good voice" in Latin.

Bonzo *Bedtime for Bonzo (1940)*
American movie, starring future president Ronald Reagan and Jiggs the chimpanzee.

Boog Boog Powell *(John Wesley Powell) (1941–)*
American baseball infielder with the Orioles, an All-Star.
"Once, just once, I'd like to play a whole season without an injury."

Booker Booker T. Washington *(Booker Taliaferro Washington) (1856–1915)*
American civil-rights worker and educator, author of the autobiography *Up from Slavery* (1901).
"You can't hold a man down without staying down with him."

Boomer Steve "Boomer" Yeager *(1948–)*
American baseball catcher for the Dodgers. He posed nude for a *Playgirl* centrefold.

Booth Booth Tarkington *(Newton Booth Tarkington) (1869–1946)*
American novelist, author of *The Magnificent Ambersons* (1918), for which he won a Pulitzer Prize.

"There are two things that will be believed of any man whatsoever, and one of them is that he has taken to drink."

Bootsy Bootsy Collins *(20th century)*
American funk bass player with George Clinton.
"There is a shortage of good funk."

Boris Boris Karloff *(originally William Henry Pratt) (1887–1969)*
British character actor noted for his role as Frankenstein's monster.

Borys Borys Conrad *(20th century)*
American son of writer Joseph Conrad and his wife, Jessie. When Jessie went into labour for his birth, Joseph locked himself in his study, saying, "I really don't care who suffers! I have enough of my own troubles!"

Boss Boss Croker *(originally Richard Croker) (1841–1922)*
Irish-born American politician, leader of the "Tammany Hall machine."

Boutros Boutros Boutros Ghali *(1922–)*
Egyptian secretary general of the United Nations, sometimes called "Boo Boo" because of his reputation for errors.
"To work here [at the U.N.] you have to be cuckoo — like me."

Bowie Bowie Kuhn *(1926–)*
American baseball executive. His officious manner won few friends; during his rule as commissioner, a journalist wrote, "This strike wouldn't have happened if Bowie Kuhn were alive today."

Boxcar "Boxcar Bertha" Thompson *(20th century)*
American campaigner for homeless women.

Boy Boy George *(George Alan O'Dowd) (1961–)*
English pop singer with the group Culture Club. He sang "Do You Really Want to Hurt Me?" (1982).

Brad Brad Pitt *(originally William Bradley Pitt) (1964–)*
American actor, the younger hunk in the movie *Interview with the Vampire* (1994).

Bradley Bradley Kincaid *(1895–)*
American folk-singer, author of the songbook *My Favorite Mountain Ballads and Old Time Songs* (1928).

Brag Brag
Norse god of eloquence.

Bram Bram Stoker (originally Abraham Stoker) (1847–1912)
Dublin-born civil servant, author of the novel *Dracula* (1897).

Branch Wesley "Branch" Rickey (1881–1965)
American baseball manager of the Dodgers, known as "The Mahatma" for his prescience in spotting fresh talent. He helped eliminate baseball's race discrimination just so he could sign Jackie Robinson.
"Luck is the residue of design."

Brandon Brandon Thomas (1849–1914)
English actor and playwright, author of *Charley's Aunt* (1892).
"I'm Charley's aunt from Brazil—where the nuts come from."

Branford Branford Marsalis (1960–)
American jazz saxophonist, brother of Wynton Marsalis.

Branwell Branwell Brontë (1817–1848)
Ne'er-do-well English brother of the more talented Anne, Charlotte, and Emily Brontë.

Branwen Branwen *trans. white crow*
Celtic wife of abusive King Matholwch. Her brother Bran tried to rescue her, and was beheaded. His head, the "Uther Ben," was dug up by King Arthur.

Breaker *Breaker Morant* (1980)
Australian film based on the adventures of Harry Harbord "Breaker" Morant (1865–1902).

Brenda Brenda Lee (originally Brenda Mae Tarpley) (1944–)
American pop and country singer.

Brendan Brendan Behan (1923–1964)
Drunken Irish author.
"I am married to Beatrice Salkend, a painter. We have no children, except me."

Bret Bret "The Hitman" Hart (1958–1993)
Canadian pro wrestler. According to *Western Report* magazine, he is "almost certainly the best known Albertan on earth."

Brett Brett Hull (1964–)
Canadian-born hockey right-winger for the St. Louis Blues. He and his father, Bobby Hull, can both shoot the puck at almost 100 mph. As Bobby was called "the Golden Jet," his son became known as "the Golden Brett."

Brian Brian Boru (c. 926–1014)
King of Ireland, defeater of the Danish invaders.

Bridey Bridey Murphy (19th century)
Irish previous incarnation of *Virginia Tighe Morrow*.

Bridget St. Bridget (or St. Brigid, or St. Bride) (453–523)
Irish abbess. She founded a monastery at Cill-Dara, now the city of Kildare.

Brigham Brigham Young (1801–1877)
American Mormon leader, the successor to Joseph Smith. At the time of his death, Young had seventeen wives and fifty-six children.

Brigid Brigid Brophy (1929–1995)
British novelist, author of *Fifty Works of English and American Literature We Could Do Without* (1967).

Brigitte Brigitte Bardot (originally Camille Javal) (1934–)
French animal-rights activist, a former sex goddess.

Briton Briton Hadden (1899–1929)
American journalist, co-founder of *Time* magazine in 1923.

Britt Britt Marie Ekland (1942–)
Swedish model and actress.
"I say I don't sleep with married men, but what I mean is that I don't sleep with happily married men."

Brittany Brittany York (20th century)
American model, the August 1990 Playmate of the Month in *Playboy* magazine.

Broderick Broderick Crawford (1911–1986)
American actor, winner of an Academy Award for his performance in *All the King's Men* (1949).

BRIGITTE BARDOT

Bronislava Bronislava Nijinska *(1891–1972)*
Russian ballet dancer, sister of Vaslav Nijinsky.

Bronwyn Bronwyn Drainie *(1945–)*
Canadian journalist.

Brook Brook Taylor *(1685–1731)*
English mathematician, author of a *Methodus incrementorum* (1715), which paved the way for calculus.

Brooke Brooke Shields *(1965–)*
American fashion model, star of the film *Pretty Baby*.

Brooks Brooks Stevens *(1911–1995)*
American industrial designer. He invented the wide-mouthed peanut butter jar.

BUDDY
HOLLY

Brownie Brownie McGhee *(originally Walter Brown McGhee) (1915–)*
American blues singer and guitarist.

Bruce Bruce Springsteen *(Bruce Frederick Joseph Springsteen) (1949–)*
American rock star, winner of an Academy Award for the title song of the film *Philadelphia* (1993).
  "I was born in the USA."

Brünnhilde Brünnhilde
Character in Wagner's opera *Götterdämmerung* (1876). In her immolation scene, she sings the longest aria in any opera, lasting more than fourteen minutes.

Bruno Bruno Gerussi *(1928–1995)*
Canadian actor. He played Nick Adonides on the TV series "The Beachcombers" (1971–1990).

Brutus Marcus Junius Brutus *(85–42 B.C.)*
Roman friend and assassin of Julius Caesar. In William Shakespeare's play, Caesar realizes his betrayal and says, "Et tu Brute, then die Caesar."

Bryan Bryan Ferry *(1945–)*
Well-dressed British rock star, a member of the group Roxy Music.

Bryher Bryher McAlmon, *née Winifred Ellerman (20th century)*
British heiress. To fulfil the terms of her father's will to inherit a fortune, she married homosexual writer Robert McAlmon. He spent his share of the loot publishing books by Ezra Pound, Gertrude Stein, and others.
  "Arranged marriages were perfectly familiar to me. It never occurred to me that there was anything irregular in my suggestion."

Bubb Bubb Dodington *(later George, 1st Baron Melcombe) (1691–1762)*
English politician, famous for switching sides.
  "Love thy country, wish it well,
  Not with too intense a care.
  'Tis enough, that when it fell
  Thou its ruin did not share."

Bubble Bubble
Ineffectual secretary of Edina on British television series "Absolutely Fabulous" (1993), known to its fans as "AbFab."
  "What's my job? I'm not quite sure. . . . To get paid?"

Buck Buck Owens *(originally Alvis Edgar Owens) (1929–)*
American country musician, leader of the Buckaroos.

Buckminster Buckminster "Bucky" Fuller *(originally Richard Buckminster Fuller) (1895–1983)*
American architect and designer, the inventor of the geodesic dome.

Bud Bud Fisher *(originally Harry Conway Fisher) (1885–1954)*
American cartoonist, the creator of "Mutt and Jeff."

Buddy Buddy Holly *(originally Charles Hardin Holly) (1936–1959)*
American rock'n'roll singer-songwriter-producer, composer of "That'll Be the Day" (1957). The Beatles named themselves in honour of his band, the Crickets.

Budge Budge Crawley *(20th century)*
Canadian animated filmmaker.

Buffalo "Buffalo Bill" Cody *(William Frederick Cody)*
(1846–1917)
American showman, creator of the Wild West
Show.

Buffy John "Buffy" Glassco *(1909–1981)*
Canadian poet, author of the definitive *Memoirs
of Montparnasse* (1970).
> *"We remained sunk in greed, sloth and sensuality
> —the three most amiable vices in the catalogue."*

Bugs Bugs Bunny *(20th century)*
American animated-film star.

Bugsy Bugsy Siegel *(originally Benjamin Siegel)*
(1906–1947)
American gangster, the founder of modern Las
Vegas. He spent $6 million building the
Flamingo Hotel, and was murdered when he
couldn't pay back his partners. His funeral was
attended by five people, all relatives.

Bulldog Jim "Bulldog" Bouton *(1939–)*
American baseball pitcher with the Yankees, an
All-Star. In retirement, he helped market "Big
League Chew," bubblegum that looks like
chewing tobacco.

Bumps Bumps Blackwell *(originally Robert A.
Blackwell) (1922–1985)*
American popular composer of "Good Golly
Miss Molly" (1957) and "You Send Me" (1957).

Bun Fred "Bun" Cook *(or Bunny Cook) (1903–)*
Canadian hockey player with the Saskatoon
Crescents. He invented both the slap shot and
the drop pass.

Bunny Bunny Wailer *(originally Neville O'Reilly
"Bunny" Livingstone) (1947–)*
Jamaican reggae musician, one of Bob Marley's
Wailers.

Burgess Burgess Meredith *(1908–)*
American character actor.

Burl Burl Ives *(originally Burle Icle Ivanhoe Ives)*
(1909–1995)
American singer and actor, immortalizer of the
song "Frosty the Snowman." He played Big
Daddy in the film *Cat on a Hot Tin Roof* (1958).

Burleigh Burleigh Grimes *(1893–1985)*
American baseball pitcher and manager, a member of the Hall of Fame, last of the legal spitball
pitchers.

Burnita Burnita S. Matthews *(1894–1988)*
American lawyer, the first female American federal district judge. She presided over the bribery
trial of James R. "Jimmy" Hoffa.

Burrhus Burrhus Frederic (B.F.) Skinner *(1904–1990)*
American behavioral psychologist, inventor of
the "Skinner box" in which he conditioned
pigeons to play Ping-Pong.
> *"Education is what survives when what has been
> learnt has been forgotten."*

Burt Burt Reynolds *(1936–)*
American film star.
> *"Nobody is worth what they pay me."*

Burton Burton Cummings *(1947–)*
Canadian singer-songwriter.

Busby Busby Berkeley *(originally William Berkeley
Enos) (1895–1976)*
American film choreographer extraordinaire,
creator of *42nd Street* (1933).

Buster Buster Keaton *(originally Joseph Francis
Keaton) (1895–1966)*
American film comedian. "Buster" was vaudeville slang for a comic fall, and Keaton got this
nickname from magician Harry Houdini, a
friend of the family, who saw him survive a
long fall unscathed at age six months.

Butch Butch Cassidy *(originally Robert Parker)*
(1896–?)
American outlaw.

Buttercup Buttercup
Heroine of the English operetta *HMS Pinafore*
(1878) by William Schwenck Gilbert and Arthur
Seymour Sullivan.
> *"Things are seldom as they seem,
> Skim milk masquerades as cream."*

Butterfingers Butterfingers Moran *(originally
Thomas B. Moran) (1892–1971)*
American pickpocket. He is estimated to have
acquired 50,000 wallets, mainly at racetracks,
setting an American career record.

Butterfly Butterfly McQueen (originally Thelma McQueen) (1911–1995)
American actress, Scarlett O'Hara's maid in the film *Gone With the Wind* (1939).

> "I hated it. The part of Prissy was so backward. I was always whining and complaining. . . . But now I'm very glad I made the film because I make a living off it. You wouldn't be here if I hadn't been Prissy."

Buzz Buzz Aldrin (originally Edwin Eugene Aldrin) (1930–)
American astronaut, the second man to walk on the moon, author of *Return to Earth* (1973).

Byron George Noel Gordon, 6th Baron Byron of Rochdale (1788–1824)
British poet.

> "I awoke one morning, and found myself famous."

Cab Cab Calloway (originally Cabell Calloway) (1907–1994)
American big-band leader. He invented the "hi-de-hi-de-ho" chorus to "Minnie the Moocher" (1931) when he forgot the real words while performing live on radio.

> "I had to fill the space, so I started to scat-sing the first thing that came into my mind."

Cain Cain *trans. spear, Genesis 4: 9*
Old Testament farmer who murdered his shepherd brother Abel in jealousy after God preferred Abel's offering over his own.

> "Am I my brother's keeper?"

Caipre Caipre
Aggressive Celtic bard, son of Ogma and Etan. He once composed a satire so rude that the victim's face broke out in blotches.

Cairine Cairine Reay Wilson *née Mackay* (1885–1962)
Canadian politician, the first female senator.

Caitlin Caitlin Thomas, *née Macnamara* (1913–1994)
Welsh wife of poet Dylan Thomas. As he lay dying in a New York hospital, she entered the room, asked, "Is the bloody man dead yet?" and bit an attendant.

Cal Cal Ripken, Jr. (1960–)
American baseball shortstop with the Orioles, an All-Star, the 1982 Rookie of the Year and Most Valuable Player in 1983 and 1991.

Calamity "Calamity Jane" Burke, *née Martha Jane Cannary* (c. 1852–1903)
American frontierswoman.

> "I'm Calamity Jane. Get the hell out of here and let me alone."

Caligula Caligula (*Gaius Caesar Augustus Germanicus*) (12–41)
Incompetent Roman emperor. His name came from his "caligae," soldier's boots. He executed as many people as he could manage, including most of his relatives, before himself being assassinated.

> "Would that the Roman people had but one neck."

Calixa Calixa Lavallée (originally Callixte Lavallée) (1842–1891)
Canadian pianist, composer of the tune to the national anthem "O Canada."

Calpurnia Calpurnia (*1st century*)
Roman wife of sickly Pliny the Younger. His letters praise her charm and attentions to him.

Calvert Calvert Vaux (1824–1895)
American landscape architect, co-designer of New York's Central Park and designer of Ottawa's parliamentary grounds.

Calvin Calvin Coolidge (*John Calvin Coolidge*) (1872–1933)
American politician, the 29th president, said to have slept more than any other president.

> "If you don't say anything, you won't be called upon to repeat it."

Calypso Calypso *trans. hidden or hider*
Mythical Greek daughter of Atlas. When Odysseus was shipwrecked on her island, she offered him immortality to stay with her, but he left anyway.

Cam Cam Neely (*Cameron Michael Neely*) (1965–)
Canadian-born American hockey right-winger for the Boston Bruins, an All-Star. He shares the 1991 National Hockey League single-season playoff record for most power-play goals (nine).

Cameron Cameron Mackintosh *(1946–)*
British stage producer.

Camilla Camilla Parker-Bowles *(20th century)*
British royal confidante. When she married Andrew Parker-Bowles, she wrote, "I suppose the feeling of emptiness will pass eventually."

Camille Camille Paglia *(20th century)*
American gonzo feminist, author of *Sexual Personae* (1990).

Campbell Campbell Swinton *(originally Archibald Campbell Swinton) (1863–1930)*
Scottish inventor in 1908 of the idea of the scanning cathode-ray tube, which would have been a television if he had built one.

Canaletto Canaletto *(real name Giovanni Antonio Canal) (1697–1768)*
Italian painter of magnificent scenic views of Venice.

Candace Candace Wheeler, *née Thurber (1827–1923)*
American textile designer, co-founder of the firm Tiffany and the Associated Artists.

Candice Candice Bergen *(1946–)*
American actress, star of the TV series "Murphy Brown."
> *"It's impossible to be more flat-chested than I am."*

Candida Candida *(1897)*
Satirical English play by George Bernard Shaw.
> *"We have no more right to consume happiness without producing it than to consume wealth without producing it."*

Candide Candide *(1759)*
Satirical French novella by François Voltaire.

Candido Candido Jacuzzi *(1903–1986)*
Italian-born American inventor of the whirlpool-bath pump. He wanted to provide hydrotherapy for his infant son's painful arthritis.

CAMILLE PAGLIA

Candy William Arthur "Candy" Cummings *(1848–1924)*
American baseball pitcher, inventor of the curveball.

Cantinflas Cantinflas *(originally Mario Moreno Reyes) (1911–1993)*
Mexican clown, acrobat, and bullfighter.

Canute Canute *(or Canut, or Knut Sveinsson) (994–1035)*
King of England, Denmark, and Norway, the uncle of St. Canute. He introduced a new title, "jarl" (earl), to replace the existing "ealdorman."

Canvass Canvass White *(1790–1834)*
American civil engineer, creator of a patented cement used in the Erie Canal.

Cap Cap Anson *(Adrian Constantine Anson) (1852–1922)*
American baseball infielder with the Cubs, the first person to get 3,000 hits in the National League, a member of the Hall of Fame. He started the ban on black players in the major leagues by pulling his team off the field against black pitcher Harry Stovey.

Capability Lancelot "Capability" Brown *(1715–1783)*
English naturalist and garden designer. He got his nickname from his habit of informing potential clients that their gardens had excellent "capabilities."

Caresse Caresse Crosby *(1892–1970)*
American inventor. In 1914 she created a "backless brassiere" out of two handkerchiefs and sold the patent for $1,500. Her autobiography, *The Passionate Years* (1953), may embroider facts; there is no outside evidence that she was the first U.S. Girl Scout.

Carey Carey Thomas *(Martha Carey Thomas) (1857–1935)*
American feminist, president of Bryn Mawr College and author of *The Higher Education of Women* (1900).
> *"I can't imagine anything worse than living a regular young lady's life."*

Cari Cari Hayer (1977–) American athlete. In 1984, at age seven, she became the youngest-ever international log-rolling champion.

Caril Caril Ann Fugate (1943–) American accomplice. She watched TV in the living-room while her boyfriend murdered her entire family.

CANDICE BERGEN

Carl Carl Gustav Jung (1875–1961) Swiss psychologist who described the "collective unconscious."

Carla Carla Bley (originally Carla Borg) (1938–) American jazz-rock fusion composer.

Carleton Carleton Stevens Coon (1904–1981) American anthropologist.

Carling Carling "Darling" Bassett (1968–) Canadian tennis player. She never won a major tournament, but retired rich anyway from endorsements.

Carlo Carlo Bugatti (1855–1940) Italian designer of excessively original Art Deco furniture, brother of better-known car manufacturer Ettore Bugatti.

Carlos Carlos Castanada (1935–) American mystic.

Carlotta Carlotta Monterey (20th century) Third wife of American playwright Eugene O'Neill. They exchanged engraved wedding rings, his reading "I am your laughter," and hers, "and you are mine."

Carly Carly Simon (1945–) American pop composer.
"You're so vain, you probably think this song is about you."

Carmelina Carmelina Fedele (20th century) Italian mother in 1955 of the world's largest known baby (22 pounds 8 oz.).

Carmen Carmen Miranda (Marie do Carmo Miranda da Cunha) (1909–1955) Portuguese-born American singer fondly remembered for her fruit-bearing hats.

Carmine Carmine Appice (1946–) American psychedelic drummer with the group Vanilla Fudge.

Carol Carol Moseley-Braun (1947–) American lawyer and politician, the first black female senator. Before the election, she said, "If I lose, I'm going to retire from politics, practice law, and wear bright leather pants."

Carole Carole Lombard (originally Jane Alice Peters) (1908–1942) American actress, the wife of William Powell and Clark Gable.

Carolina Lady Carolina Nairne, née Oliphant, (pen-name Mrs. Bogan of Bogan) (1766–1845) Scottish songwriter. She composed "Will ye no' come back again," the lament for Prince Charles Edward Stuart.

Caroline Caroline of Brandenburg-Ansbach (1683–1737) German wife of George II. On her deathbed, she urged him to remarry. Weeping, he refused, saying "J'aurai de maîtresses" ("I will have mistresses"). "Ah," she replied. "Cela non empêche pas" ("That shouldn't stop you").

Carolus Carolus Linnaeus (also known as Carl von Linné) (1707–1778) Swedish physician and naturalist, creator of the botanical nomenclature used to describe living things in terms of "class," "order," "genera" and "species."

Carolyn Carolyn Wells (1862–1942) American humorist, author of A Nonsense Anthology (1902).
"Dead men sell no tales."

Carrie Carrie Fisher (1956–) American actress, author of Postcards from the Edge (1987). Daughter of Eddie Fisher and Debbie Reynolds.
"You can't find true affection in Hollywood because everyone does the fake affection so well."

Carroll Carroll O'Connor *(1922–)*
American actor. He played Archie Bunker in the TV series *All in the Family* (1971–92).

Carry Carry Nation, *née Carry Amelia Moore (1846–1911)*
Axe-wielding American temperance worker, noted for her methodical saloon-smashing.
"Men are nicotine-soaked, beer-besmirched, whiskey-greased red-eyed devils."

Carson Carson McCullers, *née Lula Carson Smith (1917–1967)*
American Southern Gothic novelist. She wrote *The Heart Is a Lonely Hunter* (1940).

Carsten Carsten Niebuhr *(1733–1815)*
German tourist, the only member of his party to survive an expedition to the Middle East.

Carter Carter Godwin Woodson *(1875–1950)*
American historian, the "Father of Negro History." In 1926, he organized the first Negro History Week, now known as Black History Week.

Cary Cary Grant *(originally Archibald Leach) (1904–1986)*
British-born American film star.
"I play myself to perfection."

Casanova Casanova *(Giacomo Girolamo Casanova de Seingalt) (1725–1798)*
Italian sexual adventurer.

Casaubon Casaubon
Character in Umberto Eco's Italian novel *Foucault's Pendulum* (1989).
"There exists a secret society with branches throughout the world, and its plot is to spread the rumour that a universal plot exists."

Casey Casey Stengel *(Casey Charles Dillon Stengel) (c. 1890–1975)*
American baseball player, later manager of the Yankees during ten successful pennant races.
"The secret of managing is to keep the five guys who hate you away from the five guys who haven't made up their minds."

Casimir King Casimir III, the Great *(1310–1370)*
Polish ruler, last of the Piast dynasty, founder of Cracow University.

Caspar Caspar Willard Weinberger *(1917–)*
American lawyer and politician, Secretary of Defense under Reagan.

Cass Cass Elliot *(originally Ellen Naomi Cohen) (1943–1974)*
American pop singer with the group the Mamas and the Papas. She died in bed choking on a sandwich.

Cassandra Cassandra *trans. she who entangles men*
Mythical Trojan princess who promised to sleep with the god Apollo if he gave her the gift of prophecy. He did, but she refused to deliver her half of the deal, so he added a curse so that, although Cassandra would always predict the future correctly, no one would ever believe her.

Cassian St. Cassian of Tangiers *(d. c. 298)*
Moroccan court recorder at the trial of St. Marcellus the Centurian. He was put to death for protesting about the trial, and is now the patron saint of stenographers.

Cassie Cassie L. Chadwick *(d. 1907)*
Canadian-born American swindler. Her specialty was convincing banks that she was the secret daughter of Andrew Carnegie, temporarily short of funds.

Cassius Cassius Marcellus Clay *(1810–1903)*
American abolitionist leader. Cassius Clay the boxer (later Muhammad Ali) was named after him.

Caterina Caterina Cornaro *(1454–1510)*
Venetian-born Queen of Cyprus. She abdicated in favour of a republic after her husband's death.

Catfish Catfish Hunter *(James Augustus Hunter) (1946–)*
American baseball pitcher with the As and the Yankees, member of the Hall of Fame, one of the top ten players of all time. In his autobiography *Catfish: My Life in Baseball* (1988), he describes being assigned this nickname.

Catherine Catherine of Valois *(1401–1437)*
French princess, wife of English king Henry V. After his death, she secretly married Welshman Owen Tudor, the handsomest man of his time.

When her body was disinterred in the 17th century, Samuel Pepys kissed it on the forehead.

Cathleen *Cathleen ni Houlihan (1907)*
Play by William Butler Yeats. With Maud Gonne in the title role, this play probably helped spark the "Irish Rising" of Easter 1916.

Cathy *"Cathy" (20th century)*
American cartoon strip by Cathy Guisewite.

Catriona *Catriona (1893)*
Scottish novel by Robert Louis Stevenson, who also wrote *Kidnapped* (1886).

Cauac Cauac
Mayan god of the south. His colour was red.

Cecil Cecil John Rhodes *(1853–1902)*
South African politician, creator of the Rhodes scholarships to send colonial students to Oxford. His last words were "So little done—so much to do."

Cécile Cécile Dionne *(1934–)*
Canadian quintuplet, co-author with her surviving sisters, Annette and Yvonne, of the sad exposé *Family Secrets* (1995).
> *"We were too much to love."*

Cecilia Cecilia Bartoli *(20th century)*
Italian mezzo-soprano. Her concerts usually sell out within hours.
> *"I was a flamenco dancer. . . . Then I decided to have a [singing] lesson with my mother and I was discovered to have a voice. It was a big surprise to everybody—for me too."*

Cedric Cedric Errol Fauntleroy
Hero of the popular English tale *Little Lord Fauntleroy* (1886) by Frances Eliza Burnett.

Celeste Celeste Dandeher *(20th century)*
British dancer. Paralysed by a stage accident, she formed the CandoCo dance company, combining disabled and able-bodied performers.

Celestia Celestia Josephine "Jessie" Field *(1881–1971)*
American teacher; founder of the Boys Corn Club and the Girls Home Club, later the 4-H Club. She wrote *The Corn Lady: The Story of a Country Teacher's Life* (1911).

Celestine St. Celestine *(Pietr di Morrone, Pope Celestine V) (1215–1296)*
Neapolitan pope who resigned after five months. For this "great refusal," Dante depicted him at the entrance of hell.

Celia Celia Franca *(1921–)*
English-born Canadian prima ballerina.

Céline Céline Dion *(1968–)*
Quebec pop superstar, the youngest of fourteen children.

Celso Celso Russomanno *(20th century)*
Brazilian journalist, consumer affairs reporter for TV news show "Agui Agora."

Cendrith Cendrith *(7th century)*
British wife of King Cedwalla of Wessex. She rounded up the entire population of the Isle of Wight and forcibly baptized them all at once.

Century Century Millstead *(1900–1963)*
American football offensive tackle with the New York Giants. He was born on January 1 of the first year of the new century.

Cerberus Cerberus *trans. demon of the pit*
Legendary Greek three-headed dog of the Underworld; the Hound of Hell; guardian of the far side of the River Styx.

Cesar Cesar Estrada Chavez *(1927–1993)*
American farm union leader.

Cesare Cesare Borgia *(1476–1507)*
Italian ruler.
> *"Aut Caesar, aut nihil"* ("Emperor or nothing").

Chad Chad Allan *(originally Allan Kobel) (1945–)*
Canadian rock singer with the group the Guess Who.

Chaim Chaim Azriel Weizmann *(1874–1952)*
Russian-born Israeli chemist and Zionist politician, the first president after independence in 1949.

Chaka Chaka Khan *(originally Yvette Marie Stevens) (1953–)*
American soul singer, leader of the group Rufus.

Chandrasekhara Sir Chandrasekhara Venkata Raman *(1888–1970)*
Indian physicist awarded a Nobel Prize for explaining the "Raman effect," which makes water look blue.

Chang Chang and Eng Bunker *(1811–1874)*
Siamese-born American circus entertainers, the original "Siamese twins." Their names mean "left" and "right" in the Thai language. Both brothers married, and had a total of twenty-two children between them.

Charis Charis *trans. grace*
Greek goddess of grace and pleasure.

Charity Charity Cardwell *(1899–)*
American triplet. In 1995, she and her sisters, Faith and Hope, were the world's longest-lived triplets.

Charles Charles Lynch *(d. 1796)*
American magistrate, inventor of the "Lynch mob."

Charles-Geneviève Charles-Geneviève-Louise-Auguste-Andrée-Timothée d'Eon de Beaumont *(1728–1810)*
French diplomat, swordsman, and transvestite spy. He lived his last years in England on a pension from Louis XV given on the understanding that he remain a woman publicly. English sexologist Havelock Ellis coined the term "eonism" to describe cross-dressing.

Charley Charley Pride *(1938–)*
American country musician, the first black country superstar.

Charlie Charlie Chaplin *(Sir Charles Spencer Chaplin) (1889–1977)*
English-born American film genius, creator of *The Tramp* (1915).
"All I need to make a comedy is a park, a policeman, and a pretty girl."

Charlotte Charlotte Corday d'Armont *(1768–1893)*
French murderess who stabbed politician Jean-Paul Marat in his bath. (He was sitting in the bath because he was already dying of an uncomfortable disease.)

Charlton Charlton Heston *(originally Charlton Carter) (1923–)*
American epic-film actor. He won an Academy Award for his performance in *Ben-Hur* (1959).
"[Fame] is part of my job. The guy over there who turned around is one of the people who's been buying my kids' shoes for 40 years."

Charmian Charmian
Cleopatra's favourite attendant in William Shakepeare's play *Antony and Cleopatra* (1606–1607). She kills herself after Cleopatra's death.

Charon Charon *trans. fierce brightness*
Mythical miserly boatman who ferries the dead across the River Styx to the Underworld. A coin was laid under the tongue of the dead to pay Charon's fare.

Chazz Chazz Palminteri *(1951–)*
American actor, the screenwriter of *A Bronx Tale* (1993) in which he co-starred with Robert De Niro.

Che Che Guevara *(Ernesto Guevara de la Serna) (1928–1967)*
Argentinian revolutionary worker, a central figure in the Cuban Revolution with Fidel Castro.

Checker Douglas Gordon "Checker" Goody *(active 1963)*
English Great Train Robber.

Checkers Checkers *(20th century)*
American cocker spaniel, the pet of Richard Nixon.

Cheesy Gerry "Cheesy" Cheevers *(1941–)*
American hockey goalie for the Boston Bruins, a member of the Hall of Fame.
"I became a goalie because I wasn't good enough to be anything else."

Cheops King Cheops *(or Khufu) (active c. 2551 B.C.)*
Egyptian king of Memphis, second king of the fourth dynasty, builder of the Great Pyramid at Giza.

Cher Cher *(originally Cherilyn LaPiere Sarkisian) (1946–)*
American songstress and actress. She won an Academy Award for *Moonstruck* (1987).

Chéri *Chéri (1920)*
French novel by Sidonie Colette, describing the prototypical toy boy.

Cherubino Cherubino
Mezzo-soprano trouser role in Wolfgang Amadeus Mozart's opera *The Marriage of Figaro (Le nozze di Figaro)* (1786).

Cheryl Cheryl Ladd *(originally Cheryl Stoppelmoor) (1951–)*
American actress.

Chesty Chesty Love *(originally Cynthia Hess) (20th century)*
American stripper. In 1994, she successfully claimed the cost of her breast implants as a business tax-deduction, on the basis that the resulting size 55FF bust provided no personal benefit to its owner.

Chet Chet Atkins *(Chester Burton Atkins) (1924–)*
American guitarist and record producer, creator of the "Nashville sound."

Chevalier Chevalier Jackson *(1865–1958)*
American writer.
> "In teaching the medical student, the primary requisite is to keep him awake."

Chevy Chevy Chase *(originally Cornelius Crane Chase) (1943–)*
American comedian.

Chewbacca Chewbacca
Fuzzy alien sidekick of Han Solo in the American film *Star Wars* (1977).

Cheyenne Cheyenne Brando *(1970–1995)*
Tahitian daughter of American actor Marlon Brando. She committed suicide after her brother was convicted of murdering her fiancé.

Chi Chi Juan "Chi Chi" Rodriguez *(1935–)*
Puerto Rican golfer. He sued the makers of the movie *To Wong Foo, Thanks for Everything! Julie Newmar* (1995) on the basis that the drag-queen character of the same name defamed his reputation.

Chic Chic Young *(originally Murat Bernard Young) (1901–1973)*
American cartoonist, the creator of "Blondie" (1930).

Chick Chick Corea *(originally Armando Anthony Corea) (1944–)*
American jazz keyboard player.

Chico Chico Marx *(originally Leonard Marx) (1891–1961)*
American gambler and film comedian. He got his nickname, properly pronounced "Chicko," because he liked the "chicks" so much.
> "I wasn't kissing her. I was whispering in her mouth."

Childe "Childe Roland to the Dark Tower Came" *(1855)*
Scottish ballad by Robert Browning about a young man who rescues his sister from an elf's castle.
> "Dauntless the slug-horn to my lips I set, and blew."

Chili Chili Palmer *(20th century)*
American security guard and former gangster, the inspiration for the character in Elmore Leonard's novel *Get Shorty* (1993).

Chill Chill Wills *(1903–1978)*
American actor. He was the voice of Francis the Talking Mule.

Chinski Charlie "Chinski" Root *(1899–1970)*
American pitcher for the Cubs. He was pitching the day Babe Ruth "called his shot" and hit the ball out of the park. Root always denied this, claiming he would have beaned Ruth if it was true.
> "He was just saying he had one strike left."

Chips Sir Henry "Chips" Channon II *(1897–1958)*
American-born British politician. He once shared a house with a friend known as "Fish."

Chita Chita Rivera *(1933–)*
Puerto Rican–born actress.

Chiuchi Chiuchi Nagumo *(1886–1944)*
Japanese commander of the Carrier Fleet, which attacked Pearl Harbor. He committed suicide.

Chloris Chloris *trans. greenish*
Legendary Greek athlete, winner of the first Heraean games (the female Olympics).

Chris Chris Evert *(originally Christine Marie Evert, later Chris Evert Lloyd) (1954–)*
American tennis player, the "Ice Maiden." She set the second all-time record for tournament victories, but audiences seemed cool towards her because she was always so perfect.

Chrissie Chrissie Hynde *(Christine Ellen Hynde) (1951–)*
American rock guitarist, singer, and songwriter; leader of the Pretenders.
> *"It's such a forgiving audience, the rock audience. As long as you don't get fat, anything goes."*

Christabel Christabel Harriette, *née Pankhurst (1880–1958)*
English suffragist, daughter of Emmeline Pankhurst. They founded the militant Women's Social and Politican Union.

Christiaan Christiaan Huygens *(1629–1695)*
Dutch mathematician and physicist, the first to propose a wave theory of light.

Christian Christian Doppler *(1803–1853)*
Austrian physicist. His "Doppler's Principle" explains why the frequency of a sound or light appears to change when the source is moving (as when the siren changes tone when an ambulance passes).

Christie Christie Hefner *(1953–)*
American second-generation boss of the *Playboy* publishing empire.

Christina Christina Rossetti *(Christina Georgina Rossetti) (1830–1894)*
Pre-Raphaelite English poetess. Her family intended her to become a governess, but she managed to remain sick enough to stay home and write poetry instead.
> *"My heart is like a singing bird."*

Christine Christine Jorgensen *(20th century)*
Pioneering British sex-change.

CHRISSIE HYNDE

Christo Christo *(originally Christo Javacheff) (1935–)*
Bulgarian-born American environmental artist. A spectator was killed when of one of his giant umbrellas fell.

Christofor Marcis Anastasia "Christofor" Christoforides *(later Mrs. James Dunn, and later still Lady Beaverbrook) (1910–1994)*
British-born secretary and wealthy widow. Her second husband remarked that she was the only woman he knew richer than he was.

Christoph Christoph Willibald Gluck *(1714–1787)*
Bavarian-born Austro-German composer. He fought a long musical war with Niccola Piccinni, which he won by composing the triumphant *Iphigénie en Tauride* (1779), and retired.

Christopher Christopher Robin Milne *(1920–1996)*
English child, immortalized (to his later chagrin) by his father, A.A. (Alan Alexander) Milne, in the poems *When We Were Very Young* (1924).

Christy Christy Brown *(1932–1981)*
British writer, author of the autobiography *My Left Foot* (1954).

Chrysostom St. Chrysostom *(St. John Chrystostom) (c. 347–407)*
Syrian church worker, the "golden mouthed."
> *"No one can harm the man who does himself no wrong."*

Chubby Chubby Checker *(originally Ernest Evans) (1941–)*
American singer, popularizer of "The Twist" (1960).

Chuck Chuck Berry *(originally Charles Edward Anderson Berry) (1926–)*
American rock icon, composer of "Johnny B. Goode" (1958).
> *"Roll over Beethoven*
> *And tell Tchaikovsky the news."*

Cicely Cicely Tyson *(1933–)*
American actress.

Cicero Marcus Tullius Cicero *(106–43 B.C.)*
Roman orator, essayist, and lawyer.
> *"When you have no basis for an argument, abuse the plaintiff."*

Cihuacoatl Cihuacoatl
Aztec goddess of childbirth, "Serpent Woman."

Cilla Cilla Black (originally Priscilla Maria Veronica White) (1943–)
English singer, the first British host of a game-show, "Blind Date."

Cinderella Cinderella
Char-maid fiancée of handsome Prince Charming.

Cindia Cindia Huppeler (20th century)
American acting coach to Uma Thurman.

Cindy Cindy Birdsong (1939–)
American pop singer, one of the Supremes.

Cissy Cissy Pascal (20th century)
American wife of writer Raymond Chandler. She was eighteen years older than he was, and married to someone else when they met. In one of Chandler's books, a character says, "I never proposed marriage formally to anyone. My wife and I just seemed to melt into each others' hearts without the need for words."

Cito Cito Gaston (Clarence Edwin Gaston) (1944–)
The first Canadian baseball manager (and the first black manager) to win a World Series.
  "I think I get the most out of my players simply by treating them with respect."

Claes Claes Oldenburg (Claes Thure Oldenburg) (1929–1990)
Swedish-born American sculptor. He makes big soft versions of things normally hard, such as toilets.

Clara Clara Josephine Schumann, née Wieck (1819–1896)
German pianist and composer, wife of Robert Schumann, a professional from the age of eleven.
  "I once thought I possessed creative talent, but I have given up on this idea; a woman must not desire to compose—no one has ever been able to do it, and why should I expect to?"

Clare St. Clare of Assisi (1194–1253)
Religious friend of St. Francis, founder of the order of the Poor Clares, the patron saint of television.

Clarence Clarence Seward Darrow (1857–1938)
American lawyer. Teased by reporters about his appearance, he said, "I go to a better tailor than any of you and pay more for my clothes. The only difference is that you probably don't sleep in yours."

Claretta Claretta Pettacci (d. 1943)
Italian mistress of Benito Mussolini. They were killed by a mob, and their bodies hung by the feet in Milan for public display.

CHUCK BERRY

Clarice Clarice Cliff (1899–1972)
English designer of "Bizarre" ceramics.

Clarissa Clarissa Pinkola Estés (20th century)
American author of Women Who Run with the Wolves.

Clark Clark Gable (originally William Clark Gable) (1901–1960)
American actor. He played Rhett Butler in Gone With the Wind (1939).

Claude Claude Lévi-Strauss (1908–)
French social-anthropologist.

Claudell Claudell Washington (1954–)
American baseball outfielder with the Braves, an All-Star.

Claudette Claudette Colbert (originally Claudette Lily Chauchoin) (1905–)
French-born American actress. She won an Oscar for It Happened One Night (1934).

Claudia Claudia Cardinale (1939–)
Italian actress, star of Federico Fellini's film 8½ (1963).

Claudine Claudine Longet (20th century)
French actress. She appeared in the movie The Party.

Claudio Claudio Monteverdi (1567–1643)
Italian baroque composer, creator of the very first opera.

Claudius *I, Claudius (1934)*
Novel by British writer Robert Graves.

Clay Clay Allison *(1840–1877)*
American outlaw. He once shot out all the shop windows in the town of Canadian, Texas, while drunk, wearing only hat, boots, and six-guns.

Clea *Clea (1960)*
Expatriate British novel by Lawrence Durrell, the last volume of his "Alexandria Quartet."

Clem Clem Daniels *(1937–)*
American football running back for the Oakland Raiders, the National Football League 1963 Player of the Year.

Clement Clement Clarke Moore *(1779–1863)*
American writer, author of "A Visit from St. Nicholas" (1823).
> *"'Twas the night before Christmas,*
> *When all through the house,*
> *Not a creature was stirring,*
> *Not even a mouse."*

Clementina Clementina Walkinshaw *(18th century)*
English mistress of Prince Charles Edward Stuart ("Bonnie Prince Charlie"). She may have been a spy for Hanover.

Clementine Clementine Hunter *(19th century)*
American folk painter, a former slave, resident of Natchitoches, Louisiana.

Clements Sir Clements Robert Markham *(1830–1916)*
English geographer. As president of the Royal Geographic Society, he appointed Captain Robert Scott to lead his successful first Antarctic expedition. (Scott died on the second expedition.)

Clennell Clennell "Punch" Dickins *(b. 1899)*
Canadian Second World War air-ace and bush pilot, creator of the first regular air service into the Canadian north.

Cleo Cleo Laine *(originally Clementina Dinah Campbell) (1928–)*
British jazz vocalist.

Cleon Cleon *(d. 442)*
Athenian soldier.

Cleonie Cleonie Knox *(pen-name of Magdalen King-Hall) (1904–1971)*
English writer, author of *The Diary of a Young Lady of Fashion in the Year 1764–5.*

Cleopatra Cleopatra VII *(69–30 B.C.)*
Queen of Egypt, last of the Ptolemy dynasty, the fascinating lover of Julius Caesar and Mark Antony. As William Shakespeare put it, "Age cannot wither her, nor custom stale her infinite variety."

Cleotha Cleotha Staples *(1934–)*
American gospel singer with the Staples Singers.

Clerihew Edmund Clerihew Bentley *(1875–1956)*
British novelist. He invented the perky four-line "clerihew" form of biography.
> *"Brigham Young*
> *Was exceptionally high strung.*
> *He always used a chopper*
> *When a Mormon said anything improper."*

Clete Clete Boyer *(Cletis Leroy Boyer) (1937–)*
American baseball third baseman with the Yankees, winner of a Gold Glove award. In 1964, Clete and his brother Ken both hit home runs in the same game, for opposing teams.

Cleve Cleve Cartmill *(20th century)*
American writer. In 1944, he published a short story in *Astounding Science Fiction* magazine about a bomb "made of an isotope of uranium, U-235," which greatly alarmed intelligence agents, particularly when they found he'd done all his research at the public library.

Cliff Sir Cliff Richard *(originally Harry Roger Webb) (1940–)*
Indian-born English pop singer. He can be seen in the film *Expresso Bongo* (1960).

Clifford Clifford Irving *(1930–)*
American author. He served time in jail for writing a bogus Howard Hughes biography.

Clifton Clifton Chenier *(1925–1987)*
American zydeco accordian player, "King of the Bayou."

Clint Clint Eastwood *(1930–)*
American filmmaker, star of *Dirty Harry* (1971), winner of an Oscar for directing *Unforgiven* (1992).

Clive Clive James *(1930–)*
Australian-born British TV personality, author of the childhood depiction *Unreliable Memoirs* (1980).

Clodion Clodion *(real name Claude Michel) (1738–1814)*
French sculptor of the Napoleonic era specializing in small terracotta figures of nymphs and fauns.

Cloris Cloris Leachman *(1926–)*
American actress.

Clotho Clotho *trans. spinner*
Greek Fate. She spins the thread of life that is measured by her sister Lachesis and cut by deadly Atropos.

Clotilda St. Clotilda *(474–545)*
Queen of the Franks. She baptized her husband, Clovis, and 2,000 of his soldiers, all at once.

Clough Sir Clough Williams-Ellis *(1883–1978)*
British architect. He designed Portmeirion, the Italiante-style Welsh village used as the setting for the British TV series *The Prisoner* (1967).

Clovis Clovis Carl Green, Jr. *(20th century)*
American prison inmate, the initiator of a record-setting 700 civil law suits against his jailors. Recreational lawsuits are a popular American prison hobby, since inmates have time and free legal help.

Clyde Clyde William Tombaugh *(1906–)*
American astronomer, the discoverer of Pluto. He was too poor to attend college, so he built his own telescope at home.

Clyfford Clyfford Still *(1904–1980)*
American painter.

Clytemnestra
Clytemnestra *trans. praiseworthy wooing*
Legendary Greek wife of King Agamemnon. She was murdered by her son Orestes because she had helped murder her husband.

COCO CHANEL

Coatlicue Coatlicue
Aztec earth goddess.

Cochise Cochise *(1812?–1874)*
Chief of the American Apache Indians.

Coco Coco Chanel *(originally Gabrielle Bonheur Chanel) (1883–1971)*
French couturier. Among her innovations were loose clothes worn without corsets, jersey fabrics, the "twin set," quilted handbags hung on gold chains, and, of course, Chanel No. 5 perfume.

Coenraad Coenraad Jacob Temminck *(1778–1858)*
Dutch ornithologist. "Temminck's Horned Lark" is named after him.

Cole Cole Porter *(1892–1964)*
American composer of elegant songs such as "Begin the Beguine" (1934).

Coleman Coleman Hawkins *(1904–1969)*
American jazz tenor-saxophone player.

Colette Colette *(Sidonie Gabrielle Colette) (1873–1954)*
French writer, author of *Gigi* (1945), the first female writer to be given a state funeral.
"What a wonderful life I've had! I only wish I'd realized it sooner!"

Colin Colin Luther Powell *(1937–)*
American soldier, chairman of the Chief Joints of Staff, mastermind of Operation Desert Storm in Iraq.
"Avoid having your ego so close to your position that, when your position fails, your ego goes with it."

Colleen Colleen McCullough *(1937–)*
Australian novelist, author of *The Thorn Birds*.

Colley Colley Cibber *(1671–1757)*
English actor and dramatist.
"Stolen sweets are best."

Columba St. Columba *(or Colum, or Colmcille) (521–597)*
Irish apostle, the patron saint of poets.

Columbine Columbine
Traditional character in the "harlequenade," the sweetheart of Pierrot. She may be the goddess Diana fallen on hard times.

CORAZON
MARIA AQUINO

Columbus Columbus Joiner *(20th century)*
American oil wildcatter. In 1930, he sold control of his East Texas oil field for $30,000 to H.L. (Haroldson Lafayette) Hunt, who found oil and became a billionaire.

Commander Commander Cody *(originally George Frayne) (1944–)*
American boogie rocker, leader of Commander Cody and His Lost Planet Airmen.

Conan *Conan the Barbarian (1982)*
American movie starring Arnold Schwarzenegger.

Conchita Conchita Cintrón *(originally Consuela Verrill) (1922–)*
Chilean-born American bullfighter. She made her first appearance in Mexico at the age of fifteen, killing 800 bulls over the next thirteen years before retiring to get married.

Confucius Confucius *(Latin for K'ung Fu-tze, or "Master K'ung") (551–479 B.C.)*
Chinese philosopher. His descendants live today in Taiwan.

Conn Conn Smythe *(originally Constantine Falkland Cary Smythe) (1895–1980)*
Canadian sports entrepreneur.

Connee Connee Boswell *(1907–1976)*
American blues singer with the Boswell Sisters. After her childhood polio caught up with her in later years, she continued to perform from a wheelchair.

Connie Connie Mack *(originally Cornelius Alexander McGillicuddy) (1862–1956)*
American baseball owner of the Philadelphia Athletics.
"It is more profitable for me to have a team that is in contention for most of the season but finishes about fourth. A team like that will draw well enough during the first part of the season to show a profit for the year, and you don't have to give the players raises when they don't win."

Conor Conor Cruise O'Brien *(Donal Conor Dermod David Donat Cruise O'Brien) (1917–)*
Irish historian and politician, author of *To Katanga and Back* (1962). He is called "Conor Cruise O'Britain" by those who dislike his anti-IRA intellectual stance.

Conrad Conrad Nicholson Hilton *(1887–1979)*
American hotelier, author of *Be My Guest* (1957).

Constance Constance H.K. Applebee *(1874–1981)*
English-born American athlete, "the Apple," sports coach at Bryn Mawr and founder of the the first women's sports magazine, *The Sportswoman*. She introduced field hockey to the United States.

Constante Constante of "La Floridita" bar in Havana *(20th century)*
Cuban bartender, inventor during the 1930s of the daiquiri.

Constantin Constantin Brancusi *(1876–1957)*
Romanian sculptor, creator of *Bird in Space* (1925).
"Architecture is inhabited sculpture."

Constantine Constantine the Great *(Flavius Valerius Aurelius Constantinus) (c. 288–337)*
First Christian Roman Emperor. He chose Byzantium for his capital, and renamed it Constantinople in his own honour.

Constanze Constanze Mozart, *née Weber (married 1782)*
German wife of Wolfgang Amadeus Mozart.

Conway Conway Twitty *(originally Harold Lloyd Jenkins) (1934–1993)*
American country singer and songwriter.

Cool James "Cool Papa" Bell *(1903–)*
American baseball outfielder with the Pittsburgh Crawfords, a member of the Hall of Fame. Satchel Paige said, "He was so fast, he could turn out the light and be in bed before the room got dark." In fact, he did this once, but there was a fault in the wiring.

Cora Cora Taylor *(19th century)*
American prostitute, the common-law wife of writer Stephen Crane. They met in her brothel, where she expressed admiration for his novel *The Red Badge of Courage* (1895).

Coraghessan T. Coraghessan Boyle *(1948–)*
American writer, author of *East Is East* (1990).

Corazon Corazon (Cory) Maria Aquino, *née Cojuangco (1933–)*
Filipino politician. She won the election that caused the flight of Ferdinand Marcos.

Cordelia Cordelia
Misunderstood virtuous daughter in William Shakespeare's play *King Lear* (c. 1605).

Coretta Coretta Scott King *(20th century)*
American wife of theologian Martin Luther King.

Corey Corey Hart *(1961–)*
Canadian pop singer, with the hit "(I Wear My) Sunglasses at Night" (1983).

Corin Corin
Rustic shepherd in William Shakespeare's play *As You Like It* (1599–1600).

Corinna Corinna *(1st century)*
Roman mistress of the poet Ovid. He wrote his *Amores* poems to her.

Corinne *Corinne (1807)*
French novel by Madame de Staël based on the real Jeanne Récamier, who led a brilliant salon until the bankruptcy of her husband. He offered to divorce her so that she could accept marriage from Prince August of Prussia, but she refused to abandon him.
   "To understand all makes us very indulgent."

Coriolanus *The Tragedy of Coriolanus (1607–8)*
Play by William Shakespeare, inspired by the real Roman soldier Gaius Coriolanus.

Corliss *A Kiss for Corliss (1949)*
American film starring David Niven and Shirley Temple.

Cornel Cornel West *(1953–)*
American educator, writer and social activist, author of *Race Matters* (1993).
   "Black people have always been America's wilderness in seach of a promised land."

Cornelia Cornelia Otis Skinner *(1901–1979)*
American actress and writer.
   "One learns in life to keep silent and draw one's own confusions."

Cornelis Cornelis Jacobszoon Drebbel *(1572–1633)*
Dutch inventor. In 1621, he sailed a wooden submarine with a crew of twelve down the Thames from Westminster to Greenwich. King James I watched from the bank.

Cornelius Cornelius (Commodore) Vanderbilt *(1794–1877)*
American financier. He started his fortune at age sixteen, using a rowboat.

Cory Cory Wells *(1942–)*
American rock musician with the group Three Dog Night.

Cosima Cosima Wagner, *née Liszt (1837–1930)*
French illegitimate daughter of Franz Liszt and the Comtesse d'Agoult. She left her first husband to run off with Richard Wagner.

Cosimo Cosimo de' Medici *(1389–1464)*
Florentine financier and philanthropist, "Pater Patriae" of the Medici family.
   "We read that we ought to forgive our enemies, but we do not read that we ought to forgive our friends."

Cosmo Cosmo Kramer
Neighbourly sidekick on the American TV series "Seinfeld" *(b. 1990)*.

Cotton Cotton Mather *(1663–1728)*
American clergyman. His book *Memorable Providences Relating to Witchcraft and Possessions* (1685) helped to inspire the fatal Salem witchcraft mania.

Count Count Basie *(originally William Basie) (1904–1984)*
American jazz pianist and composer, leader of the Count Basie Orchestra.
   "Of course, there are a lot of ways you can treat the blues, but it will still be the blues."

Countee Countee Cullen *(1903–1946)*
American poet, a leader of the Harlem Renaissance.
   "In order for a writer to succeed, I suggest three things—read and write—and wait."

Courtney Courtney Love *(originally Courtney Menely) (1964–)*
American singer, wife of suicide Kurt Cobain, creator of the "kinderwhore" fashion look.

Madonna said, "I am fascinated by [Courtney], but in the same way I am by somebody who's got Tourette's syndrome walking in Central Park."

Coventry Coventry Patmore *(Coventry Kersey Dighton Patmore) (1823–1896)*
English librarian and Pre-Raphaelite poet, author of *The Angel in the House* (1854), a tribute to married love. He was married three times.

Coyote Coyote
Mythic native North American clever trickster.

Cozy Cozy Powell *(1947–)*
American progressive-rock drummer, with the band Emerson, Lake and Palmer.

Craig Craig Russell *(20th century)*
Canadian female impersonator. He appeared as himself in the film *Outrageous.*
"Sex is only a matter of lighting."

Crawford Dr. Crawford Williamson Long *(1815–1878)*
American surgeon, in 1842 the first person to perform surgery with a general anaesthetic, ether. In 1844, he gave his wife ether at the birth of their second child.

Crazy Frederick "Crazy" Schmidt *(1866–1940)*
American baseball pitcher. He had a poor memory, and on the mound, before a pitch, would consult a little notebook recording batter's habits.

Cristina Cristina Sanchez *(20th century)*
Mexican bullfighter, the first female bullfighter to perform in the world's largest arena, Plaz Mexico. She was awarded an ear.

Cristóbal Cristóbal Balenciaga *(1895–1972)*
Spanish couturier, noted for the unsurpassed magnificence of his ball gowns.

Croesus King Croesus *(d. c. 546 B.C.)*
Wealthy last king of Lydia. He was the patron of Aesop, who wrote the fables.

Cronus Cronus *(or Cronos) trans. crow*
Greek Titan of Saturn, ruler of the golden race of the first men. (We today belong to the inferior or third race of iron men.)

Crowfoot Chief Crowfoot *(1830–1890)*
Canadian leader, Blood-born chief of the Blackfoot Indians. He negotiated peace with both the Cree and the Canadian Pacific Railway.

Cruella Cruella de Ville
Fur-loving villainness of Dodie Smith's children's story "The Hundred and One Dalmations" (1956).

Crystal Crystal Gayle *(originally Brenda Gayle Webb Gatzimos) (1951–)*
American country music star. She sang "Don't It Make My Brown Eyes Blue" (1977).

Cual Cual Delavrancea *(1887–1991)*
Romanian pianist. She gave her last public recital at the age of 103, taking six encores.

Cudjoe Cudjoe Lewis *(d. 1935)*
Guinean-born American, the longest-lived member of the last boatload of African slaves brought to America in 1859. Their ship was burnt on the shore, and the slaves freed to settle nearby.

Cunobelin Cunobelin *(active A.D. 43)*
Celtic Iron Age ruler, possibly the original jolly "Old King Cole."

Cupid Cupid
Roman god of love.

Cupra Cupra
Etruscan goddess of fertility.

Curly Curly Howard *(Jerome Horowitz) (1903–1952)*
American actor, one of the Three Stooges.

Curt Curt Smith *(1961–)*
British pop musician with the group Tears for Fears.

Curthose Robert II "Curthose," Duke of Normandy *(1054?–1134)*
Eldest son of William the Conqueror. His hose were "curt" because he was very short.

Curtis Curtis Sliwa *(1954–)*
American founder of the do-it-yourself Guardian Angels street patrol.

Curtmantle Henry II "Curtmantle" *(1133–1189)*
English Plantagenet king. He introduced a type of short coat which came only to the knees and was more convenient for hunting.

Cuthbert Cuthbert Tunstall (1474–1559)
English Bishop of Durham. He never put anyone to death for heresy, very unusual for the
time.

Cy Cy Young (Cy Denton True Young) (1867–1955)
American baseball pitcher. The Cy Young Award
is given annually to the best pitcher in both
leagues.

Cybill Cybill Shepherd (1950–)
American actress. When the TV series
"Moonlighting" started, she was a star and
Bruce Willis unknown.

Cyd Cyd Charisse (originally Tulla Ellice Finklea)
(1923–)
American dancer and actress, star of the film
Silk Stockings (1957).

Cyndi Cyndi Lauper (originally Cynthia Anne
Stephanie Lauper) (1953–)
American rock singer.
"Girls just want to have fun."

Cynthia Cynthia Albritten (c. 1955–)
American rock star groupie, the "Plaster Caster."
"Jimi Hendrix's guitar went for $500,000. The
one-of-a-kind replica of his penis must be worth
at least that much."

Cyrano Cyrano de Bergerac (1897)
French novel by Edmond Rostand concerning
an honourable gentleman with a large nose.
"A great nose indicates a great man—
Genial, courteous, intellectual,
Virile, courageous."

Cyrene Cyrene trans. sovereign queen or mistress of
the bridle
Mythical Greek princess. Apollo fell in love
when he saw her wrestling lions, and they had
two sons.

Cyril Cyril Northcote Parkinson (1909–1993)
English political scientist, author of Parkinson's
Law, the Pursuit of Progress (1957). His rule is that
work expands to fill the time available, and that
subordinates multiply at a fixed rate, regardless
of the amount of work.

Cyrus Cyrus Hall McCormick (1809–1884)
American inventor of the mechanical reaping
machine.

Dabney Dabney Coleman (1932–)
American actor.

Daedelus Daedelus trans. bright or cunningly wrought
Legendary Greek inventor. He and his son
Icarus escaped the labyrinth of King Minos on
artificial wings. Foolish Icarus flew too close to
the sun, melting the wax holding the feathers,
and fell into the sea.

Dafne Dafne (1594)
Italian poem by Ottavio Rinucini, the first
Italian melodrama. In 1597, it was made into
the first opera by Jacopo Peri.

Dafydd Dafydd ap Gwilym (14th century)
Mythical Welsh poet created by 20th-century
Welsh poet Edward Williams, a brilliant forger
who created a vast trove of fake Welsh folklore.

Dag Dag Hammarskjöld (Dag Hjalmar Agne Carl
Hammarskjöld) (1905–1961)
Swedish diplomat, secretary general of the
United Nations. He died in an airplane crash on
his way to try to negotiate peace in the Congo,
and was awarded a posthumous Nobel Peace
Prize.

Dagmar Jennie "Dagmar" Lewis (20th century)
Busty American actress. Bullet-shaped swellings
on the bumpers of American automobiles were
called "dagmars" in her honour.

Dagwood Dagwood (20th century)
Cartoon husband of the title character in
"Blondie."

Dai Dai Ailian (1916–)
Trinidad-born Chinese dancer. He introduced
classical ballet to China.

Daisie Daisie Walker King (1901–1955)
American mother. Her son Jack Gilbert Graham
blew up a DC6B, killing all forty-four people on
board, in hopes of collecting her life insurance.

Dale Dale Carnegie (originally Dale Carnegey)
(1888–1955)
American self-improvement guru, author of the
influential How to Win Friends and Influence People.

Dalma Dalma Brown (20th century)
American author of The Erotic Silence of the
American Wife.

Dalton Dalton Trumbo *(1905–1976)*
American screenwriter blacklisted as a communist in the Joe McCarthy era. For example, he wrote "share and share alike," in the screenplay of *Tender Comrade* (1944).

Damaris Lady Damaris Masham *(1658–1708)*
English theological writer, a protégée of John Locke.

Damaso Damaso Garcia *(Damaso Domingo Garcia y Sanchez) (1957–)*
Dominican Republic–born American baseball infielder with the Blue Jays. He became unpopular after he burned his uniform in the clubhouse.

Damien Damien Parer *(1912–1944)*
Australian news photographer. His film *Kokoda Front* (1942) was the first Australian film to win an Oscar.

Damocles Damocles *(4th century B.C.)*
Greek courtier. After he described the happiness of royalty with too much enthusiasm, the local ruler invited him to dinner, seated underneath a sword suspended by only one horsehair: the original "sword of Damocles."

Damon Damon Runyon *(Alfred Damon Runyon) (1884–1946)*
American short-story writer, author of the collection *Guys and Dolls* (1931) later made into a Broadway musical.
> *"The race is not always to the swift, nor the battle to the strong—but that's the way to bet."*

Dan Dan Aykroyd *(Daniel Edward Aykroyd) (1952–)*
Canadian-born comedian, the survivor of *The Blues Brothers* (1980).

Dana Dana Zatopkova *(1922–)*
Czechoslovakian athlete. He won the 1952 Olympic gold medal in javelin.

Danforth J. Danforth "Dan" Quayle *(1947–)*
American vice-president under Bush, noted for publicly changing a schoolchild's spelling to read "potatoe" instead of "potato."

DAMON RUNYON

Daniel Daniel Defoe *(1660–1731)*
English lifelong troublemaker, author of *Robinson Crusoe* (1719).
> *"I let him know that his name should be Friday, which was the day I saved his life."*

Danielle Danielle Steele *(originally Danielle Schuelein-Steel) (1947–)*
Prolific American writer of best-sellers.
> *"A bad review is like baking a cake with all the best ingredients and having someone sit on it."*

Danny Danny Kaye *(originally David Daniel Kominski) (1913–1987)*
American entertainer, star of the film *The Secret Life of Walter Mitty* (1947). He set a 1985 Guinness record by assembling a 4,524-member marching band in Dodger Stadium, Los Angeles.

Dante Dante Alighieri *(Durante Alighieri) (1265–1321)*
Italian poet, author of *The Divine Comedy* (begun *c.* 1307), the very first work of art to be written in the new Italian language.
> *"All hope abandon, ye who enter here."*

Dany Dany Laferrière *(20th century)*
Haitian-born bad-boy of Quebec literature, author of *How to Make Love to a Negro*.

Daphne Daphne du Maurier *(Dame Daphne Francis du Maurier) (1907–1989)*
English novelist of period romances such as *Jamaica Inn* (1936) and *Rebecca* (1938).

Dar Dar Robinson *(20th century)*
American stunt man. He was paid $100,000 to jump from Toronto's CN Tower (1,100 feet).

Darby "Darby and Joan" *(1735)*
Traditional English ballad about a happy old couple.

Daren Daren Puppa *(Daren James Puppa) (1963–)*
Canadian hockey goaltender for the Buffalo Sabres, a National Hockey League All-Star.

Daria Daria Halprin *(20th century)*
American actress. She starred in the film *Zabriskie Point* (1970).

Darien Darien *(1851)*
English novel by Eliot Warburton, describing a ship on fire. He himself later died in a ship fire.

Dario Dario Fo *(1926–)*
Italian dramatist, author of *Can't Pay, Won't Pay* (1974).

Darius Darius III *(Darius Codomannus) (d. 330 B.C.)*
Last King of Persia. He was defeated by Alexander the Great.

Darla Darla Hood *(1931–1979)*
American child actress, one of *Our Gang*.

Darlene Darlene Dietrich *(20th century)*
American magician. Using a special cup, she can catch a bullet in her mouth. Houdini said he would do this trick, but never did.

Darold Darold Knowles *(1941–)*
American baseball pitcher with the Senators, an All-Star.

Darryl Darryl F. Zanuck *(Darryl Francis Zanuck) (1902–1979)*
American movie mogul, producer of *The Jazz Singer* (1927) the first movie with sound.
> *"For God's sake don't say yes until I've finished talking."*

Daryl Daryl Hall *(originally Daryl Franklin Hohl) (1949–)*
American soul singer and pianist, half of the group Hall and Oates.

Dashiell Dashiell Hammett *(Samuel Dashiell Hammett) (1894–1961)*
American detective novelist, author of *The Maltese Falcon* (1930), an ex–Pinkerton's detective.
> *"He felt like somebody had taken the lid off life and let him look at the works."*

Dave Dave Barry *(20th century)*
American humorist.
> *"Little girls are in fact smaller versions of real human beings, whereas little boys are Pod People from the Planet Destructo."*

David David Herbert (D.H.) Lawrence *(1885–1930)*
British novelist, author of the controversial *Lady Chatterley's Lover* (1928). A friend observed, "Lawrence could not buy a bicycle without investing it with a dark, mysterious, sexual significance."

Davidson Davidson Black *(known as Bu Dasheng) (1885–1934)*
Canadian-born Chinese archaeologist, the discoverer of Peking Man.

Davy Davy Crockett *(David Crockett) (1786–1836)*
American frontiersman.

Dawn Dawn Steel *(20th century)*
American film producer, author of the Hollywood memoir *They Can Kill You. . . . But They Can't Eat You.*

DeWitt DeWitt *(or Dewitt)* Wallace *(1889–1981)*
American publisher, co-founder in 1922 with his wife, Lila Bell Acheson, of *The Reader's Digest* magazine.

Deadwood Deadwood Dick *(probably Nat Love) (19th century)*
American cowboy. He got his name by winning a shooting competition in Deadwood, S.D.

Dean Dean Rusk *(David Dean Rusk) (1909–1994)*
American politician, secretary of state during the Vietnam War. During the Cuban missile crisis he said, "We're standing eyeball to eyeball and the other fellow just blinked."

Deanna Deanna Durbin *(originally Edna Mae Durbin) (1921–)*
Canadian-born American singing actress. Her first feature film, *Three Smart Girls* (1936), saved Universal Studios from bankruptcy.
> *"The character I was forced into had little or nothing in common with myself or with other youth of my generation, for that matter. . . . My fans were the parents, many of whom could not cope with their own youngsters."*

Deanne Deanne H. Russell *(20th century)*
Canadian industrial designer, creator of the "best factory-made hunting knife in the world," the Nova Scotia D.H. Russell belt knife.

Deanie Deanie O'Bannion *(Charles Dion O'Bannion) (1892–1924)*
American bootlegger. O'Bannion always sent flowers and cigars to anyone he shot accidentally.

Top 10 Baby Names for Black Activists

Althea • Aretha • Bill • Carol •

Cito • Hattie • Martin • Sojourner •

Stokely • Thurgood

Debbie Debbie Reynolds *(originally Mary Frances Reynolds) (1932–)*
American actress, star of *The Singing Nun* (1966), mother of actress/novelist Carrie Fisher.
> *"Obviously my daughter and I shouldn't make decisions about men. We should have a board of directors and they'll vote."*

Deborah Deborah Coyne *(20th century)*
Canadian politician, author of *Seven Fateful Challenges for Canada* (1993) and mother of former prime minister Pierre Trudeau's youngest child.

Debra Debra McKinney *(20th century)*
American reporter with the *Anchorage Daily News*. Discussing the myth that Alaska has a male-to-female ratio of 10:1, she wrote, "There's even a saying here. . . 'The odds are good but the goods are odd.'"

Decca Decca Mitford *(Jessica Lucy Mitford) (1917–)*
British-born American communist writer, sister of Nancy, Pamela, Tom, Diana, Unity, and Debo. Nancy moved to France, Unity was a close friend of Adolf Hitler's, and Debo was Duchess of Devonshire.

Dee Dee Dee Dee Kennibrew *(originally Delores Henry) (1945–)*
American girl singer with the Crystals. They sang "Da Doo Ron Ron" (1963).

Deford Deford Bailey *(1899–1982)*
American musician, the "Harmonica Wizard." He was the first black cast member on the Nashville radio show "The Grand Ole Opry."

Deirdre Princess Deirdre
Irish mythic heroine. She deserted her fiancé, King Conchubar of Ulster, to elope with his nephew Naoise.

Del Del Shannon *(originally Charles Westover) (1939–1990)*
American pop musician, composer of the song "Runaway" (1961).

Delarivière Delarivière Manley *(originally Mary Delarivière Manley) (1663–1724)*
British author of "scandal novels."

Delbert Delbert Mann *(1920–)*
American director, winner of an Academy Award for his film *Marty* (1955).

Delia Delia Salter Bacon *(1811–1859)*
American academic, inventor of the idea that Shakespeare's plays were written by Francis Bacon.

Delilah Delilah *Judges 16: 4-20 (12th century B.C.)*
Old Testament betraying mistress of Samson. His enemies paid her to learn the secret of his strength, which proved to be his hair.

Della Della Street
Fictional American secretary. She can be found at work in Erle Stanley Gardner's novel *The Case of the Velvet Claws* (1933).

Delmore Delmore Schwartz *(1913–1966)*
American poet and critic. He appears as a character in Saul Bellow's novel *Humbolt's Gift* (1975).

Delphine Delphine Delamare *(1822–1848)*
French model for the fictional character of Emma Bovary in Gustave Flaubert's novel *Madame Bovary* (1857).

Delta Delta Burke *(1956–)*
American actress. She played Suzanne Sugarbaker on the TV series "Designing Women" (1986–93).

Deluvina Deluvina Maxwell *(19th century)*
American girlfriend of Billy the Kid. In 1881, she paid for his gravestone after he was shot in the back by Pat Garrett.
> *"You didn't have the nerve to shoot him face to face."*

Demeter Demeter *trans. barley-mother*
Greek goddess of the cornfield, one of the twelve great Olympian gods.

Demetrius Demetrius *(Acts 19: 24)*
Ephesian silversmith. When the preachings of Paul theatened his business selling shrines in honour of the goddess Diana, he started a riot in the theatre of Ephesus. The theatre still stands, and may be visited in modern Turkey.

Demi Demi Moore *(originally Demi Guynes) (1963–)*
American actress, wife of actor Bruce Willis. In 1991, she appeared naked and pregnant on the cover of *Vanity Fair* magazine.

Demosthenes Demosthenes *(384–322 B.C.)*
Athenian orator.
> *"Though a man can escape every other danger, he can never wholly escape those who do not want a person like him to exist."*

Den Den Hegarty *(20th century)*
British doo-wap revival singer with the Darts.

Denholm Denholm Elliott *(1922–1992)*
Welsh character actor. He played a drunken director of Bar Mitzvah movies in the film *The Apprenticeship of Duddy Kravitz* (1974).

Denis Denis Diderot *(1713–1784)*
Prolific and versatile French writer, the inventor of the encyclopaedia.
> *"Men will never be free until the last king is strangled with the entrails of the last priest."*

Denise Denise Coffey *(1936–)*
English actress.
> *"I am that twentieth-century failure, a happy undersexed celibate."*

Dennis Dennis Hopper *(1936–)*
American actor. He did eighty-five takes the wrong way for director Henry Hathaway in *From Hell to Texas* (1958).

Denny Denny Doherty *(Dennis Gerard Stephen Doherty) (1940–)*
Canadian folksinger, a member of the seminal Mugwumps, as well as the Mamas and the Papas.

Denys Denys Arcand *(1942–)*
Canadian filmmaker of *The Decline of the American Empire* (1986).

Denzel Denzel Washington *(1954–)*
American actor. He played Malcolm X in the Spike Lee biopic.

Derek Derek Jarman *(1942–1994)*
British painter and filmmaker. His first film, *Sebastiane* (1975), about the saint, featured dialog in Latin.

Derick Derick Herning *(20th century)*
British linguist, resident of Shetland. In 1990, he won the Polyglot of Europe contest with twenty-two languages.

Dermot Dermot Bolger *(1959–)*
Irish writer.

Derrick Derrick *(17th century)*
English hangman, in whose honour first gallows, then all hoisting cranes in general, are called "derricks."

Dervla Dervla Murphy *(20th century)*
Irish travel writer.

Desdemona Desdemona
Abused devoted wife in William Shakespeare's play *Othello* (c. 1602).

Desi Desi Arnaz *(originally Desiderio Alberto Arnaz y de Acha III) (1917–1986)*
American band-leader, the husband of Lucy on the TV series "I Love Lucy" (1951–61), and in real life.

Desiderius Desiderius Erasmus *(c. 1466–1536)*
Dutch scholar, a pillar of the northern Renaissance.
> *"I know how busy you are in your library, which is your Paradise."*

Désirée Désirée Bernadotte *(née Eugénie Bernardine Désirée Clary) (1777–1860)*
French-born queen of Sweden, the first love of Napoleon Bonaparte.

Desmond Desmond Mpilo Tutu *(1931–)*
South African Anglican prelate, the first black bishop of Johannesburg, and winner of the 1984 Nobel Peace Prize.

Deucalion King Deucalion of Pythia *trans. new-wine sailor*
Mythical Greek ruler. After his father, Prometheus warned him of a coming flood, he and his wife, Pyrria, built an ark and survived a nine-day flood that covered the entire world.

Devon Devon White *(1962–)*
American baseball outfielder, an All-Star and winner of several Gold Glove awards.

Dewi Dewi Jones *(20th century)*
British motorcycle rider. In 1988 he set a Guinness record by steering his motorcycle backwards from the top of a ten-foot ladder for 1½ hours.

Dewi Dewi Sukarno *(1941–)*
Indonesian first lady; American jail-bird.

Dexter Dexter Keith Gordon *(1923–1989)*
American jazz tenor-saxophonist.

Di Lady Di *(Lady Diana Frances Spencer, since her marriage Diana, Princess of Wales) (1961–)*
Media favourite and thorn in the side of the British royal family. Explaining her premarital virginity, she said,
> *"I knew I had to keep myself tidy for what lay ahead."*

Diahann Diahann Carroll *(originally Carol Diahann Johnson) (1935–)*
American singer and actress.

Diamond Diamond Jim Brady *(James Buchanan Brady) (1859–1917)*
American gambler. He once tied an eating contest with singer Lillian Russell.

Dian Dian Fossey *(1932–1985)*
American zoologist, author of *Gorillas in the Mist* (1983). She was murdered by poachers.

Diana Diana Ross *(originally Diane Ross) (1944–)*
Supreme American pop singer.
> *"If I have any bad memories, I hope they're not true."*

Diane Diane Arbus, *née Nemerov (1923–1971)*
American photographer. Her work is famously depressing.

Dick Dick Turpin *(1705–1739)*
English robber, the inspiration for Alfred Noyes's poem "The Highwayman," though the real ride was probably done by "Swift John" Nevison.
> *The wind was a torrent of darkness among the gusty trees,*
> *The moon was a ghostly galleon tossed upon cloudy seas,*
> *The road was ribbon of moonlight over the purple moor,*
> *And the highwayman came riding—Riding— riding—*
> *The highwayman came riding, up to the old inn-door."*

Dickie Dickie Kerr *(1893–1963)*
American baseball pitcher for the White Sox. In 1919, he was the only honest player on the team, but quit when refused a $500 raise.

DIANA ROSS

Dickinson Dickinson Woodruff Richards *(1895–1973)*
American doctor, joint winner of the 1956 Nobel Prize for his work on cardiac catheterization.

Didi Didi *(originally Valdi Pereira) (1928–)*
Brazilian football ("soccer") player.

Dido *Dido, Queen of Carthage (1596)*
English play by Christopher Marlowe and Thomas Nash, about the rude abandonment of Dido by Aeneus.

Diego Diego Rivera *(1886–1957)*
Mexican socialist mural painter.

Dieter Dieter Rams *(1932–)*
German industrial designer, the guru of Braun.

Dilbert *Dilbert (20th century)*
American cartoon strip by Scott Adams. He gets 200 calls a day on E-mail regarding his workplace humour.
> *"Looks like an isolated case of bad attitude."*

Dimitri Dimitri Tiomkin *(1894–1980)*
Russian-born American movie composer of the score to *Town without Pity* (1961), and the theme music for the TV series "Rawhide" (1959–66).

Dimitry Dimitry Volkognov *(1928–1995)*
Soviet general. As head of the Institute of Military History, he made public records of ruthless mass murders by Joseph Stalin and Vladimir Lenin.

Dinah Dinah Shore *(originally Frances "Fanny" Rose Shore) (1917–1994)*
American popular singer, star of the TV series "Dinah" (1974–79).

Dingaan Dingaan *(or Dingane) (d. 1840)*
Zulu chief defeated by Boer colonists at Blood River on December 18, 1838, now known as "Dingaan's Day."

Dingle Sir Dingle Mackintosh Foot *(1905–1978)*
English politician.

Dingus Jesse "Dingus" Woodson James *(1847–1882)*
American outlaw. He earned this nickname, known only to close friends, when he shot off the end of his left middle finger while cleaning his gun, and exclaimed, "If that ain't the din-gus-dangast thing!"

Dino Dino Valenti *(originally Chester Powers) (1943–1994)*
American lead singer of Quicksilver Messenger Service.
> *"C'mon people now,*
> *Smile on your brother,*
> *Everybody get together*
> *Try to love one another, right now."*

Diogenes Diogenes of Sinope *(c. 412–c. 323 B.C.)*
Greek philosopher, founder of the Cynics. When Alexander the Great visited and asked if there was anything he could do for him, Diogenes replied, "You could move out of the sun and not cast a shadow on me."

Dion Dion Fortune *(19th century)*
English witch. She was a friend of Aleister Crowley.

Dionne Dionne Warwick *(originally Marie Dionne Warwick) (1940–)*
American pop singer, aunt of Whitney Houston.

Dionysus Dionysus *trans. lame god*
Greek god of wine and revelry.

Dirick Dirick Vellert *(worked 1511–1544)*
Antwerp-born stained-glass artist. He created windows for the King's College Chapel in Cambridge, England.

Dirk Sir Dirk Bogarde *(Derek Niven Van Den Bogaerde) (1921–1994)*
English actor, designer and writer. He played the dying composer in *Death in Venice* (1971).

Dismas St. Dismas *Luke 23: 39–43*
Good Thief crucified with Jesus at Calvary. A popular medieval legend said that he and Gestas were the robbers who met the Holy Family on their way to Egypt, and that Dismas had paid off Gestas to leave the family unharmed.

Divine Divine Brown *(originally Stella Marive Thompson) (20th century)*
American hooker arrested in a parked car with British actor Hugh Grant.
> *"He said to me, 'What about my money?' He wanted his money back! I said, 'Honey, we're going to jail.'"*

Dixie Dixie Walker *(Fred Walker) (1910–1982)*
American baseball outfielder with the Dodgers, an All-Star, known in Brooklyn as "the People's Cherce." His brother, father, and uncle also played professional baseball.

Dixon Dixon Denham *(1786–1828)*
English army officer and African explorer. "Denham's Bustard" is named after him.

Dizzy Dizzy Gillespie *(originally John Birks Gillespie) (1917–1993)*
American jazz trumpeter, subject of the film *A Night in Havana* (1989). His vast inflating cheeks have given the name to the medical phenomena now known as "Gillespie's pouches."

Django Django Reinhardt *(originally Jean Baptiste Reinhardt) (1910–1953)*
Belgian Gypsy jazz guitarist.

Djuna Djuna Barnes *(1892–1982)*
American poet and illustrator, author of the novel *Nightwood* (1936).

Dmitri Dmitri Dmitriyevich Shostakovich *(1906–1975)*
Russian composer.

Doc Doc Watson *(originally Arthur Watson) (1923–)*
American old-time folksinger and guitar flat-picker.

Dock Dock Ellis *(1945–)*
American baseball pitcher with the Pirates. In his autobiography, *Dock Ellis in the Country of Baseball*, he claimed to have pitched a 1970 no-hitter while under the influence of LSD.

Doctor Doctor Subtilis *(Johannes Duns Scotus)* *(c. 1266–1308)*
Latin philosopher and theologian who defended popes against the theory that kings ruled by divine right. His followers were known as "duns," later "dunces."

Dodie Dodie Smith *(pseudonym of C.I. Anthony)* *(1896–1990)*
English playwright and theatre producer, author of the children's story *The Hundred and One Dalmations* (1956).

Dollar Dollar Brand *(now Abdullah Ibrahim)* *(1934–)*
South African jazz pianist.

Dolly Dolly Madison, *née Payne Todd (1768–1849)*
American political worker, wife of president James Madison.

Dolly Dolly Parton *(1946–)*
American country superstar.
"It costs a lot to look this cheap."

Dolores Dolores Ibarruri Gomez, *(known as "La Passionaria") (1895–1989)*
Spanish communist. She won her last election at age eighty-one.
"It is better to die on your feet than to live on your knees."

Domenico Domenico Modugno *(1928–)*
Italian singer, composer of "Volare" (or "Nel Blu Dipinto di Blu") (1958).

Dominic St. Dominic *(c. 1170–1221)*
Spanish founder of the Order of Friars Preachers, or Dominicans, an enthusiastic leader of the Spanish Inquisition.

Dominick Dominick James La Rocca *(known as Nick La Rocca) (1889–1961)*
American cornet player with the Original Dixieland Jazz Band.

Dominik Dominik Hasek *(1965–)*
Czech-born American hockey goaltender with the Buffalo Sabres, an All-Star, and three-time Czech Player of the Year.

Dominique Dominique Larrey *(Baron Dominique-Jean Larrey) (1766–1842)*
French military surgeon under Napoleon. He could amputate a leg in a record-setting fifteen seconds. (Speed was essential before anaesthetics, to prevent patients dying of shock.)

Don Don Marquis *(Donald Robert Perry Marquis)* *(1878–1937)*
American poet, author of *archy and mehitabel* (1927).
"Middle age is . . . when a man is always thinking that in a week or two he will feel just as good as ever."

Donald Donald Sutherland *(1934–)*
Canadian-born actor. He played Hawkeye in the Robert Altman movie *M.A.S.H.*

Donatien Donatien-Alphonse-François, Comte de Sade *(known as the Marquis de Sade) (1740–1814)*
French writer, author of *Les 120 Journées de Sodome* (1784), which inspired the term "sadist." He died in a mental institution.

Donato Donato Bramante *(originally Donato d'Agnolo or d'Angelo) (1444–1514)*
Italian High Renaissance architect, designer of the new Basilica of St. Peter's in Rome.

Donna Donna Karan *(originally Donna Faske) (1948–)*
American fashion designer.

Donny Donny Osmond *(Donald Clark Osmond)* *(1958–)*
American pop star and actor.
"I'll be a former teen idol all my life."

Donovan Donovan Leitch *(1946–)*
Scottish flower-power singer-songwriter.
"Beatniks out to make it rich."

Donyale Donyale Luna *(20th century)*
Italian actress. She died shortly after starring in Federico Fellini's film *Satyricon* (1969).

Dooley Dooley Wilson *(originally Arthur Wilson)* *(1894–1953)*
American pianist who plays "As Time Goes By" in the film *Casablanca* (1942) when Humphrey Bogart orders, "Play it, Sam" (not "Play it again").

Dora Dora Mavor Moore *(1889–1979)*
Canadian teacher and theatre director. The Dora Awards are named after her.

Dorcas Dorcas *(also known as Tabitha), trans. gazelle (Acts 9: 36)*
New Testament woman, "full of good works."

Doreen "Doreen, My Bluegrass Queen" *(1974)*
American song by the group Banjo Dan and the Midnight Plowboys.

Dorelia Dorelia John *(19th century)*
English wife of the painter Augustus John, the subject of many of his portraits.

Dorian *The Picture of Dorian Gray (1890)*
English novel by Oscar Wilde, inspired by the poet John Gray.

Doris Doris Day *(originally Doris von Kappelhoff) (1924–)*
American big-band singer and comic actress, star of the film *Pillow Talk* (1959).

Dornford Dornford Yates *(pseudonym of Cecil William Mercer) (1885–1960)*
English novelist specializing in classy adventures like *Berry and Co* (1921).

Dorothea Dorothea Lynde Dix *(1802–1887)*
American humanitarian, a tireless worker for prison reform and humane care for the insane. As superintendent of nurses during the Civil War, she banned curly hair from the Union Army Nursing Corps.

Dorothy Dorothy Parker, *née Rothschild (Mrs. Alan Campbell) (1893–1967)*
American wit. After one of her lovers left her, she observed, "It serves me right for putting all my eggs in one bastard."

Doug Doug and the Slugs *(1977–)*
Vancouver rock band founded by Doug Bennett.
"It's your basic rock and roll but with a certain Kafka-esque, grass roots, Pavlovian, existential, Calvinistic, Zen, New York liberal Jewish intellectual kind of slant to it."

Douglas Douglas Adams *(Douglas Noël Adams) (1952–)*
English writer, creator of *The Hitchhiker's Guide to the Galaxy* science-fiction epic.
"Why bother writing a send-up of science fiction? It may give you a ten-minute sketch, but that's about all. I'd rather use the devices of science fiction to send up everything else."

Dracon Dracon *(or Draco) (active 621 B.C.)*
Athenian legislator who drafted "Draconian" laws specifying death as the penalty for things like urinating in public.

Dracula *Dracula (1897)*
Classic English horror novel by Bram Stoker.

Dragan Dragan Dzajic *(1946–)*
Yugoslavian soccer player, Player of the Year in 1963, 1966, 1968, 1969, 1970, and 1972.

DOLLY PARTON

Drake Drake Levin *(20th century)*
American pop musician with the group Paul Revere and the Raiders.

Dred Dred Scott *(c. 1795–1858)*
American hotel porter. As the plaintiff in the "Dred Scott Case," he claimed freedom from slavery on the basis that he lived in a free state. He lost, but was freed soon after by emancipation.

Drew Drew Barrymore *(1975–)*
American actress. She played a child in Steven Spielberg's film *E.T.—The Extra Terrestrial* (1982).

Drusilla Livia Drusilla *(A.D. 15–38)*
Roman sister, and probably mistress, of the Emperor Caligula.

Duane Duane Allman *(1946–1971)*
American country-rock guitarist, leader of the Allman Brothers Band.

Dud Dud Dudley *(1599–1684)*
English ironmaster, author of *Metallum Martis* (1665).

Dudley Dudley Moore *(1935–)*
British pianist and sex symbol, star of the film *10*.

Duffy Duffy Lewis *(George Edward Lewis) (1888–1979)*
American baseball outfielder for the Red Sox. Fenway Park's left-field fence became known as "Duffy's Cliff" while he ruled it.

Dugald Sir Dugald Clerk *(1854–1932)*
Scottish engineer, inventor of the Clerk two-stroke gas engine.

DUKE
ELLINGTON

Duke Duke Ellington *(originally Edward Kennedy Ellington) (1899–1974)* American jazz pianist and band-leader, composer of the song "Don't Get Around Much Any More."

"My mother told me I was blessed, and I have always taken her word for it."

Duncan Duncan Phyfe *(originally Duncan Fife) (1768–1854)* Scottish-born American furniture maker.

Dunstan St. Dunstan *(924–988)* Ango-Saxon prelate, patron of smiths and the blind. He composed the coronation rite used to crown English sovereigns.

Dustin Dustin Hoffman *(1937–)* American actor. He won an Academy Award for *Rain Man* (1988).

Dusty Dusty Springfield *(Mary O'Brien) (1939–)* English pop singer.

"You don't have to say you love me."

Dutch Dutch Schultz *(Arthur Flegenheimer) (1902–1935)* American bootlegger.

"Personally, I think only queers wear silk shirts."

Dweezil Dweezil Zappa *(1969–)* American actor, son of musician Frank Zappa.

Dwight Dwight David Eisenhower *(1890–1969)* American general and 34th president. In 1954, he resisted five separate attempts by defence experts to initiate a nuclear war against China.

"There is one thing about being president— nobody can tell you to sit down."

Dyan Dyan Cannon *(originally Samille Diane Friesen) (1937–)* American actress, the first woman to be nominated for Academy Awards for both acting— *Heaven Can Wait* (1978) best supporting actress; and directing—short film *Number One* (1976).

Dylan Dylan Thomas *(Dylan Marlais Thomas) (1914–1953)* Welsh poet, author of *Under Milk Wood*.

"Do not go gentle into that good night Old age should burn and rave at close of day; Rage, rage against the dying of the light."

Dymphna Dymphna Cusack *(originally Ellen Dymphna Cusack) (1902–1981)* Australian author.

Eadgar King Eadgar the Peaceful *(or Edgar) (944–975)* English ruler. Handsome but very short, he was insulted when a local noble substituted a serving girl for the daughter he had requested for his bed, and made the earl into a servant to the serving girl.

Eadweard Eadweard Muybridge *(originally Edward James Muggeridge) (1830–1904)* English-born American photographer. To settle an 1872 bet by Governor Leland Stanford about horses galloping, he took the photographs that first demonstrated that horses never took all four feet off the ground at the same time. You can see the difference in horse paintings before and after Muybridge.

Earle Earle C. Haas *(1885–1981)* American inventor of the menstrual tampon.

Early Early Wynn *(Gus Wynn) (1920–)* American baseball pitcher for the Indians, a member of the Hall of Fame. A pro from the age of seventeen, he referred to the pitching mound as his "office."

Earnest *The Importance of Being Earnest (1895)* English comic masterpiece by Oscar Wilde.

Eartha Eartha Kitt *(Eartha Mae Kitt) (1928–)* American singer and actress, author of the autobiography *Alone with Me* (1976).

Earvin Earvin "Magic" Johnson *(1959–)* American basketball player, bravely HIV-positive.

"You don't have to feel sorry for me. Because if I die tomorrow, I've had the greatest life that anybody can want."

Eazy-E Eazy-E *(Eric Wright) (1964–1995)* American gansta rapper, one of the Niggas with Attitude.

Eben Eben Eugene Rexford *(1848–1916)*
English poet. He wrote "Silver Threads among the Gold."

Ebenezer Ebenezer Scrooge
Notorious English miser of Charles Dickens's tale *A Christmas Carol* (1843).

Echo Echo *trans. echo*
Greek nymph of sentimental fable. She pined away with unrequited love for Narcissus, until only her voice remained.

Ed Ed Sullivan *(Edward Vincent Sullivan) (1902–1974)*
American host of the TV variety show "The Ed Sullivan Show" (1948–71). He was legendary for his stiff delivery.

Eddie Eddie Murphy *(Edward Regan Murphy) (1961–)*
American comedian, star of the movie *Beverly Hills Cop* (1984).

Eddy Eddy Merckx *(1945–)*
Belgian cyclist, five-time winner of the Tour de France.

Eden Eden Phillpots *(1862–1960)*
Indian-born English novelist and dramatist.

Edgar Edgar Allan Poe *(1809–1849)*
American writer, inventor of both the horror story and the detective thriller.
> *"The dearth of genius in America is due to the continual teasing of mosquitos."*

Edie Edie Sedgewick *(20th century)*
American socialite and Andy Warhol alumnus.

Edina Edina Monsoon *(known as Eddy)*
Heroine's sidekick on British television series "Absolutely Fabulous" (1993), known to its fans as "AbFab."

Edith Edith Wharton, *née Edith Newbold Jones (1862–1937)*
American novelist and short-story writer.
> *"I was never allowed to read the popular American children's books of my day because, as my mother said, the children spoke bad English without the author's knowing it."*

EDGAR ALLAN POE

Edme Edme Mariotte *(1620–1684)*
French priest and physicist. He coined the word "barometer."

Edmond Edmond Halley *(1656–1742)*
British astronomer. His prediction that "Halley's comet" would return proved to be accurate, after his death.

Edmund Sir Edmund Hillary *(1919–)*
New Zealand mountaineer. After his successful career, he became active in bringing social aid to the Sherpa people near Mount Everest.
> *"There is precious little in civilization to appeal to a Yeti."*

Edna Edna St. Vincent Millay *(Mrs. Eugen Jan Boissevain, known as "Vincent") (1892–1950)*
American poet, winner of the 1923 Pulitzer Prize.
> *"It is not true that life is one damn thing after another it's one damn thing over and over.'*

Edouard Edouard Manet *(1832–1883)*
French painter of the controversial nude *Olympia* (1865).

Edvard Edvard Munch *(1863–1944)*
Norwegian painter.

Edward Edward, Duke of Windsor *(formerly King Edward VIII) (1894–1972)*
British aristocrat.
> *"The thing that impresses me most about America is the way parents obey their children."*

Edwards W. Edwards Deming *(d. 1993)*
American guru of the quality-management movement. Number 4 of his "14 points to successful management" is: "End the awarding of lowest-tender contracts, which generally deliver poor quality."

Edwin Edwin Powell Hubble *(1889–1953)*
American astronomer. He proved that the spiral nebulae were separate galaxies beyond our galaxy, the Milky Way.

Edwina Countess Edwina Cynthia Annette Mountbatten, *née Ashley (1901–1960)*
British vice-reine of India, a very intimate friend of Mahatma Gandhi.

Edy Edy Williams *(20th century)*
American actress, wife of trash filmmaker Russ Meyer.

Eero Eero Saarinen *(1910–1961)*
Finnish-born American Modernist architect. He designed the TWA Terminal at the John F. Kennedy Airport, New York.

Effa Effa Manley *(1897–1981)*
American baseball executive, owner of two Negro Leagues teams, "the First Lady of Black Baseball." After the end of colour discrimination in major league ball, she was forced to disband her teams, since her best players were raided without compensation.

Effie Effie Gray *(Euphemia Chalmers Gray) (19th century)*
English bride of writer John Ruskin. On their wedding night in 1848, he assumed her pubic hair was a deformity because previously he had only seen naked women in Classical sculpture. After six years of married virginity, Effie obtained an annulment, married the painter Sir John Millais and had eight children.

Egbert King Egbert *or Ecgberht, or Ecgbryht)* *(828–839)*
First Saxon ruler of all England. He united Essex, Sussex, Kent, Mercia, East Anglia, Northumbria, and Wessex, but not Wales.

Egidio Egidio Cattaneo *(20th century)*
Swiss ski-lift operator. He commissioned a chapel to the Virgin Mary on his mountain, Mount Tamaro, designed by artist Enzo Boffo and architect Mario Botta.

Egill Egill Skallagrímsson *(c. 910–990)*
Icelandic Viking poet. He once escaped death by hastily composing a flattering poem for his aggressors.

Eglinton Lady Eglinton Wallace *(or Eglantine Wallace) (d. 1803)*
English playwright. She was arrested in France as a spy in 1789, after advising other ladies to live in "social retirement."

Egon Egon Schiele *(1890–1918)*
Austrian Expressionist painter.

Ehrengard Countess Ehrengard Melusina von der Schulenburg, *(also Duchess of Kendal)* *(1667–1743)*
German mistress of King George I of Britain. Tall and thin, she was known to his subjects as "the Maypole."

Eileen Eileen O'Casey *(originally Eileen Reynolds Carey) (1900–1995)*
Irish actress and writer. A fortune-teller told her to go to New York, where she would meet her future husband, a man with "piercing eyes and heavy boots." There, she auditioned for the play *The Plough and the Stars* (1926), and met its playwright, Sean O'Casey, who filled this bill.

Eileithyia Eileithyia *(or Ilithyia) (trans. she who comes to aid women in childbirth)*
Greek goddess of childbirth.

Einar Einar Jónsson *(1874–1954)*
Icelandic sculptor.

Ekaterina Ekaterina "Katya" Gordeeva *(1971–)*
Russian skater, an Olympic gold-medallist. Her husband and partner, Sergei Grinkov, died suddenly of heart failure at age twenty-eight while they were touring together.

El El Lissitzky *(originally Eliezar Markovitch Lissitzky) (1890–1941)*
Russian Constructivist painter.

Elaine "The Exploits of Elaine" *(1914–15)*
American cliff-hanging movie serial. It starred Pearl Fay White, who also starred in *The Perils of Pauline* (1914).

Elayne Elayne Boosler *(1952–)*
American stand-up comic. She refused to appear on the Johnny Carson show when the show's writers prepared her a monologue along the lines of, "I'm so ugly, I can't make a nickel on a battleship."

Elbert Elbert Hubbard *(1856–1915)*
American writer and printer, founder of the Roycrofters, a craft community near Buffalo, New York, which manufactured "Mission style" furniture.
"To escape criticism—do nothing, say nothing, be nothing."

Elbie Elbie Fletcher *(Elburt Preston Fletcher) (1916–)*
American baseball infielder for the Pirates, an
All-Star.

Elbridge Elbridge Gerry *(1744–1814)*
American vice-president under James Monroe.
He redrew electoral boundaries to create a sala-
mander-shaped electoral area favouring him,
thus becoming the first person to "gerrymander"
for party advantage.

Eldridge Eldridge Cleaver *(1935–)*
American activitist, author of *Soul on Ice* (1968).
> *"You're either part of the solution or part of the
> problem."*

Eleanor Eleanor Roosevelt, *née Anna Eleanor
Roosevelt (1884–1962)*
American political worker, wife of president
Franklin D. Roosevelt and niece of Theodore
Roosevelt, author of *The Lady of the White House*
(1938).
> *"Nobody can make you feel inferior without your
> permission."*

Eleanora Eleanora Duse *(known as "the Duse")
(1859–1924)*
Italian actress, a great friend of the poet
Gabriele d'Annunzio, the first woman to appear
on the cover of *Time* magazine.

Eleazar Eleazar Albin *(d. 1759)*
English naturalist and watercolourist, author of
The History of Insects (1720).

Eleonora Eleonora of Arborea *(c. 1350–1404)*
National heroine of Sardinia.

Éleuthère Éleuthère Irénée du Pont de Nemours
(1771–1834)
French-born American industrialist, founder of
the gunpowder factory which became the Du
Pont chemical company.

Eleutherius St. Eleutherius *(d. c. 189)*
Greek-born pope, known for his decree that any
food fit for humans was fit for Christians.

Elfleda Elfleda the Fair *(or Elfthryth) (10th century)*
English beauty. King Edgar the Peaceful's marriage counsellor liked her so much that he married her himself. The king discovered the trick,
killed the counsellor, and married the widow.

Eli Eli Whitney *(1765–1825)*
American inventor of the "cotton gin" machine
for separating seeds from cotton. Previously,
cotton had to be laboriously cleaned by hand,
an argument for preserving slavery.

Elia Elia Kazan *(originally Elia Zazanjogolous) (1909–)*
Turkish-born American film director of *A
Streetcar Named Desire* (1951).

Elias Elias Ashmole *(1617–1692)*
English alchemist and antiquarian. He
bequeathed a collection of rarities to Oxford
which became the basis of the Ashmolean
Museum, the oldest surviving museum in the
world.

Elie Elie Wiesel *(1928–)*
Hungarian-born French writer, author of *All
Rivers Run to the Sea* (1995). In his idyllic
prewar childhood, he unabashedly adored his
mother.
> *"Smile all you want, Mr. Freud, I would count
> the minutes I had to be away from her."*

Eliel Eliel Saarinen *(Gottlieb Eliel Saarinen)
(1873–1950)*
Finnish-born American architect, the father and
partner of architect Eero Saarinen.

Eligius St. Eligius *(or Eloi) (c. 590–c. 660)*
Gallic goldsmith and evangelist, the patron of
metalsmiths.

Elihu Elihu Root *(1845–1937)*
American lawyer, winner of a Nobel Peace Prize
for his part in founding the League of Nations.
He helped ban poison gas under the
Washington Arms Limitation Teaty of 1921.

Elijah Elijah Muhammad *(slave name Elijah Poole)
(1897–1975)*
American religious worker, co-founder of the
Nation of Islam.

Elinor Elinor Glyn, *née Sutherland (1864–1943)*
British popular writer. She used the word "it" to
describe sex appeal. A film was made about "it,"
starring Clara Bow.

Eliot Eliot Noyes *(1910–1977)*
American Modernist designer and architect,
corporate design director for IBM.

ELLA
FITZGERALD

Elioth Elioth Guner *(1882–1939)*
New Zealand–born Australian painter.

Elisabeth Dame Elisabeth Frink *(1931–1993)* British sculptress.

Elisha Elisha Gray *(1835–1901)* American inventor. His sixty-odd patents do not include one for the telephone, which he lost after a court battle to Alexander Graham Bell.

Elissa Dr. Elissa Newport *(20th century)* American researcher. She studies the effects of teaching babies sign language before they speak.

Eliza Eliza Doolittle
Cockney flower girl of George Bernard Shaw's play *Pygmalion* (1913), which in turn inspired the musical film *My Fair Lady* (1964).

Elizabeth Queen Elizabeth I *(Elizabeth Tudor Gloriana, also known as Good Queen Bess) (1533–1603)*
Ruler of England and Ireland, the "Virgin Queen."
> "I know I have the body of a weak and feeble woman, but I have the heart and stomach of a king, and of a king of England, too."

Elke Elke Sommer *(Elke Schletz) (1940–)*
German-born actress.

Elkie Elkie Brooks *(originally Elaine Bookbinder) (1945–)*
English popular singer.

Ella Ella Fitzgerald *(1918–1996)*
American jazz singer.
> "The only thing better than singing is more singing."

Ellen Ellen Church *(20th century)*
American nurse and student pilot. She successfully urged United Airlines to hire the first stewardesses in 1930, starting with her.
> "How is a man going to say he is afraid to fly when a woman is working on the plane?"

Ellery Ellery Queen *(pen-name of the team of Frederic Dannay [1905–1982] and Manfred B. Lee [1905–1971])*
American thriller writers, the founders of *Ellery Queen's Mystery Magazine*.

Ellie Ellie Norwood *(1861–1948)*
British actor who holds the record for playing the role of Sherlock Holmes more times than anyone else, in forty-seven silent films made before 1923.

Elliott Elliott Leyton *(1939–)*
Canadian social-anthropologist and journalist, author of *Sole Survivor: Children Who Murder Their Families*.

Ellis Ellis Cornelia Knight *(1758–1837)*
English scholar, historian, novelist, and poet. Samuel Johnson enjoyed teasing her about her lack of sense of humour.

Ellison Ellison Hatfield *(stabbed 1882)*
American hillbilly, the first person murdered in the famous feud of the Hatfields and the McCoys.

Ellsworth Ellsworth Kelly *(1923–)*
American hard-edge abstract painter.

Elly Elly Mae Clampette
Unwitting teenage sexpot of the American TV series "The Beverly Hillbillies" (1962–71).

Elmer C. Elmer Doolin *(20th century)*
American entrepreneur. In 1932, he ordered a sandwich in a restaurant, and enjoyed the corn chips on the side so much that he bought the recipe from the owner for $100, and started a company to manufacture them under the name "Fritos."

Elmo St. Elmo *(also known as St. Erasmus) (d. c. 303)*
Italian bishop, the patron of sailors. A blue light appearing near the mast before or after a storm is called "St. Elmo's fire" by Neapolitan sailors.

Elmore Elmore Leonard *(Elmore John Leonard) (1925–)*
American thriller writer, author of *Get Shorty*.

Éloïse Éloïse Abelard *(or Héloïse) (d. c. 1164)*
French wife of the unfortunate theologian Peter. She retired to a monastery after his castration.

Elphaba Elphaba (or "Elphie")
Revisionist heroine of *Wicked: The Life and Times of the Wicked Witch of the West* (1995) in which the Wizard of Oz is a tyrant, and Glinda an airhead.

Elsa Elsa Schiaparelli *(1896–1973)*
Italian-born fashion designer. She invented hats shaped like ice-cream cones, purses that played tunes when opened, and the colour "shocking pink."

Elsie Elsie de Wolfe *(1865–1950)*
American interior designer, author of *The House in Good Taste* (1915). Seeing the Acropolis in Athens for the first time, she exclaimed, "It's beige! My colour!"

Elspeth Elspeth Buchan, *née Simpson (1738–1791)*
Scottish founder of the Buchanite religious sect.

Elston Elston Howard *(Elston Gene "Ellie" Howard) (1929–1980)*
American baseball catcher with the Yankees, an All-Star and a Gold Glove winner, and the Yankees' first black player.

Elton Elton John *(originally Reginald Kenneth Dwight) (1947–)*
British pop singer. He met his lyricist Bernie Taupin through a newspaper ad.
> *"I've always looked like a bank clerk who freaked out."*

Elvin Elvin Jones *(1927–)*
American jazz drummer.

Elvira *Elvira, Mistress of the Dark (1988)*
American movie starring Cassandra Peterson. *Time Out* magazine observed, "Elvira is more mistress of the dork."

Elvis Elvis Presley *(Elvis Aaron Presley) (1935–1977)*
American king.
> *"I don't sound like nobody."*

Elwy Elwy McMurran Yost *(1925–)*
Canadian TV personality, the soothing host of *Saturday Night at the Movies*, which is watched weekly by every dateless person in Canada.

Elwyn Elwyn Brooks (E.B.) White *(1899–1985)*
American writer, author of the children's novel *Charlotte's Web* (1952).
> *"To perceive Christmas through its wrappings becomes more difficult with every year."*

Elzie Elzie Crisler Segar *(1894–1938)*
American cartoonist, creator of "Thimble Theatre" (1919–), where Popeye the Sailor made his entrance in 1929.

Elzire Elzire Dionne *(d. 1934)*
Canadian mother of the Dionne quintuplets. After the girls turned twenty-one, they never again returned home, except for funerals; in 1995 they broke silence to say their mother beat them.

Emerald Emerald Cunard *(20th century)*
American heiress and English socialite. *The Diaries of Chips Cannon* describes her mischievous old age.

Emil Emil Jannings *(originally Theodor Emil Janenz) (1885–1950)*
Swiss-born German actor, star of *The Blue Angel* (1930). He won the first-ever Academy Award for best actor.

Emilie Emilie Charlotte, *née Emilie Le Breton, later famous as Lillie Langtry (1853–1929)*
British actress and royal mistress. She sat for the *Jersey Lily* portrait painted by Sir John Millais.

Emile Emile Zola *(1840–1902)*
French novelist of the human condition. He wrote *J'accuse* (1898) about the Dreyfus affair. (Army officer Alfred Dreyfus had been falsely convicted of treason on the basis of forged documents.)

Emilia Emilia Mary Fitzgerald, Duchess of Leinster *(1731–1814)*
English letter writer. She was the most beautiful of her four sisters, with a happy marriage and nineteen children.
> *"The dear little brats are, thank God, so well, so merry, so riotous, so hardy, and so full of play from morning till night that it wou'd enliven the dullest of mortals to see them . . . Henry naked is the dearest little being on earth."*

Emiliano Emiliano Zapata *(c. 1879–1919)*
Mexican politician.

Emilie Emilie Flöge *(20th century)*
Austrian dressmaker, the uncredited artistic collaborator of painter Gustav Klimt.

Emily Emily Dickinson *(Emily Elizabeth Dickinson)* *(1830–1886)*
American poet, the reclusive "Belle of Amherst."

> *"How dreary to be someone*
> *How public like a frog*
> *To sing your song the livelong day*
> *To an admiring bog."*

Emlyn Emlyn Williams *(George Emlyn Williams)* *(1905–1987)*
Welsh playwright and actor.

Emma Emma Thompson *(1959–)*
British actress. Shortly before her separation from husband Kenneth Branagh, asked if the couple planned children, she replied, "Conception would be tricky. Kenneth is so tired even his sperm are on crutches."

Emmeline Emmeline Pankhurst, *née Goulden* *(1857–1928)*
English suffragist, founder of the Women's Franchise League, author of *My Own Story* (1914).

> *"We women suffragists have a great mission—*
> *the greatest mission the world has ever known. It*
> *is to free half the human race, and through that*
> *freedom to save the rest."*

Emmerson Emmerson Philips *(20th century)*
Canadian maintenance worker. In 1994, he won a court case allowing him paid sick-leave from work for a hangover he'd booked, in advance, for his daughter's wedding.

Emmett Emmett Hall *(1898–1995)*
Canadian judge, the architect of Canada's system of state medicare.

> *"I think we have accomplished the best medical-*
> *care program to be found any place in the*
> *world."*

Emmuska Baroness Emmuska Orczy *(1865–1947)*
Hungarian-born English novelist, author of *The Scarlet Pimpernel* (1905).

> *"We seek him here, we seek him there*
> *Those Frenchies seek him everywhere,*
> *Is he in heaven?—Is he in hell?*
> *That demmed elusive Pimpernel?"*

Emmy "Frau Emmy von N." *(19th century)*
Viennese patient of Sigmund Freud, one of the case-studies in *Studies on Hysteria* (1895).

Emmylou Emmylou Harris *(1947–)*
American country singer.

Ena Princess Ena *(Victoria Eugénie Julia Ena)* *(1887–1969)*
British granddaughter of Queen Victoria. At her baptism, the minister misread the handwritten name "Eva."

Endora Endora
Samantha's witchy mother on the American TV series "Bewitched" (1964–72).

Endymion Endymion Porter *(1587–1649)*
English royalist, groom of the bedchamber to Charles I. He fought for King Charles in the Civil War.

Engelbert Engelbert Humperdinck *(1854–1921)*
German composer, no relation to the pop-singer of the same name.

Enheduanna Enheduanna *(active c. 2270 B.C.)*
Mesopotamian high priestess of Ur, daughter of Sargon I. She is the earliest known composer, of two songs to the goddess Nanna.

Enid Enid Mary Blyton *(1897–1968)*
English children's author.

Ennio Ennio Morricone *(1928–)*
Italian movie composer. He wrote the score for Sergio Leone's *Per un Pugo di Dollari (A Fistful of Dollars)* (1964).

Ennoia Ennoia
Greek female figure, the embodiment of thought.

Enoch Enoch Powell *(John Enoch Powell)* *(1912–)*
English Conservative politician.

> *"I do not keep a diary. Never have. To write a*
> *diary every day is like returning to one's vomit."*

Enola *Enola Gay (flew August 6, 1945)*
American B-59 bomber aircraft that dropped the atomic bomb on Hiroshima, Japan. The airplane was named after the mother of pilot Paul Wafield Tibbets.

Enrico Enrico Caruso *(1873–1921)*
Italian opera tenor, one of the first singers to make recordings.

Enrique Enrique Fioco *(20th century)*
Peruvian founder of the successful Little Yellow
Man debt-collection agency, which sends
placard-carrying men in yellow suits to
embarrass debtors.

> *"When I think of the amount of people who hate
> me in Peru, it's scary."*

Enver Enver Hoxha *(or Hodja) (1908–1985)*
Albanian founder of the Albanian Communist
Party, a hardline Stalinist. Under his dictator-
ship, popular baby names included "Hammer,"
"Sickle," "Proletarian," "Patriot," and
"Marenglen" (Marx, Engels, Lenin).

Enzo Enzo Ferrari *(1898–1988)*
Italian racing-car manufacturer.

Eoghan Eoghan Ruadh Ó Súilleabháin *(or Red Owen
O'Sullivan) (1748–1784)*
Irish poet, teacher, sailor, and soldier. William
Butler Yeats's character "Red Hanrahan" was
based on him.

Eostre Eostre
Teutonic goddess. She gave her name to the
celebration "Easter."

Ephraim Ephraim *trans. fruitfulness, Genesis 41: 52
(c. 16th century B.C.)*
Old Testament second son of Joseph. He
received his grandfather Jacob's deathbed blessing, which was normally given to the oldest
son. Jacob explained that Ephraim's descendant
would be more important than his brother
Manasseh's.

Epictetus Epictetus *(c. 50–c. 130)*
Stoic philosopher.

> *"If you hear that someone is speaking ill of you,
> instead of trying to defend yourself you should
> say: 'he obviously does not know me very well,
> since there are so many other faults he could
> have mentioned.'"*

Epicurus Epicurus *(c. 341–270 B.C.)*
Greek philosopher, the original "epicure."

Epops Epops
Hoopoe bird consulted for advice in
Aristophanes' comic play *The Birds* (414 B.C.).
Following its directions, construction was
started on Nephelococcygia, the original
"Cloud-cuckoo-town."

Erasmus Erasmus Bartholin *(1625–1698)*
Danish physician and physicist, the discoverer
of the peculiar double refraction of light in
Icelandic feldspar that forced a re-evaluation of
the physics of light.

Erastus Erastus Brigham Bigelow *(1814–1879)*
American inventor, founder of the
Massachusetts Institute of Technology (1861).

Erconwald St. Erconwald *(7th century)*
English brother of St. Etheburga, St. Etheldred,
St. Sexburga, and St. Withburga.

Eric Eric Newby *(1919–)*
British travel-writer, author of *A Short Walk in
the Hindu Kush* (1958).

> *"The ground was like iron with sharp rocks stick-
> ing up out of it. We started to blow up our air-
> beds. 'God, you must be a couple of pansies,'
> said [Wilfred] Thesiger."*

Erica Erica Jong *(1942–)*
American feminist, author of *Fear of Flying*
(1974) in which she describes the "zipless fuck"
where "zippers fell away like rose petals, under-
wear blew off in one breath like dandelion
fluff."

Erich Erich Fromm *(1900–1980)*
German-born American psychoanalyst, author
of *Fear of Freedom* (1941).

Erik Erik Erikson *(1903–1994)*
Freudian psychoanalyst. He coined the phrase
"identity crisis."

Erle Erle Stanley Gardner *(1889–1970)*
American crime novelist, creator of Perry Mason
the lawyer/sleuth, and, in his spare time, a pioneer of the dune buggy.

Erma Erma Bombeck *(1927–1996)*
American humorist.

Ernest Ernest Hemingway *(Ernest Miller Hemingway)
(1899–1961)*
American archetypal man's man, author of *For
Whom the Bell Tolls* (1940). He won the 1954
Nobel Prize for literature.

> *"Courage is grace under pressure."*

Ernestine Ernestine Hudgins *(1983–)*
American baby, the most premature ever to survive in the United States. She weighed 17 ounces at birth.

Ernö Ernö Rubik *(1944–)*
Hungarian designer of the 1975 "Rubik's cube" toy.

Ernst Ernst Mach *(1838–1916)*
Austrian physicist. "Mach 1" is the speed of light, named after him. There is also a "Mach angle" used to describe the direction of a shock wave relative to the direction of motion.

Eros Eros *(or Phanes) trans. erotic love*
Greek god, the first to be born from the great silver egg of Night. Double-sexed and golden-winged, he was too irresponsible to be one of the twelve Olympian gods.

Errol Errol Flynn *(1909–1959)*
Tasmanian-born American film swashbuckler, the star of *Captain Blood* (1935). The expression "in like Flynn" refers to an unproven charge of rape once laid against him.
> *"My problem lies in reconciling my gross habits with my net income."*

Erskine Erskine Caldwell *(1903–1987)*
American writer, author of *Tobacco Road* (1932).

Erwin Erwin Johannes Eugen Rommel *(1891–1944)*
German Field Marshal, the "Desert Fox" of North Africa. He chose suicide when discovered in a plot to murder Adolf Hitler. The suicide was concealed and he was buried with honour.

Esau Esau *(or Edom), trans. hairy, Genesis 25: 25 (c. 17th century B.C.)*
Old Testament hungry brother of Jacob, who traded his birthright for a bowl of soup. Jacob later sneakily sealed the bargain by disguising himself in hairy clothing to pretend to be Esau to get their blind father's blessing.

Esmerelda Esmerelda
Beloved of the hunchback Quasimodo in Victor Hugo's novel *Notre Dame de Paris* (1831).

Estée Estée Lauder, *née Mentzer (1908–)*
American beautician, a pioneer of the free sample. She wrote *Estée: A Success Story* (1985).

Estella Estella
English ward of Miss Havisham in Charles Dickens's novel *Great Expectations* (1860–61).

Esther Esther Johnson *(1681–1728)*
English poet, the pupil and lover of Jonathan Swift. She is the "Stella" of his *Journal to Stella* (1710–13). They first met in a park when she was eight years old.

Estrella *Alfonso and Estrella (1800s)*
German opera by Franz Schubert.

Eth Eth Glum
Character on the English radio series "Take It from Here" (1953–60). She was played by June Whitfield, also noted for her "Carry On" films.

Ethan Ethan Allen *(1738–1789)*
American Revolutionary soldier and Green Mountain Boy.

Ethel Ethel Barrymore *(1879–1959)*
American stage actress, the sister of Lionel and John Barrymore.
> *"For an actress to be a success, she must have the face of Venus, the brains of Minerva, the grace of Terpsichore, the memory of Macaulay, the figure of Juno, and the hide of a rhinoceros."*

Ethelred King Ethelred the Unready *(or Aethelred II) (ruled 978–1016)*
Saxon king. He didn't get his name because he was unprepared, but because he lacked "rede," or good advice.

Ethyl Ethyl Sibyl Turner *(1872–1958)*
English-born Australian children's novelist, author of the classic *Seven Little Australians* (1894).

Étienne Étienne de Silhouette *(1709–1767)*
French economist and politician. He was so notoriously stingy that popular cheap profile portraits cut out of black paper were nicknamed "silhouettes" in his honour.

Etta Etta Place *(20th century)*
American schoolteacher, the girlfriend of both Butch Cassidy and the Sundance Kid. She accompanied them to Argentina in 1907.

Ettore Ettore Sottsass, Jr. *(1917–)*
Italian industrial designer, leader of the Milan design group Memphis. The group got its name for being halfway between Memphis, Egypt, and Memphis, Tennessee.

Eubie Eubie Blake *(originally James Hubert Blake)* *(1883–1983)*
American ragtime pianist, composer of the first black-produced Broadway musical, *Shuffle Along* (1927). He was the only one of ten brothers and sisters to survive childhood.
> *"If I'd known I was going to live this long, I'd have taken better care of myself."*

Euclid Euclid *(Greek Eucleides) (4th–3rd century B.C.)*
Greek mathematician, author of the earliest surviving intact book of mathematics. When Ptolemy I of Egypt wanted to study geometry, but without going over the thirteen parts of the *Elements*, Euclid replied, "There is no royal road to geometry."

Eudora Eudora Welty *(1909–)*
American novelist, author of *The Robber Bridegroom* (1942), winner of a 1973 Pulitzer Prize.

Eudoxia Empress Eudoxia *(or Eudocia, originally Athenais) (401–465)*
Byzantine princess, the wife of the Emperor Theodosius II and an active Christian.

Eugen Eugen Bleuler *(1857–1939)*
Swiss psychiatrist, the teacher of Carl Jung. He coined the word "schizophrenia."

Eugene Eugene O'Neill *(Eugene Gladstone O'Neill)* *(1888–1953)*
American playwright, author of *Long Day's Journey into Night* (1957). He was expelled from Princeton for throwing a beer bottle through the window of the university's president, Woodrow Wilson.

Eugenia Eugenia Stanhope, *née Pieters (active 1760–1786)*
English editor, the "unattractive woman of undistinguished position" who was the mother of the illegitimate grandchildren of the Earl of Chesterfield. After the Earl's death, she published the letters of worldly advice that he had written to his wretched son.

Eugénie Empress Eugénie, *née Eugénia Maria de Montijo de Guzmán (1826–1920)*
Spanish-born wife of Napoleon III.

Euhemerus Euhemerus *(3rd century B.C.)*
Greek author. In his *Sacred History* he "euhemerized" Greek mythology, claiming that the gods were human heroes distorted.

Eunice Eunice *trans. conquering well, 2 Timothy 1: 5 (1st century)*
New Testament mother of Paul's disciple Timothy. It was Timothy who was personally circumcized by Paul.

Euphemia Euphemia Alten *(b. 1861)*
English composer. At the age of sixteen, under the alias Arthur de Lull, she registered her new composition, "Chopsticks," at the British Museum.

Euripides Euripides *(484–406 B.C.)*
Greek playwright. He invented the plot device of "deus ex machina," or "God from the machine," in which a god descends from the ceiling in the last five minutes of the play and ties up all the loose ends of the plot, using a real machine to achieve this effect by lowering actors from the roof.
> *"The gods visit the sins of the fathers upon the children."*

Eurydice Eurydice *(or Agriope) trans. wide justice*
Greek nymph, wife of the poet Orpheus. When she died of a snake-bite, he was inconsolable and tried to get her back from Hades. He almost succeeded, but at the last moment looked back to see if she was following, breaking the spell so that he lost her for good.

Eustace Eustace Tilly *(1925–)*
American top-hatted mascot of *The New Yorker* magazine. He appeared on the cover of the first edition, which had 32 pages and cost 15 cents, and promised to "not be edited for the old lady in Dubuque."

Eustochium St. Eustochium (or Eustochium Julia)
(c. 370–419)
Roman daughter of St. Paula. St. Jerome wrote
Concerning the Keeping of Virginity (384) for her.

Euthymides Euthymides (6th–5th century B.C.)
Greek vase painter, a rival of Euphronius, possibly the first person to draw with foreshortening.

Eva Eva Le Gallienne (1899–1991)
English-born theatre actress, director, and producer.

Evan Evan Hunter (originally Salvatore A. Lambino;
also known as Ed McBain) (1926–)
American novelist, author of *The Blackboard
Jungle* (1954).

Evander Evander Holyfield (Budd Schulberg Evander
Holyfield) (1962–)
American boxer, twice heavyweight champion.
His mother called him "Chubby."
> "This may sound funny, but he really hated to
> fight."

Evangeline "Evangeline" (1847)
American poem by Henry Wadsworth
Longfellow about the expulsion of the French
Acadians.

Évariste Évariste Galois (1811–1832)
French mathematician, author of a small but
significant body of work written on the night
before his death in a duel.

Eve Eve trans. life, Genesis 2: 23
Old Testament first woman, the wife of Adam.
She persuaded him to eat fruit from the tree of
knowledge, which proved to be a bad idea.

Evel Evel Knievel (1939–)
American motorcycle jumper.
> "Jumping, I stand or lean on the balls of my feet.
> The motorcycle's tendency is to buck and come
> down over backwards on me. So I try and lean
> forward to hold it down. I want to go off the
> ramp right at the pop of the power curve. If I do
> it, it'll go straight through the air. If I don't, this
> motorcycle has a tendency to drift sideways and
> cross up."

Eveline Eveline Hanska (married 1850)
Polish-born wife of the novelist Honoré de
Balzac. After corresponding for more than
fifteen years, they met for the first time and got
married only three months before his death.

Evelyn Evelyn Waugh (Evelyn Arthur St. John Waugh)
(1903–1966)
British novelist, author of *Brideshead Revisited*
(1945; film 1981).
> "Assistant masters came and went . . . Some
> liked little boys too little and some too much."

Evelyn Evelyn Nesbit (c. 1885–1967)
American dancer, the "Girl in the Red Velvet
Swing." In 1906 her husband shot her former
lover, architect Stanford White, after details of
their "exotic housekeeping" got out.
> "Don't forget I was only fifteen and I enjoyed
> swinging."

Everest Mount Everest
World's tallest mountain, at 29,078 feet. It is
named after Colonel Sir George Everest
(1790–1866).

Everett Everett Lamar "Rocky" Bridges (1927–)
American baseball shortstop with the Reds, an
All-Star.
> "There are three things the average man thinks
> he can do better than anybody else: build a fire,
> run a hotel, and manage a baseball team."

Evita Evita Perón, (Maria Eva Duarte de Perón, née
Ibargusen) (1919–1952)
Argentinian Socialist party worker, the wife and
political partner of Juan Perón. She inspired
Andrew Lloyd Webber's American musical *Evita*
(1978).

Evylyn Evylyn Thomas
(19th century)
American cyclist. In
1896, she was the first
American victim of a
car accident. Her leg
was broken, and the
driver held in jail
overnight.

EVITA PERÓN

Ewa Ewa Klobukowska *(20th century)*
Polish sprinter, an Olympic medallist, and the first athlete to fail an Olympic sex test.

Ewan Ewan MacColl *(originally William Miller)* *(1915–1989)*
Scottish balladeer, composer of "The First Time Ever I Saw Your Face" (1972).

Ewell Ewell Backwell *(1922–)*
American baseball pitcher with the Reds, an All-Star, known as "the Whip" for his fast sidearm throw.

Ewen Sir Ewen Cameron *(1629–1719)*
Scottish chief of the Camerons.

Eydie Eydie Gormé *(1932–)*
American songstress.

Eyre Eyre de Lanus *(pseudonym of Elizabeth de Lanus, née Eyre) (20th century)*
American-born Parisian interior designer.

Ezekial Ezekial "Easy" Rawlins *(active 1950s)*
Fictional Los Angeles black detective, hero of Walter Mosley's novel *Devil in a Blue Dress* (1990).

Ezra Ezra Pound *(Ezra Loomis Pound) (1885–1972)*
American poet and critic. After active war work in Italy on behalf of the Fascists, he was tried for treason but judged insane, and spent thirteen years institutionalized before being released and returning to Italy.
"Literature is news that STAYS news."

Ezzard Ezzard Charles *(20th century)*
American boxer. He defeated Joe Louis, and was defeated by Jersey Joe Walcott.

Fabian Fabian Gottlieb von Bellingshausen *(1778–1852)*
Russian explorer, the discoverer of the Antarctic.

Fabio Fabio *(Fabio Lanzoni) (1961–)*
International bleach-blond bulging-muscle cover-boy spokesmodel.

Faith Faith Popcorn *(originally Faith Plotkin) (1940–)*
American self-promoter, author of *The Popcorn Report* (1991).

Falstaff Sir John Falstaff
Fat drinking pal of the heir to the throne in William Shakespeare's plays *Henry IV Part One* (*c.* 1597) and *Henry IV Part Two* (*c.* 1598).

Fania Fania Mindell *(20th century)*
American political activist, one of the two employees of Margaret Sanger's first birth-control clinic in New York. All three were arrested in 1916 for distributing "obscene material," a pamphlet titled "What Every Girl Should Know."

Fannie Fannie Merritt Farmer *(1857–1915)*
American cookbook writer, author of *The Boston Cooking-School Cook Book* (1896).
"Progress in civilization has been accompanied by progress in cookery."

Fanny Fanny Burney *(later Madame D'Arblay)* *(1752–1840)*
English novelist and diarist, author of *Cecilia* (1782).
"Travelling is the ruin of all happiness! There's no looking at a building here after seeing Italy."

Faron Faron Young *(1932–)*
American country singer.

Farouk King Farouk I *(1920–1965)*
Egyptian monarch. He became a citizen of Monaco after he was deposed by Gamal Nasser.

Fat Fat Albert *(T.J. Albert Jackson) (1944–)*
American phenomenon. In 1992 he was the largest person alive, at 891 pounds.

Fatima Fatima *(7th century)*
Youngest daughter of the prophet Muhammad.

Fatma Fatma Rushdy *(1907–1995)*
Egyptian actress, the "Sarah Bernhardt of the East."

Fats Fats Waller *(originally Thomas Wright Waller)* *(1904–1943)*
American jazz pianist, composer of "Ain't Misbehavin'" (1929). In 1950, he ended a radio broadcast by saying, "I'd like to close with a message to my dear little wife—get that man outta there, honey, 'cause I'm coming home directly."

Fatty Roscoe "Fatty" Arbuckle *(1887–1933)*
American vaudeville star, the first person to be hit in the face with a custard pie on film. His career was ruined by a false charge of rape.

Fauna Fauna
Roman wife of Faunus, god of farming. After they married, she never laid eyes on another man.

Faustine "Faustine" (19th century)
Romantic English poem by Algernon Charles Swinburne.
> "A love machine with clockwork joints of supple gold—No more, Faustine."

Fausto Fausto Coppi (1919–1960)
Italian racing bicyclist.

Faustus Doctor Faustus (1588)
English play by Christopher Marlowe.

Fay Fay Weldon (originally Franklin Birkinshaw) (1932–)
English novelist. She wrote the advertising slogan "Go to work on an egg."

Faye Faye Dunaway (1941–)
American actress, winner of an Academy Award for Network (1976).
> "It's like Jackie Onassis said: If you bungle raising your children, it doesn't matter much what else you do."

Feargal Feargal Sharkey (1958–)
Northern Irish punk rock singer with the Undertones. A critic described him as having a "face like a bucket with a dent in it."

Februus Februus (or Februa)
Roman god of purification. The month "February" is named after him.

Federico Federico Fellini (1920–1993)
Italian film director of La Dolce Vita (1960).
> "All art is autobiographical; the pearl is the oyster's autobiography."

Fee Fee Waybill (originally John Waldo) (1950–)
American pop singer with the Tubes.

Fela Fela Kuti (Fela Ransome-Kuti) (1938–)
Nigerian musician, creator of the Afrobeat style.

Felice Felice Bryant, née Scaduto (1925–)
American country songwriter. She and her husband, Boudleaux, wrote the song "Bye Bye Love" (1957).

Felicia Felicia Dorothea Hemans, née Browne (1793–1835)
English poet. She took to writing for money after her husband abandoned her.
> "The boy stood on the burning deck
> Whence all but he had fled;
> The flame that lit the battle's wreck
> Shone round him o'er the dead."

Felipe Felipe Rose (1954–)
American disco vocalist with the Village People.

Felix Felix Wankel (1902–1988)
German mechanical engineer, inventor of the Wankel rotary engine used in the Mazda RX-7.

Felizberto Felizberto Duarte (20th century)
Brazillian TV weather reporter. He wears a tuxedo and dances the tango.

Ferdinand Count Ferdinand Adolf August Heinrich von Graf von Zeppelin (1838–1917)
German army officer. He served in the Union Army during the American Civil War, and in 1900 launched his first "zeppelin" lighter-than-air rigid airship.

Ferenc Ferenc Molnár (1878–1952)
Hungarian playwright and novelist. He wore a plain suit for his second wedding, rather than formal garb, because "I only dress for premières."

Fergie Sarah "Fergie" Ferguson (1959–)
Unsatisfactory British royal wife, the "Duchess of Pork."

Fergie Dennis "Fergie" Frederiksen (1951–)
American rock musician with the group Toto.

Fergus King Fergus of Ulster
Mythic ruler who persuaded Nessa to marry him by letting her son rule for a year. However, after a year with Conchobar, Fergus's people refused to have him back.

Ferguson Ferguson Jenkins (1943–)
Canadian baseball pitcher with the Cubs, an All-Star and winner of the Cy Young Award.

Ferhat Ferhat Abbas (1890–1989)
Algerian politician. He was deposed a year after achieving his lifelong goal of separating an independent Algeria from France.

Fermin Fermin Coytisolo (1951–)
Cuban-born American disco musician with the group KC and the Sunshine Band. They performed "Shake Your Booty" (1976).

Fern Fern Arable
Close personal friend of Willard the pig in E.B. (Elwyn Brooks) White's children's novel Charlotte's Web (1952).

> *Top 10 Baby Names*
> *Chosen by*
> *Famous Parents*
>
> Dweezil • Fifi • Jade • Leopold •
>
> Mercer • Rory • Sage • Shamus •
>
> Starlite • Tori

Fernand Fernand Léger *(1881–1955)*
French cubist painter. He helped create the first art film, *Le Ballet mécanique* (1923).

Fernandel Fernandel *(stage-name of Fernand-Joseph-Désiré Contandin) (1903–1971)*
French film comedian.

Fernando Fernando de Soto *(c. 1496–1542)*
Spanish explorer.

Ferruccio Ferruccio Lamborghini *(1917–1993)*
Italian car manufacturer, the rival of Enzo Ferrari.

Ffyona Ffyona Campbell *(1967–)*
British athlete, the first woman to walk around the world. It took eleven years.

Fiacre St. Fiacre *(d. 670)*
Irish hermit, who settled in France and founded a travellers' hospice. Parisian cabs are called *fiacres*, because the first hired coach in Paris was located outside the Hôtel Saint-Fiacre.

Fidel Fidel Castro *(1926–)*
Cuban politician. He gave up a promising career in baseball, refusing a $5,000 offer from the Giants, to become a revolutionary leader.

Fidelio *Fidelio (1814)*
German opera by Ludwig van Beethoven.

Fifi Fifi Trixabelle Geldof *(20th century)*
British daughter of rock star Bob Geldof.

Figaro *The Marriage of Figaro (1786)*
Comic opera in Italian by Wolfgang Amadeus Mozart.

Figgy Figgy Duff *(1975–)*
Canadian Newfoundland folk-music group.

Filipo Filipo Brunelleschi *(1377–1446)*
Italian Renaissance architect.

Filippo Filippo Strozzi the Elder *(1426–1491)*
Florentine banker. He built the Palazzo Strozzi.

Finbar St. Finbar *(originally Lochan, also known as Bairre, or Barr) (d. c. 633)*
Irish hermit, founder of the monastery that became the city of Cork. Monks nicknamed him Fionnbharr ("white head") when he was a boy.

Fingal *Fingal: An Ancient Epic Poem in Six Books (1762)*
Ancient Scottish epic poem supposedly discovered and translated by James Macpherson. Actually, he wrote it himself.

Finley Finley Peter Dunne *(1867–1936)*
American humorist, creator of Mr. Dooley the bartender. Describing the American vice-presidency, he explained, "It isn't a crime exactly. Ye can't be sint to jail f'r it, but it's kind iv a disgrace."

Finn Finn MacCool
Irish mythic hero. Disguised as a boar, he killed Diarmait, who had eloped with Finn's love Grainne.

Fiona Fiona, Countess of Arran *(b. 1918)*
British speedboat champion who set a 1989 electrical powerboat speed record of 45.13 knots (51.97 mph).

Fiorella Dr. Fiorella Terenzi *(20th century)*
Italian astrophysicist and New Age musician.

Fiorello Fiorello La Guardia *(Fiorello Henry La Guardia) (1882–1947)*
Popular American mayor of New York City.

Firmin Firmin Didot *(1764–1836)*
French printer of fine-edition books.

Firyal Princess Firyal of Jordan *(20th century)*
Jordanian socialite.

Fisher Fisher Arnes *(1758–1808)*
English politician.
> *"A monarchy is a merchantman which sails well but will sometimes strike on a rock and go to the bottom, while a repubic is a raft, which would never sink, but then your feet are always in water."*

Fitz-Greene Fitz-Greene Halleck *(1790–1867)*
American poet.
> *"None knew thee but to love thee."*

Fitzroy Fitzroy James Henry Somerset, 1st Baron
Raglan *(1788–1855)*
English soldier. He gave the order at Balaclava
for the ill-fated charge of the Light Brigade.
Raglan-style sleeves are named after him.

Flann Flann O'Brien *(pseudonym of Brian O'Nolan)*
(1911–1966)
Irish humorist, author of the comic masterpiece
At Swim-Two-Birds (1939).

Flannery Flannery O'Connor *(originally Mary
Flannery O'Connor) (1925–1964)*
American novelist, author of the astonishing
Everything That Rises Must Converge (1965). She
died young of lupus.
> *"Everywhere I go I'm asked if universities stifle
> writers. In my view, they don't stifle enough of
> them."*

Flash "Flash Gordon" *(1933–)*
American cartoon strip created by Alex
Raymond.

Flavia St. Flavia Domitilla *(2nd century)*
Roman Christian convert, the great-niece of
Emperor Domitian.

Flavor Flavor Flav *(originally William Drayton)*
(1959–)
American comic rapper with the group Public
Enemy.

Fleet Fleet Walker *(Moses Fleetwood Walker)*
(1856–1924)
American baseball catcher. He was fired in 1887
when the official ban on black players started,
and wrote *Our Home Colony* (1908) proposing
emigration to Africa as the solution for mount-
ing racial intolerance.

Fletcher Fletcher Christian *(c. 1764–c. 1794)*
English seaman. In 1789, he led the mutiny on
the ship *Bounty*.

Fleur Fleur Forsyte
English heroine of John Galsworthy's novels in
The Forsyte Saga (1906–21).

Flinders Sir Flinders Petrie *(William Matthew
Flinders Petrie) (1853–1942)*
English Egyptologist/archaeologist, the first to
realize the importance of stratification in
ancient sites, author of *Decorative Patterns of the
Ancient World* (1930).
> *"The subject is boundless, and to wait for com-
> pletion would bar any useful result."*

Flip Flip Wilson *(originally Clerow Wilson) (1933–)*
American comedian, one of twenty-four
children in his family.
> *"The devil made me do it."*

Flo Flo Lancaster *(originally Florence Wallis) (20th
century)*
British children's author, creator of Uncle Oojah
the elephant.

Flo-Jo Florence Griffith "Flo-Jo" Joyner *(1959–)*
American track-and-field Olympic gold-medallist,
called "Fluorescent Flo" for her striking taste in
tracksuits.

Flora Flora Macdonald *(1722–1790)*
Scottish Jacobite heroine. She disguised the
Young Pretender Charles as her maid "Betty
Burke," and accompanied him on a perilous
journey.

Florence Florence Nightingale *(1820–1910)*
British army nurse and sanitary reformer; the
"Lady with the Lamp." She was named after her
birthplace in Italy.
> *"To understand God's thoughts we must study
> statistics, for these are the measure of his pur-
> pose."*

Florenz Florenz Ziegfeld *(1869–1932)*
American theatre manager, creator of the *Follies
of 1907*, and a following series of other theatri-
cal extravaganzas.

Florian "Florian, the Emperor's Stallion" *(1934)*
Austrian animal story by Felix Salten, who also
wrote *Bambi* (1929).

Florrie Florrie Forde *(originally Florence Flanagan)*
(1876–1940)
Australian-born grande dame of the British
music hall. She was the first to sing "It's a Long
Way to Tipperary" (1912).

Floyd Floyd Patterson *(1935–)*
American boxer, twice heavyweight champion.
"It's easy to do anything in victory. It's in defeat that a man reveals himself."

Floyer Floyer Sydenham *(1710–1787)*
English scholar. He failed to make money translating Plato, and died in debtors' prison. His death inspired a literary fund to help future destitute writers.

Fog Captain Mark "Fog" Philips *(1948–)*
First husband of Britain's Princess Anne, so-called because he is "thick and wet."

Fontella Fontella Bass *(1940–)*
American soul singer of "Rescue Me" (1966).

Fopling Sir Fopling Flutter, title character of *The Man of Mode; or Sir Fopling Flutter (1676)*
English play, a comedy of manners by Sir George Etherege. It was extremely popular at the time.

Ford Ford Madox Ford *(originally Ford Hermann Hueffer) (1873–1939)*
British novelist and editor.

Forest Forest E. Mars *(20th century)*
American entrepreneur, co-creator of M&M's candies that "melt in your mouth, not in your hand." They were originally invented for soldiers.

Forrest *Forrest Gump (1986)*
American novel by Winston Groom, made into a 1994 movie starring Tom Hanks.
"Stupid is as stupid does."

Fortuna Fortuna
Roman goddess of chance, the equivalent of Greek Nemesis. Her name comes from the word "vortumna," meaning "she who turns the world around."

Fortunatus Fortunatus Wright *(d. 1757)*
English pirate and privateer.

Foster Foster Hewitt *(1902–1985)*
Canadian hockey announcer.
"He shoots, he scores!"

Foulweather John "Foulweather Jack" Byron *(1723–1786)*
English naval officer. He wrote an account of his 1761 shipwreck off the coast of Chile that was used by his grandson Lord Byron in the poem *Don Juan.*

Four-Eyed Four-Eyed George *(General George Gordon Meade) (1815–1872)*
American army officer. He was the first person to earn this nickname for wearing glasses.

Fran Fran Leibowitz *(20th century)*
American humorist.
"Children ask better questions than do adults. 'May I have a cookie?' 'Why is the sky blue?' and 'What does a cow say?' are far more likely to elicit a cheerful response than 'Where's your manuscript?' 'Why haven't you called?' and 'Who's your lawyer?'"

Frances Frances Willard *(1839–1898)*
American president of the Women's Christian Temperance Union, an enthusiast of bicycle-riding.
"I finally concluded that all failure was from a wobbling will rather than wobbling wheel."

Francesco Francesco Borromini *(originally Francesco Castello) (1599–1667)*
Italian baroque sculptor and architect.

Francis Francis Bacon, Baron Verulam of Verulam, Viscount St. Albans *(1561–1626)*
British author, philosopher, and politician.
"Children sweeten labours, but they make misfortunes more bitter. They increase the cares of life, but they mitigate the remembrance of death."

Francisco Francisco Goya *(Francisco José de Goya y Lucientes) (1746–1828)*
Spanish artist, court painter to Charles IV, noted for his unflatteringly honest portraits.

Francisque Francisque Poulbot *(1879–1946)*
French cartoonist of the working classes. *Poulbot* is still slang for a street urchin. In 1979, he appeared on a postage stamp.

Franco Franco Zeffirelli *(1923–)*
Italian director of stage, opera, and film.

François François Marie Arouet de Voltaire *(1694–1778)*
French author, embodiment of the "enlightenment." Asked on his deathbed to renounce the devil, he replied, "This is no time to be making new enemies."

François-Auguste-René François-Auguste-René, Vicomte de Chateaubriand *(1768–1848)* Breton aristocrat and politician. Chef Montmireil invented for him the dish known as "beef Chateaubriand."

François-Eugène François-Eugène Vidocq *(1775–1857)* French sleuth, creator in 1832 of the world's first detective agency. His exaggerated memoirs influenced Edgar Allan Poe.

Françoise Françoise Sagan *(pen-name of Françoise Quoirez) (1935–)* French novelist. She wrote her first book, the best-selling *Bonjour tristesse* (1954), in only four weeks at the age of eighteen. Manuel Puig later called her "the oldest seventeen-year-old in France."

Franjo Franjo Tudjman *(20th century)* Croatian president.

Frank Frank Zappa *(Frank Vincent Zappa) (1940–1993)* American musician.
> "Most people wouldn't know good music if it came up and bit them on the ass."

Frankie Frankie Vaughn *(20th century)* American pop singer.
> "I'm not a crooner—I'm just a song salesman."

Franklin Franklin Delano Roosevelt *(1882–1945)* American 32nd president, inventor of the "fireside chat."
> "A man who has never gone to school may steal from a freight car, but if he has a university eduction he may steal the whole railroad."

Franz Franz Anton Mesmer *(1734–1815)* Austrian doctor, the describer of "animal magnetism."

Franz Franz Kafka *(1883–1924)* Austrian author of *The Castle* (trans. 1937). He refused to allow any of his work to be published in his lifetime.

Fraser Fraser Clark *(20th century)* Scottish "zippy," or "zen-inspired pronoia professional." He defines "pronoia" as "the sneaking suspicion that someone is conspiring to help you."

Frasier Dr. Frasier Crane Psychiatrist character on the American TV series "Cheers" (d. 1993) and "Frasier" (b. 1993).

Fred Fred Astaire *(originally Frederick Austerlitz) (1899–1987)* Legendary American dancer and actor, star of *Top Hat* (1935).
> "The hardest job kids face today is learning good manners without seeing any."

Freda Freda Washington *(20th century)* American dancer, an innovator in the Lindy Hop. The dance was named after Charles Lindbergh when couples vaulting over each other started calling out "I'm flying like Lindy!"

Freddie Sir Freddie Laker *(Sir Frederick Alfred Laker) (1922–)* British businessperson, the creator of budget transatlantic air travel.

Frédéric Frédéric Chopin *(1810–1849)* Polish pianist and composer.
> "I don't want anyone to admire my pants in a museum."

Frederick Sir Frederick Grant Banting *(1891–1941)* Canadian physiologist. He shared the Nobel Prize with J.J.R. (John James Rickard) Macleod and C.H. (Charles Herbert) Best for their discovery of insulin.

Frederik Frederik Pohl *(1919–)* American science-fiction writer.

Fredric Fredric March *(originally Frederick McIntyre Bickel) (1897–1975)* American actor, winner of an Academy Award for his performance in *Dr. Jekyll and Mr. Hyde* (1932).

Freelan Freelan O. Stanley *(1849–1940)* With his twin brother, Francis, American manufacturer of the Stanley Steamer car, which could reach 127 mph without spark plugs, gears, or transmission, burning any fuel available. Freelan and

FRANK ZAPPA

his brother never advertised, did not improve their original model, and closed their business when Henry Ford's assembly lines made their prices too high for competition.

Freeman Freeman Gosden *(20th century)*
American radio writer. He and Charles Correll created the show "Amos 'n' Andy" (1926–51), originally called "Sam and Henry" until they overheard this conversation on an elevator
> *"OPERATOR: Well, well, famous Amos.*
> *PASSENGER: Hello, handy Andy."*

Freya Freya Stark *(Dame Freya Madeline Stark) (1893–1993)*
English explorer, author of *Valley of the Assassins* (1934), about Luristan.
> *"The great and almost only comfort about being a woman is that one can always pretend to be more stupid than one is, and no one is surprised."*

Frida Frida Kahlo *(1910–1954)*
Mexican painter. She had a tempestuous marriage to fellow painter Diego Rivera.

Frideswide St. Frideswide *(d. c. 735)*
Anglo-Saxon abbess, the patron saint of Oxford. She fled her own wedding to become a religious hermit living in a pigsty at Binsey Abbey.

Fridtjof Fridtjof Nansen *(1861–1930)*
Norwegian explorer. In 1893, he almost reached the North Pole by letting his ship freeze in the ice and drift north with the ice floe, before setting off on foot.

Frieda Frieda von Richthofen Weekley Lawrence *(eloped 1912)*
German-born cousin of war ace Baron Mannfred von Richthofen. She left her husband and children for English writer D.H. (David Herbert) Lawrence, with whom she quarrelled endlessly.
> *"It's still gorgeous here," she wrote in a letter. "No it isn't," Lawrence wrote underneath, "it's cold and dark."*

Friedrich Friedrich Wilhelm August Froebel *(1782–1852)*
German educationist, inventor of the "Kindergarten" ("children's garden").

Frigga Frigga
Nordic goddess. She gave her name to "Friday."

Fritz Fritz Lang *(1890–1976)*
Austrian-born American film director, creator of *Metropolis* (1926).

Friz Friz Freleng *(originally Isadore Freleng) (1906–)*
American animated-film director, creator of Porky Pig and Sylvester the Cat.

Frodo Frodo Baggins
Intrepid Hobbit hero of J.R.R. (John Ronald Reuel) Tolkien's English fantasy trilogy *The Lord of the Rings* (1954–55).

Frost Frost McKee *(20th century)*
American prodigy. In 1992, he memorized a random sequence of 1,872 playing cards on one viewing, with only eight errors.

Fryniwid Fryniwid "Fryn" Tennyson Jesse *(pen-name F. Tennyson Jesse) (1889–1958)*
English novelist, author of the *The Lacquer Lady* describing the arrival of the British in Burma.

Fu *Dr. Fu Manchu (1913)*
English mystery novel by Sax Rohmer.

Fulbert St. Fulbert *(c. 952–1029)*
Italian-born bishop of Chartres. He rebuilt the cathedral when it burnt down.

Fulke Sir Fulke Greville, 1st Baron Brooke *(1554–1628)*
English poet and courtier to Elizabeth I. He was murdered by an old family retainer who mistakenly thought he'd been cut out of the will.

Fuller Fuller Pilch *(19th century)*
British cricket batsman. He dominated British batting for thirty years.

Fulton Fulton Allen *(known as Blind Boy Fuller) (1908–1941)*
American blues guitarist, composer of "I'm a Rattlesnakin' Daddy" (1935).

Furry Furry Lewis *(originally Walter Lewis) (1893–1981)*
American blues singer and bottleneck guitarist.

Fyodor Fyodor Mikhailovich Dostoevsky *(1821–1881)*
Russian novelist, author of *Crime and Punishment* (1866).
> *"Man is a pliable animal, a being who gets accustomed to everything."*

Gabby Gabby Hartnett *(Charles Leo Hartnett)* *(1900–1972)*
American baseball catcher with the Chicago Cubs, a member of the Hall of Fame. The whole family had the "Hartnett arm"; his father and six of his fourteen siblings (three brothers and three sisters) all played ball.

Gabriel Gabriel Daniel Fahrenheit *(1686–1736)*
German physicist, inventor of the mercury thermometer and the "Fahrenheit" scale for measuring temperature.

Gabriela Gabriela Mistral *(pseudonym of Lucila Godoy Alcayaga) (1889–1957)*
Chilean poet and diplomat, winner of the 1945 Nobel Prize for literature.

Gabriele Gabriele d'Annunzio *(1863–1938)*
Italian poet and *homme fatale*, author of *La gioconda* (1899). He had a pillow stuffed with locks of hair from a hundred women.

Gabrielle Gabrielle d'Estrées *(c. 1570–1599)*
French noblewoman, mistress of Henri IV. Henri was about to divorce his queen in order to marry her, when she died suddenly in Paris.

Gaby Gaby Concepcion *(20th century)*
Filipino actress. She was charged with fraud for allegedly falsifying the winners at the 1994 Manila Film Festival with a simple plan whereby the award-givers on stage simply announced different names.

Gae Gae Aulenti *(1928–)*
Italian designer; the only successful woman of her generation of architects.

Gaea Gaea *trans. mother earth*
Greek mother of the gods; after Chaos, the most ancient of the gods. With her son Uranus, she gave birth to the first race of men: the twelve Titans.

Gaetan Gaetan Dugas *(20th century)*
Québécois flight attendant and jet-set partyboy, known as "Patient Zero" for his suspected early role in spreading the AIDS epidemic.

Gaetano Gaetano Donizetti *(Domenico Gaetano Maria Donizetti) (1797–1848)*
Italian composer.

Gahan Gahan Wilson *(1930–)*
Macabre American cartoonist, author of *The Man in the Cannibal Pot* (1967).

Gail Gail Singer *(20th century)*
Canadian documentary filmmaker of *Wisecracks* (1991) about female stand-up comics.

Gala Gala Dalí *(20th century)*
French wife of Paul Eluard and of Salvador Dalí.

Galahad Sir Galahad
Virgin knight of the Round Table, son of Sir Lancelot. He found the Holy Grail.

Galatea *Galatea*
Greek sculpture created by Pygmalian out of ivory. When he fell in love with his statue, Aphrodite kindly brought her to life. This story inspired George Bernard Shaw's "anti-romance" *Pygmalian* (1913), and the musical *My Fair Lady* (1956, filmed 1964).

Gale Gale Sondergaard *(originally Edith Holm Sondergaard) (1899–1985)*
American actress. She played the villainess in *The Little Princess* (1939) opposite Shirley Temple.

Galeazzo Count Galeazzo Ciano *(1903–1944)*
Italian politician. As foreign minister, he signed the Axis Alliance treaty.
"As always, victory finds a hundred fathers, but defeat is an orphan."

Galen Galen of Pergamum *(or Claudius Galenus) (c. 130–c. 201)*
Greek physician, a voluminous writer.

Galileo Galileo Galilei *(1564–1642)*
Italian astronomer, mathematician, lens-grinder, and religious heretic.
"Eppur si muove" ("But it does move").

Gallio Gallio *(Lucius Junius Gallio), Acts 18: 14 (1st century)*
Roman proconsul at Corinth, elder brother of the Stoic philosopher Seneca. He declined an invitation to prosecute Paul for blasphemy.
"I refuse to be a judge of these things."

Galyon Galyon Hone *(worked 1490–1526)*
Antwerp stained-glass master. He created many of the windows in the King's College Chapel, Cambridge, England.

Gamal Gamal Abdel Nasser *(1918–1970)*
Egyptian politician responsible for the over-throw of King Farouk (1952).

Gammer *Gammer Gurton's Needle (1553)*
English play, probably by William Stevenson. It is the earliest surviving English comedy.

Ganesh Ganesh *(or Ganesha)*
Popular elephant-headed Hindu god, patron of writers. His father accidentally chopped off his original head, then, remorseful, replaced it with a new head from the first passing animal.

Ganymede Ganymede *(or Ganymedes)*
Trojan cup-bearer at Mount Olympus. According to Homer he was "the most beautiful of all mortal men."

Gareth Gareth Owen Edwards *(1947–)*
Welsh rugby union player, possibly the finest all-round scrum half in his sport.

Gargantua *Gargantua (1534)*
French satirical novel by François Rabelais, an unparalleled mix of silliness and wisdom.

Garland Garland Braxton *(1900–1966)*
American baseball pitcher with the Senators. He retired to become a golfer.

Garp *The World According to Garp (1982)*
American movie starring Robin Williams, based on the novel by John Irving.

Garrison Garrison Keillor *(1942–)*
American radio writer, inventor of the community of Lake Wobegon.
  "People have tried, they have tried, but sex is not better than sweet corn."

Garry Garry Trudeau *(1950–)*
American cartoonist, creator of the Pulitzer Prize–winning "Doonesbury" (1970–).

Gary Gary Larson *(1950–)*
American cartoonist, creator of "The Far Side." In 1995, he retired from the daily newspapers to concentrate on books.

Gaspard Gaspard-Gustave de Coriolis *(1792–1843)*
French mathematician. In 1835, he described the "Coriolis effect," where water spins in opposite directions going down the drain above and below the Equator.

Gatemouth Clarence "Gatemouth" Brown *(1924–)*
American blues guitarist.

Gatewood Gatewood Galbraith *(20th century)*
American candidate in 1991 for governor of Kentucky, on a platform to legalize marijuana.
  "You allow me to license and regulate marijua-na, and I'll fill every hotel and motel room in the state of Kentucky."

Gautama Prince Gautama Siddhartha, the Buddha
trans. enlightened one (c. 563–c. 480 B.C.)
Nepalese prince. At the age of thirty he abandoned the luxuries of court to spend six years in austerity, until, sitting beneath a banyan tree in the state of Bihar, he reached the state of enlightenment.

Gavin Gavin Maxwell *(20th century)*
British author of the memoir *Ring of Bright Water*, about his pet otters.

Gavrilo Gavrilo Princip *(1895–1918)*
Serbian revolutionary, a member of the Black Hand terrorist group. He assassinated Archduke Francis Ferdinand and his wife, Sophie, in Sarajevo, providing an excuse for the start of the First World War.

Gawain *Sir Gawain and the Green Knight (14th century)*
Traditional English tale. A 1925 edition was edited by J.R.R. (John Ronald Reuel) Tolkien.

Gay Gay Talese *(1932–)*
American journalist, a founder of the "new journalism."

Gayle Gayle Sierens *(1954–)*
American sports journalist, the first woman to broadcast NFL football play-by-play.

Gaylord Gaylord Perry *(1938–)*
American baseball pitcher for the Giants, an All-Star and winner of the Cy Young Award. He fidgeted constantly while on the mound, convincing nervous batters he was about to throw an illegal spitball. His autobiography is titled *Me and the Spitter*.

Geddy Geddy Lee *(1953–)*
Canadian heavy-metal bass player with the band Rush.

Geena Geena Davis *(originally Virginia Davis) (1957–)*
American actress, winner of an Oscar for *The Accidental Tourist* (1988).

Gefjon Gefjon
Nordic goddess, the protector of girls who died unwed.

Gelett Gelett Burgess *(1866–1951)*
American humorist and illustrator.
> *"I never saw a Purple Cow*
> *I never hope to see one*
> *But I can tell you, anyhow*
> *I'd rather see than be one."*
> *The sequel is:*
> *"Ah, yes, I wrote the 'Purple Cow'—*
> *I'm sorry, now, I wrote it!*
> *But I can tell you, anyhow,*
> *I'll kill you if you quote it!"*

Gelsey Gelsey Kirkland *(1952–)*
American dancer, author of *Dancing on My Grave* (1986).

Gemma Gemma Jones *(20th century)*
British actress, star of "The Duchess of Duke Street."

Gena Gena Rowlands *(originally Virginia Rowlands) (1934–)*
American actress.

Gene Gene Roddenberry *(originally Eugene Wesley Roddenberry) (1922–1991)*
American airline pilot, the creator of "Star Trek." His ashes were sent into space.

Geneviève St. Geneviève *(or Genovefa) (c. 422–500)*
French saint. She organized a crusade of prayer when Attila the Hun was headed towards Paris, and he did not visit.

Genghis Genghis Khan *(real name Temüjen) (c. 1162–1227)*
Mongolian cavalry genius. He created a lasting empire that extended from the Black Sea to the Pacific Ocean.
> *"The greatest happiness is to vanquish your enemies, to chase them before you, to rob them of their wealth, to see those dear to them bathed in tears, to clasp to your bosom their wives and daughters."*

Gennifer Gennifer Flowers *(20th century)*
American entertainer, alleged mistress of President Bill Clinton.

Gentleman "Gentleman Jim " Corbett *(James John Corbett) (1866–1933)*
American heavyweight boxing champ. A former bank teller, he knocked out John L. Sullivan to win the 1892 heavyweight title in the first modern match using padded gloves and the Queensberry rules (instead of bare knuckles and no rules).

GERMAINE GREER

Geoff Geoff Boycott *(1940–)*
British cricket player, the most celebrated batsman in post-war cricket.

Geoffrey Geoffrey Chaucer *(c. 1340–1400)*
English writer, author of *The Canterbury Tales* (1388), the first poet to write in the English language.
> *"To make vertu of necessitee."*

Georg Georg Simon Ohm *(1789–1854)*
German physicist. The "ohm" measurement of electric resistance is named after him.

George George Washington Carver *(c. 1860–1943)*
American botanist, the inventor of peanut butter, the "Wizard of Tuskegee."

Georgeanna Georgeanna Tillman *(1944–1980)*
American Motown singer with the Marvelettes.

Georges Georges Léon Jules Marre *(1862–1912)*
French dramatist. He was so lazy that when told that the prettiest woman ever seen had just entered the room behind him, he replied, without turning, "Describe her to me."

Georgette Madame Georgette de la Plante *(20th century)*
French dressmaker. "Georgette" crepe fabric is named after her.

Georghe Georghe Zamfir *(20th century)*
Greek musician. In 1992, his song "The Lonely Shepherd" was the most popular Muzak selection ever.

Georgia Georgia O'Keeffe *(1887–1986)*
American painter, the wife and model of photographer Alfred Stieglitz.

Georgiana Georgiana, Duchess of Devonshire *(1757–1806)*
English hostess, poet, and gambler. She started the style of wearing long feathers in the hair.

Georgie Georgie Hyde-Lees *(1902–)*
Irish wife of poet William Butler Yeats. They married when he was fifty-two and she was fifteen. He had proposed earlier, but she made him wait.

Georgie Georgie Fame *(originally Clive Powell) (1943–)*
British R&B Hammond-organist.

Gerald Gerald Durrell *(Gerald Malcolm Durrell) (1925–1995)*
English zookeeper, author of *My Family and Other Animals* (1956).
> *"How long did it take six men to build a wall if three of them took a week? I recall that we spent almost as much time on this problem as the men spent on the wall."*

Geraldine Geraldine Apponyi *(1915–)*
American-born queen. She was working in a souvenir shop at the Budapest National Museum when she met King Zog I of Albania in 1938.

Geraldo Geraldo Rivera *(1943–)*
American TV personality, a kiss 'n' tell heavy date to the stars.

Gerard Gerard Manley Hopkins *(1844–1889)*
English Jesuit priest. His poetry was not published in his lifetime.
> *"Glory be to God for dappled things—*
> *For skies as couple-coloured as a brindled cow;*
> *For rose-moles all in stipple upon trout that swim."*

Gerardo Gerardo Secundo Albina *(1921–)*
Argentinian-born Chilean husband of Leontina Albina, née Espinosa; father of her record-setting fifty-five children.

Gerardus Gerardus Mercator *(1512–1594)*
Flemish geographer and map-maker. He invented the "Mercator projection" for maps, in which the path of a ship steering at a constant bearing shows on the map as a straight line.

Gerd Field Marshal Gerd von Rudstedt *(1875–1953)*
German soldier, a calm professional who served in both World Wars.
> *"This war with Russia is a nonsensical idea, to which I can see no happy ending."*

Germaine Germaine Greer *(1939–)*
Australian feminist, author of *The Female Eunuch* (1970).
> *"Common morality now treats childbearing as an aberration. There are practically no good reasons left for exercising one's fertility."*

Germany Germany Schaefer *(Herman A. Schaefer) (1877–1919)*
American baseball infielder with the Tigers. His vaudeville act with teammate Charley O'Leary helped inspire the MGM musical *Take Me Out to the Ball Game* with Gene Kelly and Frank Sinatra.

Geronimo Geronimo *(real name Goyathlay) (1829–1909)*
American Apache chief, author of *Geronimo: His Own Story* (1906).

Gerrit Gerrit Rietveld *(Gerrit Thomas Rietveld) (1888–1964)*
Dutch architect, creator in 1918 of the uncomfortable "red blue" chair.

Gerry Gerry Ford *(Gerald Rudolph Ford) (1913–)*
American president who pardoned Richard Nixon. Lyndon Johnson said, "Gerry Ford is so dumb that he can't fart and chew gum at the same time."

Gertrude Gertrude Stein *(1874–1946)*
American writer, author of *The Autobiography of Alice B. Toklas* (1933).
> *"Rose is a rose is a rose is a rose."*

Gerty Gerty Millar *(19th century)*
British royal girlfriend. The Garrick Club still owns the metal dog-collar given to her by Edward VII.

Gervase Gervase of Tilbury *(c. 1150–c. 1220)*
English chronicler.

Gherman Gherman Stepanovich Titov *(1935–)*
Soviet astronaut. In 1961, he became the youngest person to travel into space.

Gia Gia Marie Carangi *(1960–1986)*
American supermodel and heroin addict, subject of a biography by Stephen Fried.

Giacomo Giacomo Casabianca *(d. 1798)*
French child, the real boy who stood on the burning deck of the ship *Orient*, as described in the poem by Felicia Dorothea Hemans. He stayed behind to try to help his dying father.

Giambattista Giambattista Donati *(1826–1873)*
Italian astronomer, in 1858 the discoverer of
"Donati's comet."

Giancarlo Giancarlo Giannini *(1942–)*
Italian actor, star of Lina Wertmuller's *Seven
Beauties* (1976).

Gianlorenzo Gianlorenzo Bernini *(1598–1680)*
Italian sculptor, architect, and painter, the great
master of the Baroque.

Gid Gid Tanner *(originally James Gideon Tanner)*
(1884–1960)
American country musician, leader of the influential string band the Skillet-Lickers.

Gideon Gideon Welles *(19th century)*
American politician, the inspiration for a
popular poem:
> *"Retire, O Gideon to an onion farm,*
> *Ply any trade that's innocent and slow,*
> *Do anything, where you can do no harm,*
> *Go anywhere you fancy—only go."*

Gidget *Gidget Goes Hawaiian (1961)*
Wholesome American film.

Gig Gig Young *(1913–1978)*
American actor. He won an Oscar for supporting
actor for *They Shoot Horses Don't They?* (1969).

Gil Gil Scott-Heron *(1949–)*
American poet and songwriter.
> *"It's winter in America."*

Gilbert Gilbert Hyatt *(1938–)*
American inventor in 1968 of the first modern
computer, while working at Micro Computer
Inc., Los Angeles.

Gilberte Gilberte Swann
Fascinating girl of Marcel Proust's *Remembrance
of Things Past* (1913–22).

Giles Giles Vigneault *(1928–)*
Quebec author of the song "Mon Pays" (1964).
> *"Mon pays ce n'est pays un pays, c'est l'hiver."*
> *("My country is not a country, it's winter.")*

Gilgamesh Gilgamesh
Babylonian hero of the *Epic of Gilgamesh*. After a
snake stole his plant of eternal life, he had to
make do with eternal fame instead.

Gillian Gillian Armstrong *(1951–)*
Australian film director of *Mrs. Soffel* (1984).

Gilligan *Gilligan's Island (1964–1967)*
American TV series.

Gilmer Gilmer Meriweather *(1870–1951)*
American journalist, writer of a popular column
of advice to the lovelorn.

Gilmour Gilmour "Gloomy Gil" Dobie
(1879–1948)
American college football quarterback, later a
college coach at Cornell.
> *"Just because you win this game doesn't mean
> you're going to win the next one."*

Gimpy Lloyd "Gimpy" Brown *(1904–1974)*
American baseball pitcher with the Senators. He
pitched more home runs to Lou Gehrig than
anyone else.

Gina Gina Lollobrigida *(1927–)*
Italian film star.

Ginger Ginger Rogers *(originally Virginia Katherine
McMath) (1911–1995)*
American actress and dancer, Fred Astaire's
partner.
> *"We had fun and it shows."*

Gino Gino Vanelli *(1952–)*
Canadian pop singer.

Gio Gio Ponti *(20th century)*
Italian furniture designer.

Gioacchino Gioacchino Antonio Rossini
(1792–1868)
Italian opera composer, creator of *The Barber of
Seville (Il Barbiere de Seviglia)* (1816)
> *"Give me a laundry list and I'll set it to music."*

Giordano Giordano Bruno Guerri *(1950–)*
Italian author of the religious exposé *I Absolve
You* (1993). He tape-recorded fake confessions.
> *"When I confessed to murder and told the priests
> I was about to turn myself in, every time they
> would say, 'Don't do it. God has already forgiven
> you.'"*

Giorgio Giorgio de Chirico *(1888–1978)*
Italian artist.
> *"Modernism is dying in all the countries of the
> world. Let us hope it will soon be just an unhappy
> memory."*

Giotto Giotto di Bondone *(c. 1266–1337)*
Italian artist, the finest painter of his age. He
was discovered at age ten drawing a lamb on a
flat rock while working as a shepherd.

Giovanni Giovanni Agnelli *(1866–1945)*
Italian motor-car manufacturer, the founder of
Fiat.

Gipper George "The Gipper" Gipp *(1895–1921)*
American football quarterback. Dying of pneumonia, he told coach Knute Rockne:
> *"Sometime, Rock, when things are wrong and the
> breaks are beating the boys, tell them to go in
> there with all they've got and win one just for the
> Gipper. I don't know where I'll be then, Rock, but
> I'll know about it. And I'll be happy."*

Girolamo Girolamo Fracastoro *(c. 1478–1553)*
Italian physician. He coined the word "syphilis"
to replace existing xenophobic names for the
disease, such as "French pox," "Spanish fever,"
and "Polish plague."

Gisela Gisela Fluss *(19th century)*
Viennese sister of a school friend of young
Sigmund Freud. He had a crush on her.

Giselle *Giselle (1841)*
French ballet by Adolphe Charles Adam, based
on a story by Théophile Gautier.

Giulietta Giulietta Masina *(1920–1994)*
Italian actress, wife of Federico Fellini.

Giuseppe Giuseppe Arcimboldo *(1530–1593)*
Italian artist. He painted symbolic royal portraits composed of mounds of fruit.

Gizella Gizella Witkowsky *(1957–)*
Canadian prima ballerina with the National
Ballet.

Gladys Gladys Aylward *(1902–1970)*
English missionary to China, the former par-
lour-maid who founded the "Inn of the Sixth
Happiness."

Glaucis Glaucis *trans. grey-green*
Greek peasant. She and her husband, Philemon,
were hospitable to some ragged strangers, who
proved to be the gods Zeus and Hermes in disguise, and who richly rewarded the old couple
for their kindness.

Glen Glen Campbell *(Glen Travis Campbell) (1936–)*
American country star.

Glencora Lady Glencora Palliser
Vivacious society hostess of Anthony Trollope's
English novel *Can You Forgive Her?* (1864).

Glenda Glenda Jackson *(1936–)*
British actress and politician. She won an
Academy Award for her performance in *Women
in Love* (1969).
> *"I've had more bad notices than Lipton's has tea
> bags."*

Glenn Glenn Gould *(Glenn Herbert Gould)
(1932–1982)*
Canadian classical pianist and composer.

Glennda Glennda Orgasm *(20th century)*
American drag queen, a friend of philosopher
Camille Paglia.

Glennis *Glamorous Glennis (flew 1947)*
American airplane in which Chuck Yeager flew
the world's first supersonic flight. She was a Bell
XS-1, named after his wife.

Glinda Glinda, Good Witch of the South
Beautiful benefactress of lost Dorothy Gale in L.
Frank Baum's children's novel *The Wonderful
Wizard of Oz* (1900).

Glooskap Glooskap
Mythic hero of the Algonquin Indians, twin
brother of wicked Maslum.

Gloria Gloria Steinem *(1934–)*
American feminist, co-founder of *Ms. Magazine*,
author of "I Was a Playboy Bunny."
> *"Some of us are becoming the men we wanted to
> marry."*

Gloriana Queen Gloriana
Queen of Faeryland in Edmund Spenser's poem
The Faerie Queen (1590). Her character was a
tribute to Queen Elizabeth I

Glynis Glynis Johns *(1923–)*
South African–born British actress.

Glynn Glynn de Moss Wolfe *(active 1931–1980)*
British marrying man. He married twenty-four
times, with no bride over the age of twenty-five.
He kept a number of wedding dresses on hand
in different sizes, just in case.

Godfrey Godfrey Evans (*originally Thomas Godfrey Evans*) (*1920–*)
Cricketer, one of the greatest of England's wicket-keepers.

Godiva Lady Godiva (*d. 1080*)
English noble benefactor, the patron of modern engineering students.

Godzilla Godzilla (*or Gojira*) (*b. November 3, 1954*)
Japanese cinematic film monster, star of *Gojira, Terrible Creature of the Hydrogen Bomb* (1954). For American consumption, this film was retitled *Godzilla, King of the Monsters*.

Godzooki Godzooki (*20th century*)
Japanese cinematic son of Godzilla.

Golda Golda Meir, *née Mabovich* (*1898–1978*)
Kiev-born Israeli prime minister.
> "We intend to remain alive. Our neighbours want to see us dead. This is not a question that leaves much room for compromise."

Goldie Goldie Hawn (*1945–*)
American comedienne and filmmaker.
> "My greatest regret is that I won an Oscar before I learned how to act."

Goldwin Goldwin Smith (*1823–1910*)
Canadian historian-journalist, author of *Canada and the Canadian Question*, "the most pessimistic book that has ever been written about Canada."

Goldy Goldy McJohn (*John Goadsby*) (*1945–*)
American rocker with the band Steppenwolf.

Goliath Goliath of Gath *I Samuel 17: 43 (c. 1060 B.C.)*
Biblical giant slain by David with his sling. The Bible said he was 6 cubits high (9 feet), but the historian Flavius Josephus said he was 4 cubits tall (6 feet).

Gomer Gomer *Hosea 1: 3 (c. 8th century B.C.)*
Old Testament wife of the prophet Hosea. He complained about her loose morals, but he loved her.

Gonzalo Gonzalo Quiepo de Llano, Marquis of Quiepo de Llano y Sevilla (*1875–1951*)
Spanish soldier. He invented the phrase "fifth column" to describe rebel supporters inside Madrid during the Spanish Civil War. Four official columns were attacking from outside.

Goodridge Goodridge Roberts (*20th century*)
Canadian painter.

Goody Goody Two Shoes (*c. 1750*)
English children's book, written and published by John Newbury, who was the first person to create miniature books for children. The Newbury medal for children's literature is named in his honour.

Gordie Gordie Howe (*originally Gordon Howe*) (*1928–*)
Canadian hockey legend. His career record is 801 goals with the National Hockey League, plus 174 in the World Hockey Association. When talk-show host Dick Cavett asked him why he wore an athletic protector but no helmet, Howe replied, "You can always pay people to do your thinking for you."

Gordius King Gordius of Phrygia
Legendary creator of the complicated "Gordian knot," which could only be untied by the future ruler of Asia. Alexander the Great inspected this knot, and then cut it with his sword.

Gordon Sir Gordon Reece (*20th century*)
British "image maker" employed by both Lady Thatcher and Princess Diana.

Gore Gore Vidal (*originally Eugene Luther Vidal, Jr.*) (*1925–*)
American novelist. When his old foe Truman Capote died, he described it as "a good career move."
> "Never have children, only grandchildren."

Gorgo Ricardo Alonzo "Gorgo" Gonzales (*1928–*)
American tennis player, an eight-time national champion despite his unprivileged upbringing without tennis lessons. "Gorgo" is short for "Gorgonzola"—because he became a "big cheese."

GRACE SLICK

Gorman Gorman Thomas *(1950–)*
American baseball outfielder with the Brewers, an All-Star.

Gottfried Gottfried Semper *(1803–1879)*
German architect. He designed the Victoria and Albert Museum in London, England.

Gottlieb Gottlieb Wilhelm Daimler *(1834–1900)*
German motor-car engineer, inventor of the carburettor.

Gottlob Gottlob Frege *(Friedrich Ludwig Gottlob Frege)* *(1848–1925)*
German philosopher. He created a complex theory of meaning, then became depressed when Bertrand Russell detected a logical contradiction in it.

Gough Gough Whitlam *(Edward Gough Whitlam)* *(1916–)*
Australian prime minister.

Gower Gower Champion *(1919–1980)*
Broadway director of the musical *42nd Street*. He died the day it opened, but the producer persuaded the hospital to delay announcing his death until after the reviews were written.

Grace Grace Slick *(originally Grace Barnett Wing)* *(1939–)*
American rock star with the group Jefferson Airplane.
> *"When you put six ducks and a rat on stage, the rat's going to stand out."*

Gracian Emperor Gracian *(d. 383)*
Roman ruler.

Gracie Gracie Allen *(Grace Ethel Cecile Rosalie Allen)* *(1902–1964)*
American comedienne extraordinaire, co-star of "The Burns and Allen Show" (1950–58). When George Burns died in 1996, he left instructions for his name to be written beneath hers on their tomb, so that she would always have top billing.

Grady Grady Hatton *(1922–)*
American baseball infielder for the Reds, later a manager for the Astros.

Graeme Graeme Murphy *(1951–)*
Australian dancer and choreographer.

Grafton Sir Grafton Smith *(1871–1937)*
Australian ethnologist, an expert on Egyptian mummification.

Graham Graham Chapman *(1941–1989)*
British comedian. In 1994 his long-time companion David Sherlock sprinkled his cremated ashes onto the front row of the audience at the Directors' Guild 25th anniversary salute to Monty Python's Flying Circus, saying, "I know he would have wanted to be here tonight."

Graig Graig "Puff" Nettles *(1944–)*
American baseball third baseman for the Yankees, an All-Star and winner of a Gold Glove award.
> *"When I was a little boy I wanted to be a baseball player and join the circus. With the Yankees I've accomplished both."*

Gram Gram Parsons *(originally Ingram Cecil Connor III)* *(1946–1973)*
American country-rock musician.

Grandma Grandma Moses *(Anna Mary Robertson Moses)* *(1860–1961)*
American primitive painter.
> *"I don't advise anyone to take up [painting] as a business proposition, unless they really have talent and are crippled so as to deprive them of physical labour."*

Grandmaster Grandmaster Flash *(originally Joseph Saddler)* *(1958–)*
American musician, one of the originators of hip-hop, which was the first new street-level black-culture music since 1950s doo-wap.

Grant Grant Wood *(Grant De Volsen Wood)* *(1892–1942)*
American artist. He painted the picture *American Gothic* (1930), using his sister and a dentist friend as models.

Grantland Grantland "Granny" Rice *(1880–1954)*
Definitive American sports writer, author of *The Tumult and the Shouting* (1954).
> *"When the last Great Scorer comes*
> *To mark against your name,*
> *He'll write not 'won' or 'lost'*
> *But how you played the game."*

Grantly Grantly Dick-Read *(1890–1959)*
English gynaecologist, author of the unorthodox and controversial *Natural Childbirth* (1933).

Granville Granville Sharp *(1735–1813)*
English abolitionist. Defending a black immigrant, James Sommersett, he won a judgement that any slave who set foot on England became free automatically.

Graydon E. Graydon Carter *(c. 1950–)*
Canadian-born editor of *Vanity Fair* magazine.

Gre Gre Taylor *(20th century)*
Australian sculptor, creator of *Down By the Lake with Liz and Phil*, a statue of the Queen and Prince Philip nude on a bench.

Green Green Strohmeyer-Gartside *(20th century)*
Welsh-born avant-garde dance-band singer-guitarist with the group Scritti Politti.

Greer Greer Garson *(1908–)*
Irish-born American actress. She won an Academy Award for her performance in *Mrs. Miniver* (1942).

Gregg Gregg Allman *(1947–)*
American country-rock star of the Allman Brothers Band.
> *"Before I got into rock and roll I was going to be a dentist."*

Gregor Gregor Johann Mendel *(1822–1884)*
Austrian monk. His careful observations of the peas growing in his monastery garden became the basis for modern genetics.

Gregorio Gregorio Fuentes *(b. 1898)*
Cuban friend of Ernest Hemingway, the model for the character in *The Old Man and the Sea* (1952). On Hemingway's birthday each year, he bought two bottles of whiskey—one to drink, and one to pour on the grave.

Gregorius Gregorius de Saint Vincent *(1584–1667)*
Flemish mathematician. Some of his work anticipated integral calculus.

Gregory Gregory Peck *(Eldred Gregory Peck) (1916–)*
American actor, star of *To Kill a Mockingbird* (1962).

Greta Greta Garbo *(originally Greta Louisa Gustafsson) (1905–1990)*
Swedish-born American actress. She was once approached in a coffee shop by a man who asked, "Aren't you Greta Garbo?" She answered, "What would Greta Garbo be doing in a place like this?"

Gretchen Gretchen Frasier *(1919–)*
American skier, the first American to win an Olympic gold medal in the special slalom.

Griff Griff Fender *(20th century)*
British doo-wap revival singer with the group the Darts.

Griffin Griffin Dunne *(1955–)*
American actor.

Grigorij Grigorij Efimovich Rasputin *(c. 1871–1916)*
Russian hypnotist and royal adviser, the "Mad Monk."

Grinling Grinling Gibbons *(1648–1721)*
Dutch-born English Baroque woodcarver.

Grizel Lady Grizel Baillie, *née Hume (1665–1746)*
Scottish poet. As a child, "Little Grizel" carried secret messages to the Jacobite Robert Baillie in prison. She married his son.

Gro Dr. Gro Harlem Brundtland *(1939–)*
Norwegian politician, the first female prime minister.
> *"Morality becomes hypocrisy if it means accepting mothers suffering or dying in connection with unwanted pregnancies and illegal abortions."*

Grote Grote Reber *(1911–)*
American radio engineer, builder of the first radio telescope.

Groucho Groucho Marx *(originally Julius Henry Marx) (1895–1977)*
American star of vaudeville and film.
> *"Either he's dead or my watch has stopped."*

Grover Grover Cleveland *(Stephen Grover Cleveland)* *(1837–1908)*
American president. His illegimate son was born three months before the 1884 election, inspiring the ditty:
> *"Ma! Ma! Where's my pa?"*
> *"Gone to the White House. Ha! Ha! Ha!"*

Guccio Guccio Gucci *(1881–1953)*
Italian entrepreneur. He started his fabulously successful luxury-goods firm after a job working as a hotel porter carrying luxury luggage convinced him he could do better.

Guglielmo Marchese Guglielmo Marconi *(1874–1937)*
Italian physicist, the inventor of radio.

Guido Guido Molinari *(1933–)*
Canadian stripe painter.

Guildford Lord Guildford Dudley *(d. 1554)*
English teenage husband of "Queen for a day" Lady Jane Grey. He was beheaded with her on Tower Hill.

Guillaume Guillaume Apollinaire *(originally Wilhelm Apollinaris de Kostrowitzki) (1880–1918)*
Italian-born French poet, supposedly the son of Pope Leo XIII. He invented the term "surrealism" to describe his play *The Breasts of Tiresias* (1918).
> *"The days wear on but I endure."*

Guinevere Queen Guinevere
Legendary adulterous wife of King Arthur.

Guitar Guitar Slim *(or Eddie Jones) (1926–1956)*
American gospel electric-guitarist.

Gulam Gulam Kaderbhoy Noon *(20th century)*
Indian-born British prepared-food entrepreneur.
> *"I have yet to meet an Englishman who doesn't like Indian food."*

Gummo Gummo Marx *(or Milton Marx) (1894–1977)*
American performer, the fifth Marx Brother.

Gunnar Gunnar Myrdal *(1898–1987)*
Swedish economist, winner of the 1974 Nobel Prize for his work identifying how the poor get poorer while the rich get richer.

Gunnlauth Gunnlauth
Mythical Nordic giantess. Odin seduced her in hopes of learning the secret of how to brew mead.

Günter Günter Grass *(Günter Wilhelm Grass) (1927–)*
Polish-born German novelist, author of *The Tin Drum* (1962).

Gurinder Gurinder Chadha *(1960–)*
Kenyan-born film director of *Bhaji on the Beach* (1994).

GREGG ALLMAN

Gus Gus Dorais *(Charles E. Dorais) (1891–1954)*
American football player. In the summer of 1912, he and Knute Rockne unveiled their brand-new tactic: the forward pass.

Gussy Gertrude "Gorgeous Gussy" Moran *(1923–)*
American tennis champion, winner of the 1949 singles, doubles, and mixed doubles in the National Indoor Championship. A competitor complained, "It used to bother me a bit that they didn't write up the tennis. All they wrote about was Gussy's panties."

Gustav Gustav Eiffel *(originally Alexandre Gustav Eiffel) (1832–1922)*
French engineer, designer of the Eiffel Tower, which was the tallest building in the world until 1930.

Gutzon Gutzon Borglum *(John Gutzon de la Mothe) (1867–1941)*
American sculptor of Mount Rushmore.

Guy Guy Burgess *(Guy Francis de Moncy Burgess) (1910–1963)*
British-born Soviet patriot.

Guylaine Dr. Guylaine Lancôt *(1941–)*
Canadian author of *The Medical Mafia* (1994), an attack on drug companies and the dangers of childhood immunizations, for which the Quebec College of Physicians has tried to revoke her medical licence. She points out that

North America uses 1950s-style immunization serums, not the newer purifed vaccines used in Japan and Europe.

Gwen Gwen Raverat *(1885–1957)*
English writer, granddaughter of Charles Darwin, author of *Period Piece*.

Gwendolyn Queen Gwendolyn
Legendary British ruler. She raised an army against her unfaithful husband, Locrine.

Gwladys St. Gwladys *(6th century)*
Welsh bandit. She led a riotous life with her husband, St. Gundleus, until their son, St. Cadoc, persuaded them to settle down and live separately as hermits.

Gypsy Gypsy Rose Lee *(Rose Louise Hovick) (1914–1970)*
American stripper. She started on stage in vaudeville at age four, working with her older sister. In 1957, *Fisherman's Magazine* voted her Fisherwoman of the Year.

Gywn Gywn Thomas *(1913–1981)*
Welsh comic novelist, famous as a great talker.
"Television is not decent work for a grown man."

Hablot Hablot Knight Browne *(pen-name "Phiz") (1815–1882)*
English illustrator, a favourite of Charles Dickens'.

Hades Hades *trans. sightless*
Greek god of the underworld, fourth child of Cronus and Rhea.

Hadley Hadley Richardson *(married 1921)*
American fishing enthusiast, the first Mrs. Ernest Hemingway. Asked why they divorced, Ernest replied, "Because I am a son of a bitch."

Hadrian Emperor Hadrian *(Publius Aelius Hadrianus) (76–138)*
Roman ruler. During a tour of his Empire, he built Hadrian's Wall in Britain.

Hagar Hagar Currie
Canadian heroine of Margaret Laurence's novel *The Stone Angel* (1964).

"There was I, strutting the board sidewalk like a pint-sized peacock, resplendent, haughty, hoity-toity, Jason Currie's black-haired daughter."

Hal Hal
Evil computer in the film *2001, A Space Odyssey*. Scott French gave this name to the computer he programmed to write a "rules-based" "Jacqueline Susann" novel titled *Just This Once* (1993).

Halbert Halbert Louis Hoard *(20th century)*
American journalist, editor of the *Jefferson County Union*. In 1926, he led an unsuccessful campaign to legally ban brassieres (then used to flatten breasts for the "boyish" flapper look) as "an evil that menaces the future well-being of society."

Haldan Haldan Keffer Hartline *(1903–1983)*
American physiologist, winner of the Nobel Prize for his work on the neurophysiology of vision in frogs and crabs.

Halford Sir Halford John MacKinder *(1861–1947)*
British political geographer, director of the London School of Economics, and the first person to climb Mount Kenya.

Hallgrimur Hallgrimur Pétursson *(1614–1674)*
Icelandic poet. Reykjavik cathedral is named after him.

Hallie Hallie Quinn Brown *(1850–1949)*
American teacher, co-founder of the Colored Women's League of Washington.

Halsey Halsey Hall *(1899–1978)*
American sports broadcaster. He was broadcasting a Twins game when his cigar set his papers on fire, igniting his sports jacket. He shed it without missing a word; fans bought him an asbestos jacket for future wear.

Halvard Halvard Solness
Architect hero of Henrik Ibsen's play *The Master Builder* (1892)

Hamilcar Hamilcar Barca *(c. 270–228 B.C.)*
Carthaginian soldier, father of the even more effective soldier Hannibal.

Hamilton Hamilton Othanel Smith *(1931–)*
American molecular biologist. He shared the 1978 Nobel Prize with Werner Arber and Daniel

Nathans for locating the "restriction enzymes" used in DNA sequencing.

Hamish Hamish Stuart *(1949–)*
Scottish soul guitarist with the Average White Band.

Hamlet *The Tragedy of Hamlet, Prince of Denmark (1600–1601)*
English play by William Shakespeare.

Hamlin Hamlin Garland *(originally Hannibal Hamlin Garland) (1860–1940)*
American writer, winner of a Pulitzer Prize for *A Daughter of the Middle Border* (1921).

Hammurabi Hammurabi *(ruled 1792–1750 B.C.)*
Babylonian king known for his legal code. He defined the purpose of law as "to cause justice to prevail in the land, to destroy the wicked and evil; that the strong may not oppress the weak."

Hamnet Hamnet Shakespeare *(1585–1596)*
English child, the short-lived only son of William Shakespeare.

Han Han van Meegeren *(or Henricus van Meegeren) (1889–1947)*
Dutch painter. Charged with wartime collaboration with the Germans, he confessed to having forging the "Jan Vermeer" paintings he had sold them. He was jailed as a forger, but became a popular hero.

Hank Hank Aaron *(Henry Lewis Aaron) (1934–)*
American baseball great. His lifetime batting average is .305, and his career total of 755 home runs far surpasses Babe Ruth's record.
  "The secret of hitting is to keep swinging."

Hanna Hanna Sheehy-Skeffington, *née Sheehy (married c. 1903)*
Irish wife of pacifist Francis Sheehy-Skeffington. They joined their names when they married, and became active in women's suffrage.

Hannah Hannah More *(1745–1833)*
English Bluestocking playwright.
  "He lik'd those literary cooks
  Who skim the cream of others' books;
  And ruin half an author's graces
  By plucking bon mots from their places."

Hannen Hannen Swaffer *(1879–1962)*
British journalist.
  "Freedom of the press in Britain is freedom to print such of the proprietor's prejudices as the advertisers don't object to."

Hannibal Hannibal *(c. 247–183 B.C.)*
Carthaginian expansionist.

Hannu Hannu Mikkola *(20th century)*
Finnish car driver, the "Flying Finn," the 1983 World Rally Champion.

Hans Hans Christian Andersen *(1805–1875)*
Danish author of the children's story "The Emperor's New Clothes."

Hansel Hansel
Stalwart small boy, legendary brother of intrepid Gretel.

Hanuman Hanuman
Vedic monkey-god.

Hap Hap Kliban *(known as B. Kliban) (1935–1970)*
American cartoonist, particularly of cats.
  "Don't think so hard. Your fur will fall out."

Happy Happy Rockefeller *(Mrs. Nelson Rockefeller), née Margaretta Fitler (1912–)*
American politican worker. She earned her nickname as a baby.

Harald Harald Gormsson, *"Blue-Tooth" (c. 910–985)*
First king to unify Denmark.

Harber Harber Sabané *(20th century)*
First democratically elected mayor of Timbuktu in Mali. His main municipal problem is burial by sand-dunes.

Hardecanute Hardecanute *(or Hardaknut Knutsson) (c. 1019–1042)*
Last Danish king of England, half-brother of Edward the Confessor. He died while proposing a toast at a wedding.

Harland Harland Williams *(1962–)*
Canadian comic, who said of the education problem in the States, "So what if 60% of Americans don't know where Germany is? What about the other 85% who do know?"

Harlow Harlow Shapley *(1885–1972)*
American astronomer. He measured the galaxy and discovered that our solar system is at the edge.

Harmon Harmon "Killer" Killebrew *(1936–)*
American baseball infielder with the Senators, a member of the Hall of Fame. He once hit a home run that shattered two wooden seats in the upper deck of Metropolitan Stadium.

Harold Harold Pinter *(1930–)*
English playwright, author of *The Caretaker* (1958).
> *"I've been waiting for the weather to break."*

Harper Harper Lee *(1926–)*
American novelist, author of *To Kill a Mockingbird* (1960).

Harpo Harpo Marx *(originally Adolf Marx)* *(1893–1961)*
American star of vaudeville and film. He taught himself to play the harp.

Harriet Harriet Beecher Stowe *(Harriet Elizabeth Stowe, née Beecher) (1811–1896)*
American novelist and anti-slavery worker, author of *Uncle Tom's Cabin* (1851–52)
> *"'Who was your mother?'*
> *'Never had none!' said the child with another grin.*
> *'Never had any mother? What do you mean? Where were you born?'*
> *'Never was born!' persisted Topsy."*

Harriette Harriette Wilson, *née Dubochet* *(1789–1855)*
English genteel courtesan. She published periodic instalments of a libellous *Memoirs* in order to collect blackmail. But, as Arthur, Duke of Wellington, put it, "Publish and be damned!"

Harriot Dr. Harriot Hunt, *née Kezia (1805–1875)*
American first practising female doctor. She was admitted to Harvard Medical School in 1850, the same year that black students were admitted for the first time, but the students rioted about her, and she was forced to leave.

Harrison Harrison Ford *(1942–)*
American actor, star of *The Fugitive* (1993).

Harry Harry Cohn *(1891–1958)*
American co-founder of Columbia Pictures. At his funeral, Rabbi Edgar Magnin was asked to say something good about him. The rabbi replied, "He's dead."

Hart Hart Massey *(20th century)*
Canadian founder of an agricultural equipment empire.

Hartley Hartley Coleridge *(David Hartley Coleridge)* *(1796–1849)*
English poet.
> *"She is not fair to outward view*
> *As many maidens be;*
> *Her loveliness I never knew*
> *Until she smiled on me:*
> *Oh! then I saw her eye was bright,*
> *A well of love, a spring of light."*

Hassanal Hassanal Bolkiah *(1946–)*
Sultan of Brunei, reputed to be the richest man in the world.

Hastings Dr. Hastings Kamuzu Banda *(1905–)*
Life president of Malawi.
> *"I wish I could bring Stonehenge to Nyasaland to show there was a time when Britain had a savage culture."*

Hatshepsut Queen Hatshepsut *(ruled 1473–1458 B.C.)*
Egyptian ruler of the 18th dynasty. She maintained the fiction that she was male by wearing a gold beard.

Hatti Hatti Jacques *(originally Josephine Edwina Jacques) (1924–1980)*
English actress, a stalwart of the "Carry On" films.

Hattie Hattie McDaniel *(1895–1952)*
American singer and actress, the first black person to win an Oscar for acting, for *Gone With the Wind* (1939).

Havelock Havelock Ellis *(Henry Havelock Ellis)* *(1859–1939)*
English sexologist.
> *"Without an element of the obscene there can be no true and deep aesthetic or moral conception of life."*

Haw-Haw Lord Haw-Haw *(real name William Joyce)* *(1906–1946)*
American-born Nazi wartime propaganda broadcaster. He was hanged.

HARPO MARX

Hawkshaw Hawkshaw Hawkins *(originally Harold F. Hawkins) (1921–1963)* American honky-tonk musician with the Grand Ole Opry.

Hawley Dr. Hawley Harvey Crippen *(1862–1910)* American-born wife murderer. He and his mistress, Ethel Le Neve, fled England on the SS *Montrose,* but the suspicious captain telegraphed ahead; the first use of wireless communications in a murder hunt.

Hayley Hayley Mills *(1946–)* British actress.

Hazel Hazel Scott *(1920–1981)* American jazz pianist. She auditioned for the Juilliard School when she was eight.
> *"I've always known I was gifted, which is not the easiest thing in the world for a person to know, because you're not responsible for your gift, only for what you do with it."*

Heartley Heartley "Hunk" Anderson *(1898–1978)* American football offensive guard for the Chicago Bears. He replaced Knute Rockne as the coach of Notre Dame.

Heath Heath Robinson *(William Heath Robinson) (1872–1944)* English cartoonist and illustrator, creator of extravagant contraptions.

Heather Heather Langenkamp *(1957–)* American actress, star of the film *Nightmare on Elm Street* (1984). In *Wes Craven's New Nightmare* (1994), she plays the role of an actress named Heather Langenkamp, who is the star of a horror movie.

Heber Heber Doust Curtis *(1872–1942)* American astronomer, the first person to realize that spiral nebulae lie beyond our galaxy.

Hector Hector Berlioz *(Louis-Hector Berlioz) (1803–1869)* French composer. Replying to published criticism of his music, he wrote to the editor, "I am seated in the smallest room in my house. Your article is before me. Soon it will be behind me."

Hedda Hedda Hopper *(originally Elda Furry) (1890–1966)* American gossip columnist, author of *From Under My Hat* (1952).
> *"I wasn't allowed to speak while my husband was alive, and since he's been gone no-one has been able to shut me up."*

Hedley Hedley Verity *(1905–1943)* English left-arm spin cricket bowler. He died in a Second World War prisoner-of-war camp.

Hedy Hedy Lamarr *(originally Hedwig Eva Maria Kiesler) (1913–)* Austrian-born American actress.

Heidi *Heidi* (1881) Swiss children's novel by Johanna Spyri.

Heimdall Heimdall Nordic god, the great enemy of Loki.

Heinie Heinie Manush *(Henry Emmett Manush) (1901–1971)* American baseball outfielder with the Senators, a member of the Hall of Fame. He was the first player ejected from a World Series game, after he pulled out an umpire's elastic bow-tie and let it snap back.

Heinrich Heinrich Schliemann *(1822–1890)* German archaeologist. He retired from business to pursue his childhood dream of finding Troy by following the descriptions in the poems of Homer. Much to everyone's surprise, he found Troy and more.

Heintje Heintje *(1956–)* Dutch sentimental pop singer, "Holland's Wonder Boy." In 1968, his accounted for almost 20% of all record albums sold in Germany.

Heinz Heinz Nordhoff *(1899–1968)* German engineer, the founder of Opel.

Heitor Heitor Villa-Lobos *(1887–1959)* Brazilian composer. Igor Stravinsky asked, "Why is it that, whenever I hear a piece of music I don't like, it's always by Villa-Lobos?"

Top 10 Baby Names for Future Entrepreneurs

Alcindo • Augustus • Coco • Estée •

Laura • Lydia • Melitta • Napoleone •

Phineas • Soren

Helen Helen Adams Keller *(1880–1968)*
American writer. After a childhood illness, she became both deaf and blind.
> *"Literature is my Utopia. Here I am not disenfranchised. No barrier of the senses shuts me out from the sweet, gracious discourse of my bookfriends. They talk to me without embarrassment or awkwardness."*

Helena Helena Rubinstein *(1870–1965)*
Polish-born American cosmetics queen.
> *"There are no ugly women, only lazy ones."*

Helene Helene Weigel *(1900–1971)*
Austrian-born actress, co-founder with Bertolt Brecht of the Berliner Ensemble. She played Mother Courage in *Mother Courage and Her Children* (1949).

Hélène *La Belle Hélène (19th century)*
French *opéra bouffe* by Jacques Offenbach.

Helmut Helmut Kohl *(1930–)*
German politician. Regarding the Nazis, he observed that he had the "good fortune to be born too late."

Heloisa Heloisa Eneida de Menezes Paes Pinto *(stage-name Helø Pinheiro) (1948–)*
Brazilian performer. Walking home from the beach, she inspired the song "The Girl From Ipanema" by "Tom" Jobin.

Héloïse *La Nouvelle Héloïse (1761)*
Philosophical French novel by Jean-Jacques Rousseau. The character is based on the real Sophie d'Houdetot.

Helvetia Helvetia "Vet" Boswell *(1909–1988)*
American blues singer, one of the Boswell Sisters.

Hendrik Hendrik Willem Mesdag *(1831–1915)*
Dutch marine painter. The Mesdag Museum in The Hague contains his fabulous beach panorama.

Henny Henny Youngman *(1906–)*
British-born American comedian. Attending a party in honour of his 90th birthday with a broken hip, he said, "Take my wheelchair, please."

Henri Henri de Toulouse-Lautrec *(Henri-Marie-Raymond de Toulouse-Lautrec-Monfa) (1864–1901)*
French Post-Impressionist painter and poster designer. Crippled as a child, he documented the cabaret life of Montmartre.

Henrietta Queen Henrietta Maria *(1609–1669)*
French-born consort of King Charles I, "a brave stubborn little prig."

Henriette Henriette Callaux *(20th century)*
French society beauty, wife of politician Joseph Callaux. In 1914, she shot editor Gaston Calmette of *Le Figaro* for criticizing her husband, but was acquitted when Calmette's anti-French propaganda was revealed.

Henrik Henrik Johan Ibsen *(1828–1906)*
Norwegian dramatist.
> *"You should never wear your best trousers when you go out to fight for freedom and truth."*

Henry Henry Shrapnel *(1761–1842)*
British artillery officer. He invented "spherical case shot" intended to explode into ragged pieces and cause horrible wounds.

Hephaestus Hephaestus *(or Halciber) trans. he who shines by day*
Lame Greek smith-god. He married love goddess Aphrodite, who cheated on him shamelessly.

Hera Hera *(or Here) trans. protectress*
Greek goddess of women and of childbirth.

Heracles Heracles *trans. glory of Hera*
Greek hero. He was taken from his funeral pyre and made into an immortal god.

Heraclitus Heraclitus *(c. 535–c. 475 B.C.)*
Greek philosopher.
> *"Character is destiny."*

Herb Herb Alpert *(1937–)*
American band leader, a co-founder of A&M Records.

Herbert Herbert Hoover *(Herbert Clark Hoover) (1874–1964)*
American president.
> *"Older men declare war. But it is youth that must fight and die."*

Herbie Herbie Hancock *(Herbert Jeffrey Hancock) (1940–)*
American jazz-fusion keyboard player.

Hercule Hercule Poirot *(d. 1975)*
Fictional Belgian detective created by Agatha Christie. He got a front-page obituary in the *New York Times*.

Hercules Hercules Brabazon *(1821–1906)*
French-born English watercolour painter.

Hereward Hereward the Wake *(d. c. 1090)*
English resistance fighter.

Herimann Herimann *(working c. 1170)*
German monk. In 1983, a manuscript illuminated by him was auctioned for a record-setting £8.14 million.

Herman Herman Melville *(1819–1891)*
American author of *Moby Dick* (1851).
> *"A whale ship was my Yale College and my Harvard."*

Hermann Hermann Rorschach *(1884–1922)*
Swiss psychiatrist. He created the ink-blot diagnostic "Rorschach Test."

Hermas Hermas *Romans 16: 14*
Roman friend of St. Paul. "Hermas" was a common slave's name.

Hermes Hermes *trans. cairn or pillar*
Greek messenger of the gods, inventor of the alphabet, astronomy, boxing, and the musical scale. Within hours of his birth, he was already stealing cattle.

Hernando Hernando Cortés *(1485–1547)*
Spanish conquistador of Mexico. He introduced the horse to North America.

Herod Herod the Great *(c. 73–4 B.C.)*
Roman-appointed King of Judea. One of his last acts was to organize the "murder of the innocents" at Bethlehem in an attempt to get rid of his newborn rival Jesus.

Herodotus Herodotus *(c. 485–425 B.C.)*
Greek historian. Cicero called him "the father of history."
> *"The Persian messengers travel with a velocity which nothing human can equal. . . . Neither snow, nor rain, nor heat, nor darkness, are permitted to obstruct their speed."*

Hervey William Hervey Allen *(1889–1949)*
American writer best known for his novel *Anthony Adverse* (1933).
> *"Grow up as soon as you can . . . the young are slaves to dreams; the old, servants of regrets. Only the middle-aged have all their five senses in the keeping of their wits."*

Hesiod Hesiod *(c. 8th century B.C.)*
Greek farmer and poet.
> *"Potter is jealous of potter and craftsman of craftsman; poor man has a grudge against poor man, and poet against poet."*

Hesketh Hesketh Pearson *(1887–1964)*
English popular biographer.
> *"There is no stronger craving in the world than that of the rich for titles, except for that of the titled for riches."*

Hessie Hessie Donahue *(19th century)*
American boxer. During an 1892 all-comers boxing exhibition, she knocked out champion John L. Sullivan.

Hester Mrs. Hester Lynch Thrale, *née Salusbury (later Mrs. Piozzi) (1741–1821)*
Welsh writer, a great friend of Dr. Samuel Johnson.
> *"Johnson's conversation was by much too strong for a person accustomed to obsequiousness and flattery; it was mustard in a young child's mouth."*

Hestia Hestia *trans. hearth*
Greek goddess of the domestic hearth, oldest of the twelve Olympian gods. There are no stories about her since she was too chaste to cause gossip.

Hetepheres Queen Hetepheres *(26th century B.C.)*
Egyptian mother of King Cheops, who built the Great Pyramid. Her tomb, discovered in 1925, contained the only furniture to survive from the Old Kingdom.

Hetty Hetty Green *(Henrietta Howland Green)*, née *Robinson (1835–1916)*
American heiress. She increased her US$10 million inheritance tenfold with careful management. However, her son had to have his leg amputed after delays in treating it caused by efforts to locate a free medical clinic.

Heywood Heywood C. Broun *(Matthew Heywood Campbell Broun) (1888–1939)*
American writer and critic, founder of the American Newspaper Guild.
> *"The ability to make love frivolously is the chief characteristic which distinguishes human beings from the beasts."*

Hiawatha "Hiawatha" *(1855)*
American poem by Henry Wadsworth Longfellow.

Hideki Hideki Yukawa *(1907–1981)*
Japanese physicist, the first Japanese Nobel Prize winner. He predicted the meson particle.

Hieronymous Hieronymous Bosch *(c. 1460–1516)*
Dutch painter.

Hilaire Hilaire Belloc *(originally Joseph Hilaire Pierre René Belloc) (1870–1953)*
French-born English poet, author of *A Bad Child's Book of Beasts*.
> *"Child, do not throw this book about,*
> *Refrain from the unholy pleasure*
> *Of cutting all the pictures out,*
> *Regard it as your choicest treasure."*

Hilda Hilda Chester *(20th century)*
American sports fan. After a heart attack in the 1920s, on doctor's orders she ceased banging on a frying pan with an iron ladle, and instead rang a large brass cowbell at exciting moments.

Hildegard St. Hildegard von Bingen *(1098–1179)*
German Benedictine abbess and plainsong composer. In 1995, three albums of her songs were available, with *Vision* top of the U.S. classic crossover chart.

HILLARY RODHAM CLINTON

Hildegarde Hildegarde Neil *(20th century)*
British actress. Her lead performance in William Shakespeare's play *Cleopatra* was described by *Time Out* magazine as "a suburban schoolmarm having a fling on the Nile."

Hillary Hillary Rodham Clinton *(1947–)*
American lawyer, wife of President Bill Clinton.

Hillman Hillman Frazier *(20th century)*
American politician. In 1995, he introduced a bill for the State of Mississippi to formally ratify the abolition of slavery, 130 years after the 13th amendment. It passed unanimously, without discussion.

Hilmar Hilmar Reksten *(1897–1980)*
Norwegian shipping magnate. In 1974 he was assessed income tax of 491% of his income.

Hilton Hilton Valentine *(1943–)*
British rocker with the band the Animals.

Hippocrates Hippocrates *(c. 460–c. 377 B.C.)*
Greek physician, the "father of medicine." The Hippocratic Oath taken by physicians is named in his honour.
> *"Life is short, and art long; opportunity fleeting, experiment dangerous, and judgement difficult."*

Hippolyta Hippolyta *(or Hippolyte) trans. of the stampeding horses*
Mythical Queen of the Amazons. Accounts vary as to whether she willingly gave Heracles her girdle, or if he had to kill her to get it.

Hiram Sir Hiram Stevens Maxim *(1840–1916)*
American-born British inventor of the Maxim machine-gun (1883). He also invented a mouse-trap.

Hirohito Emperor Hirohito *(1901–1989)*
Ruler of Japan, the first Japanese prince to visit the West.
> *"The war situation has developed not necessarily to Japan's advantage."*

Hiroki Hiroki Sugihara *(1934–)*
Japanese son of consul Chiune Sugihara. He inspired his father to defy orders and issue transit visas to Jewish refugees during the Second World War when he asked, "If we don't help them, won't they die?"

Hiroshi Hiroshi Oshita *(played 1946–1959)*

Japanese baseball outfielder for the Toei Flyers. His batting average of .382 stood as a record for almost fifteen years.

Hjalmar Hjalmar Schacht *(Horace Greeley Hjalmar Schacht) (1877–1970)*

German creative financier. He solved Nazi credit problems, but quarrelled with Adolf Hitler and was interned, so that in 1945 he was acquitted of war crimes at his Nuremberg trial.

EMPEROR
HIROHITO

Hnossa Hnossa

Nordic goddess, one of the Asynjor. She was so beautiful that the word "hnosir" was used to describe all lovely things.

Hoagy Hoagy Carmichael *(originally Hoagland Howard Carmichael) (1899–1981)*

American composer of "Stardust" (1929), and "Georgia on My Mind" (1930).

Hod Hod Eller *(Horace Owen Eller) (1894–1961)*

American baseball pitcher for the Reds. His team won the World Series, but only against the "Black Sox" team who had been bribed to lose.

Hogan "Hogan's Heroes" *(1965–1971)*

American TV series concerning the amusing misadventures of some zany Second World War prisoners-of-war and their comical German guards.

Holbrook Holbrook Jackson *(George Holbrook Jackson) (1874–1948)*

English bibliophile and critic.

"Intuition is reason in a hurry."

Holden Holden Caulfield

Adolescent hero of J.D. (Jerome David) Salinger's American novel *The Catcher in the Rye* (1951).

Holger Holger Nilsson *(d. 1993)*

Swedish brewing magnate and miser. To elude estate taxes, he left his money to be shared equally by the 300 residents of his town of Kracklinge.

Hollis Hollis McLaren *(20th century)*

Canadian actress. She played Liza in the film *Outrageous!* (1977).

Holly Holly Hunter *(1958–)*

American actress. She won an Oscar for *The Piano* (1993).

Holofernes Holofernes *trans. to be deceitful (c. 5th century B.C.)*

Assyrian general. His decapitation by the beautiful Judith is described in the Apocrypha.

Homer Homer *(c. 8th century B.C.)*

Greek "father of poetry," author of the *Iliad* and the *Odyssey*.

"These things surely lie on the knees of the gods."

Honami Honami Koetsu *(1558–1637)*

Japanese calligrapher and raku potter.

Honey Honey Greer *(20th century)*

American writer.

"A diary is all penned-up emotions."

Honor Honor Blackman *(1927–)*

American actress and judo expert. She played Pussy Galore in the James Bond film *Goldfinger*.

Honora Mrs. Honora Mary Parker *(d. 1954)*

New Zealand mother killed by her daughter Pauline and her close friend Juliet Holme in "an act of profoundly misplaced loyalty." Juliet is now the writer Anne Perry.

Honoratus St. Honoratus *(d. c. 303)*

African religious worker. Rue Saint-Honoré in Paris is named after him, and he is the patron saint of bakers and candy-makers.

Honoré Honoré de Balzac *(1799–1850)*

French novelist, author of *The Human Comedy*.

"There is no such thing as a great talent without great will-power."

Honus Honus Wagner *(Johannes Peter Wagner) (1874–1955)*

American baseball shortstop with the Pittsburgh Pirates, the "Flying Dutchman." He was discovered throwing rocks across a river by a scout who had come to investigate his brother, but signed him instead.

Hoot Robert "Hoot" Gibson *(1935–)*
American baseball player.
> *"In a world filled with hate, prejudice, and protest, I find that I too am filled with hate, prejudice, and protest."*

Hopalong Hopalong Cassidy *(20th century)*
American TV cowboy, played by actor William Boyd (1949–51).

Hope Hope Lange *(1931–)*
American actress.

Horace Horace Greeley *(1811–1872)*
American writer and politician. He reprinted the "Go West, Young Man" article written in 1851 by John Babsone Lane Soule.
> *"Go West, young man, and grow up with the country."*

Horatia Horatia Nelson *(b. c. 1800)*
English daughter of Emma Hamilton and Horatio Nelson.

Horatio Horatio, Baron Nelson of the Nile *(1758–1805)*
British admiral. His last words, "Kiss me, Hardy," were spoken to his flag captain Sir Thomas Hardy.

Horatius Horatius Cocles *(6th century)*
Legendary Roman patriot, who held a bridge across the Tiber River against the Etruscan commander Porsenna.

Hormuzd Hormuzd Rassam *(1826–1910)*
Turkish archaeologist. He worked on the sites of Nimrud and Nineveh with Sir Austen Layard.

Horst Horst Wessel *(1907–1930)*
German composer of the Nazi national anthem, which was known as the "Horst Wessel song."

Hortense Hortense Eugénie Cécile Beauharnais *(1783–1837)*
French Queen of Holland, sister-in-law of Napoleon. She composed the anthem of the Second Empire, "Partant pour la Syrie."

Horton Horton Smith *(20th century)*
American golfer. In 1934, he won the Masters Tournament on his first try.

Hosea Hosea *trans. salvation, Hosea 8: 7 (c. 8th century B.C.)*
Old Testament prophet. He described the nation of Israel as a faithless spouse betraying her husband, God.
> *"They sow the wind, and they shall reap the whirlwind."*

Hotspur Sir Henry "Hotspur" Percy *(or Sir Harry Percy) (1364–1403)*
Scottish skirmisher, portrayed as the honourable rebel in William Shakespeare's play *Henry IV Part One* (c. 1597).

Howard Howard Hughes *(Howard Robard Hughes) (1905–1976)*
American millionaire, film producer, aviator, and eccentric recluse. The tax collected on his estate was a Guinness-record US$336 million.

Howell Howell Heflin *(1922–)*
American senator from Alabama. After seeing a compromising photograph of Teddy Kennedy in a boat with a young woman, he said, "Well, Teddy, I see you've changed your position on offshore drilling."

Howlin' Howlin' Wolf *(originally Chester Arthur Burnett) (1910–1976)*
American Chicago blues musician.

Hoyt Hoyt Axton *(1932–)*
American country music composer.

Hubert Hubert Humphrey *(Hubert Horatio Humphrey) (1911–1978)*
American politician, vice-president to Lyndon Baines Johnson.
> *"To err is human. To blame someone else is politics."*

Hubertus Prince Hubertus von Hohenlohe *(20th century)*
Austrian rock singer.

Hubie Hubie Brooks *(Hubert Brooks) (1956–)*
American baseball third baseman with the Expos, an All-Star.

HULK HOGAN

Huckleberry *Huckleberry Finn (1884)*
American novel by Mark Twain.

Hudson Sir Hudson Fysh *(Sir Wilmot Hudson Fysh)* *(1895–1974)*
Australian aviator, founder of the airline firm now known as QANTAS.

Huey Huey P. Newton *(1942–)*
American co-founder with Bobby Seale of the Black Panther Party.
> *"Words stigmatize people. We felt that the police need a label, a label other than that fear image that they carried in the community. So we used the pig as the rather low-lifed animal in order to identify the police."*

Hugh Hugh Hefner *(Hugh Marston Hefner) (1926–)*
American journalist. He started *Playboy* magazine with a loan from his mother.
> *"When I was a little kid, my security blanket on my bed had rabbits on it."*

Hugo Hugo Wolf *(Hugo Philipp Jakob Wolf)* *(1860–1903)*
Austrian composer.

Hugues Hugues de Payens *(c. 1070–1136)*
Burgundian knight, founder of the Knights Templar.

Hulk Hulk Hogan *(20th century)*
American wrestler. A review of his film *Suburban Commando* (1991) said: "Hogan's timing makes Arnold Schwarzenegger look like Cary Grant."

Humbert Humbert Humbert
Thwarted American amour in Vladimir Nabokov's novel *Lolita* (1959).

Hume Hume Cronyn *(1911–)*
Canadian-born American actor, husband of Jessica Tandy.

Humphrey Humphrey Bogart *(Humphrey DeForest Bogart) (1899–1957)*
American actor, the star of *Casablanca* (1944).
> *"Here's looking at you, kid."*

Hunna St. Hunna *(or Huva) (d. c. 679)*
Alsatian noblewoman, known as the "holy washerwoman" for her help washing the poor.

Hunter Hunter S. Thompson *(Dr. Hunter Stockton Thompson) (1939–)*
American gonzo journalist, author of *Fear and Loathing in Las Vegas* (1972).

Huntz Huntz Hall *(1920–)*
American actor. He played a Bowery Boy in *Let's Go Navy* (1951).

Huram-abi Huram-abi, *I Kings 7: 14 (c. 10th century B.C.)*
Old Testament bronzesmith. He made basins and implements for the Temple, and two bronze pillars for the front.

Hurby Hurby Azor *(20th century)*
American manager of the best-selling female rap group Salt-n-Pepa. They met while working as telemarketers for Sears in Queens.

Hurley Hurley McNair *(1888–1948)*
American baseball outfielder in the Negro Leagues.

Hussein King Hussein *(1935–)*
Jordanian monarch.

Huw Sir Huw Wheldon *(1916–1986)*
Welsh arts television personality.

Hyacinth Hyacinth *(or Hyacinthus) trans. hyacinth*
Mythical Spartan prince, so beautiful that the poet Thamyris fell in love with him; the first to love a person of his own sex.

Hyacinthe Hyacinthe Didot *(1794–1880)*
French printer of fine-edition books.

Hyde Sir Hyde Parker *(1739–1807)*
English naval commander. He gave the order to stay out of the battle of Copenhagen, which Horatio Nelson disobeyed.

Hyman Hyman Lipman *(20th century)*
American inventor in 1958 of the eraser tip on lead pencils.

Hymen Hymen
Greek god of marriage and the wedding feast.

Hymie Hymie Weiss *(originally Earl Wajcieckowski)* *(1898–1926)*
American bootlegger. He tried to out-muscle Al Capone, with fatal results.

Hypatia Hypatia of Alexandria *(370–415)*
Egyptian astronomer, mathematician, and teacher; known for her learning, eloquence, and beauty. She was killed by a mob incited by jealous Archbishop Cyril.

Hyrum Hyrum Smith *(d.1844)*
American brother of Joseph Smith, founder of the Mormons. After he and Joseph were shot by a gang of 150 masked men in Illinois, the remaining Mormons moved west to Utah.

I

Iago Iago
Jealous villain in William Shakespeare's play *Othello* (*c.* 1602).

Ian Ian Fleming *(Ian Lancaster Fleming) (1908–1964)*
British novelist, creator of James Bond, Secret Agent 007.

Ice Ice T *(formerly Tracy Marrow) (c.1962–)*
American rapper, composer of "Copkiller."
> "I'm trying to tell you what you need to hear, not what you want to hear."

Ichabod Ichabod Crane
Sleepy character in Washington Irving's *The Legend of Sleepy Hollow* (1819–20).

Ida Ida Barnett, *née Wells (1862–1931)*
American civil-rights activist.
> "I had already found that motherhood was a profession by itself, just like schoolteaching and lecturing, and that once one was launched in such a career, she owed it to herself to become as expert as possible in the practice of her profession."

Idawalley Idawalley Zoradia Lewis *(known as Ida Lewis) (1842–1911)*
American lighthouse keeper. She took over effective operation of the Lime Rock Lighthouse in Newport, Rhode Island, after her father suffered a stroke, and saved a career total of twenty-two people from drowning, including three shepherds with sheep.

Idi Idi Amin *(Idi Amin Dada) (1925–)*
Ugandan politician. Rumours of his cannibalism may have been true.

Ieoh Ieoh Meng (I.M.) Pei *(1917–)*
Chinese-born American architect, designer of the glass-pyramid addition to the Louvre in Paris, and the Rock'n'Roll Hall of Fame in Cleveland.

IMELDA MARCOS

Iftikhar Iftikhar Ali, Nawab of Pataudi *(1910–1952)*
Indian-born British-educated cricket player, the only batsman to have played Test Matches for both England and India.

Iggy Iggy Pop *(originally James Newell Osterberg) (1947–)*
Enduring American rock icon.

Ignacy Ignacy Jan Paderewski *(1860–1941)*
Polish composer, pianist, and prime minister.

Ignatius St. Ignatius de Loyala *(originally Iñigo López de Recalde) (1491–1556)*
Spanish nobleman. Convalescing after an operation, he ran low on novels and started to read a biography of Jesus, inspiring him to found the Society of Jesus, or Jesuits.

Igor Igor Stravinsky *(Igor Fedorovich Stravinsky) (1882–1971)*
Russian composer of the controversial ballet *The Rite of Spring* (1913). On opening night, the shouting from the audience (pro and con) was so loud it drowned out the music.

Ike Ike Turner *(originally Izear Luster Turner) (1931–)*
American rock musician, the less-talented former husband of Tina Turner.

Ikto Ikto
Sioux mythic hero, the inventor of speech.

Ilie Ilie Nastase *(1946–)*
International tennis star, called "Nasty" for his temper tantrums.

Ilka Ilka Chase *(1905–)*
American actress.
> "When he said we were trying to make a fool of him, I could only murmur that the Creator had beat us to it."

Illingworth Illingworth Kerr *(1905–1989)*
Canadian abstract painter.

Illinois Illinois Jacquet *(originally Jean-Baptiste Jacquet) (1922–)*
American jazz tenor-saxophone player.

Illtud St. Illtud *(or Illtyd) (450–535)*
Welsh cousin of King Arthur. He may have been the original Sir Galahad.

Ilona Ilona Staller *(known as La Cicciolina, or "little fleshy one") (20th century)*
Italian pornographic movie star and politician, the wife of American artist Jeff Koons. As a member of Parliament in 1990, she offered to "make love with Saddam Hussein to achieve peace in the Middle East."

Ilse Ilse Koch *(d.1967)*
German wife of a Nazi concentration camp commandant, the "Bitch of Buchenwald."

Ilus Ilus *trans. he who forces back*
Legendary Greek king. He renamed his city Troy in honour of his father, Tros.

Ima Ima Hogg *(1882–1975)*
American socialite, resident of Houston, Texas.

Iman Iman *(1956–)*
Somali super-model, wife of David Bowie.

Imelda Imelda Marcos *(Imelda Romualdez Marcos) (1930–)*
Filipino political worker. In 1986, after her hasty departure revealed a huge footwear collection, she claimed, "Everybody kept their shoes there. The maids . . . everybody."

Imhotep Imhotep *(c. 2900 B.C.)*
Egyptian ruler, builder of the world's oldest existing pyramid: the Djoser step pyramid at Sakkara.

Immanuel Immanuel Kant *(1724–1804)*
Influential German philosopher, author of the *Critique of Pure Reason* (1781). His neighbours could set their watches by the regular time of his daily walk.

Imogen Imogen Cunningham *(1883–1976)*
American photographer.

Imogene Imogene Fey *(20th century)*
American writer.
> *"A man finds out what is meant by a spitting image when he tries to feed cereal to his infant."*

Imran Imran Khan *(20th century)*
Glamorous, all-round international cricket player.

Imre Imre Nagy *(1895–1958)*
Hungarian politician, hero of the Rising of 1956. He was rehabilitated after his death, and in 1989 his body dug up for a hero's reburial.

Increase Increase Mather *(1639–1723)*
American theologian, the father of writer Cotton Mather.

Indiana Indiana Jones
Archaeologist hero of the American adventure film *Raiders of the Lost Ark*, played by Harrison Ford.

Indio Manny "Indio" Trillo *(1950–)*
American baseball infielder with the Cubs, an All-Star and winner of a Gold Glove award.

INDIRA GANDHI

Indira Indira Gandhi *(Indira Priyadarshini Gandhi) (1917–1984)*
Indian politician, daughter of Jawaharlal Nehru. She was assassinated by her own bodyguards.

Indra Indra
Vedic god of battle and rain.

Inez Inez Foxx *(1944–)*
American R&B singer. She worked with her brother Charlie Foxx.

Ingeborg Ingeborg of Denmark *(married 1193–1213)*
Danish-born wife of Philip II of France. He "set aside" his marriage to her to marry Agnes of Meran, but the Vatican made him leave Agnes to take Ingeborg back.

Ingemar Ingemar Stenmark *(1956–)*
Swedish skier, the first man to win three consecutive World Cup titles in slalom skiing. He got his start at age eight, when he won a regional Donald Duck trophy.

Ingmar Ingmar Bergman *(Ernst Ingmar Bergman) (1918–)*
Swedish filmmaker.

Ingram Ingram Frisar *(16th century)*
English reputed murderer of poet Christopher Marlowe, in a 1593 tavern brawl.

Ingrid Ingrid Bergman *(1915–1982)*
Swedish actress. Her career was interrupted by the scandal of her affair with director Roberto Rossellini, but she returned to Hollywood to win an Oscar for *Anastasia* (1956).

Ingvar Ingvar Kamprad *(20th century)*
Swedish founder of the IKEA furniture stores. He confessed his pro-Nazi past in 1994, noting, "You have been young yourself."

Inigo Inigo Jones *(1573–1652)*
English architect and stage designer.

Innocent St. Innocent I *(d. 417)*
Italian pope.

Iolanda Iolanda Quinn *(1934–)*
American former wife of actor Anthony Quinn. She won a $14,000-per-month settlement when he left her for his secretary.

Iona Iona Opie *(Iona Margaret Balfour Opie), née Archibald (1923–)*
British children's-literature specialist. She and her husband, Peter Opie, edited *The Oxford Book of Nursery Rhymes* (1951). Their collection of children's books is now housed in Oxford's Bodleian Library.

Iphicrates Iphicrates *(415–353 B.C.)*
Athenian general noted for developing a new form of light infantry. Ridiculed once for being the son of a cobbler, he replied, "The difference between us is that my family begins with me, whereas yours ends with you."

Ippolito Ippolito d'Este *(1509–1572)*
Italian Cardinal and Archbishop of Milan, builder of the Villa d'Este.

Ira Ira Gershvin *(originally Israel Gershvin) (1896–1983)*
American lyricist, the older brother of George Gershwin.
>*"I got rhythm,*
>*I got music,*
>*I got my man—*
>*Who could ask for anything more?"*

Irena Irena Szewinska *(1946–)*
Russian-born Polish runner. She won medals in five different Olympiads.

Irene Irene Castle, *née Foote (1893–1969)*
English ballroom dancer, the wife of Vernon Castle. She introduced the fashion for bobbed hair to America.

Irène Irène Joliot-Curie *(1897–1956)*
French physicist, winner of a Nobel Prize and daughter of Marie Curie. When she and her husband, Frédéric, realized their research was leading towards an atomic bomb, they stopped publishing, to leave only a secret paper with the Academy of Sciences.

Iris Iris Murdoch *(Dame Jean Iris Murdoch) (1919–)*
Irish-born novelist, author of *The Bell* (1958).
>*"We can only learn to love by loving."*

Irna Irna Phillips *(1901–1973)*
American writer, creator of the first known soap opera, a series of ten-minute radio plays called *Painted Dreams* (1930).

Irving Irving Berlin *(originally Israel Isidore Baline) (1888-1989)*
Siberian-born American omnipresent composer of "God Bless America" (1939), "There's No Business Like Show Business" (1946), "White Christmas" (1942), and much, much more. He could not read music.

Irwin Irwin Schmidt *(1937–)*
German rock keyboard player with the band Can.

Iryna Iryna Senyk *(1926–)*
Ukrainian poet and embroiderer. She learned to embroider in prison camp, using fish bones for needles.

Isaac Sir Isaac Newton *(1642–1727)*
English scientist, mathematician, and alchemist, author of *Philosophiae Naturalis Principia Mathematica* (1687). He was the first to shine white light through a prism and observe the rainbow.
>*"O physics! Preserve me from metaphysics!"*

Isabel Isabel Allende *(1942–)*
Chilean novelist, author of *The House of the Spirits* (1985).

Isabelita Isabelita Perón *(real name Maria Estela Isabel Perón), née Matínez Cartas (1931–)*
Argentinian second wife of Juan Perón, after popular Eva Perón. Following his death, she took over the presidency, but ended up serving five years in prison for abuse of public property.

Isabella Isabella Mary Beeton, *née Mayson (known as Mrs. Beeton) (1836–1865)*
English cookery writer, author of the seminal *Book of Household Management* (1861).
>*"I have always thought there is no more fruitful source of family discontent than badly cooked dinners and untidy ways."*

Isabelle Isabelle Brasseur *(20th century)*
Canadian pairs skater with Lloyd Eisler. She won a 1994 Olympic bronze medal skating with broken ribs.

Isadora Isadora Duncan *(1877–1927)*
American dancer.
> *"If I could tell you what it meant I wouldn't have to dance."*

Isaiah Isaiah Patterson *(20th century)*
American gospel singer with the a capella group Five Blind Boys of Mississippi.

Isak Isak Dinesen *(pen name of Baroness Karen Blixen), née Karen Chrislence Dinesen (1885–1962)*
Danish novelist, author of *Out of Africa* (1937).

Isambard Isambard Kingdom Brunel *(1806–1859)*
English inventor.

Isamu Isamu Noguchi *(1904–1988)*
American sculptor and Modernist designer.

Iseult Iseult MacBride *(b. c. 1915)*
Irish daughter of actress Maud Gonne and hero John MacBride. Poet William Butler Yeats had a crush on both Iseult and her mother, proposing to Maud at least fifty times in fifty years, and to Iseult now and then.

Ishiro Ishiro Honda *(1912–1993)*
Japanese film director, creator of the Godzilla movies.

Ishmael Ishmael *trans. God hears, Genesis 16: 12 (c. 18th century B.C.)*
Old Testament "wild ass," the son of Abraham and his concubine Hagar cast out by jealous wife Sarah. He is the legendary ancestor of the Sinai desert nomads.

Ishtar Ishtar *trans. star*
Babylonian goddess of love, fertility, and war. Her cult spread as far as Greece.

Ishwar Dr. Ishwar Gilade *(20th century)*
Indian physician with the Indian Health Organization who uses the Kama Sutra sex manual to fight AIDS by promoting monogramy.
> *"Most men who have multiple sex partners usually use only one sexual posture."*

Isidor Isidor Feinstein (I.F.) Stone *(1907–1989)*
American radical journalist, founder with his wife, Esther, of *I.F. Stone's Weekly* magazine.

Isis Isis
Egyptian cow goddess of fertility, the sister and wife of Osiris.

Ismail Ismail Merchant *(1936–)*
British film producer, partner of James Ivory.

Ismay Ismay Ann Cruickshank *(1866–1995)*
Canadian bookkeeper who died at the age of 129.
> *"I don't understand it, I just keep on going."*

Ismene Ismene
Legendary Greek daughter of King Oedipus and his mother, Jocasta. She was conceived before Jocasta and Oedipus realized they were mother and son.

Israel Sir Israel Moses Sieff, Baron Sieff of Brimpton *(1889–1972)*
English brother-in-law of Simon Marks, with whom he founded the firm of Marks and Spencer.

Issey Issey Miyake *(1938–)*
Japanese fashion designer.

Italo Italo Calvino *(1923–1985)*
Cuban-born Italian writer, author of *If on a Winter's Night a Traveller* (1979).

Itamar Itamar Franco *(1930–)*
Brazilian politician, winner of the 1994 Macho of the Year Award for his flirtation with a teacher half his age.

Itzhak Itzhak Perlman *(1945–)*
Israeli violinist.

Ival Ival Richard "Goodie" Goodman *(1908–1984)*
American baseball outfielder with the Reds, an All-Star.

Ivan Ivan Petrovich Pavlov *(1849–1936)*
Russian physiologist. He taught dogs to salivate at the sound of a bell as part of his research into "conditioned reflexes."

Ivanhoe *Ivanhoe* (1820)
Scottish novel by Sir Walter Scott.

Ivo St. Ivo of Hélory of Kermartin *(1253–1303)*
French lawyer, the "poor man's advocate" for
his refusal to accept fees from poor clients. He is
the patron saint of lawyers.

Ivona *Ivona, Princess of Burgundia (1938)*
Surreal Polish play by Witold Gombrowicz.

Ivor Ivor Novello *(originally David Ivor Davies)*
(1893–1951)
Welsh actor, composer of the song "Keep the
Home Fires Burning" (1914).

Ivory Ivory Joe Hunter *(1911–1974)*
American blues pianist and singer.

Ivy Dame Ivy Compton-Burnett *(1892–1969)*
English novelist.
 *"Pushing forty? She's clinging on to it for
 dear life."*

Ix Ix
Mayan god of the west. His colour was black.

Iyasu Iyasu the Great *(d. 1706)*
Emperor of Ethiopia.

Izaak Izaak Walton *(1593–1683)*
English writer, author of *The Compleat Angler, or
the Contemplative Man's Recreation* (1653).
 *"Angling may be said to be so like the mathe-
 matics that it can never be fully learnt."*

Jac Dr. Jac S. Geller *(20th century)*
American doctor, in 1952 the first surgeon to
successfully separate joined twins.

Jack Jack Kerouac *(originally Jean Louis Kerouac)*
(1922–1969)
American novelist, author of *On the Road*
(1957). He once picked up a photo of his mother taken when she was young and said, "That's
the picture of the girl I want to marry some-
day."

Jackie Jackie Robinson *(Jack Roosevelt Robinson)*
(1919–1972)
American baseball infielder with the Dodgers,
the first black player in the major leagues. At his
hiring interview, manager Branch Rickey said
he needed someone "with the guts not to fight
back" in response to the abuse he knew his first

black player would face. The Rookie of the Year
Award is named in his honour.

Jackrabbit Jackrabbit Johannsen *(Herman Smith-
Johannsen) (1875–1986)*
Norwegian-born Canadian cross-country skier.
His nickname was given to him by Cree Indians
("Wapoo" in Cree).

Jackson Jackson Pollock *(Paul Jackson Pollock)*
(1912–1956)
American drip painter. He died in an auto wreck
after drinking and driving.
 "Every good painter paints what he is."

Jaco Jaco Van Dormael *(1958–)*
Belgian filmmaker of *Toto le heros* (1992).

Jacob Jacob Perkins *(1766–1849)*
American mechanical engineer. He invented the
steel-engraving technique used for printing
money, which is more difficult to copy than
copper engraving.

Jacopo Jacopo Robusti *(known as Tintoretto)*
(1518–1594)
Italian painter.

Jacqueline Jacqueline Susann *(1926–1974)*
American pop novelist, author of *Valley of the
Dolls* (1968). When her British publisher asked
permission to remove the word "fuck" from her
best-seller, she cabled back "F—K YOU. LOVE,
JACKIE SUSANN."

Jacques Jacques Cartier *(1491–1557)*
French navigator, the explorer of Canada.
 *"I am rather inclined to believe that this is the
 land God gave to Cain."*

Jacquetta Jacquetta Hawkes *(1910–)*
English archaeologist and author, wife of writer
J.B. (John Boynton) Priestley.

Jade Jade Jagger *(20th century)*
Celebrity daughter of Mick Jagger.

Jafah Jafah Panahi *(20th century)*
Iranian filmmaker. His *The White Balloon* (1995)
won a Camera d'Or award for best first film.

Jag Jag Bhaduria *(20th century)*
Canadian politician. In 1994, when a
history of writing threatening letters was
revealed, he wrote letters to the newspapers

threatening to sue if they reported he had theatened people.

Jahan Shah Jahan *(1592–1666)*
Mogul emperor. He built the white marble Taj Mahal as the tomb of his favourite wife, Mumtaz.

Jai Jai Johanny Johanson *(originally John Lee Johnson) (1944–)*
American country rocker with the Allman Brothers Band.

Jaime Jaime Jaramillo *(1956–)*
Columbian geophysicist, known as "Papa Jaime" in his spare-time role of social worker to the street children of Bogotá.

Jake Jake Shubert *(1880–1963)*
American Broadway mogul.
> *"What! An actors' union? Actors!? Spit in their faces—they'll tell you it's raining."*

Jam Maharaja Jam Saheb of Nawanagar *(1872–1933)*
Indian-born English cricketer.

Jamaica Jamaica Kincaid *(originally Eleanor Potter Richardson) (1949–)*
Caribbean-born American journalist.
> *"This is my child sitting in the shade, her head thrown back in rapture, prolonging some moment of joy I have created for her."*

James James Joyce *(James Augustine Aloysius Joyce) (1882–1941)*
Irish writer, author of *A Portrait of the Artist as a Young Man* (1916).
> *"What's in a name? That is what we ask ourselves in childhood when we write the name that we are told is ours. A star, a daystar, a firedrake rose at his birth. It shone by day in the heavens alone, brighter than Venus in the night, and by night it shone over Delta in Cassiopeia, the recumbent constellation which is the signature of his initial among the stars. His eyes watched it, lowlying on the horizon, eastward of the bear, as he walked by the slumberous summer fields by midnight, returning from Shottery and from her arms."*

(From *Ulysses.* The passage is about William Shakespeare.)

Jamie Jamie Lee Curtis *(1958–)*
American actress, daughter of Tony Curtis; star of *A Fish Called Wanda* (1988).

Jamsetji Jamsetji Nasarwanji Tata *(1839–1904)*
Indian industrialist and educational promoter.

Jan Jan Vermeer *(1632–1675)*
Flemish painter. His small output is unrivalled for quiet luminosity.

Jana Jana Sterbak *(1955–)*
Canadian artist. She made a dress out of meat, which irritated many critics.

Jane Jane Austen *(1775–1817)*
English novelist, author of *Pride and Prejudice* (1813).
> *"I do not want people to be very agreeable, as it saves me the trouble of liking them a great deal."*

Janeane Janeane Garolfalo *(1964–)*
American stand-up comic and actress.

Janene Janene Utkin *(20th century)*
American chef. In 1992, her team set a world record for potato preparation, peeling 1,064 pounds, 6 ounces, of potatoes in 45 minutes at the Annual Idaho Spud Day Celebration.

Janet Janet Becker *(20th century)*
American author of *How to Have Multiple Orgasms Easier Than You Think.*

Janey Janey Morris, *née* Burden *(1839–1914)*
English muse to the Pre-Raphaelite movement, the strikingly beautiful daughter of a stableman, wife of William Morris. She lived for some years in a *ménage à trois* with Morris and painter Dante Gabriel Rossetti, as this was felt to be less scandalous than having her visit Rossetti overnight.

Janice Janice Deveree *(b. 1842)*
American bearded lady. In 1884, her beard was 14 inches long.

Janio Janio da Silva Quadros *(20th century)*
Brazilian politician. In 1960, he tried to outlaw bikinis on the beaches of Rio.

Janis Janis Joplin *(1943–1970)*
American blues singer.
> *"Don't compromise yourself. You are all you have."*

Jann Jann Wenner *(20th century)*
American editor of *Rolling Stone* magazine.
"A thorough survey may prove that it is impossible to buy a plain white or decently tasteful shirt in the whole of Las Vegas."

Janna Janna Lambine *(20th century)*
American pilot, in 1977 the first female Coast Guard pilot.

Jano Jano
Czech shepherd boy, hero of the opera *Jenůfa* (1904) by Leoš Janáček.

János János Corvinus Hunyady *(c. 1387–1456)*
Hungarian national hero. He spent his life routing the Turks.

Januarius St. Januarius *(d. c. 305)*
Italian martyred religious worker. A vial of his still-liquid blood, preserved in Naples, sometimes seems to boil. He is the patron saint of blood banks.

Janus Janus
Roman two-faced god of beginnings and entrances.

Jared Jared Sparks *(1789–1866)*
American historian and biographer.

Jari Jari Saaelainen *(1959–)*
Finish motorcyle rider. He set a Guinness record by riding 67,109 miles across 43 countries.

Jaron Jaron Lanier *(1960–)*
Californian inventor of the term "virtual reality."

Jarvis Jarvis Cocker *(1964–)*
British pop star, lead singer of Pulp.
"It's like this, there's something freakish about you, so you either consign yourself to the margins of society or think of it as unique."

Jascha Jascha Heifetz *(1901–1987)*
Polish-born American violin virtuoso. He graduated at age eight from the Vilnius School of Music.

Jasmine Princess Jasmine
Animated heroine of Walt Disney's American film *Aladdin* (1993).

JEAN-PAUL SARTRE

Jason Jason Robards, Jr. *(1922–)*
American actor. He made his stage début at age twenty-five as the back half of the cow in *Jack and the Beanstalk*.

Jasper Jasper Johns *(1930–)*
American Pop Art painter and sculptor.

Javed Javed Faridi *(1938–)*
Indian mango mogul. He sells only the rataul type of mango because "you eat this mango and you will give up everything else."

Javier Javier Pérez de Cuellar *(1920–)*
Peruvian diplomat, Secretary General of the United Nations.

Jawaharlal Jawaharlal Nehru *(1889–1964)*
Indian politician, first prime minister of independent India, father of Indira Gandhi.
"The only alternative to coexistence is codestruction."

Jay Jason "Jay" Gould *(1836–1892)*
American financier. In 1869, his attempt to corner the gold market started the "Black Friday" stock-market crash .

Jayalalitha Jayalalitha Jayaram *(1948–)*
Indian politician, "Tamil Nadu's Iron Lady." She is worshipped as a goddess by some of her voters.

Jaye Jaye Davidson *(1967–)*
Ambiguous British star of the film *The Crying Game* (1992).

Jayne Jayne Torvill *(1957–)*
English skater, half of the acclaimed ice-dancing team of Torvill and (Christopher) Dean.

Jean Jean Harlow *(originally Harlean Carpenter)* *(1911–1937)*
American actress, the original "blonde bombshell," star of *Dinner at Eight* (1934).
"Would you be shocked if I put on something more comfortable?"

Jean-Charles Jean-Charles Pellerin *(18th century)*
French founder of l'Imagerie Pellerin, the printing house that, in 1796, created the first cut-out paper figures for children. They were paper soldiers for children who could not afford lead ones.

Jean-Claude Jean-Claude Van Damme *(originally Jean-Claude Van Verenbeerg) (1961–)*
American actor. He played twins in *Double Impact* (1992), about which *Time Out* magazine observed: "the idea of two Van Dammes must have seemed workable on paper . . . but both exude the charisma of a packet of Cup-A-Soup."

Jean-Luc Jean-Luc Godard *(1930–)*
French film director.

"Of course a film should have a beginning, a middle, and an end. But not necessarily in that order."

Jean-Paul Jean-Paul Sartre *(1905–1980)*
French existentialist philosopher and boyfriend of Simone de Beauvoir.

"[My grandmother] believed in nothing; only her skepticism kept her from being an atheist."

Jeana Jeana Yeager *(1952–)*
American pilot, the first woman to glide around the world. Her hobbies are skydiving and helicopters.

Jeanette Jeanette MacDonald *(1907–1965)*
American singing actress, star of *Rose Marie* (1936).

Jeanne Jeanne Antoinette Posson, Marquise de Pompadour *(known as Madame de Pompadour) (1721–1764)*
French queen of fashion, the influential mistress of King Louis XV. She insisted on cooling relations with Germany after Frederick II made fun of her.

"Après nous le déluge" ("After us the flood").

Jeannette Jeannette Rankin *(1880–1973)*
American politician, the first female member of Congress. She was the only Congress-person to vote against war on Japan.

"As a woman, I can't go to war, and I refuse to send anyone else."

Jeannie "Jeannie with the Light Brown Hair" *(19th century)*
American song by Stephen Collins Foster, who also wrote "The Old Folks at Home" and "Camptown Races."

"I dream of Jeannie with the light brown hair Borne like a vapor on the summer air;

I see her tripping where the bright streams play, Happy as the daisies that dance on her way."

Jed Jed Clampett
Fictional American back-woods millionaire patriarch of the 1960s TV series *The Beverly Hillbillies*.

Jedediah Jedediah Smith *(Jedediah Strong Smith) (1799–1831)*
American fur trader and explorer.

Jeff Jeff Beck *(1944–)*
British rock guitarist.

Jefferson Jefferson Davis *(1808–1889)*
American politician, president of the rebel Confederate States.

Jeffery "Sir" Jeffery Hudson *(1619–1682)*
English 3'9" tall Court Dwarf to Queen Henrietta Maria, a Captain of the Horse during the Civil War.

Jeffrey Jeffrey Nicholas *(20th century)*
American record-setting deadbeat dad. He owed $580,000 in back child support when finally cornered by his ex-wife, Marilyn Kane.

Jehane Madame Jehane Benoît *(20th century)*
Canadian author of *The Canadian Cookbook: A Complete Heritage of Canadian Cooking* (1970).

Jehudi Jehudi Ashmun *(1794–1828)*
American organizer of the African colony of Liberia. The Ashmun Institute of Chester, Pennsylvania, later Lincoln University, was named after him.

Jelly Roll Jelly Roll Morton *(originally Ferdinand Joseph La Menthe or Lemott) (1885–1941)*
American jazz pianist and composer.

"Get up from that piano. You hurtin' its feelings."

Jem James "Jem" Belcher *(1781–1811)*
English butcher and boxer, the "Napoleon of the Ring." His favourite blue neck-scarves with white spots became known as "belchers" in his honour.

Jemima Aunt Jemima Pancake Mix *(1893–)*
American food product introduced at the Chicago World's Exposition by R.T. David, who hired Nancy Green, a former slave, to demonstrate it.

Jemma Jemma Redgrave *(20th century)*
British actress, star of *Bramwell* (1994).

Jemmie James "Jemmie" Barrie *(James Matthew "J.M." Barrie) (1860–1937)*
Scottish novelist, author of *Peter Pan* (1904).
"I want always to be a little boy and have fun."

Jennet Jennet
English "lovely witch" of Christopher Fry's play *The Lady's Not for Burning* (1949).

Jennie Jennie Jerome *(later Lady Randolph Churchill) (1854–1951)*
American-born mother of Winston Churchill.
"I shall never get used to not being the most beautiful woman in the room. It was an intoxication to sweep in and know every man had turned his head."

Jennifer Jennifer Jones *(originally Phyllis Isley) (1919–)*
American actress. She won an Academy Award for *The Song of Bernadette* (1943).

Jenny Jenny Joseph *(20th century)*
American poet.
"When I am old I shall wear purple,
With a red hat which doesn't go, and doesn't suit me
And I shall spend my pension on brandy and summer gloves
And satin sandals."

Jeremias Jeremias Benjamin Richter *(1762–1807)*
German chemist, the discoverer of the law of equivalent proportions.

Jeremy Jeremy Bentham *(1748–1832)*
English philosopher and lawyer. He had his body stuffed to serve as a good example to the lower classes. It may still be seen today, though with a new wax head to replace the deteriorated original.

Jermaine Jermaine Jackson *(Jermaine La Jaune Jackson) (1954–)*
American bass player, a member of the Jackson Five.

Jeroen Jeroen Krabbe *(1944–)*
Dutch actor, the villain in the American film *The Fugitive* (1993).

Jerome Jerome K. Jerome *(Jerome Klapka Jerome) (1859–1927)*
British author of *Three Men in a Boat* (1889).
"Fox terriers are born with about four times as much original sin in them as other dogs."

Jerrell Jerrell Wilson *(1941–)*
American football punter for the Kansas City Chiefs, the "best punter in the history of the American Football League."

Jerrie Jerrie Cobb *(Geraldyn Cobb) (1931–)*
American aviator, the first woman to qualify for the astronaut program. Her Air Force father taught her to fly a biplane at the age of twelve.

Jerry Jerry Garcia *(Jerome John Garcia) (1942–1995)*
American leader of the band the Grateful Dead.
"Practice random kindness and senseless acts of beauty."

Jersey Jersey Joe Walcott *(originally Arnold Raymond Cream) (1914–1994)*
American boxer, the oldest fighter ever to win the world heavyweight championship.

Jerzy Jerzy Kosinski *(Jerzy Nikodem Kosinski) (1933–1991)*
Polish-born American novelist, author of *The Painted Bird* (1965).

Jesse Jesse Owens *(originally James Cleveland Owens) (1913–1980)*
American athlete, the "Buckeye Bullet." At the 1936 Olympics, Adolf Hitler left the stands rather than watch him win gold medals.
"After I came home from the 1936 Olympics with my four gold medals, it became increasingly apparent that everyone was going to slap me on the back, want to shake my hand, or have me up to their suite. But no one was going to offer me a job."

Jessi Jessi Winchester *(1943–)*
American prostitute, at age fifty-two an entrant in the 1995 Miss Nevada competition.
"Ladies in my profession can be just as normal as women in other fields."

Jessica Jessica Lucy Mitford *(1917–)*
British-born American communist journalist, author of *The American Way of Death* (1963).

<table>
<tr><td>

*Top 10 Baby
Names for Future
Industrialists*

André • Armand • Bertha •

Eleuthère • Enzo • Freeland •

Gottlieb • King • Lionel • Philo
</td></tr>
</table>

Jessie Jessie Newberry, *née Rowat (1864–1919)*
Scottish embroiderer. She designed the "Glasgow rose" motif usually attributed to Charles Rennie Mackintosh.

Jessye Jessye Norman *(1945–)*
American opera soprano, the inspration for Jean-Jacques Beineix's French film *Diva* (1982). Her American début was at the Hollywood Bowl.

Jesus Jesus and Mary Chain *(b. 1984)*
Scottish rock band.

Jet Jet Harris *(originally Terence Hawkins) (1939–)*
British pop bass player with the group the Shadows.

Jethro Jethro Tull *(1674–1741)*
British agricultural reformer. A 1970s rock band was named after him.

Jett Jett Williams *(stage name of Cathy Yvonne Stone) (1953–)*
American country singer, the illegitimate daughter of Hank Williams.

Jezebel *Jezebel (1938)*
American film starring Bette Davis.

Jhane Jhane Barnes *(1954–)*
American fashion designer. She specializes in men's wear.

Jiddu Jiddu Krishnamurti *(1895–1986)*
Indian theosophist. In 1925, American Annie Besant proclaimed him to be the Messiah.

Jiggs *Jiggs (1932–)*
American chimpanzee, co-star with Ronald Reagan of the film *Bedtime for Bonzo* (1951). He was confined to a cage in retirement.

"He's a mean s.o.b. He looks cute, but he's not a domestic animal. He weighs 175 pounds and has about six to eight times [a human's] strength."

Jigme Jigme Singye Wangchuck *(1953–)*
King of Bhutan. He refuses to discuss his personal life because "I would get in trouble with my four wives."

Jil Jil Sander *(full name Heidemarie Jiline Sander) (1943–)*
German fashion designer.
"I can't call it Heidi Sander. It's so German, so sweet."

Jill Jill Ker Conway *(1935–)*
Australian-born American president of Smith College, author of *The Road from Coorain* (1989).

Jim Jim Morrison *(1943–1971)*
American pop icon with the group the Doors. He sang "Light My Fire" (1967).

Jimi Jimi Hendrix *(James Marshall Hendrix, originally Johnny Allen Hendrix) (1942–1970)*
Influential American electric-guitarist, the first black rock star. The night he died of a drug overdose, he left a message on his manager's answering machine saying, "I need help bad, man."

Jimmie Jimmie Rodgers *(originally James Charles Rodgers) (1897–1933)*
American hillbilly singer, "America's Blue Yodeler."

Jimmy Jimmy Carter *(James Earl Carter) (1924–)*
American president. He was the first American president born in a hospital; his predecessors were all born at home.

Jinny Jinny Osburn *(20th century)*
American girl singer with the Chordettes.

Jiří Jiří Trnka *(1912–1969)*
Czech filmmaker. He filmed a puppet version of *The Good Soldier Schweik* (1954).

Jo Josephine "Jo" March
Character in Louisa May Alcott's American novel *Little Women* (1868).

Joachim Joachim von Ribbentrop *(1893–1946)*
German foreign minister. He helped persuade Adolf Hitler that the British would never fight.

Joan Joan Rivers (originally Joan Alexandra Molinsky) (1933–)
American comic. She recorded an album called *What Becomes a Semi-Legend Most* (1983).

Joán Joán Miró (1893–1983)
Spanish artist.
> "I want to murder painting."

Joanna Joanna Baillie (1762–1851)
Scottish dramatist poet. A stanza of her poetry was so well known that Sir Walter Scott thought it was antique, and borrowed it twice to use in his work.
> "O swiftly glides the bonnie boat
> Just parted from the shore
> And to the fisher's chorus-note
> Soft moves the dipping oar."

Joanne Joanne Woodward (1930–)
American actress. She won an Oscar for *The Three Faces of Eve* (1957).

Joaquin Joaquin Phoenix (20th century)
American actor, brother of the late River Phoenix. Asked what he'd do if he became a teen heartthrob, he replied, "I'm gonna eat a lot and gain weight. Then I'm going to scar my face."

Job Job *James 5: 11*
Hero of the Old Testament Book of Job, whose faith never wavered despite a test of undeserved torments.
> "Ye have heard of the patience of Job."

Jocelyn Dr. Jocelyn Burnell, *née Bell* (1943–)
British astronomer, the first person to observe a pulsating radio source, or "pulsar."

Jocelyne Jocelyne Grand'maison (1950–1994)
Canadian reporter with *Le Journal de Québec*. Her body was found in a smouldering ski chalet together with those of other members of the Order of the Solar Temple cult.

Jochebed Jochebed *trans. the Lord is glory, Exodus 2: 3 (c. 13th century B.C.)*
Old Testament mother. She devised a basket smeared with pitch in which to float her baby, Moses, in the bullrushes to avoid the Pharaoh's death edict against male babies.

Jock J.E.H. "Jock" MacDonald (1897–1960)
Scottish-born Canadian painter, a member of the Group of Seven.

Jodie Jodie Foster (originally Alicia Christian Foster) (1962–)
American actress and film director, winner of an Academy Award for *The Accused* (1988). By age thirteen she had appeared in forty-five television commercials.

Jody Jody Richard Davis (1956–)
American baseball catcher for the Cubs, an All-Star.

Joe Joe Louis (originally Joseph Louis Barrow) (1914–1981)
American boxer, the "Brown Bomber," in 1937 the youngest person to win the world heavyweight championship. He then held the title longer than anyone else, against twenty-five challenges. When opponent Billy Conn predicted victory before fighting him (incorrectly), Joe Louis replied, "He can run, but he can't hide."

Joel Joel Grey (1932–)
American actor. His father was comedian Mickey Katz.

Joergen Joergen Rusland (20th century)
Danish gold-medallist in the first Santa Claus games held 250 km north of the Arctic Circle; a mixed competition of chimney-climbing, tree-decorating, present-delivering, and milk-gulping.

Joey Joey Smallwood (1900–1991)
Canadian politician, premier of Newfoundland. He was the last surviving Father of Confederation.

Johann Johann Strauss the Younger (1825–1899)
Austrian composer of immortal waltzes such as "The Blue Danube" (1867). His father wanted him to be a lawyer.

Johannes Johannes Brahms (1833–1897)
German composer.

John John Bunyan (1628–1688)
English preacher, author of *Pilgrim's Progress* (1678). The introduction observes:
> "Some said, 'John, print it'; others said, 'Not so.'
> Some said, 'It might do good'; others said, 'No.'"

Johnnie Johnnie "Dusty" Baker *(1949–)* American baseball player, an All-Star, and winner of a Gold Glove award. When he was appointed manager of the San Francisco Giants, he said, "This is the greatest day of my life, so far."

Johnny Johnny Weissmuller *(Peter John Weismuller) (1903–1984)* Romanian-born American swimmer and actor. He

JONI MITCHELL was the first man to swim 100 metres in less than a minute, and is also the inventor of Tarzan's celebrated yodel.

Joice Joice Heth *(19th century)* American performer. In the 1840s, she was presented to the public by P.T. (Phineas Taylor) Barnum, as the 161-year-old black nurse of George Washington, in the very first of his popular and successful "humbugs" on the public.

Joie Joie Susannah Lee *(20th century)* American screenplay writer, the sister of director Spike Lee.

Jojo Jojo Savard *(20th century)* Canadian late-nite TV infomercial psychic.

Jokichi Jokichi Takamine *(1854–1922)* Japanese-American chemist. He isolated adrenaline, the first hormone known.

Jolene "Jolene" *(1979)* American country-western song by Dolly Parton.

Jon Jon Voight *(1938–)* American actor. He won an Oscar for *Coming Home* (1978).

Jonah Jonah *trans. dove (c. 8th century B.C.)* Adventurous hero of the Old Testament Book of Jonah. He was swallowed by a great fish while trying to avoid his God-given mission to go to wicked Nineveh and preach there.

"The waters closed in over me, the deep was round about me; weeds were wrapped about my head."

Jonas Jonas Salk *(Jonas Edward Salk) (1914–1995)* American virologist, creator of the "Salk vaccine," the first safe and effective vaccine against poliomyelitis.

Jonathan Jonathan Swift *(1667–1745)* Anglo-Irish poet and satirist, author of *Gulliver's Travels* (1726).

"So, naturalists observe, a flea
Has smaller fleas that on him prey;
And these have smaller fleas to bite 'em,
And so proceed ad infinitum.
Thus every poet, in his kind,
Is bit by him that comes behind."

Jone Jone Pearce *(20th century)* American professor of organizational behaviour.

"No research I have ever seen has been able to ascertain any benefit at all from having some famous person come in to give motivational talks to employees."

Jones Jones Morgan *(1883–1993)* American soldier, a member of the Buffalo Soldiers black cavalry unit that fought with Teddy Roosevelt in the Spanish-American war of 1898.

"I always said let my last days be my best days, and it's come true."

Joni Joni Mitchell *(originally Roberta Joan Anderson Mitchell) (1943–)* Canadian songstress.

"I think permission is far more important to an artist than encouragement."

Jonjo Jonjo O'Neill *(originally John Joseph O'Neill) (1952–)* Irish jockey. He rode 148 winners in one season.

Jools Jools Holland *(originally Julian Holland) (20th century)* British keyboard player with the band Squeeze.

Jorge Jorge Zontal *(originally George Saia) (1944–1994)* Canadian artist; member of General Idea and a co-creator of the 1984 Miss General Idea Pavilion.

Jörgen Jörgen Jörgensen *(1779–1844)* Danish adventurer, the "Dog-Days King." For six weeks in 1809 he was ruler of Iceland, until deposed by the arrival of an armed sloop.

Jorma Jorma Kaukonen *(1940–)*
American rock musician with the Jefferson Airplane.

Jørn Jørn Utzon *(1918–)*
Danish architect of the Opera House in Sydney, Australia.

José José Ferrer *(originally José Vicente Ferrer de Oteror y Cintron) (1912–)*
American actor. He won an Academy Award for *Cyrano de Bergerac* (1950).

Josef Josef Stalin *(originally Iosif Vissarionovich Dzhugashvili) (1879–1953)*
Soviet politician, the successor to Vladimir Ilyich Lenin. The key to his success was murdering all his opponents.

Joseph Dr. Joseph Ignace Guillotin *(1738–1814)*
French anatomy professor, inventor of the guillotine. He intended his invention to be a merciful alternative to the hacking off of heads by axe during the Terror of 1794.

Josepha Josepha Hale *(Sarah Josepha Hale) (1788–1879)*
American writer and first female magazine editor of *Ladies' Magazine*.
> "Mary had a little lamb,
> Its fleece was white as snow."

Josephine Josephine Baker *(originally Freda Josephine McDonald) (1906–1975)*
American-born dancer. She introduced the Charleston to Europe, dancing it in a girdle made of bananas.
> *"The rear end exists. I see no reason to be ashamed of it. It's true there are rear ends so stupid, so pretentious, so insignificant that they're good only for sitting on."*

Josephus Josephus Lembert Hassell *(1906–1983)*
Resident of the island of Saba in the Netherlands Antilles. When Dutch engineers proclaimed his home too steep for roads, he signed up for a correspondence course in road-building, and completed his first section in 1943.

Josh Josh Gibson *(1912–1947)*
American baseball catcher with the Negro Leagues, a member of the Hall of Fame, the "Black Babe Ruth." On January 20, 1947, aged thirty-five, he told his mother he was going to die that night. He went to bed, called for his trophies, and was laughing with his family gathered around when he had a stroke and died.

Joshua Captain Joshua Slocum *(1844–c. 1910)*
Canadian-born American sailor, the first person to sail alone around the world, author of *Sailing Alone Around the World* (1900). He was last seen alive in late 1909 setting off to do it a second time.

Josiah Josiah Wedgwood *(1730–1795)*
English potter. He pioneered the mass production of quality consumer goods.

Josif Josif Kobson *(20th century)*
Russian pop singer. Asked why he had decided to also run for parliament, he replied, "Honestly, who the hell knows?"

Josip Josip Broz *(known as Marshal Tito) (1892–1980)*
Yugoslav politician.

Joy Joy Adamson *(Joy Friedericke Victoria Adamson), née Gessner (1916–1980)*
Austrian-born conservationist. She describes her relationship with the lion-cub Elsa in her book *Born Free* (1960).

Joyce Joyce Cary *(Arthur Joyce Lunel Cary) (1888–1957)*
British novelist, author of *The Horse's Mouth* (1944).
> *"Remember I'm an artist. And you know what that means in a court of law. Next worse to an actress."*

Joycelyn Dr. Joycelyn Elders *(1933–)*
American politician fired as surgeon-general for agreeing that "perhaps" masturbation should be taught in school.
> *"I came to Washington as prime steak, and after being there a little while I feel like low-grade hamburger."*

Juan Juan Fernandez *(c. 1536–c. 1604)*
Spanish navigator, discoverer of Fernandez Island.

Jubal Jubal Anderson Early *(1816–1894)*
American Confederate soldier.

Judah Judah *Genesis 49: 8 (c. 16th century B.C.)*
Favoured son of Jacob, "a lion's whelp." It was Judah's idea to sell his brother Joseph to a passing slave-driver, rather than leave him to die in a dry well as the other brothers had planned.

Judas Judas Priest *(b. 1969)*
British heavy-metal band.

Judd Judd Nelson *(1959–)*
American actor.

Jude *Jude the Obscure (1895)*
English novel by Thomas Hardy.

Judi Dame Judi Dench *(originally Judith Olivia Dench) (1934–)*
English actress. As James Bond's boss in *Golden Eye* (1995), she gets to describe him as "a sexist misogynist dinosaur, a relic of the Cold War."

Judith Judith *(active c. 853)*
French great-granddaughter of Charlemagne; daughter of Charles the Bald. She married her first husband at age twelve, then one of her stepsons, then was abducted by Flemish thug Baldwin Ironhand.

Judy Judy Garland *(originally Frances Ethel Gumm) (1922–1969)*
American actress and all-round entertainer. She played Dorothy in the film *The Wizard of Oz* (1939).
"I was born at the age of twelve on a Metro-Goldwyn-Mayer lot."

Juhani Juhani Saramies *(20th century)*
Finnish taxi patron. In 1991, he and Mika Lehtonen set a Guinness record for the longest taxi ride: to Spain and back.

Jules Jules Leotard *(d. 1870)*
French trapeze artist, inventor of the stretchy one-piece suit that bears his name.

Julia Julia Child *(1912–)*
American chef.
"Life itself is the proper binge."

Julian Sir Julian Sorell Huxley *(1887–1975)*
British biologist and writer.

Juliana Queen Juliana *(Juliana Louise Emma Marie Wilhelmina) (1909–)*
Queen of The Netherlands. In 1980, she abdicated, leaving the throne to her daughter Beatrix.

Julie Julie Andrews *(originally Julia Elizabeth Wells) (1935–)*
British singer and actress. She won an Academy Award playing the title role in *Mary Poppins* (1964).

Juliet Juliet Capulet
Short-lived but articulate child bride of William Shakespeare's play *Romeo and Juliet* (1594–96).

Juliette Juliette Magill Kinzie Low, *née Gordon (1860–1927)*
American founder of the Girl Scouts of America. Her first "tenderfoot" test required tieing knots, blazing a trail, lighting a fire with one match, and making peppermint drops.

Julio Julio Iglesias *(1943–)*
Spanish singer, formerly a soccer player.

Julius Julius Rosenberg *(1917–1953)*
American spy. He and his wife, Ethel, were electrocuted for passing nuclear secrets to the Soviet Union.

June June Allyson *(originally Ella Geisman) (1917–)*
American actress, of the TV series "The June Allyson Show" (1959–61).

Junior Junior Parker *(originally Herman Parker) (1927–1971)*
American blues-harmonica player.

Jupiter Jupiter Hammon *(c. 1720–c. 1800)*
The first published black poet in the United States.

Juste Juste-Aurèle Meissonnier *(c. 1693–1750)*
French Rococo designer.

Justine *Justine (1957)*
English novel by Lawrence Durrell, the first volume of his "Alexandria Quartet."

Justinian Justinan the Great *(c. 482–565)*
Byzantine Emperor. In 529 he closed the pagan philosophical schools of Athens.

Juvenal Juvenal *(Decimus Junius Juvenalis Juvenal) (c. 55–c. 140)*
Roman lawyer and satirist.
"No one ever suddenly became depraved."

Jy Jy Chiperzak *(1948–)*
Canadian operator of the Joywind Farm Rare Breed Conservancy near Peterborough, Ontario, which rears old-fashioned breeds of farm animals.

Kaare Kaare Klint *(1888–1954)*
Danish Modernist architect and furniture designer.

Kaffe Kaffe Fasset *(20th century)*
British painter and knitting guru.

Kahlil Kahlil Gibran *(1883–1931)*
Syrian-born American poet and painter.
> *"You are the bows from which your children as living arrows are sent forth."*

Kahn-Tineta Kahn-Tineta Horn *(1940–)*
American-born Canadian fashion model and political worker, founder of the Indian Legal Defence Committee.

Kaikhosru Kaikhosru Shapurji Sorabji *(Leon Dudley Kaikhosru Shapurji Sorabji) (1892–1988)*
British composer of the world's longest piano piece, estimated at six hours in length. It has never been played.

Kaitlin Kaitlin Hopkins *(20th century)*
American actress on the TV soap-opera series "Another World."

Kaj Kaj Franck *(1911–)*
Finnish industrial designer.

Kakuei Kakuei Tanaka *(1918–)*
Japanese prime minister. He spent four years in prison for accepting bribes from the Lockheed Corporation.

Kálmán Kálmán Tisza *(1830–1902)*
Hungarian politician.

Kama Kama
Vedic god of love, son of Laksmi. He is usually depicted as a young boy carrying a bow and arrow.

Kanellos Kanellos Kanellopoulos *(1957–)*
Greek aviator. In 1988, he flew from Crete to Santorini in a human-powered aircraft, averaging 18.5 mph over the 74 miles.

Kansas Kansas Joe McCoy *(1905–1950)*
American blues artist, the husband of Memphis Minnie.

Kapax Kapax *(1944–)*
Colombian tour guide, "Tarzan of the Amazon." To bring attention to pollution, he swam 1,300 km down the Magdalena River to reach the Caribbean.

Kareem Kareem Abdul-Jabbar *(originally Ferdinand Lewis Alcindor, Jr.) (1947–)*
American basketball star, originator of the "sky hook" shot. He was over seven feet tall before he left high school.
> *"You can't win unless you learn how to lose."*

Karel Karel Čapek *(1890–1938)*
Czech journalist and playwright.
> *"If dogs could talk, perhaps we'd find it just as hard to get along with them as with people."*

Karen Karen Kain *(1951–)*
Canadian ballerina.

Karim Karim Aga Khan IV *(1936–)*
Iman of the Muslim Ismaili sect.

Karl Karl Gemzell *(1910–)*
Swedish endocrinologist. He developed pituitary growth hormone for children who would otherwise never have reached normal height.

Karl-Friedrich Karl-Friedrich Benz *(1844–1929)*
German manufacturer of the first gasoline-powered car. It could reach 10 mph.

Karle Karle Wilson Baker *(pen-name of Mrs. Thomas Ellis) (b. 1878)*
English poet.
> *"Let me grow lovely growing old—*
> *So many fine things do:*
> *Laces, and ivory, and gold,*
> *And silks need not be new."*

Karolina Karolina Sofia Key *(known as Ellen Key) (1849–1926)*
Swedish writer.
> *"At every step the child should be allowed to meet the real experiences of life; the thorns should never be plucked from roses."*

Katarina Katarina Witt *(1965–)*
East German singles figure skater, an Olympic gold-medallist in 1984 and 1988.

KATHARINE HEPBURN

Kate Kate Greenaway (*originally Catherine Greenaway*) (*1846–1901*)
British book illustrator. The Greenaway Medal for British children's books is named for her.

Kateri The Blessed Kateri Tekakwitha (*c. 1656–1680*)
American-born Canadian Algonquin Catholic-convert, the "Lily of the Mohawks."

Kath Kath Walker (*originally Kathleen Jean Walker, tribal name Oodgeroo Noonuccal*) (*1920–*)
Australian poet and political activist. She was raised among the Noonuccal tribe of Queensland.

Katharine Katharine Hepburn (*1907–*)
American actress, winner of four Academy Awards.
> *"I don't care what's written about me as long as it's not true."*

Katherine Katherine Mansfield (*Katherine Mansfield Beauchamp, or Mrs. John Middleton Murry*) (*1888–1923*)
New Zealand–born bohemian and short-story author.
> *"Regret is an apalling waste of energy; you can't build on it; it's only good for wallowing."*

Kathleen Kathleen Battle (*1948–*)
American opera soprano.
> *"Many times I am asked, 'How can you be from a small town in the Midwest and sing Mozart?' Mozart was a human being with emotions and a sense of humor . . . We all share these qualities as human beings."*

Kathrine Kathrine Switzer (*1947–*)
American athlete. In 1967, she become the first woman to run in the Boston Marathon by filling out the application form with just a "K." As she was setting out, a male official tried to rip the number off her shirt, but she broke free.

Kathy Kathy Kusner (*c. 1940–*)
American jockey, in 1968 the first woman to race thoroughbreds at major tracks. She had to go to court to get the licence.

Katia Katia Noguera Tapeti (*1953–*)
Brazilian transsexual city-councillor. She is known as "the mother and father" of the town of Colonia.
> *"I look more like a woman than most of the women here and I'm more courageous than a lot of these macho guys."*

Kato Brian "Kato" Kaelin (*1959–*)
American actor, a house-guest of O.J. (Orenthal James) Simpson on the night of his wife's murder.
> *"They said I'd get 15 minues of fame, but thanks to [TV program] "Talk Soup," I got a whole 30 minutes."*

Katy "K-K-K-K-Katy" The Stammering Song (*1918*)
Canadian comic song composed by Geoffrey O'Hara, one of the big hits of the First World War.

Kay Kay Boyle (*1902–1992*)
American novelist, co-author with Robert McAlmon of the Parisian memoir *Being Geniuses Together* (1934–68).

Kazimierz Kazimierz Pulaski (*1748–1779*)
Polish soldier. He led "Pulaski's Legion" during the American Civil War, and died in the siege of Savannah.

Kazimir Kazimir Malevich (*Kazimir Severinovich Malevich*) (*1878–1935*)
Russian Suprematist artist.

Kazuo Kazuo Yamada (*20th century*)
Japanese owner of the Convenience Business Association, which will rent fake relatives for jobs such as visiting ageing parents, tending cemeteries, weeping at funerals, or walking the dog. A presentable wedding guest costs about $195, cheaper than paying airfare for real guests.
> *"This isn't going to be printed, is it?"*

Keanu Keanu Reeves (*1965–*)
Lebanese-born Canadian-American actor.

Kees Kees Van Dongen (*1877–1968*)
Dutch painter.

Keiko Keiko (*b. c. 1967*)
Icelandic-born Mexican killer whale, star of the American film *Free Willy* (1993).

Keir Keir Hardie *(James Keir Hardie) (1856–1915)*
British labour politician.

Keith Keith Richards *(1943–)*
British rock star.
> *"The older you get, the older you want to get."*

Keitha Keitha McLean *(1971–1995)*
Canadian journalist, editor of fashion magazine *Flare* and addiction-recovery magazine *Pathways*.

Kelly Kelly Miller *(1863–1939)*
American scholar.
> *"Circumstances not only alter causes; they alter character."*

Kelly Kelly McGillis *(1957–)*
American actress.

Kelsey Kelsey Grammer *(1955–)*
American actor, Dr. Frasier Crane on the TV series "Cheers" (d. 1993) and "Frasier" (b. 1993).

Kelvin Kelvin Nagel *(1920–)*
Australian golfer.

Kemal Kemal Atatürk *(Mustafa Kemal Atatürk) (1881–1938)*
Turkish politician. He created modern Turkey out of the remains of the Ottoman Empire.
> *"It was necessary to abolish the fez, which sat on the heads of our nation as an emblem of ignorance, negligence, fanaticism, and hatred of progress and civilization; to accept in its place the hat, the headgear worn by the whole civilized world."*

Ken Ken Kesey *(Ken Elton Kesey) (1935–)*
American novelist, author of *One Flew Over the Cuckoo's Nest* (1962) and the Chief of the Merry Pranksters, as described by Tom Wolfe in *The Electric Kool-Aid Acid Test* (1967).

Kenelm Sir Kenelm Digby *(1603–1665)* English diplomat famed for his duplicity. He also wrote a cookbook called *The Closet Opened*, which instructs, "To Bake Venision . . .

KEITH RICHARDS

Before the Deer be killed, he ought to be hunted and chased as much as may be."

Kenesaw Kenesaw Mountain Landis *(1866–1944)*
American judge and baseball commissioner, a member of the Hall of Fame. He took charge after the 1919 "Black Sox" betting scandal, and suspended fifty-three players. He was named after a Civil War battle.

Kenneth Kenneth Grahame *(1859–1932)*
British author of *The Wind in the Willows* (1908).
> *"Believe me, my young friend, there is nothing—absolutely nothing—half so much worth doing as simply messing about in boats. . . or with boats. . . . In or out of 'em, it doesn't matter."*

Kenny Kenny Rogers *(originally Kenneth Donald Rogers) (1938–)*
American country balladeer.

Kent Kent Weeks *(20th century)*
American archaeologist active in excavating the tombs of the fifty sons of Ramses II in Luxor, Egypt.

Kentigern St. Kentigern *(or St. Mungo) (c. 518–603)*
Celtic hermit. He is buried in Glasgow Cathedral.

Kenzo Kenzo Tange *(1913–)*
Japanese architect of the theme pavilion for the 1970 Osaka Exposition.

Keren Keren-happuch *trans. horn of beauty, Job 42: 14*
Old Testament youngest daughter of Job. She was in his second family, born after God had killed the first family as part of an experiment to see whether Job would lose his faith as a result.

Kermit Kermit the Frog *(20th century)*
Adenoidal American amphibian hand-puppet film superstar.

Kerry Kerry Francis Bullmore Packer *(1937–)*
Australian media mogul. He organized the controversial first night-time cricket matches.

Ketèlbey Ketèlbey *(originally Albert William Ketèlbey, pseudonym of Anton Vodorinski) (1875–1958)*
British tea-dance composer.

Kevin Kevin Maxwell *(20th century)*
British businessman, son of publisher Robert Maxwell. His bankrupcy set a 1992 Guinness

record for debt of £406.8 million. Separate criminal charges were laid for theft of £135 million more.

Kevyn Kevyn Aucoin (*originally Kevin Aucoin*) (*1962–*)
American make-up artist, author of *The Art of Makeup* (1994).

Khyber Khyber (*d. 1994*)
American cat of politician Charlie Wilson. When Khyber died, his owner received a condolence note from Socks, the cat of President Bill Clinton.

Kid Charles "Kid" Keinath (*1886–1966*)
American basketball player. The rule against using both hands to dribble was invented to slow him down. He once led a 16–15 victory for Penn over Columbia in which he scored all 16 points.

Kiefer Kiefer Sutherland (*1966–*)
American actor.

Kiki Kiki of Montparnasse (*originally Marie Prin*) (*1908–1953*)
Parisian artists' model.

Kikuchi Kikuchi Kiyoma (*1971–*)
Japanese "OL," or "office lady," the first Japanese woman to bring a legal charge of sexual harassment. Her support group, the Violet's Society, publishes a monthly newsletter.
> *"I decided to give my name to the press because I wanted to give courage to other women."*

Killer Fred R. "Killer" Burke (*busy February 14, 1929*)
American gangster, the only person ever linked to the St. Valentine's Day Massacre, though never brought to trial.

Kilu-Hepa Kilu-Hepa (*married 1381 B.C.*)
Mittani princess from Mesopotamia. She married Egyptian Pharoah Amenophis II when he was ten years old.

Kim Kim Philby (*Harold Adrian Russell Philby*) (*1912–1988*)
Indian-born British double agent for the USSR, author of *My Silent War* (1968).

Kimba *Kimba, the White Lion* (1966)
American children's film, based on the Japanese comic *Jungle Emperor*.

Kimball Kimball Millikan (*20th century*)
American submarine pilot. In 1992, he and his crew set a speed record for a human-powered non-propeller submarine which used an oscillating foil.

Kin Kin Hubbard (*1868–1930*)
American humorist.
> *"If there's one thing above all a vulture can't stand, it's a glass eye."*

King King Gillette (*King Camp Gillette*) (*1855–1932*)
American inventor of the safety razor.

Kingsley Sir Kingsley Amis (*1922–1995*)
British "angry young man," author of *Lucky Jim* (1954).
> *"It was no wonder that people were so horrible when they started life as children."*

Kinko Kinko (*originally Paul Orfalea*) (*1956–*)
American founder of the successful Kinko's chain of do-it-yourself photocopying shops. He got his nickname from his hair.

Kinky Kinky Friedman (*originally Richard Friedman*) (*20th century*)
American country musician, leader of Kinky Friedman and the Texas Jewboys.
> *"I realize that anybody who uses the word 'ambivalent' should never have been a country singer in the first place."*

Kinsey Kinsey Millhone
American fictional private eye, heroine of *A Is for Alibi* (1982) through *L Is for Lawless* (1995) by Sue Grafton.

Kirby Kirby Puckett (*1961–*)
American baseball outfielder with the Twins, an All-Star and winner of a Gold Glove award.

Kiri Dame Kiri Te Kawana (*1944–*)
New Zealand honeyed soprano. She was adopted as a child.

Kirk Kirk Douglas (*originally Issur Danielovitch*) (*1916–*)
American film star. He single-handedly ended the Joe McCarthy "Hollywood blacklist" by hiring blacklisted Dalton Trumbo to write the screenplay for *Spartacus* (1960).

KIRSTIE ALLEY

Kirkpatrick Kirkpatrick Macmillan *(1813–1878)* Scottish blacksmith. He built the first machine to use connecting rods to join cranks to pedals: the bicycle.

Kirsten Kirsten Flagstad *(1895–1962)* Norwegian Wagnerian soprano.

Kirstie Kirstie Alley *(1955–)* American comic actress.

Kit Kit Carson *(originally Christopher Carson) (1809–1868)* American fur trapper.

Kitty Kitty Kelley *(20th century)* American writer, the "doyenne of dirt." After she wrote a biography of Frank Sinatra, Nancy Sinatra said, "I hope she gets hit by a truck."

Klara Klara Westhoff *(married 1901)* French pupil of the sculptor Auguste Rodin, wife of poet Rainer Maria Rilke.

Klaus Klaus Kinski *(originally Nikolaus Günther Nakszyuski) (1926–1991)* German actor.

Klement Klement Gottwald *(1896–1953)* Czech politician; president 1948–53.

Klondike Klondike O'Donnell *(William O'Donnell) (active in 1920s)* American bootlegger, a short-lived rival to Al Capone.

Klu Ted "Klu" Kluszewski *(1924–1988)* American baseball player. The Reds' uniforms were redesigned with short sleeves to allow more room for his bulging biceps.

Knowlton Knowlton Nash *(Cyril Knowlton Nash) (1927–)* Canadian news reader.

Knucksie Phil "Knucksie" Niekro *(1939–)* American baseball pitcher with the Braves, an All-Star and winner of five Gold Glove awards.

Knud Knud Johan Victor Rasmussen *(1879–1933)* Danish explorer. He crossed from Greenland to the Bering Strait by dog-sled to support his theory that the Native people of North America could be descended from migratory tribes from Asia.

Knut Knut Hamsun *(pseudonym of Knut Pedersen) (1859–1952)* Norwegian novelist, winner of a 1920 Nobel Prize.

Knute Knute Rockne *(Knute Kenneth Rockne) (1888–1931)* American football coach for Notre Dame. He delivered what may be the best-known sports pep-talk of all time, when he begged his team to "win just one for the Gipper."

Ko Ko Ko Heroine of the English operetta *The Mikado* by William Schwenck Gilbert and Arthur Sullivan.

"As some day it may happen that a victim must be found,
I've got a little list—I've got a little list.
Of society offenders who might well be under ground,
And who never would be missed—who never would be missed."

Koen Koen de Winter *(20th century)* Dutch-born Canadian industrial designer.

Kolo Kolo Moser *(originally Koloman Moser) (1868–1918)* Austrian Art Nouveau painter and designer, a founding member of the Wiener Werkstätte.

Kong *King Kong (1933)* American tragic film.

Konrad Konrad Lorenz *(Konrad Zacharias Lorenz) (1903–1989)* Austrian zoologist, winner of a Nobel Prize, author of *On Aggression* (1963). He was the first to describe "imprinting," whereby baby birds faithfully follow the first moving object they see after hatching. He imprinted the baby birds on himself.

Konstantin Konstantin Eduarovitch Ziolkovsky *(1857–1935)*
Russian engineer. He built the first Russian wind tunnel.

Koo Koo Stark *(20th century)*
British brief royal girlfriend.

Kool Kool Bell *(Robert Bell) (1950–)*
American funk musician, leader of Kool and the Gang.

Kootenai Kootenai Brown *(19th century)*
Canadian cowboy.

Korah Korah *trans. baldness, Numbers 16: 3*
Old Testament rebel against Moses.
> *"You have gone too far! " said Korah to Moses.*

Kosso Kosso Eloul *(1920–1995)*
Israeli-born Canadian sculptor, creator of the eternal-flame monument at Yad Vashem, Jerusalem.

Koumiko *The Koumiko Mystery (1964)*
American film by Chris Marker about Tokyo misfit Koumiko Muraoka. He says, "She is not an example of anything."

Krampus Krampus *(active 20th century)*
Austrian Christmas devil. Parents can call his telephone hot-line to inform on naughty children and arrange for a personal Christmastime confrontation.

Krane Ed "Krane" Kranepool *(1944–)*
American baseball infielder with the Mets, an All-Star.

Kris Kris Kristofferson *(1937–)*
American musician and film star.
> *"Nobody in this business is very stable, else we wouldn't all be up on stage making asses of ourselves."*

Kristi Kristi Yamaguchi *(20th century)*
American Olympic figure-skater, a 1988 gold-medallist.

Kristin Kristin Solvadottir *(d. 1981)*
Icelandic waitress. Working in the 1930s in Winnipeg, Manitoba, she was unsuccessfully wooed by customer Charlie Thorson, who later became a designer for Disney Studio and created the character of Snow White in her image.

Kristina Queen Kristina *(1626–1689)*
Clever and beautiful bisexual Swedish queen. She negotiated an end to the Thirty Years War, then abdicated and went to live in Rome.

Krom J. "Krom" Hendricks *(19th century)*
South African cricket player. One of the fastest bowlers in the world, he was banned from international competition 1894 because of his colour.

Krystyne Krystyne Kolorful *(1952–)*
Canadian strip-tease artist, the world's most tattooed lady. She has 95% coverage.

Kublai Kublai Khan *(1214–1294)*
Mogul Khan, grandson of Genghis Khan; and the inspiration to poet Samuel Taylor Coleridge for his English poem "Kubla Khan" (1797).
> *"In Xanadu did Kubla Khan*
> *A stately pleasure-dome decree:*
> *Where Alph, the sacred river, ran*
> *Through caverns measureless to man*
> *Down to a sunless sea."*

Kunigunde Kunigunde Macamotzki *(later Cora Crippen, stage-name Belle Elmore) (19th century)*
American-born minor singer. She married Dr. Hawley Crippen, who poisoned her, buried her in the basement, and ran off with his secretary.

Kunte Kunte Kinte *(18th century)*
African-born forefather of Alex Haley.

Kurt Kurt Vonnegut, Jr. *(1922–)*
American novelist, author of *Slaughterhouse Five* (1969).
> *"I have long felt that any book reviewer who expresses rage and loathing for a novel is preposterous. He or she is like a person who has just put on full armour and attacked a hot fudge sundae."*

Kvasir Kvasir
Mythic Nordic wiseman. After his death, his blood was distilled in a magic cauldron, and gave the art of poetry to anyone who drank it.

Kyrian Kyrian Uwandu *(1973–)*
Nigerian-born Canadian wheelchair athlete.

Laban Laban *trans. white, Genesis 31: 49 (c. 18th century B.C.)*
Old Testament father of Leah and Rachel. Jacob worked for him for seven years to earn marriage to Rachel, but Laban trickily substituted her older, plainer sister, Leah, at the wedding. Jacob then had to work another seven years to get Rachel, too.

Lachlan Lachlan Macquarrie *(1761–1824)*
Scottish soldier and colonial administrator, the "Father of Australia."

Ladislao Ladislao José Biro *(1899–1985)*
Hungarian inventor. With his brother Georg, a chemist, he invented a quick-drying ballpoint pen, still sometimes called a "biro."

Ladon Ladon *trans. he who embraces*
Mythical Greek serpent with the power of human speech. He guarded the golden apples of the Hesperides until Heracles shot him.

LaDonna LaDonna Gaines *(known as Donna Summer) (1948–)*
American disco queen, singer of "Love to Love You Baby" (1976).

Ladoris Ladoris Jackson *(20th century)*
American cook. She filed a lawsuit in 1992 when the *National Inquirer* suggested that Liz Taylor fired her for cooking fattening food.

Lady Lady Bird Johnson *(Mrs. Lyndon B. Johnson), née Claudia Alta Taylor (1912–)*
American political worker.

Laetitia Laetitia Pilkington *(1712–1750)*
English autobiographer. Jonathan Swift called her "the most profligate whore in either kingdom."

Lafayette Lafayette Ronald Hubbard *(known as L. Ron Hubbard) (1911–1986)*
American science-fiction writer, founder of Scientology, author of *Dianetics: The Modern Science of Mental Health* (1950).

Lafcadio Lafcadio Herne *(1850–1904)*
American-born Japanese patriot and journalist.

Laffit Laffit Pincay, Jr. *(1946–)*
Panamanian jockey, five-time winner of the Eclipse Award.

Laidlaw Laidlaw Fletcher (L.F.) Addison *(1878–1949)*
Canadian bandmaster. He directed the 86th Machine Gun Battalion Band in Europe during the Second World War.

Laius King Laius of Thebes *trans. having cattle*
Legendary father of Oedipus. When an oracle predicted his son would kill him, he ordered the infant killed. However, Oedipus was reared by shepherds, and later killed his father unknowingly.

Lakshmi Lakshmi
Hindu goddess of good luck and plenty.

La La Dolores "La La" Brooks *(1946–)*
American girl singer with the Crystals.

Lale Lale Anderson *(1910–1972)*
Danish-born actress. Her song "Three Red Roses" was the "A" side of surprise hit "Lili Marlene," which became popular with both sides during the Second World War.

Lamar Lamar Hunt *(1932–)*
American owner of the Dallas Texans and the Kansas City Chiefs, a member of the Hall of Fame, and one of the founders of the American Football League.

Lamashtu Lamashtu *(8th century B.C.)*
Mesopotamian lion-headed she-demon, the attacker of pregnant women and newborn babies.

Lambert Lambert Hitchcock *(1795–1852)*
American woodworker, builder of the first "designer" rocking chair.

Lamont Lamont Cranston
American "wealthy young man about town," hero of the radio program "The Shadow."
"Who knows what evil lurks in the hearts of men? The Shadow knows."

Lamoraal Lamoraal Egmont, Prince of Gavre *(1522–1568)*
Flemish statesman; hero of Goethes' play *Egmont* (1788).

Lana Lana Turner *originally Julia Jean Mildred Frances Turner (1920–)*
American actress, the original "sweater girl" who was discovered sipping a milkshake at Schwab's drugstore. Asked if she wanted to be

in the movies, she replied, "I don't know, I'll have to ask my mother."

Lance Lance Ito *(20th century)*
American judge in the O.J. (Orenthal James) Simpson murder trial. Before being appointed, he told the Los Angeles *Daily Journal*, "I think you would have to be crazy to want that case."

Lancelot Lancelot Richard Gibbs *(1934–)*
Guyanese-born international cricket player. He gave himself an enlarged knuckle on his middle index finger throwing spinners.

Landrum Landrum Shuttles *(retired 1994)*
American doctor, an expert on *in vitro* fertilization.

Landulf Count Landulf of Aquino *(13th century)*
Italian father of St. Thomas Aquinas, who sent his son to study with the Benedictines at age five.

Langdon Langdon Down *(19th century)*
English doctor, the first to describe "Down's syndrome." He also coined the phrase "idiot savant."

Langston Langston Hughes *(1902–)*
American poet, creator of "Shakespeare in Harlem." He was working as a hotel busboy when discovered by poet Vachel Washington.

> *"I swear to the Lord*
> *I still can't see*
> *Why Democracy means*
> *Everything but me."*

Laocoön Laocoön *trans. very perceptive*
Mythical Trojan son of Priam and Hecuba. When he opposed bringing the Wooden Horse into the city, Athena sent a serpent to crush him and his sons.

Lara "Lara" *(1814)*
English poem by Lord Byron.

Larissa Larissa *(pet name for Lara)*
Heroine of *Doctor Zhivago* (1957) by Boris Pasternak. The character was based on his real-life mistress, Olga Ivinskaya, who spent eight years in labour camps because of her relationship with him.

Larry Larry Holmes *(1949–)*
American boxing champion; "the Easton Assassin."

> *"It's hard being black. You ever been black? I was black once—when I was poor."*

Lars Lars Onsager *(1903–1976)*
Norwegian-born American chemist, winner of a 1968 Nobel Prize.

Lassie Lassie *(real name Pal) (20th century)*
American collie-dog movie star. Actor Peter Lawford described him as "a vicious bastard."

László László Moholy-Nagy *(1895–1946)*
Hungarian-born American photographer, founder of the New Bauhaus School of Design in Chicago.

Latif Latif Jiji *(20th century)*
American owner of a Manhattan grape vine four stories tall. It produces enough grapes to make 150 bottles of wine annually.

Latin Latin Gaius Sallustius Crispus Sallust *(86–34 B.C.)*
Roman historian and politician. He was expelled from the Senate for his decadent lifestyle.

Laucido Laucido Coelho *(20th century)*
Brazilian rancher. In 1901, he owned the world's largest ranch, covering 3,358 square miles.

Laura Laura Ashley, *née Mountney (1925–1985)*
Welsh designer. She and her husband, Bernard, started selling a line of fabric and wallpapers in 1954, but the business didn't take off until she stayed home with her baby, and started making clothes as well.

Laure Laure de Noves *(first glimpsed 1327, d. 1348)*
French aristocrat, wife of Hugo de Sade. She was probably the "Laura" to whom poet Francesco Petrarch directed his series of passionate love poems.

Laurel Laurel Aitken *(1928–)*
Cuban-born British ska singer.

Lauren Lauren Bacall *(originally Betty Joan Perske) (1924–)*
American actress. She made her film debut after director Howard Hawks's wife, Slim, liked her on the cover of *Harper's Bazaar* magazine.

Laurence Laurence Sterne *(1713–1768)*
English author of *The Life and Opinions of Tristram Shandy* (1790).

> *"Now or never was the time."*

Laurens Sir Laurens van der Post *(1906–)*
British explorer of Africa, author of *The Lost World of the Kalahari* (1958).

Laurent Laurent de Brunhoff *(1925–)*
French children's-book author, co-creator with his father, Jean, of Babar the Elephant.

Laurie Laurie Lee *(1914–)*
English poet. He wrote *Cider with Rosie* (1959).

Laurindo Laurindo Almeida *(1917–1995)*
Brazilian bossa-nova guitarist, winner of five Grammy awards.

Lauris Lauris Margaret Elms *(1931–)*
Australian opera singer.

LaVern LaVern Baker *(1928–)*
American R&B singer of "Tweedlee Dee" (1954).

Laverne Laverne Andrews *(1915–1967)*
American popular singer with the Andrews Sisters.

Lavinia Lavinia Stratton *(wed 1863)*
American short person, a performer with P.T. Barnum. She married "General Tom Thumb" (Charles Sherwood Stratton).

Lavrenti Lavrenti Pavlovich Beria *(1899–1953)*
Russian police chief. He organized the Gulag slave-labour system under Joseph Stalin.

Lawrence St. Lawrence *(d. 258)*
Spanish-born deacon of Rome, condemned to death for failing to hand over his treasure to the emperor.

Lawrencia Lawrencia "Bambi" Bembenek *(20th century)*
American convicted murderess. Doubts about her guilt have created books and movies, but not her freedom.

Layla *Layla (1970)*
American album by Derek and the Dominos, featuring the famous full-tile screech slide-guitar solo by Duane Allman.

Lazaro Lazaro Spallanzani *(1729–1799)*
Italian biologist. He discovered the function of spermatozoa and ova.

Lazarus Lazarus Ludwig Zamenhof *(1859–1917)*
Polish peace worker. He invented the language Esperanto (which means "one who hopes").

Top 10 Musical Baby Names

Alexina • Duke • Enheduanna • Euphemia • Frank • Georghe • Hector • Hildegard • Kinky • Luciano

Leadbelly Leadbelly *(originally Huddie Ledbetter) (1889–1949)*
American folk-song colossus.
"I always sings too long and too loud."

Leah Leah Fox *(Ann Leah Fox) (c. 1918–)*
Canadian-born American nurse. After the 1941 attack on Pearl Harbor, she received the first Purple Heart medal given to a woman.

Leander Leander
Mythical Greek lover of lovely Hero. He drowned while swimming across the Strait of Dardanelles to see her.

Lear *The Tragedy of King Lear (1605)*
English play by William Shakespeare.
"How sharper than a serpent's tooth it is to have a thankless child."

Learned Learned Hand *(Billings Learned Hand) (1872–1961)*
Influential American judge. He heard the case for Samuel Goldfish's request to change his name to Samuel Goldwyn.
"A self-made man may prefer a self-made name."

Lebert Lebert Lombardo *(20th century)*
Canadian musician in the Royal Canadian Orchestra led by his brother Guy Lombardo.

Lech Lech Walesa *(1943–)*
Polish trade-union electrician and politician, winner of the Nobel Peace Prize. After hosting George and Barbara Bush at his home in 1989, he commented, "I'm hungry. I was very stupid and talked all the time during the lunch instead of eating."

Leda Leda *trans. lady*

Mythical Spartan queen. She was ravished by the god Zeus after he took the form of a swan.

Lee Lee Iacocca *(Lido Anthony Iacocca) (1924–)*

American head of the Chrysler Corporation.

> *"Being waited on and having your royal ass kissed for so long by so many people can leave you a little helpless."*

Leeza Leeza Gibbons *(1957–)*

American TV host.

Legs Legs Diamond *(originally John Thomas Diamond) (1896–1931)*

American gangster.

Leia Princess Leia

Intrepid heroine of the American science-fiction film *Star Wars* (1977).

Leif Leif Eriksson *(10th century)*

Norwegian sailor. About the year 1000 he landed in "Vinland" in North America.

Leigh Leigh Hunt *(James Henry Leigh Hunt) (1784–1859)*

English poet and essayist.

> *"Abou ben Adhem (may his tribe increase)*
> *Awoke one night from a deep dream of peace,*
> *And saw, within the moonlight in his room,*
> *Making it rich, and like a lily in Bloom*
> *An angel, writing in a book of gold."*

Leland Leland Stanford *(Amasa Leland Stanford) (1824–1893)*

American railway magnate and politician. He and his wife endowed Leland Stanford, Jr., University (now Stanford University) in memory of their only son.

Lella Lella Vignelli *(c. 1935–)*

Italian-born American architect and designer.

Lemon Blind Lemon Jefferson *(originally Clarence Couchman) (c. 1897–1930)*

American blues musician.

Lemuel Lemuel Gulliver

English hero of *Gulliver's Travels* (1726) by Jonathan Swift.

Len Len Deighton *(Leonard Cyril Deighton) (1929–)*

English spy-thriller writer.

Lena Lena Horne *(1917–)*

American performer. She began dancing at the Cotton Club at age sixteen.

> *"You have to be taught to be second class; you're not born that way."*

Leni Leni Riefenstahl *(originally Berta Helene Amalie Riefenstahl) (1902–)*

German actress and filmmaker, notorious for her fabulously effective Nazi propaganda film *Triumph of the Will* (1936).

Lennart Lennart Nilsson *(1922–)*

Swedish photographer, a pioneer of endoscope photography inside the human body.

Lenny Lenny Bruce *(originally Leonard Alfred Schneider) (1925–1966)*

American comedian. Discussing his drug use he said, "I'll die young, but it's like kissing God."

Lenora *Lenora, or the World's Own (1857)*

American book of poetry by Julia Howe, who later wrote "The Battle Hymn of the Republic" (1862).

Lenton Lenton Johnson *(1888–1958)*

American poet.

> *"I am tired of work; I am tired of building up somebody else's civilization."*

Leo Count Leo Nikolayevich Tolstoy *(1828–1910)*

Russian writer and mystic, author of *War and Peace* (1865–69).

> *"All happy families resemble one another, but each unhappy family is unhappy in its own way."*

Leofric Leofric, Earl of Chester *(d. 1057)*

Legendary British husband of Lady Godiva. She rode naked through Coventry to persuade him to lower his taxes.

Leon Leon Spinks *(1953–)*

American boxing champion.

> *"I'm not the greatest, I'm the latest."*

Leona Leona Helmsley *(1920–)*

American hotel owner and tax evader, the "Queen of Mean."

> *"Only the little people pay taxes."*

Leonard Leonard Cohen *Leonard Norman Cohen (1934–)*

Canadian writer and singer, author of *Death of a Ladies' Man* (1978).

> *"Every time I pick up a pen to write something, I don't know if it's going to be a poem, a song or a novel."*

LIBERACE

Leonardo Leonardo da Vinci *(1452–1519)*
Italian architect, engineer, and painter of the *La Gioconda ("Mona Lisa")*, the original "Renaissance Man."
"Intellectual passion drives out sensuality."

Leonhard Leonhard Fuchs *(1501–1566)*
German botanist. The genus "fuchsia" is named after him.

Leonid Leonid Ilyich Brezhnev *(1906–1982)*
Ukrainian-born Soviet politician, the last Stalinist.

Leonidas Leonidas Polk *(1806–1864)*
American soldier. He died opposing the successful march of General William Sherman.

Leontina Leontina Albina, *née Espinosa (1925–)*
Chilean mother of a record-setting fifty-five children, including five sets of triplets.

Leontyne Leontyne Price *(Mary Violet Leontyne Price) (1927–)*
American operatic-soprano.
"Verdi and Mozart are the best vocal pals I have. They like me and I like them."

Leopold Prince Leopold *(1853–1884)*
English son of Queen Victoria. He was born with the help of chloroform anaesthetic, making painkillers socially acceptable for the first time.

Les Les Paul *(originally Lester Polfus) (1916–)*
American guitarist, "the Wizard of Waukesha," inventor of the solid-body electric guitar, and a pioneer of overdubbing.

Lesley Lesley Gore *(1946–)*
American pop singer. She sang "It's My Party" (1963).

Leslie Leslie Howard *(originally Leslie Steiner) (1893–1943)*
British actor, star of the film *The Scarlet Pimpernel* (1935). He initially refused the role of Ashley Wilkes in the film *Gone with the Wind* (1939) on the basis he was too old, but finally accepted, saying, "Money is the mission here, and who am I to refuse it?"

Lester Lester B. Pearson *(Lester Bowles "Mike" Pearson) (1897–1972)*
Canadian prime minister, winner of a Nobel Peace Prize.

Letizia Letizia Bonaparte *(Maria Letizia Bonaparte, née Ramolino) (c. 1749–1836)*
French mother of Napoleon.

Lettice Lettice Cooper *(b. 1897)*
English novelist.
"A cat that lives with a good family is used to being talked to all the time."

Leucosia Leucosia
Mythical Greek Sirens, one of three sisters who sat on the rocky shore and lured sailors to their deaths by singing sweet songs. When Odysseus blocked his sailors' ears with wax to get past, all three sirens drowned themselves in frustration.

Levee Levee
American character in August Wilson's play *Ma Rainey's Black Bottom* (1984).
"Me and my horn . . . we tight. If my daddy knowed I was gonna turn out like this, he would've named me Gabriel."

Levon Levon Helm *(1935–)*
American drummer with the Band.

Lew General Lew Wallace *(Lewis Wallace) (1827–1905)*
American soldier, author of the novel *Ben-Hur* (1880).

Lewis Lewis Carroll *(pen name of Charles Lutwidge Dodgson) (1832–1898)*
British mathematician, author of *Alice's Adventures in Wonderland* (1865).
"'What is the use of a book,' thought Alice, 'without pictures or conversation?'"

Liam Liam Cosgrave *(1920–)*
Irish politician; prime minister 1973–77.

Libby Libby Riddles *(c. 1957–)*
American athlete, the first woman to win the 1,100-mile Alaskan Iditarod Trail Sled Dog Race.

Liberace Liberace *(originally Wladziu Valentino Liberace) (1919–1987)*
American entertainer, maestro of the candelabra. After bad reviews of a 1954 concert, he said,
"What the critics said hurt me very much. I cried all the way to the bank."

Lida Lida Baday *(20th century)*
Canadian fashion designer.

Lighton Lighton Ndefway *(20th century)*
Zambian tennis player.
> *"He beat me because my jock strap was too tight, and because when he serves he farts, and that made me lose my concentration for which I am famous."*

Lil *Diamond Lil (1928)*
American stage play, written and first performed by Mae West.

Lila Lila Bell Wallace, *née Acheson (1889–1984)*
Canadian-born American co-founder, with her husband, DeWitt Wallace, of *The Reader's Digest* magazine.

Lili Lili de Alvarez *(20th century)*
Wimbledon tennis competitor. In 1931, she shocked fans by wearing short trousers instead of a skirt.

Lilian Lilian Mary Baylis *(1874–1937)*
British theatre owner and producer, owner of the Sadler's Wells Theatre.
> *"Oh God, send me some good actors—cheap."*

Liliuokalani Queen Liliuokalani *(Lydia Paki Liliuokalani) (1838–1917)*
Ruler of Hawaii. She was deposed by the United States.

Lillian Lillian Hellman *(Lillian Florence Hellman) (1905–1984)*
American playwright, author of *Pentimento* (1973). Dashiell Hammett portrayed her as detective Nora Charles in his novel *The Thin Man* (1932).
> *"I cannot and will not cut my conscience to fit this year's fashions."*

Lillie Lillie Langtry *(originally Emilie Charlotte, née Le Breton) (1853–1929)*
British actress and royal mistress. She sat for the *Jersey Lily* portrait painted by Sir John Millais.

Lily Lily Tomlin *(Mary Jean Tomlin) (1939–)*
American comedian and actress.
> *"The trouble with the rat race is that even if you win, you're still a rat."*

Lilya Lilya Litvak *(d. 1943)*
Soviet air force pilot. She was awarded the Order of the Red Banner for downing twelve German aircraft.

Lin Lin Bolen *(1941–)*
American television executive, the first female head of daytime programming at a major American network. As a child, she used to create radio dramas with paper dolls.

Lina Lina Basquette, *née Lena Baskette (1907–1994)*
French silent-film star and dog breeder. She claimed to have kicked Adolf Hitler in the groin in 1937 to discourage a sexual advance.
> *"He had a terrible body odour, he was flatulent."*

Lincoln Lincoln C. Andres *(20th century)*
American general. In 1925, he told a congressional committee that 696,933 illegal stills had been seized during four years of Prohibition, observing, "This means that a great many people are distilling."

Linda Linda Lovelace *(20th century)*
American porn actress, star of *Deep Throat*.

Lindsay Lindsay Anderson *(1923–1994)*
Indian-born British film director. He made *If . . .* (1968) about a boarding-school revolt.

Lino Lino Lopez *(1911–1993)*
American rancher, the first American victim of a killer-bee attack.

Linus Linus Pauling *(Linus Carl Pauling) (1901–1994)*
American chemist, winner of a Nobel Prize for chemistry, and a Nobel Peace Prize, the only person to win two unrelated Nobel prizes. He also wrote *Vitamin C and the Common Cold* (1970).

Lionel Sir Lionel Alexander Bethune Pilkington *(also known as Sir Alastair Pilkington) (1920–)*
British inventor of float glass, where molten glass is poured onto a bath of liquid tin to cool, creating a perfect flat finish.

LILY TOMLIN

Lisa Lisa Alther *(1944–)*
American writer, author of *Kinflicks* (1976).
> *"If this was adulthood, the only improvement she could detect in her situation was that she could now eat dessert without eating her vegetables."*

Lise Lise Meitner *(1878–1968)*
Austrian-born physicist, co-discoverer of radioactive protactinium.

Liselotte Charlotte Elizabeth "Liselotte," Duchess of Orleans *(18th century)*
French aristocrat.
> *"The English have always been a wicked race . . . islanders are always more treacherous and wicked than the inhabitants of terra firma."*

Lisette Lisette Lapointe *(20th century)*
Canadian political worker, wife of separatist Quebec premier Jacques Parizeau. Their house was known as the "Elysette" in honour of their extravagant lifestyle.

Lister Lister Sinclair *(1921–)*
British-born Canadian writer, host of the CBC Radio show *Ideas*.
> *"There's a saying that people on their deathbeds never say they wish they spent more time at the office. Except for artists!"*

Little Little Richard *(Richard Wayne Penniman)* *(1932–)*
American rock'n'roll pianist, composer of "Tutti Frutti" (1955).

Liubov Liubov Popova *(Liubov Sergeyevna Popova, née Eding) (1889–1924)*
Russian painter and set designer. She designed textiles for the First State Textile Print Factory in Moscow.

Liv Liv Ullmann *(Liv Johanne Ullmann) (1939–)*
Norwegian actress and film director.

Livy Livy *(Titus Livius) (59 B.C.– A.D. 17)*
Roman historian.
> *"Woe to the vanquished."*

Liz Liz Taylor *(Elizabeth Rosemond Taylor) (1932–)*
English-born American star, winner of an Oscar for *Who's Afraid of Virginia Woolf?* (1966).

Liza Liza Minnelli *(Liza May Minnelli) (1946–)*
American all-round entertainer, winner of an Oscar for her performance in *Cabaret* (1972).
> *"Reality is something you rise above."*

Lizzie Lizzie Borden *(1860–1927)*
American alleged murderess. She was acquitted of the brutal axe-slaying of her father and step-mother, but the poem survives:
> *"Lizzie Borden took an ax*
> *And gave her mother forty whacks*
> *And when she saw what she had done*
> *She gave her father forty-one."*

Llewellyn Llewellyn ap Iorwerth *(1173–1240)*
Welsh prince, battler of the Normans.

Lodovico Lodovico Visconti *(Lodovico Tullio Gioacchino Visconti) (1791–1853)*
Italian architect. He is responsible for Napoleon's liver-coloured tomb in Paris.

Lodowicke Lodowicke Muggleton *(1609–1698)*
English Puritan tailor, founder of the religious sect of Muggletonians. They denied the Holy Trinity.

Logan Logan Pearsall Smith *(Lloyd Logan Pearsall Smith) (1865–1946)*
American-born British writer.
> *"People say that life is the thing, but I prefer reading."*

Loie Loie Fuller *(originally Marie Louise Fuller) (1862–1928)*
American dancer, the sensation of Paris. She developed a special phospho-rescent treatment for her costumes.
> *"I suppose I am the only person known as a dancer who has a personal prefer-ence for science."*

Lois Lois Lane
American journalist, the fiancée of Clark Kent despite her secret passion for Superman, and without knowing that *Clark Kent is really Superman.*

LIZA MINNELLI

Loki Loki
Nordic tricky mythic hero.
Lola Lola Montez *(originally Marie Delores Eliza Rosanna Gilbert) (1818–1861)*
Irish-born dancer and international adventuress.
  "I was always notorious, never famous."
Lolita Lolita *(1959)*
American novel by Vladimir Nabokov, a *succès de scandale.*
Lolly Lolly Willowes, or the Loving Huntsman *(1926)*
American novel by Sylvia Townsend Warner. It was the first selection of the Book-of-the-Month Club.
Lon Lon Chaney *(Alonzo Chaney) (1883–1930)*
American silent screen star, "the Man of a Thousand Faces." He played the title role in *The Hunchback of Notre Dame* (1923).
Lonesome "Lonesome" George Weiss *(1894–1972)*
American baseball executive, member of the Hall of Fame; a shy, dull, penny-pincher who led the Yankees to win ten of twelve pennants. It was his wife who said, "I married George for better or worse, but not for lunch."
Longstreet Longstreet *(pen-name of Mrs. C. Gildersleeve) (19th century)*
English poet.
  "She's no prouder with her coachman
  Than am I
  With my blue-eyed, laughing baby
  Trundling by.'
Longus Longus *(5th century)*
Greek author of *Daphnis and Chloë,* the only known Greek romance in prose rather than poetry.
  "He is so poor that he could not keep a dog."
Loni Loni Anderson *(1946–)*
American actress, author of *My Life in High Heels* (1995); Burt Reynolds responded to her appearance in their bedroom one night clad in new fancy lingerie with, "What the hell do you think I am? A stud service?"

Lonnie Lonnie Donegan *(originally Anthony James Donegan) (1931–)*
Scottish teen idol, singer of "Does Your Chewing Gum Lose Its Flavour?" (1961).
Lonny Lonny Frey *(Linus Richard Frey) (1910–)*
American baseball infielder with the Reds, an All-Star.
Lorelei Lorelei Lee
American heroine of Anita Loos's novel *Gentlemen Prefer Blondes.*
  "Diamonds are a girl's best friend."
Lorena "Lorena" *(18th century)*
Popular American Civil War song by Henry de Lafayette Webster.
  "The years creep slowly by, Lorena,
  The snow is on the grass again."
Lorenz Lorenz Hart *(1895–1943)*
American songwriter, composer of "Bewitched, Bothered and Bewildered" and "The Lady Is a Tramp," from the musical *Babes in Arms.*
Lorenzo Lorenzo de Medici *(1449–1492)*
Renaissance ruler of Florence, "il Magnifico."
  "How beautiful is youth, that is always slipping away."
Lores Lores Bonney *(1898–1994)*
English-born Australian aviator who flew alone from London to Australia in 1933. Before leaving, she prepared advance menus for all of her husband's meals during her absence.
Loretta Loretta Lynn *(originally Loretta Webb) (1935–)*
American country singer, author of the autobiography *Coal Miner's Daughter* (1980). Married at age thirteen, she became the first female millionaire in country music.
Lorna Lorna Mills *(1916–)*
American banker, the first female president of an American federal savings and loan company. She started work as a stenographer.
Lorne Lorne Greene *(1915–1987)*
Canadian actor. He ruled the ranch on the American TV series "Bonanza" (1959–73).
Lorraine Lorraine Hansberry *(1930–1965)*
American playwright, author of *Raisin in the Sun* (1959).

Lot Lot *trans. a covering, Genesis 11: 27*
(c. 18th–16th century B.C.)
Old Testament nephew of Abraham who protected two strangers from a lusty crowd. The
strangers proved to be angels, who warned him
to flee the destruction of Sodom. Lot obeyed,
but his wife looked back and was turned into a
pillar of salt.

Lothar Lothar Lambert *(20th century)*
German film director.

Lothario Lothario
Decadent English character in Nicholas Rowe's
novel *The Fair Penitent* (1703). His character
inspired equally rakish Lovelace in Samuel
Richardson's *Clarissa* (1748).

Lothrop Lothrop Withington, Jr. *(20th century)*
American student. In 1939, he swallowed a live
goldfish to win a ten-dollar bet, starting a
national craze.

Lotta Lotta Dempsey *(1905–1983)*
Canadian journalist. One of her first interviews
was with politician Charlotte Whitton, who
kindly supplied both questions and answers
when she realized how inexperienced Lotta was.

Lottaringo Lottaringo Stufa *(13th century)*
Italian Servite prior, the successor of St. Philip
Benizi.

Lotte Lotte Lenya *(originally Karoline Wilhelmine
Blamauer) (1898–1981)*
Austrian cabaret star, the wife of Kurt Weill. Her
voice was described as "one octave lower than
laryngitis."

Lottie Lottie Dod *(Charlotte Dod) (1872–1960)*
English tennis player.
*"Pray do not call me 'Lottie.' My name is
Charlotte and I hate to be called 'Lottie' in public."*

Lou Lou Gehrig *(Henry Louis Gehrig, originally
Ludwig Heinrich Gehrig) (1903–1941)*
American first baseman for the Yankees, a member of the Hall of Fame. He played 2,130 consecutive games before falling ill with motorneuron
disease, now known as "Lou Gehrig's disease."

Loudon Loudon Wainwright II *(1946–)*
American country singer, composer of "Dead
Skunk in the Middle of the Road" (1972).

Louella Louella Parsons, *née Oettinger (1893–1972)*
American gossip columnist, author of *The Gay
Illiterate* (1944). Writer Paul O'Neil described her
sitting up all night on the telephone, "interpret-
ing the denials of those she was interrogating as
the great horned owl interprets the squeaking
of distant mice."

Louis Louis Pasteur *(1822–1895)*
French chemist, the father of bacteriology and
the inventor of both vaccination and "pasteur-
ized" milk.
*"Wine is the most healthful and most hygienic
of beverages."*

Louis-Ferdinand Louis-Ferdinand Céline *(pseudonym
of Dr. L.-F. Destouches) (1894–1961)*
French doctor, Nazi collaborator, and black
visionary novelist, author of *Death on the
Installment Plan* (1936).
"I piss on you all—from a considerable height."

Louisa Louisa May Alcott *(1832–1888)*
American novelist, author of *Little Women*
(1868). She once described her work as "moral
pap for the young."

Louise Louise Poirier *(20th century)*
Canadian designer in 1994 of the Wonderbra, a
push-up engineering assembly of fifty-four
pieces of strap and fabric. In England it is marketed with the slogan, "Look me in the eyes and
tell me you love me."

Lourdes Lourdes Flores *(1959–)*
Peruvian politician.
*"The question I am asked most often is,
'Why aren't you married?' People tell me if I
want to win I should project a more motherly
image. Well I'm not a mother and I am still
very happy."*

Lowell Lowell George *(1945–1979)*
American guitarist and songwriter with the
band Little Feat.

Luc Luc Montagnier *(1932–)*
French virologist. He and American Robert C.
Gallo simultaneously discovered the AIDS virus.

Luca Luca della Robbia *(c. 1400–1482)*
Florentine Renaissance sculptor.

LUCILLE
BALL

Lucan Lucan *(Marcus Annaeus Lucanus) (39–65)*
Roman poet, a foe of the Emperor Nero.
"Boldness is a mask for fear."

Lucasta "To Lucasta on Going to the Wars" *(1649)*
English Cavalier poem by Richard Lovelace, written for Lucy Sacheverell.

Luchino Count Luchino Visconti *(1906–1976)*
Italian film director, creator of *Death in Venice* (1971).

Lucia *Lucia di Lammermoor (1835)*
Popular Italian opera by Gaetano Donizetti.

Lucian Lucian Freud *(1922–)*
German-born British painter, grandson of Sigmund Freud.

Luciano Luciano Pavarotti *(1935–)*
Italian tenor. He gave up schoolteaching to become an international star.

Lucie Lucie Rie *(1902–)*
Austrian-born English potter.

Lucien Lucien Bouchard *(1938–)*
Canadian politician, an avid Quebec separatist.
"[My young sons] hate the word 'referendum.' They hate it. They spit when they pronounce it."

Lucienne Lucienne Day *(20th century)*
English textile designer of the *Calyx* pattern (1951).

Lucile Lucile Grahn *(1819–1907)*
Danish ballerina. A street in Munich is named for her.

Lucilia Lucilia *(1st century B.C.)*
Roman wife of poet Lucretius. She may have accidentally killed him with a love potion.

Lucille Lucille Ball *(Lucille Désirée Ball) (1910–1989)*
American situational comedienne, star of "I Love Lucy" (1951–55).
"The secret of staying young is to live honestly, eat slowly, and lie about your age."

Lucinda Lucinda
Close friend of Don Quixote in Miguel de Cervantes's novel *Don Quixote* (1605).

Lucius Lucius O'Brien *(19th century)*
Canadian landscape painter.

Lucky Lucky Luciano *(originally Salvatore Luciania) (1897–1962)*
Sicilian-born American gangster. He died of a heart attack in an airport in Naples while meeting a movie producer to discuss making a film of his life.

Lucretia Lucretia Mott, *née Coffin (1793–1880)*
American activist, a Quaker minister, abolitionist, and women's suffrage worker.
"We hold these truths to be self-evident, that all men and women are created equal."

Lucrezia Lucrezia Borgia *(1480–1519)*
Italian patron of the arts. She probably never poisoned anyone, despite her reputation.

Lucy Lucy Stone *(1818–1893)*
American feminist. "Doing a Lucy Stone" became slang for keeping your own name after marriage, after she married Henry Brown Backwell yet kept her original name.

Ludolph Ludolph Christian Treviranus *(1779–1864)*
German naturalist. He discovered intercellular spaces.

Ludovico Ludovico Ariosto *(1474–1533)*
Italian poet, author of *Orlando Furioso* (1532).
"Natura il fece, e poi ruppe la stampe."
("Nature made him, then broke the mould.")

Ludwig Ludwig van Beethoven *(1770–1827)*
German composer extraordinaire.

Lui Lui Saulian *(20th century)*
Chinese mother in 1953 of record-setting quintuplets, who weighed a total of 25 pounds.

Luigi Luigi Galvani *(1737–1798)*
Italian physiologist, the discoverer of animal electricity through his experiments making frog legs jump with electric shocks. Hence, the verb "to galvanize."

Luis Luis Buñuel *(1900–1983)*
Spanish film director.
"I am still an atheist, thank God."

Luise Luise Rainier *(1909–)*
Austrian-born American actress, winner of an Academy Award for *The Great Ziegfeld* (1936).

Lujo Lujo Brentano *(1844–1931)*
German political economist, winner of the 1927 Nobel Peace Prize.

Luke St. Luke *(1st century)*
Greek doctor, painter, and gospel writer, patron of painters and physicians.

Lula Lula
American road-queen heroine of the David Lynch film *Wild at Heart* (1990).

Lulu Lulu *(originally Marie McDonald McLaughlin Lawrie)* *(1948–)*
Scottish pop singer, co-star of *To Sir with Love* (1967), for which she sang the title song.

Lumpy Edward "Lumpy" Stevens *(18th century)*
English Surrey cricket player. He introduced the third stump.

Lute Lucius Curtis "Lute" Pease *(1869–1963)*
American cartoonist, winner of the Pulitzer Prize. Most of his work is set in the Klondike.

Luther Luther Burbank *(1849–1926)*
American naturalist, breeder of new varieties of fruits and flowers.
> *"It is well for people who think to change their minds occasionally to keep them clean."*

Luziah Luziah Ismail-Hennessy *(1955–)*
Parisian socialite.

Lya Lya Graf *(d. c. 1937)*
German-born American circus dwarf. She returned home to Germany in 1933, to be dispatched to a concentration camp for the crime of being short.

Lydia Lydia E. Pinkham *(1819–1883)*
American patent-medicine creator of 40-proof alcoholic "Lydia E. Pinkham's Vegetable Compound." In 1925, annual revenues were US$3.8 million.

Lyle Lyle Lovett *(1958–)*
American country singer.

Lyman Lyman Beecher *(1775–1863)*
American Presbyterian, father of Harriet Beecher Stowe.

Lyn Lyn "Broadway" Lary *(1906–1973)*
American baseball shortstop with the Yankees. In 1931, he made a mistake that cost Lou Gehrig the home run title for the season, when he left the basepath and crossed his path.

Lynda Lynda Barry *(20th century)*
American cartoonist, creator of *Ernie Pook's Comeek.*

Lyndon Lyndon Johnson *(Lyndon Baines Johnson)* *(1908–1973)*
American president.
> *"Being president is like being a jackass in a hailstorm. There's nothing to do but stand there and take it."*

Lynette Lynette "Squeaky" Fromme *(1948–)*
American failed assassin. In 1975, she tried to kill President Gerald Ford.

Lynn Lynn Redgrave *(1943–)*
British actress, star of *Georgy Girl* (1966).

Lynryd Lynryd Skynryd *(1970–1987)*
American rock band.

Lynton Lynton Boggess *known as Dusty Boggess* *(1904–1968)*
American baseball umpire. He was buried with a souvenir baseball autographed by every umpire he'd worked with.

Lyonel Lyonel Charles Adrian Feininger *(1871–1956)*
American cartoonist, a teacher at the Bauhaus.

Lysander Lysander
Athenian lover of Hermia in William Shakespeare's play *A Midsummer Night's Dream* (1595–96).

Lysistrata Lysistrata *(411 B.C.)*
Greek play by Aristophanes. The heroine persuades all the women of Athens and Sparta to refrain from sex until their husbands stop the war.

Lytton Lytton Strachey *(Giles Lytton Strachey)* *(1880–1932)*
English biographer, author of the disrespectful *Eminent Victorians* (1918).
> *"Discretion is not the better part of biography."*

M

M 'M'
British civil servant, the associate of Secret Agent 007, James Bond.

Ma Ma Rainey *(originally Gertrude Melissa Nix Pridgett (1886–1939)*
American singer, the first great female blues singer.
> *"I can't tell you about my future, so I'm going to tell you about my past."*

Mab "Queen Mab" *(1813)*
Idyllic English poem by Percy Bysshe Shelley.

Mabel Mabel Gillespie *(1877–1923)*
American secretary, first president of the Stenographers' Union.

Mac Mac Wiseman *(originally Malcolm B. Wiseman) (1925–)*
American country-folk singer.

Macaulay Macaulay Culkin *(1980–)*
American child actor.

Macbeth *The Tragedy of Macbeth (1605)*
English play by William Shakespeare. It is considered bad luck by actors to mention the name of this "Scottish play."

Maccabeus Judas Maccabeus *(2nd century B.C.)*
Judean rebel leader of the Maccabean revolt against the Seleucids. His name means "the hammer."

MacDonald MacDonald Carey *(1913–1994)*
American actor. He played the same character on the soap opera "Days of Our Lives" from 1965 until his death twenty-nine years later.

Macfarlane Sir Macfarlane Burnett *(originally Frank Macfarlane Burnett) (1899–1985)*
American immunologist, co-winner of a Nobel Prize for his work on antibody production.

Machine Machine Gun Kelly *(originally George R. Kelly) (1897–1954)*
American bootlegger. His wife, Kathryn, bought him a machine-gun because he was such a notorious cream puff; later he became known as "Pop Gun Kelly."

Mack Mack Sennett *(originally Mikall Sinnott) (1880–1960)*
Canadian-born American slapstick filmmaker, creator of the Keystone Kops. He discovered Charlie Chaplin and Fattie Arbuckle.

Mackay Mackay Hugh Baillie Scott *(1865–1945)*
English Art Nouveau architect.

MacKinlay MacKinlay Kantor *(1904–)*
American writer, winner of a 1956 Pulitzer Prize.

Macrina St. Macrina the Elder *(c. 270–340)*
Roman grandmother of St. Basil the Great and St. Gregory of Nyssa.

Macvey Macvey Napier *(1776–1847)*
Scottish lawyer and editor, the first professor of conveyancing at Edinburgh.

Maddalena Maddalena *(20th century)*
Italian cook of Gertrude Stein. She once cured Gertrude of the hiccups by pretending to break a very valuable black Renaissance plate.

Maddy Maddy Prior *(1947–)*
British electric-folk musician with the group Steeleye Span.

Madeleine Madeleine Vionnet *(1876–1975)*
French fashion designer. She invented the bias cut.

Madelon *The Sin of Madelon Claudet (1931)*
American movie. After star Helen Hayes saw its first screening, she begged the studio to sell it to her so that no one would see her shameful performance. They refused, and she won the Oscar.

Madge Madge Bester *(1963–)*
South African short person, at 25½ inches tall the smallest living woman in the world in 1994. Her mother Winnie is 27½ inches tall.

Madhur Madhur Jaffrey *(20th century)*
Indian-born British cook, winner of the James Beard Foundation award for her cookbook *A Taste of the Far East* (1994).

Madonna Madonna *(Madonna Louise Veronica Ciccone) (1958–)*
American rock star. She researched and wrote the book *Sex* (1992).

Mae Mae West *(1893–1980)*
American sex goddess, inventor of the shimmy dance. She

MADONNA

wrote, produced, and directed most of her own material.

> *"I used to be Snow White, but I drifted."*

Maestro Martin "El Maestro" Dihigo *(1905–1971)*
Cuban-born all-round baseball star. He is the only player to have been elected to the Sports Hall of Fame in three different countries: Mexico, Cuba, and the United States.

Maeve Queen Maeve *(or Mab)*
Mythic Celtic fairy ruler.

Maggie Dame Maggie Smith *(1934–)*
British actress, winner of an Oscar for her performance in *The Prime of Miss Jean Brodie* (1969). Watch for her drinks-cart scene in *A Private Function* (1984).

Magister Magister Islebius *(or Johann Agricola, real name Johann Schnitter) (1492–1566)*
German reformer, a Protestant zealot despite his dispute with Martin Luther.

Magne Magne Fuoruholmen *(1962–)*
Norwegian soft-rock keyboard player with the group a-ha.

Magnes Magnes
Mythical Greek youth. He was trapped by the iron nails in his shoe-soles when he walked over a stone mine; hence, the word "magnet."

Magnus Magnus Hirschfeld *(1868–1935)*
German psychiatrist, the proprietor of Magnus Hirschfeld's Institute for Sexual Sciences, noted for its well-equipped S&M parlours.

> *"Love is conflict between reflexes and reflections."*

Mahalia Mahalia Jackson *(1911–1972)*
American gospel singer.

> *"It's easy to be independent when you've got money. But to be independent when you haven't got a thing— that's the Lord's test."*

MAHATMA GANDHI

Mahathir Mahathir bin Mohamad *(ruling 1979–)*
Malaysian prime minister, "the Mad Mahathir." He initiated a "Buy British Last" policy, and initiated trade sanctions against Australia after spotting unflattering Malaysian characters in the film *Turtle Beach* (1992).

Mahatma Mahatma Gandhi *(Mohandâs Karamchand Gandhi) (1869–1948)*
Indian leader and peace worker, assassinated by a Hindu fanatic for urging religious toleration for Muslims in India. Asked for his view on Western civilization, he replied, "I think it would be a good idea."

Mahlon Mahlon Bush Hoagland *(1921–)*
American biochemist. He isolated t-RNA.

Mai Mai Zetterling *(1925–1994)*
Swedish-born actress and film director.

Maila Maila Nurmi *(1921–)*
Finnish-born American actress. She played the role of Vampira in *Plan 9 from Outer Space* (1959), the worst movie ever made according to the Golden Turkey Awards.

Maimonides Maimonides *(Moses Ben Maimon) (1135–1204)*
Spanish-born Egyptian doctor and Jewish philosopher.

> *"Anticipate charity by preventing poverty; assist the reduced fellowman, either by a considerable gift, or a sum of money, or by teaching him a trade, or by putting him in the way of business, so that he may earn an honest livelihood."*

Mainbocher Mainbocher *(originally Main Rousseau Bocher) (1891–1976)*
American fashion designer. He created the colour "Wallis Blue" for the wedding gown worn by Mrs. Simpson for her marriage to the former king of England.

Mairead Mairead Corrigan-Maguire *(1944–)*
Irish peace activist, co-winner of the 1976 Nobel Prize for founding the Northern Ireland Peace Movement.

Maisie "Proud Maisie" *(c. 1828)*
English poem by Sir Walter Scott.

Makiko Makiko Tanaka *(1946–)*
Japanese daughter of a notoriously corrupt politician. In a 1994 poll, she was voted one of the two most trusted people in the country.

Malachi Malachi Favors *(1937–)*
American bass player with the avant-garde jazz group Art Ensemble of Chicago.

Malachy St. Malachy *(or Malachy O'More, or Mael Maedoc Ua Morgair) (1095–1148)*
Irish religious worker, the first Irish-born saint. (St. Patrick was Welsh.)

Malchus Malchus *John 18: 10*
Hebrew slave. The Apostle Peter cut off his right ear during the skirmish at the garden of Gethsemane, and Jesus healed the ear.

Malcolm Malcolm X *(originally Malcolm Little, later El-Hajj Malik El-Shabazz) (1925–1965)*
American black-power activist.
> *"We didn't land on Plymouth Rock, my brothers and sisters—Plymouth Rock landed on us!"*

Malietoa Malietoa I *(19th century)*
Samoan high chief. He banned cricket for being too popular. District teams of two or three hundred men played extended feuds featuring three simultaneous batsmen and fresh bowlers for each ball.

Malik Malik al-Kamil *(18th century)*
Palestinian sultan. He surrendered Jerusalem in the Sixth Crusade.

Malvina Malvina Hoffman *(20th century)*
American sculptor.

Malvolio Malvolio
Cross-gartered, yellow-stocking'd, would-be lover of Olivia in William Shakespeare's *Twelfth Night* (1599–1600).

Mamah Mamah Cheney *(d. 1914)*
American wife of a neighbour of architect Frank Lloyd Wright in Oak Park, Illinois. She ran off with Wright.

Mame *Mame (1974)*
American movie starring Lucille Ball. According to critic Geoff Brown this film had "an elephantine budget matched with miniscule imagination."

Mamie Mamie Eisenhower *(Mamie Doud Eisenhower) (20th century)*
American political worker, wife of President Dwight Eisenhower.

Mamillius Mamillius
Young prince in William Shakespeare's play *The Winter's Tale* (1610–11).
> *"A sad tale's best for winter."*

Man Man Ray *(originally Emmanuel Rudnitsky) (1890–1976)*
American modernist painter and photographer, the inventor of "rayographs" in which objects are placed onto photographic paper, which is then exposed to plain light to develop a pattern of shadows.
> *"All critics should be assassinated."*

Mance Mance Lipscombe *(1895–1976)*
American rural guitarist, the subject of Les Blank's documentary film *A Well-Spent Life* (1971).

Mancocoapac Mancocoapac
Legendary Peruvian founder of the Inca race. He and his sister/wife Mama Oulla Huaca founded the city of Cuzco.

Mandell Mandell Creighton *(1843–1901)*
English historian and bishop.
> *"No people do so much harm as those who go about doing good."*

Mandy Mandy Rice-Davies *(originally Marilyn Rice-Davies) (1944–)*
Welsh call-girl, a friend of Christine Keeler's during the 1963 "Profumo affair." Told at the trial that Lord Astor denied knowing her, she replied, "He would, wouldn't he."

Manfred Baron Manfred von Richthofen *(1882–1918)*
German airman, the "Red Baron," leader of Richthofen's Flying Circus.

Manny Manny Fernandez *(1946–)*
American football defensive tackle with the Miami Dolphins.

Manolo Manolo Barendra *(20th century)*
American jazz-rock fusion musician with the group Spyro Gyra.

Manon Manon Rhéaume *(20th century)*
Canadian hockey player, the world's first professional female goalie. Her father greeted her tears during childhood hockey practice with, "Manon, macramé isn't painful. Choose!"

Mantovani Mantovani *(originally Annunzio Paolo)* *(1905–1980)*
British orchestra leader, composer, and arranger.

Manuel General Manuel Noriega *(Manual Antonio Morena Noriega) (1939–)*
Panamanian politician.

Manuela Manuela Sáenz *(18th century)*
South American mistress of Simón Bolívar.

Manya Manya Joyce *(1905–)*
American reporter, founder of the Florida Senior Olympics.

Marabel Marabel Morgan *(20th century)*
American anti-feminist, author of *The Total Woman*.

Marc Marc Chagall *(1887–1985)*
Russian-born French painter.
> *"Art is the unceasing effort to compete with the beauty of flowers—and never succeeding."*

Marcel Marcel Proust *(1871–1922)*
French writer, author of *À la recherche du temps perdu (Remembrance of Things Past)* (1913–27). He began his self-appointed task of transforming inner reality into written art after the death of his beloved mother.
> *"Happiness is beneficial for the body but it is grief that develops the powers of the mind."*

Marcelle Marcelle St. Cyr *(20th century)*
Canadian sports reporter. In 1975, she and Robin Herman were the first female reporters invited to join the players in the locker room after the game.

Marcello Marcello Mastroianni *(1924–)*
Italian actor, star of *La Dolce Vita* (1960).

Marci Marci Lipman *(1948–)*
Canadian mail-order art T-shirt entrepreneur.

Marcia Marcia Clarke *(20th century)*
American lawyer, the prosecution attorney in the O.J. (Orenthal James) Simpson trial. Asked who her childhood role models were she said, "This is so embarrassing. All I can think of is . . . Hayley Mills."

Marcian Marcian E. "Ted" Hoff *(1937–)*
American inventor. Working at Intel, he decided to break with tradition and pack all of the computer's central processing functions onto a single chip, to be known as a "central processing unit" or CPU. The result was the successful "4004."

Marco Marco Polo *(1254–1324)*
Venetian merchant traveller and author. He was a guest of Kublai Khan in China.

Marcus Marcus Aurelius Antonius *(121–180)*
Roman emperor.
> *"All is ephemeral—fame and the famous as well."*

Marcy Marcy Schwam *(19th century)*
American athlete, the first woman to run up all the stairs at the Empire State Building.

Marduk Marduk
Mesopotamian god of the spring sun, chief deity of the city of Babylon.

Margaret Margaret Sanger *(Margaret Louise Sanger), née Higgins (1883–1966)*
American nurse and activist, creator of the first birth-control clinic after own mother died at age forty-nine, exhausted by eighteen pregnancies. She was jailed at least nine times for distributing contraceptive information.

Margareta Margareta, Queen of Denmark, Norway and Sweden *(1353–1412)*
Danish-born monarch, married at the age of ten to the king of Norway. After her father's death, she was offered the throne of Denmark, and then the throne of Sweden as well.

Margaretha Margaretha Geertruide MacLeod, *née Zelle (stage-name Mata Hari) (1876–1917)*
Dutch-born femme fatale and would-be spy. She was shot by the Germans.

Margarethe Margarethe Meyer Schurz *(1833–1876)*
German-born American child-care worker, the first person to open a private kindergarten. She was inspired by Friedrich Froebel.

Margaux Margaux Hemingway *(1955–1996)*
American actress. Her parents drank a bottle of
Château Margaux wine on the evening of her
conception.

Marge Marge Grenier *(20th century)*
Canadian dairy farmer, inventor of Marge's
Muffs (polar-fleece ear warmers for cows) and
Oyster Ovens (polar-fleece scrotum warmers for
bulls).
> *"It never occurred to me there might be a market
> for them. I was just looking after my own
> babies."*

Margery Margery Allingham *(1904–1966)*
English thriller writer, the creator of detective
Albert Campion.

Margherita Margherita Sarfatti *(1880–1961)*
Italian writer and critic, the influential mistress
of Benito Mussolini. She had the good sense to
dump him before the war ended.

Margot Margot Asquith *(1864–1945)*
English wife of Prime Minister Herbert Henry
Asquith, famous for her lack of tact.
> *"What a pity when Christopher Columbus dis-
> covered America that he ever mentioned it."*

Margriet Margriet Francisca *(1943–)*
Princess of the Netherlands, sister of Queen
Beatrix. She was born in Canada during the war,
in a room declared official Dutch soil by the
Canadian government so that she would
remain eligible for royal succession.

Marguerite Marguerite de Navarre *(or Margaret of
Angoulême, Queen of Navarre) (1492–1549)*
French Renaissance woman, a writer and a
patron of writers.

Maria Dr. Maria Montessori *(1870–1952)*
Italian physician and child educator, the first
woman in Italy to receive a medical degree. In
1907 she opened the first Montessori school for
children in the slums of Rome.
> *"We teachers can only help the work going on, as
> servants wait upon a master."*

Mariamne *Mariamne (1724)*
French play by François Voltaire about the wife
of King Herod.

Marian Marian Wright Edelman *(1939–)*
American civil-rights worker, founder of the
Children's Defense Fund.
> *"The question is not whether we can afford to
> invest in every child; it is whether we can afford
> not to."*

Marianne Marianne Moore *(1888–1972)*
American poet, winner of a Pulitzer Prize. She
loved the Yankees.
> *"Mickey, leaping like the devil, why gild it,
> although deer sound better, snares what was
> beating towards its treetop nest, one-handing
> a souvenir to be, meant to be caught by you
> and me."*

Mariano Mariano de la Paz Graells *(1809–1898)*
Spanish naturalist, discoverer of the Spanish
Moon Moth.

Marie Marie Curie *(originally Manya, or Marja,
Sklodowska) (1867–1934)*
Polish-born French scientist, inventor of the
word "radioactive," co-winner of the 1911
Nobel Prize. She willed a gram of radium to the
University of Paris, on condition that her
daughter have the first right to use it for
research.
> *"One never notices what has been done; one can
> only see what remains to be done."*

Marietta Marietta Peabody Tree *(1917–1991)*
American politician and ambassador.

Marilla Marilla Ricker *(1840–1920)*
American lawyer, in 1871 the first woman to
have her vote accepted in an election. In 1910,
she attempted to run for governor, but her filing
was rejected.

Marilyn Marilyn Monroe *(originally Norma Jean
Mortenson, or Baker) (1926–1962)*
American cinematic sex goddess.
> *"I've been on a calendar but never on time."*

Marin Marin Mersenne *(1588–1648)*
French mathematician and scientist. He
designed the first reflecting telescope.

Marina Marina Warner *(1946–)*
English writer, author of *Alone of All Her Sex* (1976).
> *"Given the Catholic Church's contemporary view
> of the sanctity of marriage, it comes as a surprise*

that matrimony was only definitively proclaimed a sacrament and the Church ceremony decreed an indispensable condition of validity as late as 1563 at the Council of Trent."

Marino Marino Marini *(1901–1980)*
Italian sculptor, noted for his horses with riders.

Mario Mario Puzo *(1920–)*
American novelist, author of *The Godfather* (1969).

> *"He's a businessman. I'll make him an offer he can't refuse."*

Marion Marion Donovan *(20th century)*
American inventor in 1951 of the disposable diaper. She used padding and a piece of shower curtain for the prototype, and marketed it herself when turned down by manufacturers.

Marisela Marisela *(20th century)*
Would-be American immigrant, the illegal employee of political aspirant Michael Huffington, who in 1994 responded to questions about her by saying, "Who among us has not broken the law?"

Marita Marita Bonner *(1899–1971)*
American writer, author of *On Being Young—A Woman—and Colored* (1925).

Marius Marius Petipa *(1818–1910)*
French choreographer. He staged the original *Sleeping Beauty* (1890) for Piotr Tchaikovsky.

Marjo Marjo *(originally Marjolène Morin) (1953–)*
Canadian model and singer-songwriter.

Marjorie Marjorie Faith Barnard *(1897–1987)*
Australian novelist and historian.

Mark Mark Twain *(pen name of Samuel Langhorne Clemens) (1835–1910)*
American river-boat pilot, author of *Huckleberry Finn* (1884).

> *"Among the three or four million cradles now rocking in the land are some which this nation would preserve for ages as sacred things, if we could know which ones they are."*

Marky Marky Mark *(originally Mark Wahlberg) (1971–)*
American hip-hop hunk.

Marla Marla Maples *(1964–)*
American wife of Donald Trump.

Marlee Marlee Matlin *(1965–)*
American actress, winner of an Oscar for *Children of a Lesser God* (1986).

Marlene Marlene Dietrich *(originally Maria Magdalena von Losch) (1901–1992)*
German-born American actress, star of *The Blue Angel* (1930).

> *"Most women set out to try to change a man, and when they have changed him they do not like him."*

Marlin Marlin Hurt *(20th century)*
American radio actor. He played the maid Beulah on "Amos 'n' Andy" (1926–51).

Marlo Marlo Morgan *(b. c. 1950–)*
American doctor, author of the memoir *Mutant Message Down Under* (1991) in which she describes flying to the outback for an Aborigine "awards ceremony," where her hosts burnt her clothes, jewellery, and passport before leading her into the desert.

> *"The woman's facial expression indicated her action was not malicious. It was done in the manner one might offer a stranger some unique sign of hospitality."*

Marlon Marlon Brando *(Marlon "Bud" Brando, Jr.) (1924–)*
American actor, winner of Academy awards for *On the Waterfront* (1954) and *The Godfather* (1972).

> *"An actor's a guy who, if you ain't talking about him, ain't listening."*

Marmaduke Viscount Marmaduke Furness *(1883–1940)*
English shipowner of the Furness Line.

Marni Marni Nixon, *née McEathron* (1929–)
Hollywood ghost singer. She can be heard in *The King and I*, *West Side Story*, and *My Fair Lady*.

Marozia Marozia *(d. 938)*
Roman religious worker, mistress of Pope Serguius II, mother of Pope John XI and grandmother of Pope John XII. She died in prison.

Marquise Marquise Lepage *(20th century)*
Canadian filmmaker of *The Lost Garden: The Life and Cinema of Alice Guy-Blaché* (1995). Alice Guy-Blaché was the first director to make a fictional film—a fairy story about a baby found under a cabbage.

Mars Mars
Roman god of war. The month of March is named after him.

Marsden Marsden Hartley *(1877–1943)*
American painter, the friend of Gertrude Stein and Alfred Steiglitz, a chronic malcontent.

Marse "Marse" Joe McCarthy *(1887–1978)*
American baseball manager for the Yankees, a member of the Hall of Fame. He won three consecutive American League pennants, but his players were so good that opinion held the batboy could have done it.

Marshall Marshall McLuhan *(originally Herbert Marshall McLuhan) (1911–1980)*
Canadian philosopher who claimed that "the medium is the message."
> *"The name of a man is a numbing blow from which he never recovers."*

Mart Mart Stam *(Martinus Adrianus Stam) (1899–1986)*
Dutch architect, designer of a tubular metal chair identical to the one later popularized by Mies van der Rohe.

Martha Martha Stewart *(1942–)*
American "hostess from hell," creator of *Martha Stewart Living* magazine (1994–). She sleeps four hours a day, and gardens by flashlight.
> *"Hyperactivity is not a major fault in anyone."*

Martial Martial *(Marcus Valerius Martialis) (c. 40–c. 103)*
Roman poet and epigrammatist.
> *"Pigeons check and blunt the manly powers: let him not eat this bird who wishes to be amorous."*

Martin Martin Luther King, Jr. *(1929–1968)*
American minister, winner of the 1964 Nobel Peace Prize.
> *"I have a dream that my four little children will one day live in a nation where they will not be judged by the color of their skin but by the content of their character."*

Martina Martina Navrátilová *(1956–)*
Czech-born American tennis player. She ranked No.1 in the world for 381 weeks. Her last game was a black-tie event at Madison Square Garden.

Marty Marty Feldman *(1933–1983)*
American comedian.
> *"Comedy, like sodomy, is an unnatural act."*

Martyn Martyn Ware *(1956–)*
British post-punk ex–computer-nerd synthesizer player with the band the Human League.

Maruthas Maruthas *(d. c. 415)*
Bishop of the city of Maiferkat in Mesopotamia. He brought home so many relics of martyrs that Maiferkat became known as Martyropolis.

Marvin Marvin Gaye *(Marvin Pentz Gay, Jr.) (1939–1984)*
American soul singer and songwriter, composer of "What's Going On" (1971). He was shot by his father.

Mary Lady Mary Wortley Montagu, *née Pierrepont (1689–1762)*
English aristocrat and writer, one of the original intellectual "Bluestockings." She wrote *A Summary of Lord Lyttelton's Advice*:
> *"Be plain in dress, and sober in your diet;*
> *In short, my deary, kiss me, and be quiet."*

Mary Ann Mary Ann Evans *(or Marian Evans, pen-name George Eliot) (1819–1880)*
English novelist, author of *Middlemarch* (1872).
> *"I have a conviction that excessive literary production is a social offence."*

Maryon Maryon Pearson *(20th century)*
Canadian political worker, the wife of Prime Minister Lester B. Pearson.
> *"Behind every successful man stands a surprised woman."*

Masayaki Masayaki Koyama *(played 1952–1975)*
Japanese pitcher for the Hanshin Tigers. In 1965, he walked Daryl Spencer four times with sixteen consecutive balls to ensure that teammate Katsurya Nomura would win the home-run title instead.

Masha Masha (b. 1986)
Russian nickname for the rooftop of Chernoble Unit No. 3, the deadliest reactor. Clean-up volunteers in protective clothing can spend sixty seconds on Masha.

Mashel Mashel Teitelbaum (1921–1985)
Canadian abstract painter.

Masilio Masilio Ficino (1433–1499)
Italian scholar employed by Cosimo de' Medici, translator of the Roman magic guidebook the *Corpus Hermeticum* (1463).

Mason Mason Locke Weems (known as Parson Weems) (1759–1825)
American clergyman and writer, the biographer of George Washington.
> "'George,' said his father, 'do you know who killed that beautiful little cherry tree yonder in the garden?'. . .
> 'I can't tell a lie, Pa; you know I can't tell a lie. I did cut it with my hatchet.'"

Massasoit Massasoit (d. 1661)
American chief of the Wampanoag Indians of Massachusetts. He and his son Metacomet were killed fighting the colonists and his nine-year-old grandson sold into slavery.

Massimo Massimo Vignelli (20th century)
American interior designer.

Mastram Mastram Bapu (camped 1960–82)
Indian fakir. He set a Guinness record for camping out: twenty-two years beside a road in Chitra.

Mathias Mathias Rust (1968–)
West German aviator. On "National Border Guards' Day" 1987 he landed a light plane in Red Square in Moscow, highlighting serious deficiencies in the Soviet air defense system. He was foung guilty of "malicious hooliganism."

Mathilda Mathilda Whistler (Anna Mathilda McNeill Whistler) (19th century)
Whistler's mother. She was painted by her son as *An Arrangement in Grey and Black* (1872).

Matilda Matilda of Tuscany, the "Great Countess" (c. 1046–1115)
Italian ruler. She led her own troops into battle, and at age forty-three married seventeen-year-old Guelf of Bavaria.

Matt Sir Matt Busby (1909–)
British soccer manager.

Matthaeus Matthaeus Pöppelmann (1662–1736)
German architect, designer of the Taschenberg Palais in Dresden.

Matthew Matthew Arnold (1822–1888)
English poet.
> "So Tiberius might have sat,
> Had Tiberius been a cat."

Matthias Matthias Grünewald (real name Matthias Nitharator Gothardt) (c. 1480–c. 1528)
German artist, architect, and engineer.

Matthieu Matthieu Joseph Bonaventure Orfila (1787–1853)
French chemist, the founder of toxicology.

Matti Matti Nykaenen (20th century)
Finnish skier, winner in 1988 of two Olympic gold medals.

Mattie Mattie Silks (1848–1929)
American brothel owner. In 1877, she won a duel fought over her fiancé.

Maud Maud MacBride, née Gonne (1866–1953)
Irish Sinn Féin nationalist, a friend of the poet William Butler Yeats.

Maureen Maureen Forrester (Maureen Katherine Stewart Forrester) (1930–)
Canadian contralto.

Maurice Maurice Chevalier (Maurice-Auguste Chevalier) (1888–1972)
French boulevardier. He sang the song "Thank Heaven for Little Girls" in the film *Gigi* (1958).
> "Old age isn't so bad when you consider the alternative."

Maurillio Maurillio de Zolt (1950–)
Italian cross-country skier. He prepared for his gold medal–winning 1994 relay race by drinking red wine.
> "It is difficult to say how many glasses of wine. If I knew it I would probably get into trouble with my association."

Mauritz Mauritz Stiller *(1883–1928)*
Swedish film director. He discovered Greta
Garbo and took her to Hollywood.

Maury Maury "Mousey" Wills *(1932–)*
American baseball shortstop with the Dodgers,
later a manager for the Mariners. In the minor
leagues, he was so bad that the Topps Chewing
Gum Inc. refused to make a baseball card for
him, but in 1962 in the major leagues he stole
104 bases and was named Most Valuable Player.

Mausolus Mausolus *(d. 353 B.C.)*
Ruler of Caria in Swasia. His widow, Artemisia,
built his design for his "Mausoleum" tomb at
Halicarnassus. It was one of the Seven Wonders
of the ancient world.

Mavis Mavis Gallant, *née Young (1922–)*
Canadian novelist.

Max Max Beerbohm *(Sir Henry Maximilian Beerbohm)*
(1872–1956)
English writer and caricaturist.
> "He was fond of quoting those incomparable
> poets, Homer."

Maxfield Maxfield Frederick Parrish *(1870–1966)*
American painter and cartoonist. Reproductions
do not do justice to his colours.

Maxim Maxim Gorky *(pen name of Aleksei
Maksimovich Peshkov) (1868–1936)*
Russian realist writer, author of *My Childhood*
(1913–14). Visiting the United States, he
described it as "the garbage bin of Europe."

Maximilian Maximilian Schell *(1930–)*
American actor and director, winner of an Oscar
for Best Supporting Actor for *Judgment at
Nuremberg* (1961).

Maximilien Maximilien-François-Marie-Isidore de
Robespierre *(1758–1794)*
French revolutionary. A public accuser early in
the Revolution, he himself died on the guillotine.

Maxine Maxine Hong Kingston *(20th century)*
American writer, author of *The Woman Warrior*.

Maxwell Maxwell Anderson *(1888–1959)*
American playwright.

May May Morris *(1862–1938)*
English designer and embroidery expert, daughter of William Morris.

Maya Maya Lin *(1962–)*
American architect, designer of the low black
Vietnam Memorial in Washington, D.C.

Maybelle Maybelle Mitchell *(1872–1918)*
American feminist, mother of Margaret Mitchell,
who wrote *Gone With The Wind* (1936).
Margaret based the character of Rhett Butler on
Maybelle.

Maybelline "Maybelline" *(1955)*
American rock 'n' roll song by Chuck Berry, his
first big hit.

Maynard Maynard Keynes *(John Maynard Keynes,
1st Baron) (1883–1946)*
English economist.

Mayte Mayte Garcia *(20th century)*
Puerto Rican dancer, in 1996 the bride of the
singer formerly known as Prince.

Maz Lee "Maz" Mazzilli *(1955–)*
American baseball outfielder with the Mets, an
All-Star.

Mazo Mazo de la Roche *(1885–1961)*
Canadian epic novelist.

McLelland McLelland Barclay *(20th century)*
American magazine illustrator. In a 1935 poll of
Princeton University students, he beat out
Rembrandt as the best painter ever.

Meadowlark Meadow George "Meadowlark"
Lemon *(1933–)*
American basketball centre with the Harlem
Globetrotters.

Meat Meat Loaf *(originally Marvin Lee Aday) (1947–)*
American heavy rock singer. He appeared in the
film *The Rocky Horror Picture Show* (1975) as a
corpse served on a platter. Cult audiences
watching shout, "What's for dinner? Oh, no,
Meat Loaf again!"

Medgar Medgar Wiley Evers *(1926–1963)*
American civil-rights worker. He was shot in the
back outside his home.
> "I'm looking to get shot any time I step out of my
> car. . . . If I die, it will be in a good cause. I've
> been fighting for America."

Medusa Medusa *trans. cunning one*
Legendary Greek snake-haired Gorgon whose
glance turned anyone to stone. Perseus managed

to behead her by aiming his sword while looking in a mirror. Greek bakers put her face on ovens to discourage busy-bodies opening the door.

Meg Meg March
One of the sisters in Louisa May Alcott's *Little Women* (1868).

Megan Megan Austin *(1982–)*
American child. She set a world record for number of ancestors alive at her birth: nineteen grandparents, great-grandparents and great-great-grandparents.

Meggie Meggie
Heroine of Colleen McCullough's Australian novel *The Thorn Birds* (1977).

Meghnad Meghnad Saha *(1893–1956)*
Indian astrophysicist. In "Saha's equation" he demonstrated that elements in stars are ionized in proportion to their temperature.

Mehetabel Mehetabel "Hetty" Wright, *née Wesley (1697–1750)*
American poet, the sister of John and Charles Wesley, who founded the Methodist movement. Mehetabel could read the Bible in Greek at age six, but her father married her to an uneducated drunk.

Mel Mel Brooks *(originally Melvin Kaminsky) (1926–)*
American film director, creator of *The Producers* (1968).

Melanie Melanie *(originally Melanie Safka) (1947–)*
American peacenik pop singer.

Melba Melba Pattillo Beals *(c. 1943–)*
American academic, one of the nine children escorted to school by the National Guard in Arkansas in 1957 after the state government refused to allow black children entry.

Melchior King Melchior
Traditionally, one of the Three Magi who visited Jesus as a baby. He brought the gold. Their names are not mentioned in the Bible.

Melina Melina Mercouri *(originally Anna Amalia Mercouri) (1925–1994)*
Greek actress and politician, minister of culture.
"I fell in love with the camera and I think the camera fell in love with me—but I still think my mouth is too big."

Melitta Mrs. Melitta Benz *(20th century)*
German housewife and coffee entrepreneur. In 1908, she cut her first, archetypal, coffee filter from a circle of blotting paper.

Mellissa Mellissa Sanders *(sat 1986–88)*
American performer. She spent 512 days in a room on top of a pole in Indianapolis, setting a Guinness record.

Melmoth *Melmoth, the Wanderer* (1820)
English Gothic novel by Charles Robert Maturin.

Melpomene Melpomene
Legendary Greek Muse of tragedy, one of the nine Muses of the arts. Her symbols are the tragic mask and the platform-soled "buskin" boot worn by Greek actors to make themselves look taller.

Melva Melva
Scottish name invented by James McPherson in his forgeries of "ancient" Ossian poems.

Melvil Melvil Dewey *(1851–1931)*
American librarian, inventor of the "Dewey Decimal" library cataloguing system.

Melville Meville Bissell *(19th century)*
American inventor in 1878 of the carpet sweeper.

Melvin Melvin Franklin *(originally David English) (1943–1995)*
American singer with the Temptations. They sang "My Girl" (1965).

Melvyn Melvyn Douglas *(originally Melvyn Edouard Hesselberg) (1901–1981)*
Hollywood leading man.

Memphis "Memphis" Bill Terry *(1896–1989)*
American baseball first baseman with the Giants, a member of the Hall of Fame. His 1930 batting average was .401.

Memphis Memphis Minnie *(or Lizzie Douglas) (1897–1973)*
American blues guitarist and singer.

Mena Mena
Roman goddess of the monthly periods of women. The words "menses" and "menstruate" derive from her name.

Menachem Menachem Begin *(1913–1992)*
Polish-born Israeli politician. He shared the 1978 Nobel Peace Prize with Anwar Sadat for the Camp David Accords establishing peace with Egypt.

MERYL STREEP

Menaechmus Menaechmus *(4th century B.C.)*
Greek mathematician, tutor to Alexander the Great. He was the first to describe "conic" curves as sections of a cone.

Menander Menander *(342–292 B.C.)*
Greek playwright, creator of the "New Comedy" popular at the time of Alexander the Great.
"I call a fig a fig, a spade a spade."

Mendelson Mendelson Joe *(originally Birrel Josef Mendelson) (1944–)*
Canadian singer-songwriter, artist, and political activist.

Menelaus Menelaus, King of Sparta *trans. might of the people*
Mythical Greek brother of Agamemnon. He was the first husband of the beautiful Helen before she was abducted to Troy, starting the Trojan War.

Merald Merald "Bubba" Knight *(1942–)*
American soul vocalist with Gladys Knight and the Pips.

Merce Merce Cunningham *(1919–)*
American dancer and choreographer.

Mercedes Mercedes Cabanillas *(1948–)*
Peruvian politician.

Mercer Mercer Ellington *(1919–)*
American trumpet player, son of Duke Ellington.

Mercutio Mercutio
Brave friend of Romeo in William Shakespeare's play *Romeo and Juliet* (1594–96).

Mercy Mercy Otis Warren *(1728–1814)*
American poet and historian, author of *History of the Rise, Progress and Termination of the American Revolution* (1805).

Meredith Meredith F. Small *(20th century)*
American anthropologist, author of *What's Love Got to Do with It: The Evolution of Human Mating* (1995)

Meret Meret Oppenheim *(20th century)*
French surrealist artist.

Merian Merian C. Cooper *(1893–1973)*
American filmmaker, co-creator of *King Kong* (1933).

Meriwether Meriwether Lewis *(1774–1809)*
American explorer, one of the leaders of the 1804-1806 Lewis and Clark expedition west of the Mississippi.

Merle Merle Travis *(1917–1983)*
American country composer. His "Travis-style" guitar picking, using the palm of the hand to damp the strings, was widely imitated.

Merlin Merlin
Mythical Welsh bard, magician to King Arthur.

Merovech Merovech *(or Merovias) (5th century)*
Frankish ruler, grandfather of Clovis, and founder of the Merovingian dynasty.

Merric Merric Boyd *(William Merric Boyd) (1888–1959)*
Australian ceramicist.

Merrill Merrill Osmond *(1953–)*
American teen idol, one of the Osmonds.

Merthyr *The Former Miss Merthyr Tydfil (1976)*
Welsh novel by Alun Richards.

Merv Merv Griffin *(1925–)*
American talk show host.

Mervyn Mervyn LeRoy *(1900–1987)*
American film producer, director of the definitive gangster flick *Little Caesar* (1931).

Meryl Meryl Streep *(originally Mary Louise Streep) (1951–)*
American actress, winner of an Oscar for *Sophie's Choice* (1982).

Meshach Meshach *(Babylonian name of Mishael, Daniel 1) (c. 6th century B.C.)*
Old Testament friend cast with Daniel into a fiery furnace by Nebuchadnezzar, and delivered by an angel.

Meskhenit Meskhenit
Egyptian goddess of birth and child rearing.

Methuselah Methuselah *trans. man of the javelin, Genesis 4: 18*
Old Testament oldest person, 969 years old at his death. He had his first son at age 187.

Meyer Meyer Lansky *(1902–1983)*
American gangster.
> *"We're bigger than U.S. Steel."*

Mia Mia Farrow *(originally Maria de Lourdes Villiers Farrow) (1945–)*
American actress. Her failed romance with Woody Allen was the subject of a comic book as well as lawsuits.
> *"I can match bottoms with anyone in Hollywood."*

Micah Micah *(735–665 B.C.)*
Old Testament minor prophet, resident of Judah.

Michael Michael Jackson *(1958–)*
American pop singer.
> *"I'm totally at home on stage. That's where I live. That's where I was born. That's where I'm safe."*

Michaelangelo Michaelangelo Antonioni *(1912–)*
Italian film director of *Blow-Up* (1966).

Michel Michel Foucault *(1926–1984)*
French philosopher.

Michelangelo Michelangelo *(Michelagniolo di Lodovico Buonarroti Simoni) (1475–1564)*
Italian sculptor, painter, and poet, inventor of the "giant order" of classical columns. As a baby, he lived with a nursemaid near a quarry.
> *"I sucked in chisels and hammers with my mother's milk."*

Michelle Michelle Pfeiffer *(1957–)*
American actress.
> *"I used to beat up all the boys. Whenever there was a problem, they would come to me. I was like the Mafia Don of my elementary school."*

Michelozzo Michelozzo di Bartolommeo *(1396–1472)*
Italian architect and sculptor.

Michie Michie Makatani *(20th century)*
Japanese punk bass player, one of the girl trio Shonen Knife.

Mick Mick Jagger *(Michael Philip Jagger) (1943–)*
British rock star.
> *"It's all right letting yourself go, as long as you can let yourself back."*

Mickey Mickey Mantle *(Mickey Charles Mantle) (1931–)*
American switch-hitting baseball player, the fast-living "Commerce Comet." He was clocked at 3.1 seconds from home plate to first base.
> *"For the kids out there . . . don't be like me."*

Mickie Mickie Most *(Michael Peter Hayes) (1938–)*
British pop-music producer of "Mellow Yellow" (1967) for Donovan.

Midas Midas, King of Phrygia *(8th century B.C.)*
Phrygian ruler. It was a different Midas who had the power to turn everything he touched to gold.

Midge Midge Ure *(originally James Ure) (1953–)*
Scottish-born electro-pop singer with the band Ultravox.

Midori Midori Ito *(20th century)*
Japanese figure-skater. She and Tonya Harding were the first women to land triple-axel jumps in competition.

Mieczyslaw Mieczyslaw Horszowski *(1892–1993)*
Polish pianist. His professional career began at age seven with a performance for the Emperor Franz Joseph.

Miep Miep Gies *(c. 1905–)*
Dutch housewife. She smuggled food to Anne Frank and her family in hiding, and after their arrest in 1944, found Anne's diary on the floor.

Mighty Mighty Mouse *(1942–)*
American cartoon superhero created by Paul Terry.
> *"Superheroes get free donuts."*

Mignon Mignon McLaughlin *(20th century)*
American writer, author of *The Second Neurotic's Notebook*.
> *"Nobody listens to anyone else, and if you try it for a while you'll see why."*

Miguel Miguel de Cervantes Saavedra *(1547–1616)*
Spanish poet and soldier. He wrote *Don Quixote* (1605–15) while in prison in La Mancha.
> *"Required in every good lover . . . the whole alphabet . . . Agreeable, Bountiful, Constant, Dutiful, Easy, Faithful, Gallant, Honourable, Ingenous, Kind, Loyal, Mild, Noble, Officious, Prudent, Quiet, Rich, Secret, True, Valiant, Wise . . . Young and Zealous."*

Mik Mik Kaminski *(1951–)*
British rock violinist with the Electric Light Orchestra or "ELO."

Mika Mika Lehtonen *(20th century)*
Finnish taxi patron. In 1991, she and Juhani Saramies set a Guinness record for the world's longest taxi ride: to Spain and back.

Mikasa Prince Mikasa *(1926–)*
Japanese brother of Emperor Hirohito, author of *Reflections of a Japanese on the Sino-Japanese War.*

Mike Mike Nesmith *(1942–)*
American performer, one of the lads in the TV series "The Monkees" (1966–68).
> "You can't get the Monkees back together as a rock'n'roll group. That would be like Raymond Burr opening up a law practice."

Mikhail Mikhail Timofeyevich Kalashnikov *(1920–1993)*
Soviet inventor of the "Avtomat Kalashnikova," AK-47 machine gun.

Mikis Mikis Theodorakis *(originally Michael Theodorakis) (1925–)*
Greek political activist and film composer. He wrote the music for *Zorba the Greek* (1964) while in prison.

Miklós Miklós Rózsa *(Miklós Nicholas Rózsa) (1907–)*
Hungarian Hollywood composer. He composed music for the film *The Lost Weekend* (1945), and the theme for the TV series "Dragnet" (1952–70).

Mila Mila Mulroney, *née Pivnicki (20th century)*
Canadian political worker, wife of Prime Minister Brian Mulroney, noted for paying her bills late.

Milan Milan Kundera *(1929–)*
Czechoslovakian novelist, author of *The Unbearable Lightness of Being* (1984).

Milburga Milburga *(d. c. 700)*
English abbess. She had the gift of levitation.

Mildred Mildred E. Gillars *(originally Mildred Elizabeth Sisk) (1900–1988)*
American propaganda worker, "Axis Sally." She was convicted of wartime treason for her broadcasts on behalf of the Nazis and served twelve years in prison.
> "Hello, gang. Throw down those little old guns and toddle off home. There's no getting the Germans down."

Miles Miles Davis *(Miles Dewey Davis) (1926–1991)*
American jazz trumpeter, one of the founders of bebop.
> "When you work with great musicians, they are always a part of you . . . their spirits are walking around in me, so they're still here and passing it on to others."

Miles Miles Franklin *(originally Stella Maria Sarah Miles Franklin) (1879–1954)*
Australian novelist. She wrote *My Brilliant Career* (1901).

Mileva Mileva Maric *(divorced 1919)*
Serbian wife of Albert Einstein. She joined a physics class late, so he lent her his notes to let her catch up. She returned them with an error corrected.

Millard Millard Fillmore *(1800–1874)*
American politician, the thirteenth president.
> "It is not strange . . . that such exuberance of enterprise should cause some individuals to mistake change for progress, and the invasion of the rights of others for national prowess and glory."

Millicent Dame Millicent Fawcett, *née Garrett (1847–1929)*
British suffragist and educational reformer.
> "We believe that men cannot be truly free so long as women are held in political subjection."

Milner Milner Connorton Gray *(1899–)*
British graphic designer.

Milo Milo of Croton *(6th century B.C.)*
Greek wrestler. He won five successive Olympic Games.

Miloš Miloš Forman *(1932–)*
Czechoslovakian-born American filmmaker. He won an Oscar for *One Flew Over the Cuckoo's Nest* (1975).

Milou Milou *"Snowy" (1940s–)*
Belgium cartoon dog, the companion of Tintin.

Milt Milt Jackson *(originally Milton Jackson) (1923–)*
American jazz vibraphone player.

Milton Milton Obote *(Apollo Milton Obote) (1924–)*
Ugandan politician. He was deposed by Idi
Amin, then returned after Amin was removed.

Mimi Mimi Pond *(20th century)*
American writer, author of *The Valley Girl's
Guide to Life* (1982).
> *"Being popular is important. Otherwise, people
> might not like you."*

Mina Mina Curtiss *(20th century)*
American biographer of Marcel Proust. She had
sex with the aged Prince Bibesco just to get his
Marcel Proust letters.
> *"After all, I figured, the letters are unique and
> there are plenty of women who must like this
> kind of approach or he wouldn't have continued
> using it."*

Minerva Minerva
Roman goddess of wisdom.

Minette Minette *(Henrietta Anne, Duchess of Orléans)
(1644–1670)*
French sister of Charles II, who helped conspire
with the French.

Minik Minik, "New York's Eskimo Boy"
(1891–1918)
Greenland-born Inuit taken from the High
Arctic by Robert Peary and displayed for money.
After the death of his father, Qisuk, Minik was
adopted by the Superintendent of the American
Museum of Natural History, where, unknown to
Minik, his father's bones were stored as artifacts.
See *Give Me My Father's Bones* (1986) by Kenn
Harper.

Minnehaha Minnehaha
Character in Henry Wadsworth Longfellow's
poem "Hiawatha" (1855). He invented the
name.

Minnie "Minnie the Moocher" *(1931)*
American song by Cab Calloway. He invented
the "hi-de-hi-de-ho" chorus when he forgot the
words while performing live on radio.
> *"I had to fill the space, so I started to scat-sing
> the first thing that came into my mind."*

Minor Minor White *(1908–1976)*
American photographer and editor.

Minos King Minos II of Crete *trans. the moon's
creature*
Mythical Cretan ruler, husband of Pasiphae,
father of Ariadne, and the creator of the maze
for the bull monster Minotaur.

Mira Mira Sorvino *(20th century)*
American actress. Originally rejected for the
hooker role in *Mighty Aphrodite* (1995), she flew
to London on her own and appeared at Woody
Allen's hotel convincingly dressed as a prostitute.

Miranda Miranda
Charming daughter of Prospero in William
Shakespeare's play *The Tempest* (1611–12).

Miriam Miriam O'Brien Underhill *(1900–1976)*
American mountaineer, author of *Give Me the
Hills* (1971). She and Alice Damesme were the
first women to climb the Matterhorn.

Miroslav Miroslav Vitous *(1947–)*
Czech-born jazz-rock musician with the group
Weather Report.

Misha Sir Misha Black *(1910–1977)*
Russian-born British design educator and writer.

Mishael Mishael *trans. who is God's, Exodus 6: 22
(c. 13th century B.C.)*
Old Testament uncle of Moses. He removed the
bodies of Aaron's sons from the Tabernacle after
they were struck dead for using the wrong
incense.

Misia Misia Sert *(originally Marie-Sophie-Olga
Zénaïde Godebska) (20th century)*
Russian-born Polish-French society hostess, a
"rough and ready princess." She inspired Marcel
Proust's Madame Verdurin, and was present at
the deathbed of Serge Diaghilev.

Mississippi Mississippi John Hurt *(1893–1966)*
American finger-picking guitarist.

Mister Mister Ed *(active 1961–1965)*
American horse actor, star of his own TV series.
> *"This is America, you can't make a horse testify
> against himself."*

Mistinguett Mistinguett *(stage-name of Jeanne-Marie
Bourgeois) (1875–1956)*
French music-hall artiste.

Mitch Mitch Miller (*originally Mitchell William Miller*) (*1911–*)
American sing-along musician and record producer.
> *"Rhythm and blues is not music, it's a disease."*

Mitchell Mitchell Feigenbaum (*1945–*)
American mathematician, the discoverer of the Feigenbaum Number, universal chaotic constant (approximately 4.669201609102990).

Mithras Mithras *or Mitra*
Persian god. His worship, Mithraism, was overtaken in popularity only by Christianity. It was a men-only religion; women worshipped Cybele.

Mitsou Mitsou (*originally Mitsou-Miel-Rioux Gélinas*) (*1970–*)
Québécois chanteuse.

Mitzi Mitzi Gaynor (*originally Franceska Mitzi Marlene de Chamey von Gerber*) (*1930–*)
American performer, star of *South Pacific* (1958)

Mnemosyne Mnemosyne *trans. memory*
Mythical Greek mother of the nine Muses of the arts.

Moana Moana Pozzi (*1961–1994*)
Italian hard-core porno-film actress. She died redeemed, reading the *Confessions of Saint Augustine*.

Moby Moby Grape (*1967–1993*)
American pop band.

Mocker Mocker (*1914–1935*)
American carrier pigeon. He earned the American Distinguished Service Cross and the French Croix de Guerre in the First World War for delivering a vital message from the Hindenburg line despite a shrapnel wound.

Modest Modest Petrovich Mussorgsky (*1839–1881*)
Russian composer.

Moe Moe Koffman (*Morris Koffman*) (*1928–*)
Canadian bebop jazz flautist and composer.

Mohammad Shah Mohammad Reza Pahlavi (*1919–1980*)
Iranian ruler. He died in exile.

Moira Moira Knox (*20th century*)
British city councillor. The Edinburgh Festival awards an annual Moira Award in honour of her sight-unseen condemnations of many "fringe" acts.
> *"A sticker saying 'disapproved of by Moira Knox' is a sure-fire way to sell tickets."*

Moises Moises Simons (*1888–1945*)
Cuban composer of the song "El Manisero" ("The Peanut Vendor") (1931).

Molefi Dr. Molefi Kete Asante (*originally Arthur Lee Smith*) (*1942–*)
American scholar, founding editor of *The Journal of Black Studies*.

Molière Molière (*pseudonym of Jean Baptiste Poquelin*) (*1622–1673*)
French playwright.
> *"She is laughing in her sleeve at you."*

Molly Molly Brown, *née Tobin* (*1867–1932*)
American nouveaux-rich social climber, the "Unsinkable Molly Brown." In her hour of triumph, she bullied ladies on the sinking *Titanic* into boarding a lifeboat.
> *"Sure, I'm eccentric. But I have a heart as big as a ham."*

Momo Sam "Momo" Giancana (*1908–1975*)
American gangster. He was arrested seventy times, and convicted thrice.

Momus Momus
Mythical Greek critic. He lived on Mount Olympus, where he constantly found fault with all of the gods until they banished him.

Mona "Mona Lisa" (or *La Giaconda*) (*c. 1540*)
Ageless portrait by Leonardo da Vinci.

Monbo Bill "Monbo" Monboquette (*1936–*)
American baseball pitcher for the Red Sox, an All-Star.

Mongin Mongin-Ferdinande de Saussure (*1857–1913*)
Swiss founder of modern linguistics with its emphasis on language as a system of signs.

Monica Monica Seles (*1973–*)
German tennis player. In 1992, a deranged fan stabbed her with a kitchen knife.

Montague Montague Alfred "Monty" Noble (*1873–1940*)
Australian cricket player. A maverick, he kept his face clean-shaven during the 1900s, despite the fashion for large moustaches.

Montezuma Montezuma II *(1466–1520)*
Last Aztec emperor of Mexico. His last descendant died in New Orleans in 1836.

Montgomery Montgomery Clift *(originally Edward Montgomery Clift) (1920–1966)*
American actor specializing in brooding outsiders. See *From Here to Eternity* (1953).

Monty "Monty Python's Flying Circus" *(20th century)*
British cult television program.
　　"Nobody expects the Spanish Inquisition."

Moon Unit Moon Unit Zappa *(1968–)*
American daughter of Frank Zappa, the vocalist on his hit song "Valley Girl" (1982).
　　"My father used to tour six or nine months of the year."

Moose Moose Krause *(Ed Krause) (1913–1992)*
American football player, later a basketball player for Notre Dame. The three-second rule was developed specifically to stop him.

Morarji Morarji Desai *(1896–1995)*
Indian prime minister. He attributed his long life to celibacy and a diet of fruit, milk, and his own urine.

Morand St. Morand *(d. c. 1115)*
German noble-born Benedictine monk. He is the patron of wine growers because he ate nothing except a bunch of grapes during one Lent fast.

Mordecai Mordecai Richler *(1931–)*
Canadian novelist, author of *The Apprenticeship of Duddy Kravitz* (1959).
　　"Kids find adults frightening."

Morg Morg Murphy *(1867–1938)*
American baseball catcher for the Reds. He is best remembered for using a buried wire to relay "stolen" signals to the third-base coach.

Morgan Morgan Forster *(better known as Edward Morgan "E.M." Forster) (1879–1970)*
English novelist and critic.

MUHAMMAD ALI

"I seem fated to pass through the world without colliding with it or moving it. . . . I don't die—I don't fall in love."

Morgan Morgan la Fée *(or Morgan le Fay)*
Mythic English villainess, half-sister of good King Arthur.

Moritz Moritz Traube *(1826–1894)*
German chemist. He created semi-permeable membranes to measure osmotic pressure.

Mork Mork
American TV alien, star of the series "Mork and Mindy" (1978–82).
　　"One man's ceiling is another man's floor."

Morley Morley Callaghan *(Morley Edward Callaghan) (1903–1990)*
Canadian novelist.

Morrie Morrie "Snooker" Arnovich *(1910–1959)*
American baseball outfielder with the Phillies, an All-Star.

Morris Morris William Travers *(1872–1961)*
British chemist. He and Sir William Ramsay discovered the inert gases krypton, xenon, and neon.

Mort Mort Shuman *(1938–1991)*
American songwriter, half of the team of Pomus and Shuman, who wrote "Save the Last Dance for Me" (1960).

Morticia Morticia Addams
Fictional macabre matriarch. She may be seen in the film *Addams Family Values* (1993).
　　"Life is not all thorns and singing vultures."

Mortimer Sir Mortimer Wheeler *(Robert Eric Mortimer Wheeler) (1890–1976)*
English archaeologist, author of the autobiography *Still Digging* (1955).

Morton Morton Shulman *(1926–)*
Canadian doctor and pharmaceutical entrepreneur.

Mose Mose Allison *(1927–)*
American blues pianist, creator of "Middle-Class White Boy" (1982).

Moses Moses Znaimer *(20th century)*
Canadian television mogul, the creator of Toronto's CITY-TV.

Moshe Moshe Dayan *(1915–1981)*
Israeli soldier and politician.

Mosquito Sir Patrick "Mosquito" Manson *(1844–1922)*
Scottish doctor, the first person to suspect that the mosquito played a role in spreading malaria.

Moss Moss Hart *(1904–1961)*
American playwright, winner of a Pulitzer Prize. He wrote the screenplay for *A Star Is Born* (1954).

Mother Mother Jones *(or Mary Jones, née Harris) (c. 1830–1930)*
American political activist, "the most dangerous woman in America."
"You don't need a vote to raise hell."

Motilal Motilal Nehru *(1861–1931)*
Indian journalist, father of Jawaharlal Nehru and grandfather of Indira Gandhi.

Moulay Moulay Ismail *(1672–1727)*
Last Sharifian emperor of Morocco. He fathered his 500th son in 1721.

Mountain Mountain Charley *(originally Elsa Jane Guerin) (b. 1837)*
American railway brakeman and saloon owner. Widowed with two small children at age sixteen, she started dressing as a man to earn a living.

Mountolive *Mountolive (1958)*
English novel by Lawrence Durrell, the third in his "Alexandria Quartet."

Muammar Colonel Muammar Gadaffi *(1942–)*
Notoriously loony Libyan politician. He lives in a Bedouin tent pitched beside his house on a mound of imported desert sand.

Muda Sir Muda Hassan al Bolkiah Mu'izz-ud-Din-Waddaulah *(1946–)*
Sultan of Brunei, the world's richest person.

Mudcat Mudcat Grant *(James Timothy Grant) (1935–)*
American baseball pitcher for the Indians, an All-Star.

Muddy Muddy Waters *(originally McKinley Morganfield) (1915–1983)*
American blues musician, composer of "Hoochie Coochie Man" (1954).
"Those whites can play instruments real fine. But there's something missing in their singing. They just don't eat enough pinto beans; they haven't had enough hard times."

Muhammad Muhammad Ali *(originally Cassius Marcellus Clay, Jr.) (1942–)*
American heavyweight boxing champion. He won his first title at age fourteen.
"Float like a butterfly, sting like a bee."

Mulciber Mulciber
Satanic architect of the "high capital" Pandemonium in John Milton's *Paradise Lost* (1665).

Mumtaz Mumtaz *(d. 1631)*
Mogul wife of emperor Shah Jahan. He built the Taj Mahal as her tomb after she died giving birth to their fourteenth child. He started to build a matching black tomb for himself across the river, with a joining silver bridge, but was deposed by their sons.

Mungo Mungo Park *(1771–1806)*
Scottish explorer, author of *Travels in the Interior of Africa* (1799).

Muriel Dame Muriel Spark *(Muriel Sarah Spark, née Camberg) (1918–)*
Scottish writer, author of *The Prime of Miss Jean Brodie* (1961).
"One's prime is elusive. You little girls, when you grow up, must be on the alert to recognize your prime at whatever time of your life it may occur. You must then live it to the full."

Murphy "Murphy Brown" *(b. 1988)*
American TV series starring Candice Bergen.

Murray Murray Rose *(Iain Murray Rose) (1939–)*
Australian swimmer. In 1956 he became the youngest person to win three Olympic gold medals.

Murry Murry Dickson *(1916–)*
American baseball pitcher with the Pirates, an All-Star.

Musette Musette
Coquette in Giacomo Puccini's Italian opera *La Bohème* (1896).

Mutsuhito Emperor Mutsuhito *(Meiji Tenno Mutsuhito) (1852–1912)*
Aggressive and successful emperor of Japan.

Muv Sydney "Muv" Mitford *(née Bowles, Lady Redesdale) (1880–1963)*
British mother of Nancy, Pamela, Tom, Diana, Unity, Jessica, and Deborah Mitford.
> *"Whenever I see the words 'Peer's daughter' in a headline, I know it's going to be something about one of you children."*

Muzio Muzio Attendolo *(1369–1424)*
Italian peasant and successful soldier of fortune. He was awarded the new family name of "Sforza," or "stormer of cities."

Myles Myles na Gopaleen *(pseudonym of Brian O'Nolan) (1911–1966)*
Irish "nom de guerre" of Brian O'Nolan for his inflammatory newspaper columns for *The Irish Times*.

Myra *Myra Breckenridge (1968)*
Ambiguous American novel by Gore Vidal.

Myrddin Myrddin
Mythical Celtic bard and magician, legendary builder of Stonehenge. He may be Merlin.

Myriam Myriam Bédard *(1970–)*
Canadian biathlete, winner of two 1994 Olympic gold medals.

Myrna Myrna Loy *(originally Myrna Adele Williams) (1905–)*
American actress, co-star of the "Thin Man" movies. Her father named her after a sign in a railway station.

Myron Myron *(5th century B.C.)*
Greek sculptor. He created "The Discus Thrower."

Myrtis Myrtis Genthner, *née Favor (20th century)*
American friend of actress Bette Davis's mother, Ruthie. She read Honoré de Balzac's novel *La Cousine Bette*, and then suggested that young Betty change her name, "to set you apart, my dear."

Myrtle Myrtle Maclagan *(20th century)*
English cricket player, the first woman to score a century in Test cricket. In 1934, she was on the first female British team to tour Australia and New Zealand. The team paid their own travel costs.

Nabal Nabal *trans. fool, I Samuel 25: 10 (c. 11th century B.C.)*
Old Testament sheep farmer whose wife, Abigail, gave provisions to David against his orders, averting an armed attack. Learning of his close miss, Nabal died of fright, and Abigail married David.

Nabucco *Nabucco (1842)*
Italian opera by Giuseppe Verdi, his first big success.

Nacio Nacio Herb Brown *(Ignacio Herbert Brown) (1896–1964)*
American film composer.

Nadar Nadar *(pen-name of Gaspard-Félix Tournachon) (1820–1910)*
French caricaturist, journalist, photographer, and early balloon enthusiast. Honoré Daumier published a lithograph titled *Nadar Raising Photography to the Height of Art*.

Nadia Nadia Comaneci *(1961–)*
Romanian gymnast, in 1976, at age fourteen, the first to be awarded an Olympic perfect 10.0.

Nadine Nadine Gordimer *(1923–)*
South African novelist, winner of the 1991 Nobel Prize for literature.

Naguib Naguib Mahfouz *(1911–)*
Egyptian author, winner of the 1988 Nobel Prize for literature.

Nahum Nahum Tate *(1652–1715)*
English poet and playwright; poet laureate in 1692.

Nahun Nahun *trans. comforted, Nahum 2: 10 (c. 7th century B.C.)*
Old Testament prophet. He predicted the destruction of Nineveh.
> *"Horsemen charging, flashing sword and glittering spear, hosts of slain, heaps of corpses, dead bodies without end—they stumble over the bodies."*

Nails Nails Norton *(d. 1924)*
American gangster killed in a riding fall. His fellow gangsters executed the horse.

Namby Namby Pamby (or Ambrose Philips) (c. 1674–1749)
English poet and politician, famous for his insipid sentimentality.

Nana Nana Mouskouri (1936–)
Greek ballad singer.

Nance Nance O'Neill (20th century)
American actress noted for her love-affair with alleged axe-murderess Lizzie Borden.

Nancy Nancy Mitford (Nancy Freeman Mitford) (1904–1973)
British francophile aristocrat, author of The Pursuit of Love (1945).
   "I love children—especially when they cry, for then someone comes and takes them away."

Nandi Nandi
Snow-white bull of Siva, calf of Surabhi, the Cow of Plenty.

Nanette Nanette Fabray (originally Ruby Bernadette Nanette Fabares) (1920–)
American actress.

Nannerl Maria-Anna "Nannerl" Mozart (1751–1829)
Austrian pianist, the sister of Wolfgang Amadeus Mozart. They performed together as children.

Nanni Nanni Moretti (1953–)
Italian film director of Dear Diary (1994), the "Italian Woody Allen."

Nannie Nannie Burroughs (Nannie Helen Burroughs) (1883–1961)
American teacher, founder of the National Training School for Girls.
   "We specialize in the wholly impossible."

Naomi Naomi Wolf (1962–)
Attractive American author of The Beauty Myth (1990).

Nap Nap Lajoie (Napoleon "Larry" Lajoie) (1875–1959)
American baseball second baseman with the Cleveland Indians. His 1901 batting average was a record-setting .422.

Naphtali Naphtali (Genesis 49: 21)
Articulate son of Jacob.

Napoléon Napoléon Bonaparte (1769–1821)
Corsican-born French politician; the Emperor Napoleon I. He was exiled to St. Helena Island.
   "Whatever shall we do in that remote spot? Well, we will write our memoirs. Work is the scythe of time."

Napoleone Count Napoleone Rossi Di Montelera (1902–1994)
Italian wine entrepreneur, popularizer of the Martini e Rossi brand of beverages.

Napper Napper Tandy (James Napper Tandy) (1740–1803)
Irish politician. He was sentenced to death for treason, but escaped to France.

Narcissus Narcissus trans. benumbing
Mythical Greek son of Cephisus and Leiriope. He fell in love with his own reflection, pined away with unrequited longing, and was changed into a flower so he could bend over the water to adore himself always.

Naruhito Crown Prince Naruhito (1960–)
Japanese heir.

Nat Nat King Cole (originally Nathaniel Adams Coles) (1917–1965)
American jazz pianist and singer.

Natalia Natalia Goncharova (Natalia Sergeyevna Goncharova) (1881–1962)
Russian-born French revolutionary artist, and designer for Diaghilev's Ballets Russes. She got married on her seventy-fourth birthday.

Natalie Natalie Wood (originally Natasha Gurdin) (1938–1981)
American actress. She married actor Robert Wagner twice.

Natasha Natasha Rambova (originally Winifred Shaunessy) (1897–1969)
Interfering American wife of Rudolph Valentino. His later film contracts barred her from entering his film sets.

Nathalia Nathalia Crane (1913–)
American writer. Her poem "The Janitor's Boy" was published when she was eleven.
   "Oh, I'm in love with the janitor's boy,
   And the janitor's boy loves me;
   He's going to hunt for a desert isle
   In our geography."

Nathalie Nathalie du Pasquier *(1957–)*
French-born textile designer for the Italian
group Memphis.

Nathan Nathan Hale *(1755–1776)*
American spy, executed by the British. A statue
of him stands outside CIA headquarters in
Langley, Virginia.
> *"I only regret that I have but one life to lose for
> my country."*

Nathanael Nathanael Pringsheim *(1823–1894)*
German botanist, the first person to observe
sexual reproduction in algae.

Nathaniel Nathaniel Hawthorne *(1804–1864)*
American writer, author of *The Scarlet Letter*
(1850).
> *"It is not the statesman, the warrior, or the
> monarch that survives, but the despised poet,
> whom they may have fed with their crumbs,
> and to whom they owe all that they now are
> or have—a name."*

Naum Naum Gabo *(originally Naum Neemia Pevsner)*
(1890–1977)
Russian-born American Constructivist sculptor.
He helped write the 1920 Constructivist manifesto, titled *The Realistic Manifesto*.

Nazaire Nazaire LeVasseur *(Louis Nazaire Zéphirin
LeVasseur) (1848–1927)*
Canadian organist and composer.

Nazarin *Nazarin (1959)*
Mexican film by Luis Buñuel.

Ndugu Ndugu Ali Hassan Mwinyi *(1925–)*
Tanzanian president.

Neal Neal Cassady *(Neal Leon Cassady)*
(1924–1969)
American hobo, icon of the Beat Generation.
His biography, by William Plummer, is called
The Holy Goof (1981).

Nebuchadnezzar Nebuchadnezzar II *(or
Nebuchadressar) (ruled 604–562 B.C.)*
Assyrian king of Babylon. Under his rule the
city was restored to its former glory, and the
Processional Way leading to the Ishtar Gate
decorated with the famous glazed relief figures
of lions.

Ned Ned Kelly *(1855–1880)*
Australian outlaw.

Nedra Nedra Talley *(1946–)*
American girl singer with the Ronettes.

Neena Neena Choudhury *(20th century)*
Indian car driver. In 1991, she and Saloo
Choudbury set a Guinness speed record by driving across six continents in 39 days and 20
hours.

Nefertiti Queen Nefertiti *(4th century B.C.)*
Queen of Egypt, consort of the heretic
Akhenaton. The beautiful carving of her head is
in Berlin.

Neil Neil Armstrong *(Neil Alden Armstrong) (1930–)*
American astronaut. On July 20, 1969, he
became the first person to step onto the moon.
> *"That's one small step for a man, one giant leap
> for mankind."*
More recently, he remarked about his footprints,
> *"I kind of hope that somebody goes up there one
> of these days and cleans them up."*

Nelda Nelda Roger *(1952–)*
Canadian magazine editor, of *Azure* (1985–)

Nell Nell Gwyn *(originally Eleanor Gwyn)*
(c. 1650–1687)
English fruit-seller and actress, mistress to
Charles II, and mother of the first Duke of St.
Albans. Caught in an anti-Catholic riot during
the Popish Terror, she told the crowd, "Pray,
good people, be civil. I am the Protestant whore."

Nella Nella Larsen *(1891–1964)*
American writer of the Harlem Renaissance, the
first black woman to receive a Guggenheim
Fellowship. She supported herself as a nurse.
> *"Why couldn't she have two lives, or why
> couldn't she be satisfied in one place?"*

Nellie Nellie L. McClung *(Nellie Letitia McClung)*
(1873–1951)
Canadian novelist, feminist, and politician.

Nels Nels Potter *(1911–)*
American baseball pitcher for the Browns, the
only pitcher caught throwing a spitball after
they were made illegal.

Nelson Nelson Mandela (*Nelson Rolihlahla Mandela*) *(1918–)*
South African politician. He was imprisoned for twenty-seven years as an opponent of apartheid.

Nemesis Nemesis *trans. divine vengeance*
Greek goddess. She humiliates those who boast of their good fortune without making proper sacrifice to the gods or helping the poor.

Nemo Nemo Leibold (*Harry Loran Leibold*) *(1892–1977)*
American baseball outfielder for the White Sox. He was named after the cartoon character Little Nemo.

Nena Nena Thurman, *née von Schlebrugge (20th century)*
Mexican-born American model, wife of Tibetan monk Bob "Tenzin" Thurman, mother of actress Uma Thurman.
> *"There is a verse in the Tao Te Ching that pretty well summarizes how we view our role: parents are like innkeepers at the crossroads, and children are the travellers who use the facilities and move on."*

Neoptolemus King Neoptolemus of Epirus *(3rd century B.C.)*
Grandfather of Alexander the Great.

Nero Nero Wolfe
Jumbo fictional American detective, star of Rex Stout novels such as *Malice in Wonderland* (1940).

Nerys Nerys Hughes *(20th century)*
Welsh actress.

Nessie Nessie
Scottish sea monster frequenting Loch Ness.

Nesta Nesta *(12th century)*
Welsh grandmother of the chronicler Giraldus Cambrensis (or Gerald the Welshman).

Nesuhi Nesuhi Ertegun *(1919–1989)*
Turkish-born American record producer, co-founder of Atlantic Records.

Netta Netta Rheinburg *(1911–)*
British journalist, editor of *Women's Cricket* magazine.

Nettie Nettie Stevens *(1861–1912)*
American geneticist. In 1903, both she and Edmund Beecher Wilson, working separately, discovered that a baby's sex is determined by whether the ovum is fertilized with an X or a Y chromosome sperm.

Netty Netty Kim *(1977–)*
Canadian figure-skater, the 1995 National Champion.

Nevil Nevil Shute (*pen name of Nevil Shute Norway*) *(1899–1960)*
English novelist and aeronautical engineer. His autobiography *Slide Rule* (1954) is mainly about the R100 balloon airship.

Neville Neville Chamberlain (*Arthur Neville Chamberlain*) *(1869–1940)*
British politician.
> *"I believe it is peace for our time . . . peace with honour."*

Newk Don "Newk" Newcombe *(1926–)*
American pitcher for the Dodgers, an All-Star and winner of the first Cy Young Award.

News News Bunny *(1995–)*
British human-sized rabbit. Standing beside the news anchorman on the Live TV channel, he claps, bows, or wiggles his ears to comment on stories. Fellow journalists have laid official complaints about working with him.

Newt Newt Gingrich *(1943–)*
American Conservative futurist, creator of turgid "Newtspeak" jargon.
> *"People assume I'm some right-wing, out-of-touch Neanderthal who doesn't get it."*

Newton Newton Cleaveland *(19th century)*
American mining engineer, husband of Agnes Morley Cleaveland, who wrote the autobiography *No Life for a Lady*.

Neysa Neysa McMein (*originally Margary Edna McMein*) *(1888–1949)*
American artist. She painted all the covers for *McCall's* magazine between 1923 and 1937. She changed her name to "Neysa" on the advice of a numerologist.

Ngaio Dame Ngaio Marsh *(1899–1982)*
New Zealand detective-storywriter; creator of Roderick Alleyn.

Niamh Niamh Chinn Óir
Legendary Celtic queen of the Tir na n-Óg (land of eternal youth). The poet Ossian left her after they had lived together for 300 years. Consult James Macpherson's *Fingal: an ancient Epic Poem in Six Books* (1762) for details.

Niccolò Niccolò di Bernardo dei Machiavelli *(1469–1527)*
Italian politician, author of the strategic classic *The Prince* (published posthumously in 1532).
"When neither their property nor their honour is touched, the majority of men live content."

Nichelle Nichelle Nichols *(20th century)*
American actress. She played Lieutenant Uhura on "Star Trek" (1966–69), and was later hired by NASA for public promotions.

Nicholas St. Nicholas *(300–399)*
Russian bishop of Myra in Lycia, the patron saint of children, merchants, sailors, travellers, and thieves. He is called "Sankt Niklaus" in German, "Sinte Clause" in Dutch, "Santa Claus" in America. He gave a gold dowry to three poor girls, starting the habit of gift-giving at Christmas.

Nick Nick Park *(20th century)*
British film claymation genius. He won an Oscar for *The Wrong Trousers* (1993).

Nickolas Nickolas Ashford *(1943–)*
American jazz dancer and Motown songwriter, co-composer of "Ain't No Mountain High Enough" (1967).

Nico Nico *(originally Christa Päffgen) (1938–1988)*
German born rock musician with the Velvet Underground.

Nicodemus Nicodemus *trans. ruler over the people* *(John 7: 51)*
Pharisee elder who defended Jesus in council.
"Does our law judge a man without first giving him a hearing and learning what he does?"

Nicola Nicola Sacco *(1891–1927)*
American anarchist, executed with his friend Bartolomeo Vanzetti for allegedly robbing a bank. At their trial, they were referred to as "dagos" and "anarchistic bastards." In 1977, they were officially exonerated by the governor of Massachusetts.

Nicolae Nicolae Ceauşescu *(1918–1989)*
Romanian politician, last of the Communist dictators.

Nicolas-François Nicolas-François Appert *(c. 1750–1841)*
French chef and inventor of canning, author of *The Art of Preserving All Kinds of Animal and Vegetable Substances for Several Years* (1810).

Nicolaus Nicolaus Copernicus *(1473–1543)*
Polish inventor of modern astronomy. He proved that the sun is the centre of the solar system.

Nicole Nicole Germain *(originally Marcelle Landreau) (1917–1994)*
Canadian French-language superstar, the "Queen of Radio." She changed her name because nice girls were not actresses and she didn't want to embarrass her family.

Nicolete Nicolete Gray *(1911–)*
English designer and lettering historian.

Nicolette "Aucassin and Nicolette"
Popular mediaeval romance.

Niels Niels Bohr *(Niels Henrik David Bohr) (1885–1962)*
Danish physicist, winner of the 1922 Nobel Prize. Fleeing Denmark during the Second World War he hid his gold Nobel medal by dissolving it in acid. After the war, he precipitated the gold out of solution and recast it in the original shape.
"An expert is a man who has made all the mistakes which can be made in a very narrow field."

Nigel Nigel Hawthorne *(20th century)*
British actor, the unctuous sidekick on the TV series "Yes, Minister." Nominated for an Oscar for *The Madness of King George* (1995), he became the first person to bring a same-sex date to the Academy Awards.

Nik Nik Kershaw *(1958–)*
British teen idol.

Niki Niki Lauda *(1949–)*
Austrian racing-car driver, winner of three Formula One World Championships.

Nikita Nikita Khrushchev *(Nikita Sergeyevich Khrushchev) (1894–1971)*
Soviet politician.
"When you are skinning your customers, you should leave some skin to grow so that you can skin them again."

NIKITA KHRUSHCHEV

★★ **Nikola** Nikola Tesla *(1856–1943)*
Yugoslav-born American physicist. He invented the high-frequency Tesla coil.

Nikolaas Nikolaas Tinbergen *(1907–1988)*
Dutch ethnologist, winner of the Nobel Prize for his work on animal behaviour. He observed that ritual dance or display averts physical combat.

Nikolai Nikolai Vasilievich Gogol *(1809–1852)*
Russian novelist, author of *The Diary of a Madman* (1835).

Nikolaus Sir Nikolaus Pevsner *(Nikolaus Bernhard Pevsner) (1902–1983)*
German-born English design historian.

Nila Nila Mark *(20th century)*
American radio director of the children's program "Let's Pretend."

Nile Nile Rodgers *(1952–)*
American guitarist and record producer.

Nils Nils Nilsson Skum *(1872–1951)*
Lapland artist of the native Sami people. He was the first person in his nomadic family to draw pictures.

Nilsson Nilsson *(originally Harry Edward Nelson III) (1941–1994)*
American pop songwriter.

Nimrod Nimrod *(Genesis 10: 9)*
Old Testament hunter, ruler of a large kingdom in Iraq.

Nina Nina Bawden *(Nina Mary Bawden) (1925–)*
English novelist.
"I bought a special cream supposed to restore elasticity to the skin, but I destroyed the wrapper on the jar and the accompanying, incriminating literature, as furtively as I had, when young, removed the cover of a book on sex."

Ninette Dame Ninette de Valois *(original name Edris Stannus) (1898–)*
Irish ballerina, founder of what is now the Royal Ballet.

Ninhursag Ninhursag *(3rd millennium B.C.)*
Mesopotamian goddess of childbirth.

Nino Nino Ricci *(1959–)*
Canadian novelist, author of *Lives of the Saints* (1990).

Ninon Ninon de Lenclos *(originally Anne de Lenclos) (1616–1706)*
French prostitute, celebrated for her taste, style, and good manners.
"Love never dies of starvation, but often of indigestion."

Ninotchka Ninotchka *(1939)*
American romantic comedy film, written by Billy Wilder, starring Greta Garbo.

Nis Nis Petersen *(1897–1943)*
Danish poet, vagabond, and novelist.

Nixon Nixon Waterman *(b. 1859)*
English poet.

Nkensen Nkensen Arkaah *(1927–)*
Ghanaian vice-president. In 1995, he accused President Jerry Rawlings of kicking him in the groin during a cabinet meeting.

Noah Noah Webster *(1758–1843)*
American lexographer, author of the book now known in its revised edition as *Webster's New International Dictionary of the English Language*. When his wife caught him kissing the maid, he corrected her language, saying, "No, my dear, it is I who am surprised; you are merely astonished."

Noam Noam Chomsky *(Avram Noam Chomsky) (1928–)*
American linguist.
"Colourless green ideas sleep furiously."

Noddy Noddy Holder *(originally Neville Holder) (1950–)*
British rock singer with the group Slade.

Noël Sir Noël Coward *(Noël Pierce Coward) (1899–1973)*
British author.
"Only mad dogs and Englishmen go out in the mid-day sun."

Top 10 Names for Baby Politicians

Absolutely • Adolf • Corazon • Fidel

• Gatewood • Harber • Howell •

Lyndon • Petrona • Vyacheslav

Noisy Johnny "Noisy" Kling *(1875–1947)*
American baseball catcher with the Chicago
Cubs. In 1908, he was also the world pocket-
billiard champion.

Nokie Nokie Edwards *(1939–)*
American pop musician with the Ventures.

Nolan Nolan Bushnell *(1943–)*
American inventor in 1972 of the seminal computer game Pong.

Nona Nona Hendryx *(1945–)*
American pop singer with Patti Labelle and the
Blue Belles.

Nonius Nonius Marcellus *(c. 4th century)*
Latin grammarian. He wrote a dull lexicon
which is useful for its descriptions of archaic
word meanings.

Nonnatus St. Raymond Nonnatus *(c. 1204–1240)*
Spanish religious worker. After his mother died
in childbirth, he was delivered by a Caesarian
operation, which is why he was called "non
natus" ("not born").

Noor Queen Noor *(20th century)*
American-born wife of King Hussein.

Nora Nora Ephron *(1947–)*
American cook, novelist, and movie-maker,
author of *Heartburn* (1983).
  *"If pregnancy were a book, they would cut the
  last two chapters."*

Norbert Norbert Wiener *(1894–1964)*
American mathematician. He wrote *I Am a
Mathematician—the Later Life of a Prodigy* (1956).

Noreen Noreen Cocheran *(20th century)*
American performer, a Mousketeer on "The
Mickey Mouse Club."

Norma Norma Talmadge *(1893–1957)*
American actress. In 1927, she accidentally
stepped onto wet concrete outside Grauman's
Chinese Restaurant in Hollywood, starting the
press-agent ritual of having stars make footprints there.

Norman Norman Mailer *(1923–)*
American writer, author of *The Naked and the
Dead* (1948). Asked why he got married so
often, he replied, "To get divorced. You don't
know anything about a woman until you meet
her in court."

Norodom Prince Norodom Sihanouk *(1922–)*
Cambodian politician and elected king.

Norrie Norrie Paramor *(1913–1979)*
British pianist and pop producer.

Norris Norris Church *(1949–)*
American wife of writer Norman Mailer. Their
marriage ceremony featured readings from his
book *The Prisoner of Sex* (1971).

Norris Norris Dewar McWhirter *(1925–)*
British publisher of the best-selling *Guinness
Book of Records*, the world's second–best-selling
book, after the Bible. The 1955 first edition was
funded by the Guinness Brewery.

Northcote C. Northcote Parkinson *(Cyril Northcote
Parkinson) (1910–1993)*
British historian, the discoverer in 1957 of
Parkinson's Law that "work expands so as to fill
the time available for its completion."

Northrop Northrop Frye *(Herman Northrop Frye)
(1912–1991)*
Canadian literary critic and teacher.
  *"We are being swallowed up by the popular
  culture of the United States, but then the
  Americans are being swallowed up by it, too.
  It's just as much a threat to American culture
  as it is to ours."*

Norval Norval Morrisseau *(1932–)*
Canadian painter.

Nosferatu *Nosferatu (1923)*
German silent film, the first vampire movie.

Nostradamus Nostradamus *(or Michel de Nostredame) (1503–1566)*
French doctor and astrologer. His rhyming predictions of the future are still popular today.

Ntozake Ntozake Shange *(originally Paulette Williams) (1948–)*
American poet and playwright, author of *for colored girls who have considered suicide when the rainbow is enuf* (1976).

> *"Mamas only do things cause they love you so much. They can't help it. . . . No matter how old you get, how grown and on your own, your mama always loves you like a newborn."*

Nuala Nuala Beck *(20th century)*
Canadian management consultant, author of *Shifting Gears*.

Numina Numina *(or Pomona)*
Greek goddess, protective spirit of gardens and spring.

Nunnally Nunnally Johnson *(1897–1977)*
American screenwriter of *The Dirty Dozen* (1967).

Nuria Nuria Espert *(1935–)*
Spanish actress and stage director.

Nyahbinghi Queen Nyahbinghi *(19th century)*
Rastafarian warrior queen. There are Nyahbinghi cults.

Nyree Nyree Dawn Porter *(1940–)*
New Zealand actress.

Nzinga Nzinga *(baptized as Dona Aña de Souza) (d. 1663)*
Queen of Matamba. Driven out of her native Ndongo by the Portuguese, she established independent Matamba, trained an effective military force, and allied herself with the Dutch.

O O Henry *(pen name of William Sydney Porter) (1862–1910)*
American short-story writer, author of *Cabbages and Kings* (1904). He adopted his pseudonym while serving a three-year jail sentence for "borrowing" money from the bank where he'd worked as a teller. He used the money to start a literary magazine.

Obadiah Obadiah Slope
Unctuous chaplain of Anthony Trollope's *Barchester Towers* (1857).

Obed Obed Hussey *(1792–1860)*
American inventor of a reaping machine.

Oberon Oberon, King of the Fairies
Attractive character in William Shakespeare's play *A Midsummer Night's Dream.*

Octave Octave Feuillet *(1821–1890)*
French novelist and playwright.

Octavia Octavia *(d. 11 B.C.)*
Roman sister of the Emperor Augustus, noted for her beauty and virtue.

Octavio Octavio Paz *(1914–)*
Mexican poet, winner of a Nobel Prize, author of *The Labyrinth of Solitude* (1950).

Oddone Oddone Piazza *(lost title 1932)*
American boxer, the world middleweight champion until he was knocked out by Gorilla Jones.

Odetta Odetta *(originally Odetta Holmes) (1930–)*
American club singer and folk revivalist.

Odette Odette Hallowes *(1903–1995)*
British secret agent to France. She was awarded both the George Cross and the Legion of Honour after surviving capture and torture by the Gestapo.

Odile Odile
Fated swan princess of Piotr Tchaikovsky's ballet *Swan Lake* (19th century).

Odilon Odilon Redon *(1840–1916)*
French painter and lithographer.

Odin Odin
Nordic god, lord of Valhalla, son of Thor and Besla.

Odo Odo *(c. 1036–1097)*
Anglo-Norman prelate, half-brother of William the Conqueror. He may have commissioned the Bayeux Tapestry.

Odysseus Odysseus *trans. angry*
Legendary Greek hero of the Trojan war, star of *The Iliad* and *The Odyssey.* He is noted for his prudence, wisdom, and valour.

Oedipus King Oedipus of Thebes *trans. swellfoot or child of the swelling wave*
Legendary Greek ruler who accidentally married his mother, Jocasta, and fathered several children

with her. Upon learning the truth about his wife, he put out his own eyes, banished himself, and was swallowed by the earth. Sigmund Freud named a complex after him.

Offa King Offa of Mercia *(757–796)*
English ruler, creator of Offa's Dyke along the Welsh border. He considered himself to be as important as Charlemagne.

Ogden Ogden Nash *(Frederic Ogden Nash)* *(1902–1971)*
American poet.
> *"The trouble with a kitten is*
> *THAT*
> *Eventually it becomes a*
> *CAT."*

Ogma Ogma
Celtic chief, inventor of the "Ogma alphabet."

Okakura Okakura Kabuzo *(20th century)*
Japanese author of the perennial best-selling *The Book of Tea*.

Oksana Oksana Baiul *(1977–)*
Ukrainian figure-skater, a 1994 Olympic gold-medallist. Her father deserted the family when she was two; her mother died when she was thirteen; and then she lived with her coach.

Olaf Olaf II Haraldsson *(later St. Olaf the Fat)* *(c. 995–1030)*
King of Norway, a mercenary from the age of twelve. He was in charge of the celebrated attack on London in 1010 when the bridge was torn down with grappling irons, as recorded in the children's song "London Bridge Is Falling Down."

Olaus Olaus Roemer *(1644–1710)*
Dutch astronomer. He measured the finite velocity of light by watching Jupiter's satellites.

Ole Ole Worm *(1588–1654)*
Danish scholar of Old Icelandic lore.

Oleanna Oleanna *(1994)*
American play by David Mamet.

Oleg Oleg Gordievsky *(20th century)*
Soviet spy. He defected to Britain in 1985 and unveiled the secret "fifth man," John Cairncross, of the spy ring that included Kim Philby, Guy Burgess, Donald Maclean, and Anthony Blunt.

Olga Olga Korbut *(1955–)*
Russian gymnast, dazzler of the 1972 Olympics.

Oliver Oliver Cromwell *(1599–1658)*
English revolutionary politician.
> *"Necessity hath no law."*

Olivia Olivia Manning *(1908–1980)*
Anglo-Irish novelist.

Oliviero Oliviero Toscani *(20th century)*
Italian art director for Benetton. He also created the campaign slogan for Jesus jeans: "Qui m'aime me suive" ("Who loves me will follow me").

Ollie Ollie Johnson *(1912–)*
American cartoon animator with Walt Disney.
> *"There's four and a half billion people in the world, and half of them have seen at least a scene from one of our movies. It's hard to understand that. I can't grasp it, really."*

Olof Olof Rudbeck *(1630–1702)*
Swedish researcher. The botanical genus *Rudbeckia* is named after him.

Olympe Olympe de Longes *(d. 1793)*
French revolutionary feminist, a butcher's daughter. She rewrote the Declaration of the Rights of Man and Citizen into a radical manifesto calling on women to constitute their own national assembly, and was guillotined.

Olympia Olympia Dukakis *(1931–)*
American actress, the cousin of politician Michael Dukakis.

Olympias Olympias *(d. 316 B.C.)*
Macedonian queen, mother of Alexander the Great.

Omar Omar Khayyám *(or 'Umar Khayyám)* *(c. 1048–c. 1131)*
Persian mathematician and astronomer, author of the 250 poetic quatrains freely translated by English poet Edward Fitzgerald.
> *"A Book of Verses underneath the Bough,*
> *A Jug of Wine, a Loaf of Bread—and Thou*
> *Beside me singing in the Wilderness—*
> *Oh, Wilderness is paradise enow!"*

Omer Omer Dumas *(Joseph Omer Dumas)* *(1889–1980)*
Canadian old-time fiddle player.

Omobono Omobono Stradivari *(1679–1742)*
Italian violin-maker, son of the great Antonio Stradivari.

Omrie Omrie J. Silverthorne *(1909–1994)*
Canadian film censor, "Mr. Silvershears."

Onan Onan *Genesis 38: 9 (c. 16th century B.C.)*
Old Testament masturbater. Dorothy Parker named her canary Onan, "because he spills his seed on the ground."

One One-Leg Paget *(Henry William Paget, 1st Marquess of Anglesey) (1768–1854)*
English cavalry officer at the Battle of Waterloo, where the lost leg was given burial in a garden.
> *Paget: "By God, Sir, I've lost my leg!"*
> *Wellington: "By God, Sir, so you have!"*

Onnie Onnie McIntyre *(1945–)*
Scottish rock musician with the Average White Band.

Oojah Uncle Oojah *(real name Flip-Flap the Great Oojah) (1919–1951)*
British cartoon elephant created by Flo Lancaster. He was replaced in the public's affection by Babar.

Oona Oona Chaplin *(1925–1991)*
American daughter of playwright Eugene O'Neill and child-bride of Charlie Chaplin.

Opechancanough Opechancanough *(d. 1644)*
American Tidewater chief. He succeeded Pocahontas's father, Powhatan, as leader of the Powhatan Confederacy.

Opha Opha M. Johnson *(20th century)*
American soldier, in 1918 the first female member of the Marine Corps Reserve.

Ophelia Ophelia
Doomed lover in William Shakespeare's play *Hamlet* (1600). After her big mad scene, she drowns herself.

Oprah Oprah Winfrey *(1954–)*
American talk-show hostess.
> *"You can have it all. You just can't have it all at one time."*

Opus Opus the Penguin *(20th century)*
Hero of the American comic strip "Bloom County."

Oral Oral Roberts *(Granville Oral Roberts) (1918–)*
American TV evangelist. The *Boston Globe* noted that "he has no intention of living in the ghetto of heaven or even its suburbs."

Orange "Orange" Peel *(better known as Sir Robert Peel) (1788–1850)*
English politician. As home secretary he reorganized the London Police force, hence the names "Peelers" and "Bobbies" for police officers.

Orazio Orazio Gentileschi *(1562–1647)*
Italian painter employed in England by Charles I; father of painter Artemisia Gentileschi.

Ordoney Ordoney de Montald *(16th century)*
Spanish writer of *Las Sergas Esplanadian* (1510), which describes an imaginary land named "Californe." Spanish settlers named California after this land.

Orel Orel "Bulldog" Hershiser *(1958–)*
American baseball pitcher for the Dodgers, an All-Star and a Gold Glove winner.

Orenthal Orenthal James (O.J.) Simpson *(1947–)*
American football running back with the Buffalo Bills, "the Juice," tried for the murder of his wife.

Orestheus King Orestheus of the Ozolian Locrians
trans. dedicated to the mountain goddess
Mythical Greek ruler. He planted the stick that grew into the first grape vine.

Orfeo *Orfeo (1607)*
Italian opera by Claudio Monteverdi.

Orian Orian *(20th century)*
French performance artist. She underwent extensive plastic surgery to transform herself into a "Renaissance-style" beauty.

Oriana Oriana Fallaci *(20th century)*
Italian journalist. She interviewed Muammar Gadaffi in 1980 without gaining a single sensible comment.

Oriane Oriane, Duchesse de Guermantes
Supreme French social butterfly of Marcel Proust's *Remembrance of Things Past* (1913–22).

Oribe Oribe *(1956–)*
American hairdresser to the supermodels.

Origen Origen *(c. 185–c. 254)*
Alexandrian-born Christian scholar noted for having castrated himself.

Orinda Orinda *(pseudonym of Katherine Philips, née Fowler) (1631–1664)*
English poet, the first woman poet published in England.

Orion Orion *trans. dweller on the mountain*
Mythical Greek hunter. After death, he was doomed to the cheerless Asphodel Fields as being neither good nor bad.

Orlando Orlando *(1928)*
English novel by Virginia Woolf.

Orlandus Orlandus Wilson *(active 1940s)*
American "jubilee" gospel singer with the Golden Gate Quartet.

Orlo Orlo Miller *(1911–1993)*
Canadian historian, author of *The Donnellys Must Die* (1962).

Ornette Ornette Coleman *(1930–)*
American jazz tenor-sax player.
> "I only knew blues in B-flat. I was a B-flat man."

Orpheus Orpheus *trans. of the riverbank*
Legendary Greek poet. The Muses taught him to play his lyre so well that the rivers stopped, beasts tamed themselves, and the mountains themselves moved closer to listen.

Orrin Orrin Tucker *(1911–)*
American dance-band leader.

Orsino Orsino, Duke of Illyria
Self-indulgent lover in William Shakespeare's play *Twelfth Night* (1602).

Orson Orson Welles *(George Orson Welles) (1915–1985)*
American filmmaker, creator of *Citizen Kane* (1941).
> "Gluttony is not a secret vice."

Orville Orville Redenbacher *(1907–1995)*
American entrepreneur. He grew and taste-tested more than 30,000 corn hybrids before choosing one for his gourmet popcorn.

OSCAR WILDE

Orvon Orvon "Gene" Autry *(1907–)*
American singing cowboy, star of the film *Tumblin' Tumbleweeds* (1933).

Osami Osami Nagano *(1880–1947)*
Japanese naval officer. He planned and ordered the attack on Pearl Harbor (1941).

Osbert Sir Osbert Lancaster *(1908–1986)*
Class-conscious British cartoonist, author of *Here of All Places*.
> "'Fan vaulting'. . . an architectural device which arouses enormous enthusiasm on account of the difficulties it has all too obviously involved, but which from an aesthetic standpoint frequently belongs to the 'Last-Supper-carved-on-a-peach-stone' class of masterpiece."

Osborne Osborne Reynolds *(1842–1912)*
English engineer. He specialized in centrifugal pumps. The "Reynolds number" ratio describing fluid characteristics is named after him.

Oscar Oscar Wilde *(Oscar Fingal O'Flahertie Wills Wilde) (1854–1900)*
British author and wit.
> "Children begin by loving their parents; as they grow older they judge them; sometimes they forgive them."

Oscaria Dolly "Oscaria" Wilde *(20th century)*
Irish niece of Oscar Wilde. She lived in Paris to be closer to Gertrude Stein, on whom she had a crush.

Oseola Oseola McCarty *(1908–)*
American washerwoman. She donated her life savings of $150,000 to fund a scholarship in Southern Mississippi.
> "Maybe I can make it so the children don't have to work like I did."

Osip Osip Mandelstam *(1891–1938)*
Possibly the greatest Russian poet of the century. He died of a heart attack en route to one of Josef Stalin's internment camps.

Osiris Osiris
Egyptian god of the underworld and judge of the dead.

Oskar Oskar Schindler *(1908–1974)*
Polish factory owner. "Schindler's List" of vital employees saved more than 1,000 Jews from the

Holocaust, inspiring a 1993 Steven Spielberg movie.

Osko Osko (or Bhagwan Shree Rajneesh) (d. 1980)
Indian guru, author of *From Sex to Superconscious*. The American government expelled him from his Oregon commune.

Osmel Osmel Sousa (20th century)
Venezuelan "father of the beauty industry." He personally rehearses Venezuelan competitors for the Miss Universe competition.

Ossee Ossee Schreckengost (1875–1914)
American baseball catcher for the As. He had it written into his contract that roommate Rube Waddell was not allowed to eat crackers in bed.

Ossian Ossian (or Oisín Mac Fhinn Mhic Cumhail Mhic Tréanmóir Uí Baoisne)
Legendary Celtic bard, son of Finn. He spent 300 years in the Tir na n-Óg (land of eternal youth). Consult *Fingal: An Ancient Epic Poem in Six Books* (1762) by James Macpherson.

Ossie Ossie Bluege (1900–)
American third baseman for the Senators for seventeen years. The Senators tried to make him quit his off-season job as an accountant for fear of ruining his eyes, but since he earned less than $10,000 a year playing ball, he refused.

Oswald Oswald the Rabbit (b. 1927)
American cartoon bunny, Walt Disney's first attempt at a cute cartoon character.

Oswaldo Oswaldo Jose Guillen Barrios (known as Ozzie Guillen) (1964–)
American baseball shortstop for the White Sox, an All-Star.

Othello The Tragedy of Othello, the Moor of Venice (1602)
Play by William Shakespeare.

Otis Otis Redding (1941–1967)
American soul singer. His song "Dock of the Bay" was a No. 1 hit after his death in a plane crash.

Otranto The Castle of Otranto (1765)
Gothic English novel by Horace Walpole.

Ottmar Ottmar Mergenthaler (1854–1899)
German-born American inventor of the Linotype typesetting machine.

Otto Otto von Bismarck (Otto Eduard Leopold von Bismarck) (1815–1898)
German politician, the "Iron Chancellor."
  "Never believe in anything until it has been officially denied."

Ottoline Lady Ottoline Violet Anne Morrell, née Cavendish-Bentinck (1873–1938)
British literary hostess.

Otzi Otzi (c. 3000 B.C.)
Austrian hunter. In 1991, his body was discovered frozen in a glacier.

Ouida Ouida (pen name of Marie Louise de la Ramée) (1839–1908)
English popular novelist. "Ouida" was her own attempt as a baby to say "Louisa."

Ousmane Ousmane Toure (20th century)
Casamance-born French pop musician with the group Toure Kunda.

Ove Sit Ove Arup (1895–1988)
British structural engineer. He helped create the roof of the Sydney Opera House.

Overend Overend Pete Watts (1947–)
British rock musician with the band Mott the Hoople.

Oveta Oveta Hobby, née Culp (1905–)
American reporter. She served with the WAC in the Second World War, and became the first woman to receive the U.S. Army Distinguished Service Medal.

Ovid Ovid (Publius Ovidius Naso) (43 B.C.– A.D. 17)
Roman lawyer and poet, author of *Metamorphosis*.
  "Who would have known of Hector if Troy had been happy? The road to valor is built by adversity."

Owen Owen Wister (1860–1938)
American writer, author of *The Virginian* (1902).
  "When you call me that, smile."

Oyo Oyo Nyimba Kabamba Iguru Rukidi IV (1992–)
King of Uganda, the 12th king of the Toro Kingdom. His 1995 coronation made him the youngest king in the world.

Oz The Wizard of Oz (1900)
American children's novel by L. Frank Baum.

Ozymandias "Ozymandias" *(19th century)*
English poem by Percy Bysshe Shelley.
*"My name is Ozymandias, king of kings
Look on my works, ye Mighty, and despair!"*

Ozzy John "Ozzy" Osbourne *(1948–)*
English heavy-metal singer with the band Black
Sabbath. In 1982, he had to have rabies shots
after an ill-advised stage performance featuring
a dead bat.

Paavo Paavo Nurmi *(1897–1973)*
Finnish track star, the "Flying Finn," the first
athlete to use a stopwatch for scientific training.
In 1924, he won the 1,500-metre race and the
5,000-metre race within an hour, setting two
world records.

Pablo Pablo Picasso *(1881–1973)*
Spanish artist.
*"To search means nothing in painting. To find is
the thing."*

Paco Paco Ignacio Taibo II *(20th century)*
Mexican novelist, creator of the detective
Hector Belascoavian Shayne, as in *No Happy
Endings* (1993).

Paddles Dick "Paddles" Butkus *(1942–)*
American Hall of Fame football linebacker with
the Bears. He was called "Paddles" for his size
11½ EEE shoes.

Paddy Paddy Chayefsky *(originally Sidney Chayefsky)*
(1923–1981)
American playwright, writer of the film *Network*
(1976).
"Television is democracy at its ugliest."

Padraic Padraic Colum *(1881–1972)*
Irish poet.
*"A song is more lasting than the riches of the
world."*

Pahlan Pahlan Ratanji "Polly" Umrigar *(1926–)*
Indian cricket player. He set a record for Test
runs unbroken until 1978.

Pakenham Pakenham Beatty *(19th century)*
English poet.
"By thine own soul's law learn to live."

Pål Pål Waaktar *(1961–)*
Swedish soft-rock guitarist with the group a-ha.

Paladin Paladin
Cowboy-poet hero of the American TV series
"Have Gun Will Travel" (1957–63).
"No river is shallow to a man who can't swim."

Pallas Pallas *trans. maiden or youth*
Legendary Greek friend of Athene, who was
accidentally killed by her in mock combat, after
which remorseful Athena took the name "Pallas
Athena."

Palmer Palmer Cox *(1840–1924)*
American illustrator, creator of the "Brownie"
books for children.

Palmiro Palmiro Togliatti *(1893–1964)*
Italian politician, founder of the Italian
Communist Party, the largest Communist Party
outside the USSR and Chinese blocs.

Paloma Paloma Picasso *(20th century)*
Spanish jeweller, daughter of painter Pablo
Picasso.

Palti Palti *(or Paltiel)*, 1 Samuel 25: 44
Old Testament first husband of King Saul's
daughter Michal. When David became king, he
married Michal. Palti followed them, weeping,
until ordered to leave.

Pamela *Pamela (1749)*
English novel by Samuel Richardson. The heroine is astonishingly virtuous, but it does her no
good.

Pamina Pamina
Hero's love interest in Wolfgang Amadeus
Mozart's wonderful opera *The Magic Flute*
(1791).

Pan Pan *trans. pasture*
Greek goat god, inventor of the reed Pan-pipe.
He gave such a great shout in the battle with
the Titans that it scared them into running
away, inspiring the word "panic."

Pancho Pancho Lowe Barnes *(Florence Lowe Barnes)*
(1901–1975)
American pilot; the first woman to work as a
stunt pilot in the movies, starting with Howard
Hughes's *Hell's Angels* (1930).

161 / **Pancho–Parsifal**

Pancho Pancho Villa (*originally Doroteo Arango*) *(1878–1923)*
Mexican bandit-statesman. His last words were: *"Don't let it end like this. Tell them I said something."*

Pancras St. Pancras (*d. c. 304*)
Syrian orphan beheaded at age fourteen. He is a patron saint of children.

Pandora Pandora *trans. all-giving*
Greek mortal woman made out of clay by Hephaestus. She opened the jar in which her husband, Epimethus, had managed to imprison the Spites that plague mankind, including Old Age, Sickness, and that old liar, Delusive Hope.

Pandosto *Pandosto (16th century)*
Elizabethan English play by Robert Green, about a jealous husband.

Pāṇini Pāṇini *(5th or 7th century B.C.)*
Indian Sanskrit grammarian.

Pansy Pansy
The original name of the heroine of Margaret Mitchell's novel *Gone With the Wind* (1936). Her name was changed to Scarlett, and her house's name to Tara (from Fontenoy Hall) only at the editing stage.

Pantagruel Pantagruel
Mediaeval comic giant. He specialized in belching and farting.

Panteleon Panteleon Perez Prado (*known as Perez Prado*) *(1916–1989)*
Mexican popular pianist, "El Rey del Mambo."

Paolo Paolo Uccello *(c. 1396–1475)*
Florentine painter of the early Renaissance.
"What a delightful thing this perspective is!"

Papa Papa John Creach *(1917–1994)*
American musician. He played with the Jefferson Airplane.

Papa Doc François "Papa Doc" Duvalier *(1907–1971)*
Haitian doctor and politician. He started the notorious Tonton Macoutes secret police.

PABLO PICASSO

Papillon Henri "Papillon" Charrière (*convicted 1931*)
French safe-cracker and murderer. In 1945, after eight attempts, he escaped from Devil's Island prison in French Guyana on a raft of coconuts. (His nickname came from the butterfly tattooed on his chest.)

Pappus Pappus of Alexandria *(4th century)*
Greek mathematician. His writings helped inspire René Descartes.

Pär Pär Fabian Lagerkvist *(1891–1974)*
Swedish novelist, winner of the 1951 Nobel Prize for literature.

Paracelsus Paracelsus (*real name Philippus Aureolus Theophrastus Bombastus von Hoehenheim*) *(1493–1541)*
Swiss German alchemist and doctor, the first person to associate goitre with minerals in drinking water.
"Every physician should be rich in knowledge . . . his patients should be his book, they will never mislead him."

Paris Paris (*or Alexander*) *trans. wallet*
Trojan shepherd, son of King Priam of Troy, destined from birth to ruin his country. He managed this by running off with King Menelaus's wife, Helen, starting the Trojan War.

Parke Parke Thompson *(20th century)*
World traveller. He has visited 309 countries.

Parmeno Parmeno
Greek slave in Menander's play *Samia* (c. 300 B.C.). He tells the cook, "I'm damned if I know why you carry knives with you. Your chatter would reduce anything to mincemeat."

Parmigiano Parmigiano (*or Parmigianino, properly Girolamo Francesco Maria Mazzola*) *(1503–1540)*
Italian painter of the Lombard school.

Parnelli Parnelli Jones *(20th century)*
American racing-car driver, winner of the 1963 Indianapolis 500.

Parrhasius Parrhasius *(4th century B.C.)*
Italian painter celebrated as the first to use shading.

Parsifal *Parsifal (staged 1882)*
German opera by Richard Wagner, his last. It is based on the legend of the Holy Grail.

Parsley Parsley Peel *(Robert Peel) (1750–1830)*
English cotton manufacturer, father of the
politician Sir Robert "Orange" Peel. One of his
best-selling fabrics had a parsley pattern.

Parthenope Parthenope *trans. maiden face*
One of the three Sirens who lured Greek sailors
to their deaths with sweet singing. All three
flung themselves into the sea when Odysseus
evaded their lure by blocking his sailors' ears
with wax.

Pascale Dr. Pascale Sicotte *(1962–)*
Canadian anthropologist, head of the mountain-
gorilla reseach station in Rwanda founded by
Dian Fossey.

Pasi Pasi Kuoppamaki *(20th century)*
Finnish economist. At Web site
http://www.etia.fi/pkm/joke.html, he collects
jokes about economists.

Pasiphaë Pasiphaë *trans. she who shines for all*
Cretan wife of king of Minos II, the mother of
the Minotaur and Ariadne.

Pat Pat Nixon *(originally Thelma Catherine Ryan)
(1912–1993)*
American political worker, wife of Richard
Nixon. She was nicknamed "Pat" because she
was born the day before St. Patrick's Day.

Patañjali Patañjali *(3rd century)*
Italian founder of Hindu Yoga philosophy.

Patience Patience Wright, *née Lovell (1725–1786)*
American-born wax sculptor. Her exhibition of
famous people in London pre-dated Madame
Tussaud by thirty years; one figure is still displayed in Westminster Abbey.

Patrice Patrice Hemery Lumumba *(1925–1961)*
Zairean politician, in 1958 the founder of the
Congolese National Movement.

Patricia Patricia Highsmith *(1921–1995)*
American thriller writer, author of *Strangers on a
Train* (1950) made into a film by Alfred
Hitchcock.
*"Is there anything more boring and artificial
than justice?"*

Patrick St. Patrick *(in Irish, Padraig, nickname Succat)
(c. 389–461)*
Welsh-born apostle, the patron saint of Ireland.

Pats Pats *(or Patsy, character performed and
written by Jennifer Saunders) (20th century)*
Heroine of the British television series "Absolutely
Fabulous" (1993), known to its fans as "AbFab."
*"You've been a fantastic mother. You've let them
ruin your figure. Your stomach's stretched beyond
recognition. You've got boobs down to your
knees. And for what? For a pot-holer who's worn
nothing but a purple nylon track suit and a
Gazza T-shirt for the past two years, and a grem-
lin who lives her life at a level of boredom that
would make a battery chicken take up an evening
class. Cut the cord, sweetie!"*

Patsy Elias Henry "Patsy" Hendren *(1889–1962)*
English cricket player. Barclay's *World of Cricket*
describes his "sharply protruding rump pro-
claiming his resolution."

Patterson Patterson Ewen *(1925–)*
Canadian abstract painter.

Patti Patti Page *(originally Clara Ann Fowler) (1927–)*
American popular singer.

Patty Patty Smith Hill *(19th century)*
American Sunday-school teacher. She and
Mildred Hill composed "Happy Birthday to
You," the world's most-sung song, which
remains under copyright until the year 2010.

Paul Paul Gaugin *(Eugène-Henri-Paul Gaugin)
(1848–1903)*
French painter. He is the subject of Somerset
Maugham's novel *The Moon and Sixpence* (1919).
"To have lived is to want revenge."

Paul-Émile Paul-Émile Borduas *(1905–1960)*
Canadian abstract painter.

Paula Paula Abdul *(1962–)*
American pop singer and choreographer. She
started her career as a Laker Girl cheerleader.

Paule Paule Marshall *(1929–)*
American writer, author of the novel *Brown Girl,
Brownstones* (1959).

Paulette Paulette Goddard *(originally Pauline Marion
Levy) (1905–1990)*
American actress. She lost a chance at the role
of Scarlett O'Hara in *Gone With the Wind* (1939)
because of her rumoured romance with Charlie
Chaplin.

Top 10 Baby Names for Future Table Dancers

Chesty • Divine • Fabio • Gennifer •

Gypsy • Ilona • Kyrstyne •

Laetitia • Lola • Mandy

Pauline Pauline Marie Bonaparte, Princess Borghese *(1780–1825)*
Favourite sister of Napoleon. She posed memorably for the sculptor Antonio Canova.

Paulo Paulo Coelho *(1948–)*
Brazilian self-help guru, author of the best-selling *The Alchemist* (1993). He doesn't personally answer his 1,000 daily fan letters, but kisses each one before giving it to his secretary.

Pauly Pauly Shore *(20th century)*
American performer, the irritating "Weasel" on MTV. The *Globe and Mail* newspaper called him "a pioneer in Hollywood's ongoing quest to give stupid a good name."

Pavel Pavel Geordiyenko *(20th century)*
Russian explorer, in 1943 a member of the first party to reach the North Pole on foot.

Peadar Peadar O'Donnell *(Peter O'Donnell) (1893–1986)*
Irish revolutionary and writer.

Pearl Pearl S. Buck *(Pearl Sydenstricker Buck, or Mrs. Richard J. Walsh) (1892–1973)*
American missionary, author of the best-selling *The Good Earth* (1931) and winner of the 1938 Nobel Prize for literature.

> *"How could an actual person fit into the covers of a book? The book is not a continent, not a definite geographical measure, it cannot contain so huge a thing as an actual full-size person. Any person has to be scaled by elimination to fit the book world."*

Pedro Pedro Carolino *(19th century)*
Portuguese author of the classic *The New Guide of the Conversation in Portuguese and English* (1869) republished as *English as She Is Spoke*. Recommended phrases include, "If you like, I will hot it."

Pee Wee Pee Wee Herman *(alter ego of Paul Reubens) (1952–)*
American comic, proprietor of TV's "Pee Wee's Playhouse."

> *"What could be more fun than history? The chills, the spills, the spendor of it all."*

Peg Peg Woffington *(Margaret Woffington) (1720–1760)*
Irish actress. Charles Reade's novel *Peg Woffington* (1835) was inspired by her action-packed life.

Pegasus Pegasus *trans. of the wells*
Fabulous Greek winged horse, born from the blood of Medusa after her head was severed.

Peggy Peggy Ashcroft *(Dame Edith Margaret Emily Ashcroft) (1907–1991)*
British stage actress. She won an Oscar for *A Passage to India* (1984).

Pelagius Pelagius *(c. 360–c. 420)*
British monk, inventor of the popular Pelegian heresy in which original sin and predestination are rejected in favour of free will and the ability to do good.

Pelé Pelé *(originally Edson Arantes de Nascimento) (1940–)*
Brazilian soccer genius.

Peleg Peleg Arkwright *(pen-name of David Law Proudfit) (1842–1897)*
English poet.

Peleus King Peleus of the Myrmidons *trans. muddy*
Thessalian ruler, father of Achilles by the goddess Thetis. He was the only mortal ever to marry a goddess, though others had affairs.

Pelham Sir Pelham Grenville (P.G.) Wodehouse *(1881–1975)*
English writer, creator of the inimitable Jeeves. Critic Sean O'Casey called him "English literature's performing flea."

"I believe there are two ways of writing novels. One is mine, making a sort of musical comedy without music and ignoring real life altogether; the other is going deep down into life and not caring a damn."

Pellinore King Pellinore
Wandering king in T.H. (Terence Hanbury) White's version of the Arthurian legend, *The Once and Future King* (1958).

Penelope Penelope *trans. with a web over her face*
Greek weaver, the faithful wife of Odysseus, for whom she resisted 108 suitors for twenty years until he finally returned home from his voyages.

Penn Penn Jillette *(20th century)*
American postmodern conjurer, half of the team of Penn and Teller, co-author of *How to Play with Your Food* (1992).

Penny Penny Ann Early *(20th century)*
American jockey. In a 1969 publicity stunt, she became the first woman to play professional basketball.

Penrod *Penrod (1914)*
American novel by Booth Tarkington.

Penthesileia Penthesileia *trans. forcing men to mourn*
Amazon Queen slain by Achilles. He stripped the armour from her body, saw her lovely face, and began to weep. When Thersites laughed at this, Achilles killed him too.

Pep Pep *(20th century)*
American Labrador dog who in 1924 killed the cat belonging to neighbour Governor Gifford Pinchot, was tried for murder and sentenced to life in jail, where he became a popular resident, answering roll-call faithfully every morning.

Pépé Pépé le Pew *(1944–)*
Amorous American cartoon skunk, winner of an Oscar for *For Scenti-mental Reasons* (1949). He bears a striking resemblance to Charles Boyer as Pépé le Moko in *Algiers* (1938).

PETE ROSE

"Ah, ah, she is playing hard to get, that little coquette."

Pepin Pepin the Short *(c. 715–768)*
King of the Franks, father of the great Charlemagne.

Pepper Pepper Martin *(Johnny Martin) (1904–1965)*
American baseball outfielder with the Cardinals, an All-Star with a career batting average of .418. He once threw a ball that was followed by yards of bandage from a broken finger. Questioned by reporters, he said, "It's only a small bone."

Per Per Lindstrand *(20th century)*
British aviator. In 1987, he and his partner were the first people to cross the Atlantic in a balloon.

Percival Percival C. (P.C.) Wren *(20th century)*
English author of the novel *Beau Geste* (1924).

Percy Percy Bysshe Shelley *(1792–1822)*
English poet.
"Familiar arts are beautiful through love."

Perdita Perdita *(originally Mary Darby Robinson) (1758–1800)*
English actress and writer, mistress of the future George IV when he was seventeen and she was thirty. She got her name playing Perdita in William Shakespeare's play *The Winter's Tale* (c. 1610–11).

Peregrine *Peregrine Pickle (1751)*
English novel by Tobias Smollett.

Peregrinus Peregrinus *(d. c. 79)*
Inhabitant of Pompeii. Graffiti drawings found there ridicule his big nose.

Pericles Pericles *(c. 490–429 B.C.)*
Athenian politican. He brought down the ruling oligarchy of Athens, but failed to achieve a great confederation of all the Hellenic states.

Perkin Perkin Warbeck *(1474–1499)*
English impersonator of young Prince Richard, who was smothered in the Tower. He was hanged.

Perpetua St. Perpetua *(d. 203)*
Matron martyr of Carthage, stabbed to death after an unsuccessful attempt to persuade wild beasts to eat her in the amphitheatre. The tale of her martyrdom became so popular that St.

Augustine complained it was read in churches along with Scripture.

Perry Perry Como *(originally Pierino Como) (1912–)*
American baritone crooner.

Persephone Persephone *(formerly Cora, or Core) trans. bringer of destruction*
Legendary Greek daughter of Zeus and Demeter. When Pluto kidnapped her, sorrowful Demeter plunged the world into winter until she was found. Persephone now spends six months of the year with Pluto, and every year Demeter creates winter until she returns.

Pert Pert Kelton *(1907–1968)*
American actress. She played Alice on Jackie Gleason's original TV show "The Honeymooners", but was dropped from "The Jackie Gleason Show" in 1952 as a suspected communist.

Perugino Perugino *(real name Pietro di Cristoforo Vannucci) (c. 1450–1523)*
Italian painter. His murals were destroyed to make space for Michelangelo to redecorate the Sistine Chapel with the *Last Judgement*.

Pervis Pervis Staples *(1935–)*
American gospel singer with the Staple Singers.

Pete Pete Rose *(Peter Edward Rose) (1941–)*
American record-setting baseball infielder for the Reds, later a manager. In 1989, he earned a lifetime suspension for gambling.

Peter *Peter Pan (original title: Peter and Wendy) (1911)*
English children's story by J.M. (James Matthew) Barrie.
> *"To die will be an awfully big adventure."*

Pétomane Le Pétomane *(real name Joseph Pujol) (1857–1945)*
French entertainer who had an extremely successful music-hall act based on novelty farting. He once sued a female "Pétomane" for copying him, but before the trial she was exposed as a fraud who concealed whistles and bellows under her skirt.

Petra Petra Kelly *(1947–1992)*
German environmental worker.

Petrarch Petrarch *(Francesco Petrarca) (1304–1374)*
Italian poet, second only to Dante in his time.
> *"A shortcut to riches is to subtract from our desires."*

Petrona Petrona Lashley *(1941–)*
British Lord Mayor of Liverpool and former prostitute.
> *"I am surprised that so much attention has been paid to spent convictions, the majority of which happened 20 years ago."*

Petruchio Petruchio
Romantic tamer of Kate in William Shakespeare's play *The Taming of the Shrew* (1593–94).

Petrus Petrus Peregrinus *(or Peter the Pilgrim, or Peter of Maricourt) (13th century)*
French Crusader and scientist. He was the first person to mark the two sides of the round magnetic compass as "north" and "south."

Petrushka *Petrushka (1911)*
Russian ballet by Igor Stravinski. The title role was danced by Vaslav Nijinski.

Petula Petula Clark *(1932–)*
British pop singer, known for the hit "Downtown." She made her début at age nine.

Peyton Peyton Randolph *(1721–1775)*
American politician, president of the Continental Congress.

Phaedrus Phaedrus *(Gaius Julius Phaedrus) (1st century)*
Thracian slave, the translator of Aesop's fables into Latin.
> *"A fly bit the bare pate of a bald man, who in endeavouring to crush it gave himself a hard slap. Then said the fly jeeringly, "You wanted to revenge the sting of a tiny insect with death; what will you do to yourself, who have added insult to injury?""*

Pheidippides Pheidippides *(5th century B.C.)*
Greek athlete. He ran 150 miles in two days to ask the Spartans to send help fighting the Persians at the Battle of Marathon. Modern marathon races are only 26.2 miles.

Phidias Phidias *(or Pheidias) (d. 432 B.C.)*
Greek sculptor, the greatest of his age. He created the gold and ivory statue of Athena Parthenos for the Parthenon, which survived intact until destroyed by mediaeval Christian Crusaders.

Phil Phil Spector (*originally Philip Harvey Spector*)
(*1940–*)
American rock-record producer, creator of "Phil
Spector's Wall of Sound."
> "*The people of America are just not born with
> culture.*"

Phileas Phileas Fogg
Intrepid French traveller of *Around the World in
Eighty Days* (1873) by Jules Verne.

Philibert Philibert, Comte de Gramond
(*1621–1707*)
French court favourite of Louis XIV, author of a
scandalous *Mémoires* (1713).

Philip Philip K. Dick (*Philip Kindred Dick*)
(*1925–1982*)
American science-fiction master, author of
Do Androids Dream of Electric Sheep? (1967)
and a cult figure to the "Dick Head" fans of
California.

Philipp Philipp Rosenthal (*1855–1937*)
Bavarian porcelain manufacturer.

Philippa Philippa of Hainault (*c. 1314–1369*)
English wife of Edward III. She asked him to
show mercy to the burghers of Calais. Queen's
College, Oxford, is named for her.

Philippe Philippe Starke (*20th century*)
French trendoid designer of status consumer
goods.

Philippine The Blessed Philippine Duchesne
(*originally Rose-Philippine Duchesne*) (*1769–1852*)
French religious worker. In 1818, she brought
the Society of the Sacred Heart of Jesus to the
United States.

Philips Philips Brooks (*1835–1893*)
American bishop and songwriter.
> "*O little town of Bethlehem*
> *How still we see thee lie*
> *Above thy deep and dreamless sleep*
> *The silent stars go by.*"

Phillida Phillida Erskine-Brown
Fictional British lawyer, the professional associate of Old Bailey reprobate Horace Rumpole in
the detective series by John Mortimer.

Phillis Phillis Wheatley (*c. 1753–1784*)
Senegal-born American child kidnapped into
slavery. She was taught English by her American
owners, within sixteen months could read the
Bible, and by age thirteen was writing poetry.

Philo Philo Remington (*1816–1889*)
American inventor. He and his father, Eliphalet,
perfected the breech-loading rifle.

Philocleon Philocleon
Elderly Athenian in Aristophanes' satiric play
The Wasps (422 B.C.) who loves courtrooms.
Confined to the house by his son, he puts the
dog on trial for stealing cheese.

Phineas Phineas T. Barnum (*Phineas Taylor Barnum*)
(*1810–1891*)
American circus owner.
> "*Every crowd has a silver lining.*"

Phineus Phineus *trans. sea-eagle*
Greek fiancé of Andromeda. He did not try to
save her from an attacking sea monster but,
when Perseus killed the monster, tried to
reclaim her. Perseus turned him into a stone.

Phoebe Phoebe Cary (*1824–1871*)
English poet.
> "*And though hard be the task,*
> *Keep a stiff upper lip.*"

Phoenix Phoenix
Fabulous Egyptian bird, the only one of its kind.
It lived for six hundred years, then lit its own
funeral pyre, and was reborn from the ashes.

Phoumi Phoumi Vongvichit (*1910–1994*)
Laotian revolutionary and politician.

Phyllida Phyllida
English character in the *Ballad of Beau Brocade*
by Hugh Dobson.
> "*Phyllida my Phyllida*
> *She dons her russet gown*
> *And runs to gather maydew*
> *Before the world is down.*"

Phyllis Phyllis Diller (*originally Phyllis Driver*) (*1917–*)
American comedian.
> "*Cleaning the house while the kids are still grow-*
> *ing is like shoveling the walk before it stops*
> *snowing.*"

Phyrne Phyrne *(4th century B.C.)*
Greek courtesan accused of profaning the Eleusian mysteries. Her lawyer won the case by stripping her naked in court, revealing her loveliness.

Piapot Piapot *(or Payepat) (1816–1908)*
Canadian Cree chief. The Piapot Reserve in Saskatchewan is named after him.

Piast Piast *(9th century)*
Polish ploughman, legendary ancestor of the Piast princes.

Pick Pick Withers *(20th century)*
British drummer briefly with the group Dire Straits.

Pico Pico Iyer *(20th century)*
British-born author of *Video Night in Kathmandu* (1988). He carries an Indian passport and lives in California and Japan.
　　"I was a foreigner from the time I was born."

Pier Pier Paolo Pasolini *(1922–1975)*
Italian filmmaker, author of *Un Vita Violenta* *("A Violent Life")* (1959).

Pierce Pierce Brosnan *(1951–)*
Irish-born British actor, the 1995 James Bond.

Piero Piero della Francesca *(c. 1420–1492)*
Italian painter.

Pierpont Pierpont Morgan *(John Pierpont Morgan) (1837–1913)*
American financier and art collector.

Pierre Pierre Elliott Trudeau *(1919–)*
Canadian politician. As prime minister, he rolled down the window of his limousine near some demonstrators, and said, "Mange de la merde."

Piers Piers de Gaveston *(c. 1284–1312)*
English nobleman, the very close personal companion of King Edward II.

Piet Piet Mondrian *(Pieter Cornelis Mondriaan) (1872–1944)*
Dutch artist.

Pieter Pieter Zeeman *(1865–1943)*
Dutch physicist. He discovered the "Zeeman effect," where a ray of light from a source in a magnetic field has its spectroscopic line widened (or even doubled).

Piggy Robert "Piggy" Muldoon *(Robert David Muldoon) (1921–)*
Porcine New Zealand accountant and prime minister. The round shape of his parliament building inspired graffiti reading, "New Zealanders are dumb. We are the only country that has put a pig in a beehive."

PHYLLIS DILLER

Pigpen Ron "Pigpen" McKernan *(1945–1973)*
American psychedelic keyboard player with the band the Grateful Dead.

Pilar Pilar
Guerrilla wife in Ernest Hemingway's novel *For Whom the Bell Tolls* (1940).

Pilate Pontius Pilate *(1st century)*
Fifth Roman procurator of Judea. "Pontius" was his family name; "Pilate" means "pikeman."

Pina Pina Bausch *(originally Phillippine Bausch) (1940–)*
German choreographer and dancer.

Pincher Pincher Martin *(Admiral Sir William F. Martin) (active 1860)*
English disciplinarian sailor.

Pinckney Pinckney Benton Stewart (P.B.S.) Pinchback *(1837–1921)*
American politician. He was elected to the Senate in 1872, but refused his seat by colleagues because of his mixed racial origins.
　　"I am groping about through this American forest of prejudice and proscription, determined to find some form of civilization where all men will be accepted for what they are worth."

Pindar Pindar *(or Pindaros) (c. 522–c. 440 B.C.)*
Greek lyric poet, creator of forty-four odes to the winners of the Panhellenic Festivals expressing pious admiration for bodily beauty, which the Greeks felt to be a sacred gift from the gods.

Ping Ping Bodie *(Frank Stephan Bodie, originally Francesco Stephano Pezzolo) (1887–1961)*
American baseball outfielder with the White Sox. He also played with the Yankees, where he was the room-mate of fast-living Babe Ruth.
"I don't room with Ruth; I room with his suitcase."

Pink The Pink Panther *(1964–)*
American cartoon star. He got his start in the credits of Blake Edwards's American movie *The Pink Panther* (1964).

Pinky Pinky Lee *(originally Pincus Leff) (1908–1993)*
American vaudeville performer.

Pinocchio *Pinocchio (1940)*
American animated film by Walt Disney, based on a story by Carlo Collodi.

Pio Pio Fortunato Castellani *(1793–1865)*
Roman goldsmith. He rediscovered the secret of Etruscan filigree.

Pip Pip *(full name Philip Pirrip)*
English hero of Charles Dickens' novel *Great Expectations* (1861).

Pipeline Harry "Pipeline" Cooper *(1904–)*
English golfer. He earned his nickname because his shots were so straight it seemed he had a pipeline to the hole.

Piper Piper Laurie *(originally Rosetta Jacobs) (1932–)*
American actress. She played Paul Newman's girlfriend in *The Hustler* (1961).

Pippa *Pippa Passes (1841)*
English play by the poet Robert Browning.
"God's in his heaven—
All's right with the world!"

Pippi *Pippi Longstocking (1945)*
Swedish children's novel by Astrid Lindgren.

Pisistratus Pisistratus *(or Peisistratos) (600–527 B.C.)*
Greek tyrant of Athens. In 534 B.C. he established the first dramatic festival, where Thespis, inventor of acting, won a prize.

Pitirim Pitirim Alexandrovich Sorokin *(1889–1968)*
Russian-born American sociologist, author of *Fads and Foibles of Modern Sociology* (1956).

Placido Placido Domingo *(1941–)*
Spanish opera tenor and conductor.

Plantagenet Plantagenet *(nickname of Geoffrey, Count of Anjou) (1113–1151)*
British father of King Henry II. His nickname from wearing in his hat a sprig of broom (*planta genista orgenet*) became the name of his dynasty.

Plato Plato *(427–347 B.C.)*
Greek master philosopher, author of the *Republic*.
"A boy, of all wild beasts, is the most difficult to manage."

Pliny Pliny *(Gaius Plinius Secundus Pliny, "The Elder") (23–79)*
Roman writer on natural sciences. He died overcome by toxic fumes while trying to observe a volcano.
"In comparing various authors with one another, I have discovered that some of the gravest and latest writers have transcribed, word for word, from former works, without making acknowledgement."

Plon-Plon Plon-Plon *(Prince Napoleon Joseph Charles Paul Bonaparte) (1822–1891)*
French nephew of Napoleon. In the Crimea he was accused of cowardice ("craint-plomb," or "fear of lead").

Plutarch Plutarch *(or Ploutarchos) (c. 46–c. 120)*
Greek philosopher and historian. He wrote a series of *biographies* of noted historical figures.
"He is a fool who lets slip a bird in the hand for a bird in the bush."

Pluto Pluto *(1930–)*
Animated American dog, pet of Mickey Mouse.

Plutus *Plutus (388 B.C.)*
Greek play by Aristophanes concerning the adventures of Plutus, blind god of wealth, who is the original "plutocrat."

Pocahontas Pocahontas *(original name Matoaka, later Mrs. Rebecca Rolfe) (1595–1617)*
American Indian princess, daughter of chief Powhatan and the saviour of John Smith when his life was threatened by her tribe. She later converted to Christianity, married a different Englishman, and died while visiting England.

Poison Mike "Poison" Ivie *(1952–)*
American baseball infielder with the Padres. His promising career was damaged by his attitude, or as one critic put it, "Mike Ivie is a forty-million-dollar airport with a thirty-dollar control tower."

Poker "Poker Alice" Tubbs *(1851–1930)*
American card-sharp, noted for her trademark pistol and cheroot. During a married interval, she raised seven orphans.

Pokey Pokey Watson *(Lillian Debra Watson) (1950–)*
American athlete. She won her first Olympic gold medal, for freestyle relay swimming, at age fourteen.

Pol Pol Pot *(originally Saloth Sar) (1926–)*
Cambodian politician, mastermind of the "Killing Fields."

Pola Pola Negri *(originally Barbara Apolonia Chalupiec) (1894–1987)*
Polish-born American movie femme fatale, the "magnificent wildcat." She fainted at a New York memorial service for Rudolph Valentino, and awoke to describe their secret love affair. His wife, Natasha Rambova, retaliated by contacting Rudolph in the spirit world for assurance he loved no one else.

Polly Polly Kinnan *(originally Mary Kinnan) (1763–1848)*
American frontierswoman. She wrote a memoir of her three years' captivity with the Delaware Indians.

Pollyanna Pollyanna *(1913)*
American children's novel by Eleanor Porter. It was an immediate and lasting success.

Polybius Polybius *(c. 205–c. 123 B.C.)*
Greek historian. He witnessed firsthand the Roman destruction of Carthage in 146 B.C.

Polyhymnia Polyhymnia *(or Polymnia)*
Greek Muse of sacred song and rhetoric.

Pomona Pomona
Roman goddess of gardens and fruit trees.

Pongo Pongo
Dalmation daddy in the Walt Disney film *Hundred and One Dalmations* (1961).

Pontiac Pontiac *(c. 1720–1769)*
Chief of the Ottawa Indians. He besieged Detroit for five months.

Pooka Pooka *(later known as Puck)*
Pre-Celtic English god. He later degenerated into a mere goblin.

Pookie James "Pookie" Hudson *(1934–)*
American doo-wop singer with the Spaniels.

Poor Poor Fred *(Frederick, Prince of Wales) (1706–1751)*
British heir to King George II, a passionate cricket amateur who died of an abscessed bruise from a cricket ball.

Pop John Henry "Pop" Lloyd *(1884–1965)*
American baseball player in the Negro Leagues, the "Black Honus Wagner." Babe Ruth described him as the greatest player of all time in any league.

Popeye Popeye the Sailor *(1929–)*
American cartoon character. He started life as a supporting character in Elzie Crisler Segar's cartoon strip "Thimble Theatre."

Poppaea Poppaea *(d. c. 66)*
Roman wife of the Emperor Nero. He killed her by kicking her while she was pregnant.

Popski Vladimir "Popski" Peniakoff *(1897–1951)*
Belgian soldier. In 1942 he formed Popski's Private Army to operate behind the German lines in North Africa, for which he was decorated by Britain, France, and Belgium. He wrote *Private Army* (1950).

Porfirio Porfirio Rubirosa *(married 1951)*
Dominican Republic playboy, briefly the husband of Woolworth heiress Barbara Hutton. Zsa Zsa Gabor said that "[Rubirosa] is to lovemaking what Tiffany is to diamonds."

Porgy Porgy and Bess *(1935)*
American opera by George and Ira Gershwin.

Porky Porky Pig *(1935–)*
American animated character, first seen in Friz Frelong's *I Haven't Got a Hat* (1935). Over the years he has become shorter and prissier.

Porphyry Porphyry (*originally Malchus*)
(*c. 232–c. 305*)
Syrian Neoplatonist philosopher. A brilliant
student, he was known as "a living library and a
walking museum."

Porter Porter Wagoner (*1927–*)
American country singer.

Portia Portia
Heiress-lawyer in William Shakespeare's play
The Merchant of Venice (1596–97).
> *"The quality of mercy is not strained . . .*
> *It blesseth him that gives and him that takes."*

Postverta Postverta
Roman goddess, guardian of childbirth.

Potato Mr. Potato Head (*1952–*)
American toy. It originally featured a real
potato.

Poul Poul Anderson (*20th century*)
American science-fiction writer.

Poundmaker Chief Poundmaker (*1826–1886*)
Canadian Crowfoot leader. He helped to negotiate Treaty 6 for the Plains Cree.

Poutinette Poutinette (*20th century*)
Québécois cartoon superheroine, ally of
"cranially dense" superhero Angloman. She is
armed with a cholesterol gun. ("Poutine" is a
Québécois delicacy consisting of french fries
garnished with grated cheese and gravy, served
in a cardboard container from a roadside "chip
wagon" with vinegar and ketchup optional.)

Prairie Prairie Prince (*1950–*)
American pop musician with the band Journey.

Praxiteles Praxiteles (*active 370–330 B.C.*)
Greek sculptor. He created the first nude female
carving, a statue of Aphrodite.

Prempeh Prempeh (*d. 1931*)
Last king of Ashanti, in 1896 deposed by the
British. Years later, he was quietly allowed to
return.

Preston Preston Sturges (*originally Edmund Preston
Biden*) (*1898–1959*)
American filmmaker and the inventor of
"kiss-proof" lipstick.

Pretty Pretty Boy Floyd (*Charles Arthur Floyd*)
(*1901–1934*)
American bank-robber. He used to rip up mort-
gages in banks, hoping to save farmers' home-
steads.

Priapus Priapus *trans. pruner of the pear tree*
Greek god of fertility, the ugly large-genitalled
son of Aphrodite by Dionysus. He became a
gardener.

Prideaux Prideaux John Selby (*1788–1857*)
English naturalist, author of *A History of British
Forest Trees* (1842).

Primo Primo Levi (*1919–1987*)
Italian writer and chemist. He wrote *If This Is a
Man* (1947) about his experiences in Auschwitz.

Prince Prince (*originally Prince Rogers Nelson*)
(*1958–*)
American pop composer. He now represents
himself with a graphic symbol instead of a written name.

Prinny Prinny (*Prince George, later King George IV*)
(*1762–1830*)
British Prince Regent during his father's madness. He disliked his wife, Caroline, so much
that he refused to let her attend his coronation,
on the excuse she didn't have a ticket.

Priscilla Priscilla Presley *née Beaulieu* (*1945–*)
American wife of Elvis Presley, star of the
"Naked Gun" movies.

Prissy Prissy
American fictional maid, played by Butterfly
McQueen in the film *Gone With the Wind*
(1939).
> *"Mizz Scarlett, I don't know nothin' 'bout
> birthin' babies!"*

Procrustes Procrustes *trans. stretcher-out*
Greek bad host, a legendary obsessive-
compulsive. To make visitors fit his bed, he
either stretched their legs longer, or cut them
off. Theseus killed him.

Professor Professor Longhair (*Henry Roeland Byrd*)
(*1918–1980*)
New Orleans piano stylist.

Prometheus Prometheus *trans. forethought*
Greek Titan. Cleverer than the gods, he stole fire from Mount Olympus to give to mankind, and for this crime was chained by Zeus to a mountain for thirty years while a vulture ate his liver by day and it regenerated by night. He was freed by Heracles.

Propertius Propertius *(50–15 B.C.)*
Roman elegiac poet, a friend of Ovid's and Virgil's.
> *"Never change when love has found its home."*

Prosper Prosper Mérimée *(1803–1870)*
French novelist. He was very proud of having slept with Mary, widow of the poet Shelley.

Prospero Prospero Alpini *(1553–1616)*
Italian botanist, the discoverer of the sex life of plants.

Prudence Prudence Fenton *(c. 1950–)*
American animator. She did the title sequence for "Pee Wee's Playhouse" (1986).

Prue Miss Prue
Character in the English play *Love for Love*. Actress Frances Abington was painted in the role by Sir Joshua Reynolds.

Prunella Prunella Scales *(originally Margaret Rumney) (1945–)*
English actress. She played Mrs. Fawlty on the TV series "Fawlty Towers."

Ptolemy Ptolemy *(Claudius Ptolemaeus) (c. 90–168)*
Egyptian astronomer. The Ptolemaic System remained a standard concept until the 16th century.

Puabi Queen Puabi *(c. 2600–2400 B.C.)*
Mesopotamian queen. She was splendidly buried with gold and followers in the Royal Cemetery of Ur.

Pud Pud Galvin *(James Francis Galvin) (1856–1902)*
American baseball pitcher and manager for Buffalo, a member of the Hall of Fame.

Pudd'nhead Pudd'nhead Wilson
Fictional American created by Mark Twain.
> *"Cauliflower is nothing but cabbage with a college education."*

Pudlo Pudlo Pudlar *(1917–1993)*
Canadian Inuit artist. She was the first Inuit to have a one-person show at the National Gallery of Canada.

Pug Pug Ismay *(Lionel Hastings Ismay, 1st Baron) (1887–1965)*
English soldier.

Pumpsie Pumpsie Green *(originally Elijah Jerry Green) (1933–)*
American baseball shortstop, the first black player with the Boston Red Sox.
> *"Some day I'll write a book and call it* How I Got the Nickname Pumpsie *and sell it for a dollar and if everybody who ever asked me that question buys the book, I'll be a millionaire."*
(It came from his mother shortening the endearment "Pumpkin.")

Punch Punch Imlach *(originally George Imlach) (1918–)*
Canadian hockey manager for the Toronto Maple Leafs.
> *"As a coach—or general manager for that matter —you must always remember that when you're on your way in, you're on your way out. It all depends on how fast your old wheel is turning because your only end is the boot into the street."*

Pussyfoot W.E. "Pussyfoot" Johnson *(1862–1945)*
American law-enforcement officer, famous for his stealth and persistence in pursuing illegal alcohol.

Pygmalion King Pygmalion of Cyprus *trans. Shaggy-first*
Mythic Greek sculptor who carved an ideal woman, fell in love with his creation, and prayed to the goddess Aphrodite to bring her to life, which she did. (*See* Galatea.)

Pyotr Pyotr Grushin *(1905–1993)*
Russian rocket scientist. He designed the V-750 ground-to-air missile that brought down American pilot Francis Gary Power over the Urals in 1960s.

Pyramus Pyramus

Babylonian lover of Thisbe. Forbidden to meet by their parents, they arranged to meet at an abandoned tomb. Thisbe arrived first, but had to flee a lioness, dropping her veil. The lioness mauled the veil, so that when Pyramus arrived he thought Thisbe was dead, and killed himself in sorrow. Thisbe returned, found his body, and killed herself too. The blood of the lovers, soaking into the ground, turned the white flowers of mulberry purple.

Pyrrhus King Pyrrhus of Epirus *(c. 318–272 B.C.)*

Greek general. In 280 B.C., he won a long battle at the River Siris with such heavy casualties that his forces were crippled, so that we now talk of "Pyrrhic victories" when the cost of winning is too high.

Pythagoras Pythagoras *(6th century B.C.)*

Greek philosopher and mathematician, the discoverer of "Pythagoras's theorum" that the square of the length of the hypotenuse is equal to the sum of the square of both the short sides. He wrote nothing himself, but was the leader of a group of followers. His second most famous theory is "Do not eat beans."

Python Python

Greek serpent. The Pythian games were named in memory of its killing by Apollo.

Quade Quade Winter *(20th century)*

American tenor.

Quadequina Quadequina *(17th century)*

Native American farmer. In 1630, he introduced popcorn to the Pilgrims.

Quark Quark

Ferengi bartender in the American TV series "Star Trek: Deep Space Nine" (b. 1992).

Qubilah Qubilah Shabazz *(1961–)*

American daughter of Malcolm X. In 1995, she was arrested on charges of plotting to kill Louis Farrakhan, who has been suspected of involvement in the death of her father.

Queen "Queen Ida" Guillory *(1927–)*

American musician, the Creole queen of Zydeco accordion.

Quentin Quentin Crisp *(1908–)*

British homosexual author of *The Naked Civil Servant*. He describes himself as "one of England's stately homos."

Quett Quett Ketumile Joni Masire *(1925–)*

Botswana politician.

Quetzalcoatl Quetzalcoatl

Toltec mythic hero, represented by a feathered serpent. He brought the arts and crafts to humans.

Quickly Mistress Quickly

Hostess of the Boar's Head Tavern frequented by Falstaff in William Shakespeare's plays *Henry IV Part One* (c. 1597) and *Henry IV Part Two* (c. 1598).

Quincy Quincy Jones *(1933–)*

American musician. He had to give up trumpet playing after a brain operation left his head sensitive to pressure.

Quindrida Quindrida *(married c. 757)*

English wife of King Offa of Mercia, who built Offa's Dyke.

Quintilian Quintilian *(Marcus Fabius Quintilianus) (c. 35–c.100)*

Roman orator. His pupils included Pliny the Younger.

"A liar should have a good memory."

Quintin Quintin McGarel Hogg, 2nd Vicount Hailsham *(1907–)*

English Conservative politician.

"The best way I know to win an argument is to start by being in the right."

Quintus Quintus Roscius Gallus *(c. 134–62 B.C.)*

Roman slave-born comic actor. He gave elocution lessons to Cicero.

Quirinius Quirinius *(Luke 2: 2)*

Governor of Syria. It was his edict that forced Joseph and his pregnant wife, Mary, to travel to Bethlehem.

Quiz Dan "Quiz" Quisenberry *(1953–)*

American baseball pitcher for the Royals, an All-Star.

Ra Ra
Egyptian sun god.

Rabbit Rabbit Maranville *(Walter James Vincent Maranville) (1891–1954)*
American baseball shortstop for the Braves, a member of the Hall of Fame. He was noted for antics such as twisting the bill of his cap sideways over one ear and then leaping into the arms of a bigger teammate.

Rabindranath Rabindranath Tagore *(1861–1941)*
Indian author and painter, winner of the 1913 Nobel Prize for literature.
> *"I do not love him because he is good, but because he is my little child."*

Rabon Rabon Delmore *(1916–1952)*
American boogie-woogie singer and guitarist, one of the Delmore Brothers.

Rachael Rachael Heyhoe *(captain 1966–1978)*
English cricket player.

Rachel Rachel Carson *(1907–1964)*
American naturalist, author of the influential *Silent Spring* (1962) describing the effects of pesticides.

Radclyffe Radclyffe Hall *(Marguerite Radclyffe Hall) (1886–1943)*
English novelist, author of the lesbian classic *The Well of Loneliness* (1928).

Radmila Radmila Mays *(1950–)*
Australian mother of the world's first test-tube twins, Stephen and Amanda.

Radovan Radovan Karadzic *(1944–)*
Bosnian Serb leader.

Rafael Rafael Sabatini *(1875–1950)*
Italian-born romantic novelist, author of *Scaramouche* (1921).

Rafer Rafer Johnson *(20th century)*
American actor and bodyguard. In 1968, he was standing beside Robert Kennedy when he was shot by Sirhan Sirhan.

Raffi Raffi *(originally Raffi Cavoukian)(1948–)*
Canadian singer-songwriter. He created the industry of original music for children with *Singable Songs for the Very Young* (1976).

> *"It was an idea whose time had come. Some things are as simple as that."*

Raffles Frank "Raffles" Boucher *(1901–1977)*
Canadian hockey player, a seven-time winner of the Lady Byng Trophy for gentlemanly behaviour.

Ragnar Ragnar Anton Kittil Frisch *(1895–1973)*
Norwegian economist, winner of a 1969 Nobel Prize.

Raguel Raguel *(c. 8th century B.C.)*
Hebrew relative of Tobit, as mentioned in the Apocrypha. His beautiful daughter Sarah killed seven bridegrooms on their wedding nights before Tobit's son Tobias married her and exorcized her demon with the help of an angel.

Rahab Rahab *trans. wide, Joshua 6: 25 (c. 13th century B.C.)*
Old Testament prostitute who hid two spies of Joshua in the city wall. Rahab and her family were spared the burning of Jericho.

Rahere Rahere *(d. 1144)*
English religious worker. He founded St. Bartholomew's Hospital in London.

Rahsaan Rahsaan Roland Kirk *(1936–1977)*
American jazz flautist.

Raimu Raimu *(originally Jules Auguste César Muraire) (1883–1946)*
French actor. He got his first professional job at the age of sixteen.

Rain Rain Phoenix *(20th century)*
American actress, sister of River Phoenix.

Raine Raine, Countess Spencer *(1930–)*
British stepmother of Diana, Princess of Wales, who calls her "Acid Raine."

Rainer Rainer Maria Rilke *(1875–1926)*
Austrian poet. He scheduled two hours for love on his honeymoon, with the rest of the time for writing.

Rainier Rainier III *(Rainier Louis Henri Maxence Bertrande de Grimaldi, prince of Monaco) (1923–)*
Ruler of Monaco, the 26th prince of the House of Grimaldi, husband of Grace Kelly.

Raisa Raisa Gorbachev *(20th century)*
Russian political worker, wife of Mikhail Gorbachev.

RAQUEL WELCH

Rajiv Rajiv Gandhi *(1944–1991)* Indian politician. He and his mother were both victims of assassination.

Ralf Ralf Hutter *(1946–)* German electronic musician with the group Kraftwerk.

Ralph Ralph Ellison *(Ralph Waldo Ellison) (1914–1994)* American writer, author of *The Invisible Man* (1952).

"*When it comes to chillen, women just ain't gentlemen.*"

Ram Ram Dass *(formerly Richard Alpert) (20th century)* American guru.

Rama Rama
Indian hero of the epic *Ramayama* (4th century). Rama tells his friend Hanuman, the monkey god, "As long as men and women tell your story, you will live, indestructible and invincible."

Ramblin' Ramblin' Jack Elliott *(originally Elliott Charles Adnopoz) (1931–)* American folk guitarist. Woody Guthrie said of his singing, "He sounds more like me than I do."

Rambo *Rambo: First Blood (1982)* American movie starring Sylvester Stallone.

Rameses Rameses II *(or Ramses) (ruled 1304–1237 B.C.)* Egyptian ruler, third king of the 19th dynasty, the long-lived megalomaniacal builder of Abu Simbel. His mummy was uncovered in 1881 and moved to a museum.

Ramiro Ramiro Caballero *(20th century)* Mexican baseball star. He hit thirty-five home runs in 1964, with a batting average of .380.

Ramon Ramon Navarro *originally Ramon Samaniegos (1899–1968)* American actor, star of the silent-film version of *Ben-Hur* (1926).

Ramona *Ramona (1884)* American novel by Helen Hunt Jackson.

Ramsay Ramsay MacDonald *(James Ramsay MacDonald) (1866–1937)* Scottish prime minister of Britain.

Ran'l Randolph "Ran'l" McCoy *(bereaved 1882)* American hillbilly. His three sons were murdered by Anderson "Devil Anse" Hatfield in retaliation for the murder of Ellison Hatfield, starting the famous feud of the Hatfields and the McCoys.

Ranan Ranan R. Lurie *(1932–)* American political cartoonist, the most widely syndicated cartoonist in the world.

Randall Randall "Tex" Cobb *(20th century)* American boxer.
"*Sports writers are probably the only individuals in our universe who actually have less constructive jobs than I do. I don't do nothing but hit people. And they don't do nothing but talk about what I do.*"

Randolph Randolph Caldecott *(1846–1886)* English illustrator of children's books. The Caldecott Medal is named after him.

Randy Randy Newman *(1944–)* American pop musician.
"*I have enormous respect for the power of faith — as I would for anything that's a big hit.*"

Ransom Ransom Eli Olds *(1864–1950)* American automobile manufacturer, founder of the Olds Motor Vehicle Company.

Raoul Raoul Wallenberg *(1912–1947)* Swedish diplomat. He managed to rescue thousands of people from the Holocaust before himself vanishing into a Russian prison.

Rap H. Rap Brown *(new name Jamil Abdullah Al-Amin) (1943–)* American political worker, head of the Students' Non-Violent Coordinating Committee in the 1960s.
"*Violence is as American as cherry pie.*"

Raphael Raphael *(or Raffaello Santi, or Raffaello Sanzio) (1483–1520)* Italian master painter and architect.

Raquel Raquel Welch *(originally Rachel Tejada) (1940–)* American sex goddess.

Ras Ras Tafari (*originally Lij Tafari; later the Emperor Haile Selassie*) (*1892–1975*)
Emperor of Ethiopia, the Lion of Judah, a direct descendant of the Queen of Sheba. His name as emperor means "Might of the Trinity."

Rashid Rashid Varachia (*Mohammed Rashid Varachia*) (*20th century*)
Founding president of the multiracial South African Cricket Union, which was created in 1977 after twenty years of negotiation.

Rasselas *Rasselas: The Prince of Abyssinia* (*1759*)
English fable written by Samuel Johnson in one week to pay the cost of his mother's funeral.

Rat Rat Scabies (*originally Chris Miller*) (*1957–*)
British punk drummer with band the Damned.

Ratso Ratso Rizzo
Small-time urban loser of the American film *Midnight Cowboy* (1969), played by Dustin Hoffman.

Rattlesnake Rattlesnake Dick (*originally Richard Baarter*) (*1834–1859*)
American robber. He planned a perfect gold robbery, but missed the pay-off rendezvous when he was arrested for a lesser crime.

Raul Raul Julia (*originally Raul Rafael Carlos y Arcelay*) (*1940–1994*)
Puerto Rican–born American actor. He starred in *Kiss of the Spider Woman* in both the Broadway and the film version.

Ravenna "Ravenna" (*1878*)
English poem by Oscar Wilde, for which he won the Newdigate Prize.

Ravi Ravi Shankhar (*1920–*)
Indian sitar player and composer.

Ray Ray Charles (*Ray Charles Robinson*) (*1930–*)
American soul pianist, blind since the age of seven.
> "*Going blind. Sounds like a fate worse than death, doesn't it? Seems like something which would get a little kid down, make him afraid and leave him half-crazy and sad. Well, I'm here to tell you that it didn't happen that way—at least not with me.*"

Rayfield Rayfield Wright (*1945–*)
American football offensive tackle with the Dallas Cowboys.

Raymond Raymond Chandler (*Raymond Thornton Chandler*) (*1888–1959*)
American detective novelist, author of *The Big Sleep* (1939).
> "*I was neat, clean, shaved and sober, and I didn't care who knew it.*"

Rayner Baron Rayner Goddard (*1877–1971*)
English judge, a believer in the death penalty.
> "*Punishment must punish.*"

Razvi Razvi Asif Iqbal (*1943–*)
Pakistani record-setting cricket player, noted for never unbuttoning his sleeves.

Reba Reba McEntire (*1954–*)
American country star, author of *Reba: My Story* (1995).

Rebecca Rebecca West (*pen-name of Dame Cicily Isabel Andrews, née Fairfield*) (*1892–1983*)
Irish novelist and journalist. At age eighty-five, she asked to try on a green caftan in a shop, was told it was a maternity dress, and replied, "One can always hope for miracles."

Rebekah Rebekah *Genesis 22: 23* (*c. 17th century B.C.*)
Old Testament matriarch, mother of the twins Esau and Jacob.

Red "Red Emma" Goldman (*1869–1940*)
Lithuanian-born American anarchist, author of *My Disillusionment in Russia* (1923).

Redburga Redburga (*active c. 838*)
English wife of King Egbert. She was a racist who persuaded him to ban Welsh immigration.

Redd Redd Foxx (*1923–1991*)
American comedian.

Redferne Redferne Hollinshead (*Percy Redferne Hollinshead*) (*1885–1937*)
English-born Canadian tenor. In 1912, he recorded some of the earliest sound cylinders for Thomas Edison.

Reece Reece "Goose" Tatum (*1922–1969*)
American basketball centre with the Harlem Globetrotters, the "Clown Prince of Basketball."

REDD FOXX

Reed Reed Waddell *(1859–1895)*
American swindler. He owned a lead brick covered with triple gold plate.

Reg Reg Smythe *(originally Reginald Smith) (1917–)*
British cartoonist, the creator of Andy Capp.

Regan Regan
Flattering two-faced daughter in William Shakespeare's play *King Lear* (c. 1605).

Reggie Reggie Kray *(1933–)*
English gangster, twin brother of gangster Ronnie Kray.

Regina Regina Barreca *(20th century)*
American writer, author of *Perfect Husbands (& Other Fairy Tales): Demystifying Marriage, Men and Romance* (1995).
> *"How come there's no 'I'm 35 and I still live with my parents' Ken [doll]? Or 'Six-pack a day' Ken?"*

Reginald Reginald J. Mitchell *(1895–1937)*
British aircraft engineer, designer of the Spitfire. He died before the Spitfire's winning performance in the Battle of Britain.

Regine Regine Debora Freud *(b. 1860)*
Viennese sister of Sigmund Freud.

Reinhold Reinhold Messner *(1944–)*
Italian mountain climber. He made the first ascent of Mount Everest without oxygen.

Reinier Reinier de Graaf *(1641–1673)*
Dutch physician. The Graafian vesicles of the ovary are named after him.

Reinold St. Reinold *(d. c. 960)*
German monk in charge of renovating St. Pantaleon Monastery. He was killed by stonemasons irritated that he worked harder than they did, and is the patron of stonemasons.

Reizi Reizi Bozyk *(1914–1993)*
Polish-born American actress. She played the Bubie in *Crossing Delancey* (1988).

Rem Rem Koolhaus *(20th century)*
Trendy Dutch designer and architect.

Rembrandt Rembrandt *(Rembrandt Harmensz van Rijn) (1606–1669)*
Dutch painter. He is considered the first modern painter for his series of revealing self-portraits.

Remi St. Remi *(or Remigius) (c. 437–530)*
French religious worker. He became bishop of Rheims at age twenty-two.

Remington "Remington Steele" *(1982–1987)*
American TV series starring Pierce Brosnan.
> *"Man can only doodle on his napkin for so long."*

Remus Remus
Mythical twin brother of Romulus, co-founder with him of Rome. The twins were both thrown into the river Tiber by their uncle, but were saved and suckled by a she-wolf.

Rémy Rémy de Gourmont *(1858–1915)*
French poet and novelist.
> *"Very simple ideas lie within the reach only of complex minds."*

Rena Rena Owen *(20th century)*
New Zealand actress, star of *Once Were Warriors* (1994).

Rénald Rénald
Irritatingly needy son in the Quebec sit-com "La Petite Vie" (The Banal Life) (1992–95). His father, Popa, agrees not to ridicule him any more, then adds, "You don't mind if I fall asleep while you're talking?"

Renaldo Renaldo "Obie" Benson *(20th century)*
American soul singer with the Four Tops.

Renata Renata Tebaldi *(1922–)*
Italian opera soprano.

Renato Renato Dulbecco *(1914–)*
Italian-born American molecular biologist, winner of a Nobel Prize.

René René Descartes *(1596–1650)*
French father of modern philosophy.
> *"I think, therefore I am."*

Renenit Renenit
Egyptian goddess of birth and child-bearing.

Renzo Renzo De Vacchi *(1894–1967)*
Italian soccer player. He was so popular with fans that they called him "Il Figlio di Dio" ("the Son of God").

Retta Retta Younger *(19th century)*
American sister of the Younger brothers, who rode with the outlaw Jesse James.

Reuben Reuben *trans. see a son, Genesis 49: 3 (c. 16th century B.C.)*
Old Testament first-born son of Jacob and Leah, "unstable as water." He saved Joseph from the jealous brothers by suggesting they put him in a pit to die rather than killing him outright; but by the time he snuck back to rescue him, Joseph had been sold to a slave driver.

Rewin Rewin Stresemann *(1889–1972)*
German ornithologist, author of the definitive *Aves* (1927–34).

Rex Sir Rex Harrison *(originally Reginald Carey Harrison) (1908–1990)*
British actor, "Sexy Rexy." He won an Academy Award for his performance as Professor Higgins in *My Fair Lady* (1964) .

Reynaldo Reynaldo de Oliveira *(20th century)*
Brazilian personality, the 227-kilogram King of the Rio Carnival.

Reyner Reyner Banham *(20th century)*
English architectural historian.

Rezim Rezim Bowie *(1793–1841)*
American inventor of the "Bowie knife," which was popularized by his brother Jim at the Battle of the Alamo.

Rhazes Rhazes *(or Räzi) (9th century)*
Persian alchemist, the greatest physician of his age. He was the first person to distinguish between measles and smallpox.

Rhea Rhea *trans. earth*
Mythical Greek sister/wife of Cronus, "mother of the gods."

Rheticus Rheticus *(real name Georg Joachim von Lauchen) (1514–1574)*
Austrian-born German astronomer noted for creating the trigonometrical tables used by Copernicus.

Rhiannon Rhiannon
Mythical Celtic mother of Pryderi. When he was stolen at birth, she was suspected of murdering him, and was given seven years' penance.

Rhino Larry "Rhino" Reinhardt *(1948–)*
American heavy-metal guitarist with the band Iron Butterfly. They played the classic "In-a-Gadda-Da-Vida" (1968).

Rhoshandiatellyneshiaunneveshenk
Rhoshandiatellyneshiaunneveshenk Koyaanfsquatsiuty Williams *(1984–)*
American child. Since she was named, her father, James, has legally lengthened her name further, to a Guinness record–setting 1,019 letters.

Ric Ric Prichard Throssell *(1922–)*
Australian writer. He wrote a biography of his mother, Katharine Prichard, titled *Wild Weeds and Wind Flowers* (1975).

Rich Rich Little *(20th century)*
Canadian comic impersonator.

Richard Richard Pryor *(Richard Franklin Lenox Thomas Pryor III) (1940–)*
American comic. He grew up in his grandmother's brothel.
> *"It's so much easier for me to talk about my life in front of two thousand people than it is one-to-one. I'm a real defensive person, because if you were sensitive in my neigbourhood you were something to eat."*

Richmal Richmal Crompton, *née Lamburn (1890–1969)*
English teacher, writer of the fabulously successful *Just William* children's books.
> *"She's my best friend. I hate her."*

Rick Rick Blaine
Proprietor of Rick's Café Américain in the film *Casablanca* (1942).
> *"The Germans wore grey, you wore blue."*

Rickey Rickey Henderson *(Rickey Henley Henderson) (1957–)*
American baseball outfielder, known as "Style Dog" for his stylish base-stealing.

Ricky Ricky Nelson *(originally Eric Hilliard Nelson) (1940–1985)*
American musician and teen idol. He was the son of Ozzie and Harriet Nelson, stars of the TV series "The Adventures of Ozzie and Harriet" (1952–66).

Rico Rico Carty (*Ricardo Adolfo Jacobo y Carty*) (*1938–*)
Dominican Republic–born American baseball outfielder. In 1960, not knowing any better, he signed ten different professional contracts.

Ridgely Ridgely Torrence (*1875–1950*)
English poet.
"I was weak as a rained-on bee."

Ridley Ridley Scott (*1937–*)
American film director of the movie *Alien* (1979).

Rigoberto Rigoberto Menchú (*1959–*)
Guatemalan-born Mexican maid and human-rights activist, winner of the 1992 Nobel Peace Prize for her work defending Guatemala's indigenous people. She has created a Rigoberto doll, because "Barbie needs a servant."

Rigoletto Rigoletto (*1851*)
Italian opera by Giuseppe Verdi.

Rikki Rikki Fulton (*1924–*)
Scottish actor and pantomime dame.

Rima Rima
Bird-girl of the English novel *Green Mansions* (1904) by William Henry Hudson. A statue of her by Jacob Epstein stands in the bird sanctuary in Hyde Park, London.

Rimush Rimush (*ruled 2278–2270 B.C.*)
King of Agade in Mesopotamia.

Rin Rin Tin Tin (*1916–1932*)
German-born American shepherd-dog movie star. During the 1920s, he got the top billing at Warner Brothers. In 1976, his estate sued the makers of the film *Won Ton Ton, The Dog That Saved Hollywood*, alleging that the story was based on Rin Tin Tin's life. Filmmaker Michael Winner said, "It's absurd to be sued by a dog, especially by a dog who's been dead for the past twenty years."

RINGO STARR

Rinaldo "Rinaldo" (*c. 1560*)
Romantic Italian poem by Torquato Tasso.

Ring Ring Lardner (*Ringold Wilmer Lardner*) (*1885–1933*)
American writer.
"A good many young writers make the mistake of enclosing a stamped, self-addressed envelope, big enough for the manuscript to come back in. This is too much of a temptation to the editor. Personally I have found it a good scheme to not even sign my name to the story, and when I have got it sealed up in its envelope and stamped and addressed, I take it to some town where I don't live, and mail it from there. The editor has no idea who wrote the story, so how can he send it back? He is in a quandary."

Ringo Ringo Starr (*originally Richard Starkey*) (*1940–*)
British drummer for the Beatles. He got his name by wearing rings.

Rip Rip Torn (*originally Elmore Rual Torn*) (*1931–*)
American actor. He plays the producer on "The Larry Sanders Show."

Ripley Ripley
Tough, space-going heroine of the American film *Alien*, played by actress Sigourney Weaver.

Rita Rita Hayworth (*originally Margarita Carmen Cansino*) (*1918–1987*)
American actress. Actor Peter Lawford described her as "the worst lay in the world—she was always drunk and never stopped eating."

Ritchie Ritchie Valens (*originally Richard Stephen Valenzuela*) (*1941–1959*)
American Chicano teen rocker. He recorded "Let's Go" and "Donna" before dying in a plane crash with the Big Bopper and Buddy Holly.

Rivella The Adventures of Rivella (*1714*)
British fictionalized autobiography by Delarivière Manley.

River River Phoenix (*originally Rio Jude Phoenix*) (*1970–1993*)
American actor, star of *My Own Private Idaho* (1991). He died young of a drug overdose.

Rivka Rivka Golani *(1946–)*
Israeli-born Canadian violinist and artist. She plays a unique hand-made viola.
> *"When the music is there before me I feel as if I could go anywhere."*

Roadrunner Ralph "Roadrunner" Garr *(1945–)*
American baseball outfielder with the Braves, an All-Star.

Roald Roald Engelbreth Gravning Amundsen *(1872–1928)*
Norwegian explorer who beat Robert Scott to the South Pole. He used dogs to pull sleds, which the British refused to do for reasons of honour.

Rob Rob Roy *(Gaelic for "Red Robert," the nickname of Robert MacGregor) (1671–1734)*
Scottish freebooter. His career was popularized by Sir Walter Scott in *Rob Roy* (1818).

Robbie Robbie Robertson *(1943–)*
Canadian guitarist, leader of the Band.

Robert Robert Louis Stevenson *(Robert Louis Balfour Stevenson) (1850–1894)*
Scottish poet, author of *Kidnapped* (1886) and *A Child's Garden of Verses* (1885).
> *"In winter I get up at night*
> *And dress by yellow candle-light*
> *In summer, quite the other way—*
> *I have to go to bed by day."*

Roberta Roberta Bondar *(Dr. Roberta Lynn Bondar) (1945–)*
First Canadian woman astronaut.

Roberto Roberto Rossellini *(1906–1977)*
Italian film director, lover of Ingrid Bergman.

Robertson Robertson Davies *(William Robertson Davies) (1913–1995)*
Canadian writer and critic, author of *Fifth Business* (1970).

Robin Robin Hood *(c. 1250–c. 1350)*
Legendary English robber. There is no evidence he really existed.

Robina Robina Laidlaw *(19th century)*
Scottish pianist. In 1838, she had a brief liaison with Robert Schumann during a quarrel with his wife-to-be, Clara Wieck.

Robinson *Robinson Crusoe (1719–20)*
Satiric English novel by Daniel Defoe, based on the adventures of the real Alexander Selkirk, who was set ashore on uninhabited Juan Fernandez Island after arguing with his captain.

Rocco Rocco Zingar di San Fernando *(20th century)*

MAURICE "ROCKET" RICHARD

Italian grand master of the Knights Templar. In August 1995, he unveiled the Holy Grail at a press conference in Rome.
> *"We have decided it is time the world knew about the Grail's true whereabouts."*

Rochelle Rochelle Pittman, *née Darlene Rochelle Winault (1939–1995)*
Canadian activist, the 1995 *Chatelaine* magazine Woman of the Year. She won a court settlement against her husband's doctor, who allowed her to catch AIDS when he decided not to inform her husband that he had contracted the virus through a transfusion. The doctor felt the couple did not have sex, but did not ask.

Rock Rock Hudson *(originally Roy Harold Scherer, Jr.) (1925–1985)*
American actor, the first major Hollywood star to die of AIDS.

Rocket Maurice "Rocket" Richard *(1921–)*
Canadian hockey right-wing for the Montreal Canadiens. Boston Bruins' goalie Glenn Hall recalled: "when [Richard] came flying towards you with the puck on his stick, his eyes were all lit up, flashing and gleaming like a pinball machine. It was terrifying."

Rockley Rockley Wilson *(Evelyn Rockley Wilson) (1879–1957)*
English cricket bowler and coach. His collection of cricket memorabilia is kept at Lord's.

Rockwell Rockwell Kent *(1882–1971)*
American artist. He was awarded the Lenin Peace Prize in Moscow in 1967.

Rocky Rocky Marciano *(originally Rocco Francis Marchegiano) (1923–1969)*
American boxer. He retired undefeated after forty-nine professional bouts.

Rod Rod Serling *(Rodman Serling) (1924–1975)*
American creator of the TV series "The Twilight Zone" (1959–64). He wrote 90 of the 156 episodes.

Roddy Roddy Doyle *(1958–)*
Irish writer, author of *The Commitments* (1987).

Roderick *Roderick Random (1748)*
English novel by Tobias Smollett.

Rodney Rodney Dangerfield *(1922–)*
American comedian.

Rodolfo Rodolfo Gucci *(20th century)*
Italian tycoon, son of founder Guccio Gucci.

Rodolphe Rodolphe Töpffer *(1799–1846)*
Swiss short-story writer and cartoonist, author of *Voyages en zig-zag* (1843–53).

Rodrigo Rodrigo Borgia *(1431–1503)*
Pope Alexander VI. He was the father of Cesare and Lucrezia Borgia.

Rodrigue Rodrigue Tremblay *(1939–)*
Canadian politician, industry minister of the province of Quebec.
> *"Quebec has been disadvantaged in the auto industry since Confederation." (Confederation was in 1867.)*

Roebuck Roebuck "Pops" Staples *(1915–)*
American singer with the Staples Singers.

Roger Roger Tory Peterson *(1908–)*
American ornithologist. His 1934 field guide to the birds of North America established the format for all bird books.

Roger Roger Bacon *(c. 1214–1294)*
English philosopher, scientist, and alchemist.

Rogers Rogers "Rajah" Hornsby *(1896–1963)*
American baseball infielder for the Cardinals, a member of the Hall of Fame. One of the greatest right-handed hitters of all time, he refused to read or watch movies for fear of ruining his eye.

Roland Roland *(or Rolando) (d. 778)*
Legendary French knight, a nephew of the great Charlemagne. His exploits were described in the 11th century in the *Chanson de Roland*.

Rolf Rolf Boldrewood *(pseudonym of Thomas Alexander Browne) (1826–1915)*
Australian novelist, author of *Babes in the Bush* (1900).

Rolin Rolin Eslinger *(20th century)*
American logger. He set a 1987 Guinness record by buck-sawing a 20-inch-diameter white pine log in 18.96 seconds.

Rollie Rollie Fingers *(Roland Glen Fingers) (1946–)*
American baseball pitcher for the As, an All-Star, and winner of the Cy Young Award.

Rollin Rollin Kirby *(20th century)*
American cartoonist, winner of the 1922 Pulitzer Prize for editorial cartooning.

Rollo Rollo May *(1909–1994)*
American humanist psychologist, author of *The Meaning of Anxiety* (1950), in which he argues that anxiety is normal in our dangerous age.

Roloff Roloff Beny *(originally Wilfred Roy Beny) (1924–1984)*
Canadian photographer and social climber, noted for his coffee-table books subsidized by the Shah of Iran. In later life, he pronounced the name of his home town (Medicine Hat, Alberta) as if it was Italian: "Medicheenay Hat."

Roman Roman Polanski *(1933–)*
French-born Polish film director, of *Chinatown* (1974).

Romeo Romeo Montague
Moody yet romantic hero of William Shakespeare's play *Romeo and Juliet* (1594–96).

Romer Romer Grey *(or Romer Pearl) (19th century)*
American baseball player with the Pirates, brother of novelist Zane Grey

Romy Romy Schneider *(originally Rosemarie Albach-Retty) (1938–1989)*
Austrian actress.

Ron Ron Arad *(20th century)*
Israeli designer noted for his welded sheet-metal armchairs.

Rona Rona Barrett *(1936–)*
American TV gossip.

Ronald Ronald Reagan *(Ronald Wilson Reagan) (1911–)*
American politician and actor, the 40th president.
> *"You can tell a lot about a man's character by the way he eats jelly beans."*

Ronnie Ronnie Kray *(1933–1995)*
English gangster, twin brother of equally notorious Reggie Kray, with whom he ruled the East End during the 1960s. He spent twenty-six years in jail for killing gangster George Cornell for calling him a "fat poof."

Rook David "Rook" Goldflies *(20th century)*
American country-rock musician with the Allman Brothers Band.

Rooster Rick "Rooster" Burleson *(1951–)*
American baseball infielder for the Red Sox, an All-Star and a Gold Glove winner.

Roque The Blessed Roque Gonzalez *(1576–1628)*
Paraguayan missionary tomahawked to death, one of the first beatified martyrs in America.

Rory Rory Flynn *(20th century)*
American daughter of actor Errol Flynn. He used to organize mouse races for her, giving the mice the names of fellow Hollywood stars.

Rosa Rosa Parks *(1913–)*
American bus rider. In 1955 she sparked the modern civil-rights movement by refusing to give up her seat to a white man when he demanded it, as was his legal right at the time in Montgomery, Alabama.

Rosalie *The Sorrows of Rosalie (1829)*
Popular book of English verse written by Caroline Norton, née Sheridan. She started writing to support her dissolute husband.

Rosalind Rosalind Elsie Franklin *(1920–1958)*
English crystallographer. She created X-ray diffraction photography.

Rosalinde Rosalinde
Ingenious heroine of William Shakespeare's play *As You Like It* (1599–1600).

Rosalyn Rosalyn Yalow, *née Sussman (1921–)*
American physiologist noted for her work measuring hormones in blood. She shared a 1977 Nobel Prize with Roer Guillemin and Andrew Schally.

Rosalynde *Rosalynde (1590)*
English play by Thomas Lodge, the inspiration to William Shakespeare for *As You Like It* (1599-1600).

Rosalynn Rosalynn Carter *(1927–)*
American political worker, the wife of President Jimmy Carter.

Rosamond "Rosamond" *(1860)*
Extravagantly sentimental English poem by Algernon Charles Swinburne.

Rosamund Rosamund Clifford *(or "The Fair Rosamond") (d. 1116)*
Celebrated English beauty, mistress of Henry II. She was supposedly murdered by Eleanor of Aquitaine. There is a rose named for her.

Rosanna "Rosanna" *(1982)*
American hit song by the band Toto, in honour of actress Rosanna Arquette.

Rosanne Rosanne Cash *(1955–)*
American country singer, daughter of Johnny Cash.

Rosario Rosario Bayeur *(1875–1944)*
Canadian violin maker. Rosario-Bayeur Street in Montreal is named after him.

Roscoe Roscoe Pound *(1870–1964)*
American botanist. A rare lichen is named after him.

Rose Rose Macaulay *(1881–1958)*
English novelist.
> *"'Take my camel, dear,' said by Aunt Dot as she climbed down from this animal upon her return from High Mass."*

Roseanne Roseanne Barr *(also briefly Roseanne Arnold) (1953–)*
American star of the TV series "Roseanne" (b. 1988).
> *"The thing women have to learn is that nobody gives you power. You just take it."*

Rosella Rosella Hightower *(1920–)*
American ballerina.

Roselle Roselle Mercier Montgomery *(1874–1933)*
American writer, author of *The Fates.*
> *"The fates are not quite obdurate;*
> *They have a grim, sardonic way*
> *Of granting them who supplicate*
> *The thing they wanted yesterday."*

Rosemary Lady Rosemary du Cros *(1900–1992)*
British Air Transport Auxiliary Pilot, or "ATA girl." She flew ninety-one different types of aircraft during the war, sometimes after only reading the manual. She got a postwar commercial pilot's licence despite bad eyesight by memorizing all possible eye charts.

Rosencrantz Rosencrantz
Old school chum in William Shakespeare's play *Hamlet* (1600–10).

Rosie Rosie Day *(20th century)*
American sailor. She spent two years sailing around the world with her husband and young sons. The eight-year-old was caught stuffing a note into a bottle reading "Help! I've been kidnapped by my parents and forced to take a trip around the world!"

Rosina Rosina B. Bonavita *(20th century)*
American factory worker, the original "Rosie the Riveter." In 1943, she and a co-worker set 3,345 rivets in six hours.

Rosita Rosita Forbes *(Joan Rosita Forbes) (1893–1967)*
English writer and traveller, author of *From Red Sea to Blue Nile* (1928).

Ross Ross Perot *(Henry Ross Perot) (1930–)*
American computer executive and one-man third political party.

Rossano Rossano Brazzi *(1916–1994)*
Italian actor. You can see him in *The Barefoot Contessa* (1954).

Roswlia Roswlia Mielezarak *(1868–1981)*
Oldest person recorded in Poland.

Roualeyn Roualeyn George Gordon-Cumming *(1820–1866)*
British lion-hunter, author of *Five Years of a Hunter's Life* (1850).

Rough Bill "Rough" Carrigan *(1883–1969)*
American baseball catcher for the Red Sox, later a manager.

Roundell Roundell Palmer, 1st Earl of Selbourne *(1812–1895)*
English judge. He reorganized the English court system into the Supreme Court of Judicature.

Rowan Rowan Atkinson *(1955–)*
English comic actor, star of "Blackadder" and "Mr. Bean."

Rowdy Rowdy Joe Lowe *(Joseph Lowe) (d. 1880)*
American brothel-keeper. His wife was called Rowdy Kate.

Rowena Rowena *(active c. 475)*
Saxon beauty, given in marriage by her father, King Hengist, to King Vortigern in exchange for Kent.

Rowland Sir Rowland Hill *(1795–1879)*
English inventor of postage stamps.

Roxana Princess Roxana *(4th century)*
Sogdianian wife of Alexander the Great.

Roxanne *Roxanne (1987)*
American movie by Steve Martin, based on Edmond de Rostand's novel *Cyrano de Bergerac* (1897).

Roy Roy C. Sullivan *(working 1942–1977)*
American park ranger. He has been struck seven times by lightning, losing several hats.

Royce Royce Middlebrook Youngs *(known as Ross Youngs) (1897–1927)*
American baseball outfielder for the Giants, a member of the Hall of Fame. He maintained a .306 batting average while dying of Bright's disease. The Giants hired a full-time nurse to travel with him.

Rube Rube Marquard *(Richard William Marquard) (1899–1980)*
American baseball pitcher with the Giants, a member of the Hall of Fame. He also performed on the vaudeville stage.
> *"You wished it on yourselves, and I got nerve enough to sing it."*

Rubin Rubin "Hurricane" Carter *(1937–)*
American boxer falsely convicted of murder. His misfortunes were turned into a song by Bob Dylan, but he was ultimately freed from jail through the efforts of a group of Canadians.

Ruby Ruby Bridges Hall *(1954–)*
American civil-rights worker. Norman Rockwell painted a picture of her at age six being escorted into her school by U.S. marshals. She now works to improve parent involvement at the same school.
> *"I feel like my life has started at 40, like I just woke up and understand. It's quite an experience, I have to say."*

Rud Rud Laederach *(20th century)*
Swiss confectioner. He revolutionized the chocolate-truffle industry in the 1960s with a premade truffle shell.

Rudolf Rudolf Nureyev *(1938–1993)*
Phenomenal Tartar dancer. In later life, he claimed that Miss Piggy of the Muppets was his favourite partner. They danced *Swine Lake*.

Rudolph Rudolph Christian Karl Diesel *(1858–1913)*
German engineer, inventor of the diesel engine.

Rudy Rudy Vallee *(Hubert Prior Vallee) (1901–1986)*
American actor, the first popular "crooner."

Rudyard Rudyard Kipling *(1865–1936)*
Indian-born British author, author of the *Just So Stories* (1902).
> *"A woman is only a woman, but a good cigar is a Smoke."*

Rufus Rufus Choate *(1799–1859)*
American politician.
> *"The final end of government is not to exert restraint but to do good."*

Ruhollah Ayatollah Ruhollah Hendi Khomeini *(1900–1989)*
Iranian political and religious leader.

Rumer Rumer Godden *(Margaret Rumer Godden) (1907–1951)*
British writer, author of *The Mousewife*.

Rumina Rumina
Roman goddess of suckling babies.

Rumpelstiltskin Rumpelstiltskin
Legendary entrepreneurial dwarf.

RuPaul RuPaul *(RuPaul André Charles) (c. 1960–)*
American cult performer.
> *"You're born naked and the rest is drag."*

Rupert Rupert Brooke *(Rupert Chawner Brooke) (1887–1915)*
English poet.
> *"If I should die, think only this of me:*
> *That there's some corner of a foreign field*
> *That is forever England."*

Rush Rush Limbaugh *(Rush Hudson Limbaugh) (1951–)*
American radio monologist, the "patron saint of chauvinists."

Russ Russ Meyer *(b. 1922–)*
American sexploitation filmmaker, "King of the Nudies," creator of *Beyond the Valley of the Dolls* (1970) and other even bigger films.

Russell Russell Baker *(1925–)*
American columnist. Regarding Richard Nixon, he observed, "a group of politicians deciding to dump a President because his morals are bad is like the Mafia getting together to bump off the Godfather for not going to Church on Sunday."

Rusticiano Rusticiano of Pisa *(13th century)*
Italian companion of Marco Polo in prison in Genoa. In 1299, he helped Marco write up the notes of his travels to China.

Rusty Rusty Staub *(Daniel Joseph Staub) (1944–)*
American baseball outfielder with the Mets, an All-Star. He is called "Rusty" for his red hair, or "Le Grande Orange" in Montreal.
> *"I discovered at a very early age that nothing was going to come easy for me, that I'd have to work for my success."*

Rutebeuf Rutebeuf *(c. 1230–1286)*
French entertainer, author of the *Miracle de Théophile* (c. 1260), an early version of the Faust story.

Ruth "Baby" Ruth Cleveland *(b. 1891)*
American political worker; the first child born to a president in the White House. The Curtiss Candy Company renamed its Kandy Kake chocolate bar as the "Baby Ruth" in her honour, or so they claimed when baseball player Babe Ruth sued them for royalties for the use of his name.

Rutherford Rutherford B. Hayes *(Rutherford Birchard Hayes) (1822–1893)*
American politician, the 19th president, called "the Fraud" or "President De Facto" because he managed to win the election with fewer popular votes than his opponent, Samuel Tilden, thanks to the electoral college winner-take-all system.

Ruthie Ruthie Davis *(20th century)*
Intrepid American mother of actress Bette Davis.

Ry Ry Cooder *(originally Ryland Peter Cooder) (1947–)*
American guitarist, a living encyclopaedia of folk-songs.

Ryan Ryan O'Neal *(originally Patrick Ryan O'Neal) (1941–)*
American actor. He played Rod Harrington on the TV series *Peyton Place* (1964–69), opposite Mia Farrow as Alison McKenzie.

Ryne Ryne "Ryno" Sandberg *(1959–)*
American baseball infielder for the Cubs, an All-Star and winner of nine Gold Glove awards.

Ryoei Ryoei Saito *(20th century)*
Japanese paper manufacturer. In 1990, he paid US$82.5 million for Vincent Van Gogh's painting *The Portrait of Dr. Gachet* (1890).

Sabazius Sabazius *trans. breaker in pieces*
Greek barley and beer god, a precursor to Dionysus the wine god.

Sabin Sabin Berthelot *(1794–1880)*
French naturalist.

Sabine Sabine Baring-Gould *(1834–1924)*
English hymn author.
> "Onward, Christian soldiers,
> Marching as to war,
> With the Cross of Jesus,
> Going on before."

Sabrina Sabrina
Legendary Celtic character. The River Severn is named after her, or vice versa.

Saburo Saburo Lenaga *(b. c. 1910)*
Japanese historian. He has launched three lawsuits against the Department of Education for sanitizing textbook accounts of the Second World War.

> "I am ashamed because I was against the war, yet I did not say anything during the war. This is why I went to court; I wanted people to know what happened.'

Sacha Sacha Guitry *(originally Alexandre Georges Guitry) (1885–1957)*
French actor and dramatist.

Sacherson Sacherson *(or Sackarson) (16th century)*
English performing bear mentioned by William Shakespeare.

Sacheverell Sacheverell, 6th Baron Sitwell *(1897–1988)*
English writer, brother of Dame Edith Sitwell.
> "Poetry is an absolutely dead art—like taking up archery."

Sadaharu Sadaharu Oh *(1940–)*
Japanese baseball first baseman with the Yomiuri Giants who set the Japanese record of 868 home runs. He rehearsed his batting stance with samurai sword practice.

Saddam Saddam Hussein *(1937–)*
Iraqi politician. About a month before invading Kuwait in 1990 he said:
> "We don't want war. We hate war. We know what war does."

Sade Sade *(originally Helen Folasade Adu) (1959–)*
Nigerian-born British soul-pop singer.

Sadie Sadie Allen *(b. c. 1868)*
American thrill-seeker. She rode the Niagara Rapids in a barrel, accompanied by her friend George Hazlett and 500 pounds of sand.

Saemundur Saemundur Sigfússon *(1056–1133)*
Icelandic scholar, the first historian of Iceland.

Saffron Saffron *(or Saffy)*
Studious daughter of Eddy on the British television series "Absolutely Fabulous" (1993), known to its fans as "AbFab."
> "[My mother] has tried every fad drug and diet that has ever existed. She's a mad, fat old cow, and she's trying to make me just like her. For my last birthday I got a copy of the Kama Sutra *and a Dutch cap.*"

Sage Sage Stallone *(active 1990s)*
American actor, son of Sylvester Stallone, with whom he appeared in *Rocky V* (1990).

Reviewing this movie, *Time Out* magazine claimed, "There are more perceptive insights into parent–child relationships in an Oxo ad."

Saidye Saidye Rosner Bronfman *(1897–1995)*
Canadian patron of the arts.

Saint-John Saint-John Perse *(pen-name of Marie-René Auguste-Alexis Saint-Léger) (1887–1975)*
French poet, winner of the 1960 Nobel Prize.

Saki Saki *(pen-name of Hector Hugh Munro) (1870–1916)*
Burmese-born British short-story writer.
> *"In baiting a mousetrap with cheese, always leave room for the mouse."*

Sal Sal Bando *(Salvatore Leonard Bando) (1944–)*
American baseball third baseman with the Oakland As, an All-Star.

Saladin Saladin *(real name Salah al-Din al-Ayubi) (1137–1193)*
Sultan of Egypt and Syria. He was defeated by Richard Coeur de Lion.

Sallie Sallie Tisdale *(20th century)*
American journalist, author of *Talk Dirty to Me* (1994).
> *"I had this guy the other day ask me if women really like sex. I mean, helloo, are we from the same planet? I just said the obvious. We women are human beings, you know."*

Sallust Sallust *(In Latin, Gaius Sallustius Crispus) (86–34 B.C.)*
Roman historian and politician.
> *"Every man is the architect of his own fortune."*

Sally Sally Ride *(Sally Kristen Ride) (1951–)*
American astronaut, in 1983 the first American woman to go to space.

Salman Salman Rushdie *(Ahmed Salman Rushdie) (1947–)*
Indian-born British author of the novel *Midnight's Children* (1981). He has been in hiding since 1989 with a $1 million bounty on his life. Despite the stress, Rushdie has never consulted a therapist, saying,
> *"My therapy is talking to journalists and answering intimate questions."*

Salmon Salmon Portland Chase *(1805–1873)*
American politician, Secretary of the Treasury of the Union during the Civil War.

> *"I would rather that the people should wonder why I wasn't President than why I am."*

Salomé Salomé *(1st century, possibly Mark 6: 21)*
Judean princess, granddaughter of Herod the Great. The historian Josephus identified her as the unnamed girl who danced for Herod Antipas and demanded the head of John the Baptist on a plate, inspiring a play by Oscar Wilde and an opera by Richard Strauss. The real Salomé married and lived quietly ever after.

Salote Queen Salote Tupou III *(1900–1965)*
Ruler of Tonga. She had a prosperous and happy reign.

Salvador Salvador Dalí *(Salvador Felipe Jaunto Dalí) (1904–1989)*
Spanish surrealist painter. Writer Clive James said about his autobiography that, "faced with a virtually complete record of the old phoney's unswerving bathos, it was impossible not to burst out yawning."

Salvator Salvator Rosa *(1615–1673)*
Italian landscape painter.

Salvatore Salvatore Ferragamo *(1898–1960)*
Italian designer, inventor of the wedge heel and the platform sole, and 300 shoe-related patents.

Sam Sam Bernstein *(20th century)*
Immigrant father of American maestro Leonard Bernstein. He did his best to discourage his young son's interest in music.
> *"How could I know my son was going to grow up to be Leonard Bernstein?"*

Samantha Samantha Stevens
Witchy wife on the American TV series "Bewitched" (1964–72)

Sambo *The Story of Little Black Sambo (1899)*
Children's tale by Helen Brodie Bannerman, based on illustrated letters she wrote her children from India. The story was condemned as racist only after her death.

SALVADOR DALI

Sammy Sammy Davis, Jr. *(1925–1990)*
American singer, dancer, actor, and entertainer.
> *"Being a star has made it possible for me to get insulted in places where the average Negro could never hope to get insulted."*

Samson Samson *trans. man of the sun, Judges 13–16 (c. 12th century B.C.)*
Old Testament boyfriend of Delilah. An angel warned his mother about the side-effects of cutting his hair.

Samuel Samuel Butler *(1835–1902)*
English writer, author of the classic dystopian novel *Erewhon* (1872).
> *"A hen is only an egg's way of making another egg."*

Sancho Sancho Panza
Rotund sidekick in Miguel de Cervantes's novel *Don Quixote* (1605–15).

Sanctorius Sanctorius *(Santorio Santorio) (1561–1636)*
Italian doctor, inventor of the clinical thermometer.

Sandie Sandie Shaw *(originally Sandra Goodrich) (1947–)*
British popular singer.

Sandor Sandor Peröfi *(1823–1849)*
Hungarian poet and patriotic soldier.

Sandra Sandra Shamas *(active 1990s)*
Canadian comedian, author of the one-woman play *My Boyfriend's Back and There's Gonna Be Laundry*, which was followed by *Wedding Bell Hell*.

Sandro Sandro Botticelli *(originally Alessandro di Mariano Filipepi) (c. 1444–1510)*
Florentine painter of the *Birth of Venus*.
Peter Ustinov said, "If Botticelli were alive today, he'd be working for Vogue."

Sandy Sandy Cook *(20th century)*
The Singing Dentist of Baltimore. He does sing. His publicity motto is, "Let me torture you as I torture you."

Sanford Sir Sanford Fleming *(1827–1915)*
Scottish-born Canadian railway engineer. His triumph was the crossing Kicking Horse Pass in the Rocky Mountains.

Sanjay Sanjay Gandhi *(1946–1980)*
Indian airline pilot, heir apparent to his mother, Indira Gandhi, until his death in an airplane crash.

Santa Santa Claus
Dutch name for St. Nicholas. The popular American Santa Claus owes a lot to the god Thor, who was also associated with winter, Yule logs, and flying chariots.

Santiago Santiago Ramón y Cajal *(1852–1934)*
Spanish doctor. He shared the 1906 Nobel Prize for his work isolating the neuron cell.

Sapphire Sapphire
American radio associate of "Amos 'n' Andy" (1926–51).

Sappho Sappho *(b. c. 650 B.C.)*
Greek lyric poet from the island of Lesbos. The term "lesbian" was coined in her honour.
> *"Ah, once I loved thee, Atthis, long ago,*
> *The fields about the farm are silent now."*

Sarah Sarah Bernhardt *(originally Henriette Rosine Bernard) (1844–1923)*
French actress, "the Divine Sarah."
> *"For the theatre one needs long arms; it is better to have them too long than too short. An artiste with short arms can never, never make a fine gesture."*

Sarianna Sarianna Browning *(19th century)*
English sister of the poet Robert Browning. She kept house for him, and spoke with a lisp.

Sarojini Sarojini Naidu, *née Chattopadhyay (1879–1949)*
Indian feminist poet, the "nightingale of India."

Saskia Saskia Wickham *(active 1990s)*
British actress, the heroine in the BBC adaptation of Samuel Richardson's novel *Clarissa, or the History of a Young Lady* (1748).

Sassy Sarah "Sassy" Vaughan *(1924–1990)*
American jazz singer and pianist.
> *"I'd like to go broke again, and this time I'd like to spend all the money myself."*

Satyajit Satyajit Ray *(1921–1992)*
Indian film director.

Satchel Satchel Paige *(Leroy Robert Paige) (1906–1982)*
American baseball pitcher, author of the autobiography *Maybe I'll Pitch Forever* (1962). The first six of his "Ten Rules for Success" are:

"1. Avoid fried meats which angry up the blood.
"2. If your stomach disputes you, lie down and
pacify it with cool thoughts.
"3. Keep the juices flowing by jangling around
gently as you move.
"4. Go light on the vices, such as carrying on in
society. The social ramble ain't restful.
"5. Avoid running at all times.
"6. Don't look back. Something might be gaining
on you."

Satchmo Louis "Satchmo" Armstrong *(or Daniel Louis "Pops" Armstrong) (1900–1971)*
American jazz great.
  "There are some people that if they don't know, you can't tell 'em."

Saul Saul Bellow *(1915–)*
Canadian-born American author, winner in 1976 of a Nobel Prize and a Pulitzer Prize.
  "She was what we used to call a suicide blonde—dyed by her own hand."

Savinien Savinien Cyrano de Bergerac *(1619–1655)*
French soldier and writer.

Savva Savva Mamontov *(19th century)*
Russian railway tycoon. He set up an artist's community at Abramtsevo which became "the cradle of modern Russian art," frequented by Ilya Repin and other members of the Realist group.

Sax Sax Rohmer *(pseudonym of Arthur Sarsfield Ward) (1886–1959)*
English mystery writer, the creator of sinister *Dr. Fu Manchu* (1913).

Saxe Saxe Holm *(pen name of Helen Maria Hunt Jackson (1831–1885)*
American writer.
  ". . . that indescribable expression peculiar to people who hope they have not been asleep, but know they have."

Saxo Saxo Grammaticus *(c. 1150–c. 1220)*
Danish chronicler, the first national historian of Denmark.

Scarecrow Scarecrow
Clever stuffed companion of Dorothy in L. Frank Baum's children's novel *The Wonderful Wizard of Oz* (1900).

"Everything in life is unusual until you get used to it."

Scarface Scarface *(nickname of Alphonse Capone) (1894–1947)*
Chicago gangster. The scar was on the left side.
  "Canada? I don't even know what street it's on."

Schlemiel *Schlemiel the First (1974)*
American Yiddish book by Isaac Bashevis Singer.

Schofield Schofield Haigh *(1871–1921)*
English cricket player, a member of the Yorkshire team which won four championships in five years.

Schuyler Schuyler Colfax *(1823–1885)*
American vice-president. He retired in 1873 amid allegations of crookedness.

Scott Scott Young *(1919–)*
Canadian journalist, the father of singer Neil Young.
  "I think being Neil Young's dad is great. Somebody said to me once, 'You're really lucky. Your son might have turned out to be Neil Sedaka.'"

Scottie Scottie Pippen *(20th century)*
American basketball forward for the Chicago Bulls, an All-Star.

Scylla Scylla *trans. she who reads*
Mythical Greek sea nymph. A love rival poisoned her bath, turning her into a monster with barking dog heads around her waist. Scylla then threw herself into the sea and became a shoal of dangerous rocks.

Sean Sean Connery *(originally Thomas Connery) (1930–)*
Scottish actor, six-times James Bond, in 1989 the sexiest man alive according to *People* magazine.
  "More than anything else, I'd like to be an old man with a good face, like Hitchcock or Picasso."

Sebastian Sebastian Cabot *(c. 1475–1557)*
Venetian navigator.

Top 10 Baby Names for Future Theologians

Aimée • Aleister • Ann • Cotton

• Lafayette • Lodowick • Oral •

Palagius • Sun • Tammy

Sebastiano Sebastiano Serlio *(1475–1554)*
Italian painter and architect. He pioneered U-shaped floor-plans for Parisian town-houses.

Sedna Sedna
Inuit sea goddess. Seals and whales were born from the segments of her fingers.

Seebohm Seebohm Rowntree *(Benjamin Seebohm Rowntree) (1871–1954)*
British chocolate manufacturer, an enlightened manager who wrote on social problems.

Sejanus *Sejanus, His Fall (1603)*
English tragedy by Ben Jonson.

Sekwan Sekwan Auger *(1984–)*
Canadian actress, the lead child in the movie *Legends of the Fall* (1995). Her name, pronounced "seeguin," means "spring" in Cree.

Selena Selena *(Selena Quintanilla Peréz) (1972–1995)*
American Tejano singer. (Tejano is a modern version of traditional Tex-Mex accordian conjunto music.) Her fan club president was convicted of her murder.

Selima Selima *(18th century)*
Oliver Goldsmith's cat, who "drowned in a tub of goldfish."

Selina Selina Scott *(20th century)*
British television newsreader.

Seljük Seljük *(10th century)*
Turkish ancestor of the Seljük dynasty.

Selma Dr. Selma Barkham *(20th century)*
Canadian historian, the world expert on 16th-century Basque explorers in Labrador. A widow with four children and no money, she moved her family to Mexico to learn Spanish on the cheap before going to Spain to study original archival material.

Selman Selman Abraham Waksman *(1888–1973)*
Russian-born American biochemist, winner of a Nobel Prize for discovering the antibiotic streptomycin.

Selwyn John Selwyn Brooke Lloyd, Baron Selwyn-Lloyd *(1904–1978)*
British politician.

Semiramis Semiramis *(9th century B.C.)*
Legendary Queen of Assyria who built the hanging gardens of Babylon. She may be the real Queen Sammu-ramat (811–808 B.C.).

Senator Steve "Senator" Garvey *(1948–)*
American baseball infielder with the Dodgers, an All-Star, and a Gold Glove winner. In 1989 he was the target of two different paternity suits.

Senda Senda Berenson *(originally Senda Valvrojenski) (1868–1954)*
Lithuanian-born American athlete. She developed the rules for women's basketball.

Seneca Lucius Annaeus Seneca *(known as Seneca the Younger) (48 B.C.–A.D. 65)*
Roman Stoic philosopher and tragician.
"Conversation has a kind of charm about it, an insinuating and insidious something that elicits secrets from us just like love or liquor."

Senerat King Senerat *(d. 1636)*
Ruler of Kandy (later Ceylon, now Sri Lanka).

Sequoyah Sequoyah *(or George Guess) (c. 1770–1843)*
American half-Cherokee scholar. He invented a written Cherokee alphabet with eighty-five characters. The *sequoia* genus of coniferous trees is named after him.

Serafín Serafín Álvarez Quintero *(1871–1938)*
Spanish playwright.

Serah Serah *trans. lady, Genesis 46: 17 (c. 16th century B.C.)*
Old Testament granddaughter of Jacob. She is the only woman mentioned in the genealogy of the tribes of Israel while they were in the wilderness.

Serena Serena Stanhope *(1970–)*
British royal fiancée.

Serge Serge Diaghilev *(Sergei Pavlovich Diaghilev)* *(1872–1929)*
Russian impresario, founder of Les Ballets Russes.
> *"It is success and only success, my friend, that saves and redeems all."*

Sergei Sergei Sergeyevich Prokofiev *(1891–1953)*
Ukrainian-born Russian composer of *Peter and the Wolf* (1936).

Sergey Sergey Vasilyevich Rachmaninov *(1873–1943)*
Russian-born composer of lushly romantic music.

Sergio Sergio Leone *(1921–1989)*
Italian film director, creator of "spaghetti western" movies such as *A Fistful of Dollars* (1964).

Sese Sese Seko Kuku Ngbendu Wa Za Banga Mobutu *(formerly Joseph Désiré Mobutu) (1930–)*
Zairean soldier and politician.

Seth Seth Starkadder
Resident English hunk of Stella Gibbons's gothic parody *Cold Comfort Farm* (1933).
> *"He came over to her with the lounging grace of a panther, and leaned against the mantlepiece. Flora saw at once that he was not the kind that could be fobbed off with offers of tea. She was for it."*

Seti Seti I
Egyptian warrior king. His mummy can be seen in Cairo, complete with six toes.

Severiano Severiano "Sewy" Ballesteros *(1957–)*
Spanish golfer, the "Car Park Golfer" for making wild drives that looked like they were headed for the parking lot.

Severo Severo Ochoa *(1905–1993)*
Japanese biochemist, a Nobel Prize winner for his work in synthesizing RNA.

Sexburga St. Sexburga *(d. c. 699)*
English daughter of King Anna of the East Angles, the sister of St. Erconwald, St. Ethelburga, St. Ethereda, and St. Withburga.

Seymour Seymour R. Cray *(1925–)*
American designer of the early Cray "supercomputer."

Shad Shad Barry *(John C. Barry) (1879–1936)*
American baseball player. During the First World War he was in charge of baseball for the American Expeditionary Force.

Shadow Shadow Morton *(originally George Morton) (1942–)*
American record producer.

Shahnaz Princess Shahnaz *(1940–)*
Persian daugher of Shah Mohammad Reza Pahlavi.

Shailer Shailer Mathews *(1863–1941)*
American educator.
> *"An epigram is a half-truth so stated as to irritate the person who believes the other half."*

Shaker Lloyd "Shaker" Moseby *(1959–)*
American baseball outfielder for the Blue Jays, an All-Star.

Shakin' Shakin' Stevens *(originally Michael Barrett) (1948–)*
British teen idol singer.

Shakuntala Shakuntala Devi *(active 1980)*
Indian math prodigy. She can mentally multiply any two thirteen digit numbers.

Shamash Shamash
Assyrian sun god, son of Sin and Ningal, brother of Ishtar.

Shamus Shamus Farrow *(formerly Satchel Farrow) (20th century)*
American former son of director Woody Allen by actress Mia Farrow.

Shane *Shane (1953)*
American movie starring Alan Ladd.

Shania Shania Twain *(originally Eileen Twain) (1966–)*
Canadian singer.

Shannon Shannon W. Lucid *(1943–)*
Chinese-born American astronaut, the first woman to make three space flights.

Shanty Shanty Hogan *(James Francis Hogan) (1906–1967)*
American baseball catcher with the Giants who recorded 120 consecutive errorless games. He got his nickname because he was so large he resembled a small building.

SHIRLEY TEMPLE

Shaquille Shaquille O'Neal *(1972–)* American basketball player, creator of the "Shaq attack." He was forbidden from playing on the Olympic team by his personal sponsor, Pepsi, lest his face appear on the official Olympic cup from McDonald's, containing Coke.

Shari Shari Lewis *(1934–)* American puppeteer, the creator of Lambchop. She was introduced to Princess Anne as someone who had learned ventriloquism from her father. Princess Anne observed, "One does tend to get involved in the family business, doesn't one?"

Sharon Sharon Pratt Kelly *(1944–)* American politician. In 1990, she was elected mayor of Washington, D.C., the first black female mayor of a major U.S. city.

Shashi Shashi Kapoor *(20th century)* Indian film star.

Shaun Shaun Lacker *(20th century)* American mountaineer, one of a team who in 1991 made a Guinness record–setting climb of all the high spots of forty-eight states in 30½ days.

Shavsha Shavsha *(or Sheva, Shisha or Seraiah)*, *2 Samuel 8: 17 (c. 10th century B.C.)* Old Testament secretary to King David. His sons became secretaries to King Solomon.

Shaw Shaw Taylor *(1924–)* British TV commentator with the program "Police Five."

Shawon Shawon Dunston *(Shawon Donnell)* *"Thunder Pup" Dunston (1963–)* American baseball shortstop with the Cubs, an All-Star.

Shechem Shechem *trans. shoulder (c. 16th century B.C.)* Old Testament Canaanite lover of Jacob's daugher Dinah. Her father agreed to their marriage on condition that Shechem and all his family get circumcised, but while they were recovering from their operations Dinah's brothers killed them.

Sheena Sheena Easton *(originally Sheena Orr) (1959–)* Scottish pop singer.

Sheila Sheila Minto *(d. 1994)* British secretary to eight prime ministers at No.10 Downing Street, after she started working there as a temp. Her rule for discussing politics away from the office was, "Keep quiet and look rather stupid."

Sheilah Sheilah Graham *(originally Lily Sheil)* *(1904–1988)* British movie columnist, the girlfriend of writer F. Scott Fitzgerald after his wife, Zelda, was permanently hospitalized.

Shelagh Shelagh Delaney *(1936–)* English writer, author of the play *A Taste of Honey* (1958).
 "The one thing civilization couldn't do anything about—women."

Shelby Shelby Steele *(1946–)* American writer and educator, author of the controversial *The Content of Our Character: A New Vision of Race in America* (1990).

Sheldon Sheldon Lee Glashow *(1932–)* American physicist, winner of a Nobel Prize.

Shelley Shelley Winters *(originally Shirley Schrift)* *(1922–)* American actress.
 "I did a picture in England one winter and it was so cold I almost got married."

Shemp Shemp Howard *(originally Samuel Horowitz)* *(1895–1955)* American actor, one of the Three Stooges.

Shep James "Shep" Sheppard *(1936–1970)* American doo-wop composer, leader of Shep and the Limelites.

Sherard Sherard Osborn *(1822–1875)* Indian-born English naval officer. "Osborn Deep" in the Indian Ocean was named after he helped lay the telegraph cable between Australia and England.

Sheridan Sheridan Whiteside Character in the American play *The Man Who Came to Dinner* (1939) by George Kaufman and

Moss Hart, based on the real Alexander Woolcott.

Sherilyn Sherilyn Fenn *(1965–)*
American actress. She took the unappealing role in *Boxing Helena* after Kim Bassinger bowed out.

Sherlene Sherlene O'Brien *(active 1986)*
British farmer. One of her Holstein cows gave birth to a Guinness record–setting 270-pound calf.

Sherlock Sherlock Holmes
British fictional private investigator, the creation of Sir Arthur Conan Doyle.
  "When you have excluded the impossible, whatever remains, however improbable, must be the truth."

Sherri Sherri Spillane *(20th century)*
American talent agent for "scandal icons" like Kato Kaelin, Joey Buttafuoco, Gennifer Flowers, Sidney Biddle Barrows, and John Wayne Bobbit. She claimed that client Tonya Harding turned down an offer from Woody Allen, "because she didn't like his morals."

Sherrie Sherrie Schneider *(20th century)*
American co-author with Ellen Fein of the book *The Rules: Time-Tested Secrets for Capturing the Heart of Mr. Right.* Rule No. 5 is, "Don't call him and rarely return his calls."

Sherwood Sherwood Anderson *(1876–1941)*
American writer, author of *Tar, A Midwest Childhood* (1926). He died after swallowing the toothpick in a party hors d'oeuvre.

Sheryl Sheryl Swopes *(1971–)*
American basketball player, the first woman to have a Nike shoe named after her.
  "Growing up, I never thought anything like this would happen."

Shigechiyo Shigechiyo Izumi *(1865–1971)*
Japanese old person, the oldest person known at the time of his death. He took up smoking at age 70, retired at 105, and attributed his long life to "god, Buddha and the sun."

Shikibu Shikibu Murasaki *(978–c. 1031)*
Japanese novelist. She wrote *The Tale of Genji.*

Shimei Shimei *trans. famed, I Kings 2: 9 (c. 10th century B.C.)*
Old Testament aged member of Saul's family. He threw stones and dirt at David.
  "Begone, begone, you man of blood, you worthless fellow."

Shimon Shimon Peres *(originally Shimon Persky) (1923–)*
Polish-born Israeli politician, the successor to Yitzak Rabin.

Shirley Shirley Temple *(later Mrs. Shirley Temple Black) (1928–)*
American child actress. She earned $1 million before she was ten.

Shivaji Shivaji *(1627–1680)*
Marathan emperor of northern India. He successfully defied the Mughals until his death.

Shock Thomas "Shock" White *(active 1770s)*
English cricket player, a celebrated batsman for Surrey. When he appeared with a bat as wide as the stumps, the rule was created restricting bats to 4¼ inches wide.

Shoe Willie "Shoe" Shoemaker *(1931–)*
American jockey. He weighed only 2½ pounds at birth, and was kept in a shoebox near the stove.

Shoeless Shoeless Joe *(Joseph Jefferson Jackson) (1887–1951)*
American baseball outfielder for the Indians. Despite a .375 hitting average, he supposedly cheated to lose the World Series, and was permanently barred from playing. During this scandal a tearful young fan stopped him on the courthouse steps and said, "Say it ain't so, Joe."

Shogo Shogo Tomiyama *(20th century)*
Japanese producer in 1995 of the last Godzilla movie, in which Godzilla dies.
  "As long as Godzilla is a star, he could make a comeback."

Sholem Sholem Aleichem *(pseudonym of Solomon J. Rabinowitz) (1859–1916)*
Russian author of the short story on which the musical *Fiddler on the Roof* was based.

Shoney Shoney
British Celtic sea deity. Sacrifices to him were still being offered on the Isle of Lewis in the nineteenth century.

Shridhar Shridhar Chillal *(1937–)*
Indian person with the longest fingernails in the world; 48 inches in 1993. He last cut them in 1952.

Shuggie Shuggie Otis *(originally Johnny Otis, Jr.) (1953–)*
English guitarist briefly with the Rolling Stones.

Shulgi Shulgi *(ruled 2094–2047 B.C.)*
Sumerian king, author of the oldest surviving code of laws, a precursor to Hammurabi's code. He also established the world's first collection of live animals.

Shute Shute Barrington *(1734–1826)*
English educator and bishop.

Shyam Shyam Selvadurai *(1965–)*
Sri Lankan–born Canadian novelist, author of *Funny Boy* (1994).

Shylock Shylock
Thwarted businessman in William Shakespeare's play *The Merchant of Venice* (1596–97).
> *"Hath not a Jew eyes, if you prick him does he not bleed?"*

Siaka Siaka Probin Stevens *(1905–1988)*
Sierra Leone politician, the first president.

Sib Sib Hashian *(1949–)*
American drummer with the band Boston.

Sid Sid Vicious *(originally John Beverley) (1957–1979)*
British punk rocker. He died of a drug overdose while awaiting trial for murder. Fellow Sex Pistol Johnny Rotten said, "Sid was nothing more than a coat hanger to fill an empty space on the stage."

Sidney Sidney Poitier *(1924–)*
American actor, and director, the mystery date in *Guess Who's Coming to Dinner?* (1963). Girlfriend Diahann Carroll called him "the most beautiful male specimen I have ever seen."

Sidney Sidney Biddles Barrow *(20th century)*
American sexual entrepreneur, the "Mayflower Madam."

Sidonie Sidonie Gabrielle Colette *(pen-name Colette) (1873–1954)*
French novelist, author of *Gigi* (1945).

Siegfried Siegfried Sassoon *(Siegfried Lorraine Sassoon) (1886–1967)*
English poet and novelist, author of *Memoirs of a Fox-Hunting Man* (1928), a veteran of the First World War.
> *"If I were fierce and bold and short of breath*
> *I'd live with scarlet Majors at the Base,*
> *And speed glum heros up the line to death."*

Sierra Sierra Sneith *(1984–)*
American child, the first person born in the United States to a mother with an organ transplant (a new heart).

Sigismondo Sigismondo *(1815)*
Serious Italian opera by Giocchino Rossini, almost the only thing he wrote that was not fabulously successful.

Sigismund Sigismund *(1368–1437)*
Holy Roman Emperor.
> *"Do always in health what you have often promised to do when you are sick."*

Sigmund Sigmund Freud *(originally Sigismund Schlomo Freud) (1856–1939)*
Austrian inventor of psychoanalysis.
> *"The first human being who hurled a curse instead of a weapon was the founder of civilization."*

Signe Signe Hasso *(originally Signe Larssen) (1910–)*
Forceful Swedish character actress.

Sigrid Sigrid Undset *(1882–1949)*
Norwegian novelist, winner of the 1928 Nobel Prize for literature.

Silas Silas Marner *(1861)*
English novel by George Eliot (pen name of Mary Ann Evans). W.C. Fields claimed he was "probably one of the few people outside an institution who can outline the various plots of *Silas Marner*."

Silenus Silenus *trans. moon-man*
Greek satyr, the brother (or possibly son) of Pan, usually depicted as a fat old drunk on a donkey.

Silk Silk O'Loughton *(Frank O'Loughton) (worked 1902–1918)*
American baseball umpire. He used to tell argumentative batters, "I have never missed one in my life, and it's too late to start now. The Pope for religion, O'Loughlin for baseball. Both infallible."

Silvana *Silvana (1800)*
German opera by Carl Weber.

Silvanus Silvanus Phillips Thompson *(1851–1916)*
English physicist, author of the witty *Calculus Made Easy* (1910).

Silver Silver King *(originally Charles Frederick Koenig) (1868–1938)*
American baseball pitcher for St. Louis. In 1888 he led the American League in games, innings pitched, shut-outs, and ERA.

Silvia Silvia Matos *(parked 1985–1988)*
American car owner. She accumulated a Guinness record 2,800 unpaid parking tickets, using 36 different licence plates and 19 addresses.

Silvio Silvio Berlusconi *(1936–)*
Italian media mogul and politician.

Simba Simba
Orphaned lion prince hero of Walt Disney's animated movie *The Lion King* (1994).

Simeon St. Simeon Stylites, the Elder *(387–459)*
Syrian ascetic, the original Christian pillar-saint. His pillar can still be visited today in the city of Aleppo.

Simon Simon Fraser *(1776–1862)*
American-born Canadian fur trader. The Fraser River and Simon Fraser University are named after him.

Simone Simone de Beauvoir *(1908–1986)*
French existentialist novelist and feminist, author of *The Second Sex* (1949). Have a drink in her honour at the Café Deux Magots in Paris.
"One is not born a woman, one becomes one."

SINÉAD O'CONNOR

Simonetta Simonetta Calteano *(1456–1476)*
Italian artists' model. She posed for Botticelli's painting *Birth of Venus*.

Simonides Simonides of Ceos *(c. 556–c. 468 B.C.)*
Greek lyric poet. He wrote the epitaph for the fallen soldiers of Thermopolae.
"Go tell the Spartans, thou that passeth by, That here, obedient to their laws, we lie."

Sinclair Sinclair Lewis *(Harry Sinclair Lewis) (1885–1951)*
American novelist, winner of the 1926 Pulitzer Prize and the 1930 Nobel Prize for literature.
"In America the successful writer or picture-painter is indistinguishable from any other decent businessman."

Sindy Sindy *(1961–)*
American doll, Hasbro's competitor to Mattel's Barbie. Mattel won a copyright lawsuit in 1992 forcing Hasbro to remodel Sindy's face.

Sinéad Sinéad O'Connor *(1966–)*
Irish singer-songwriter. In 1992, she ripped up a photo of the Pope on live television.
"Know the real enemy."

Sinon Sinon *trans. plunderer*
Mythical Greek friend of Odysseus. At the climax of the Trojan War, as the Greeks sailed away, he approached the city of Troy with his hands tied, and informed the Trojans that the Greeks has left behind this wooden horse as an offering, to be dragged into the city. Of course, the wooden horse was filled with warriors, and the Greek ships waiting just out of sight.

Siouxsie Siouxsie Sioux *(originally Susan Dallion) (1958–)*
British punk singer, leader of Siouxsie and the Banshees.

Sirhan Sirhan Sirhan *(Sirhan Bishara Sirhan) (1945–1969)*
Palestinian-born American assassin of Robert Kennedy.

Siricius St. Siricius *(d. 399)*
Roman pope, the first pope to demand celibacy in clergy.

Sirius Sirius *trans. Dog-star*
Mythical Greek hound of Orion. He was placed in the heavens as the Dog star, Canis Major.

Sissy Sissy Spacek *(originally Mary Elizabeth Spacek) (1949–)*
American actress. She won an Oscar for *Coal Miner's Daughter* (1980).

Sisyphus Sisyphus *trans. very wise*
Mythical Greek wicked person. In the underworld he is doomed to eternal labour, forever rolling uphill a large rock which always falls back.

Sitting Bull Sitting Bull *(Tatanka Iyotake) (1834–1890)*
Dakota Sioux chief, leader of the celebrated attack on Colonel George Armstrong Custer at the 1876 Battle of the Little Big Horn, and star of Buffalo Bill Cody's Wild West Show.
"The white man knows how to make everything, but he does not know how to distribute it."

Siva Siva
Vedic god associated with the powers of reproduction and dissolution.

Sixto Sixto Lezcano *(1953–)*
American baseball outfielder for the Brewers, winner of a Gold Glove award.

Skates Lonnie "Skates" Smith *(1955–)*
American baseball outfielder for the Cardinals, an All-Star.

Skink Skink
Fictional road-kill-eating swamp-dwelling ex-governor of Florida, hero of the novel *Stormy Weather* (1995) by Carl Hiaasen.

Skip Skip James *(originally Nehemiah James) (1902–1969)*
American blues musician.

Skoonj Carl "Skoonj" Furillo *(1922–)*
American baseball outfielder, one of the Dodgers' "Boys of Summer." He successfully sued the Dodgers for dropping him after an injury, but was unable to get work with any other team, and ended up working as an elevator installer.

Skuld Skuld
Nordic mythic Fate. She sometimes slipped off to ride with the Valkyries.

Sky Sky Gilbert *(20th century)*
Canadian theatre actor, director, producer, writer, and cross-dresser.

Slade Slade Corter *(Thomas Slade Corter) (1928–)*
American Republican senator from Washington, "Slippery Slade." He is one of a very small number of senators to win a return to office after being voted out.

Slappy Melvin "Slappy" White *(1921–1995)*
American comic.
"My landlord said he's going to raise the rent. 'Good,' I said, "cause I can't raise it.'"

Slapsie Slapsie Maxie Rosenbloom *(1904–1976)*
American boxer, the 1932 World light heavyweight champion. He tended to punch with his hands open.

Slash Slash *(Saul Hudson) (1966–)*
American guitarist with the group Guns 'n' Roses.

Sleepy Sleepy *(1935–)*
American animated film dwarf, co-star of Walt Disney's *Snow White and the Seven Dwarfs* (1935).

Slim Slim Gaillard *(originally Bulee Gaillard) (1916–1991)*
American scat singer and comedian. His first act involved playing a guitar while tap-dancing.

Sloppy Sloppy Thurston *(Hollis John Thurston) (1899–1973)*
American baseball pitcher for the White Sox. He inherited his nickname from his father, a restaurant owner who gave out free soup to the poor.

Sly Sly Stone *(originally Sylvester Stewart) (1944–)*
American pioneer of funk music.

Smartyboots Cyril "Smartyboots" Connolly *(Cyril Vernon Connolly) (1903–1974)*
British author and snob. This nickname was invented by Virginia Woolf.

Smaug Smaug the Dragon
Perilous foe of Bilbo Baggins in J.R.R. (John Ronald Reuel) Tolkien's English novel *The Hobbit* (1937).

Smiley Smiley Lewis *(originally Overton Amos Lemons) (1913–1966)*
American R&B guitarist.

Smithson Smithson Tennant *(1761–1815)*
English chemist. He proved that diamonds are carbon.

Smoke Smoke Jaguar *(ruled 628–695)*
Mayan ruler of the city of Copán, which is known as the "Athens of the New World."

Smokey Smokey Robinson *(originally William Robinson) (1940–)*
American Motown singer and songwriter, leader of the Miracles.

Smokin' Smokin' Joe Frazier *(1944–)*
American boxer, an Olympic gold-medallist and heavyweight champion. He entered the ring "smoking"—throwing punches.
> *"I don't want to know my opponent's out, I want to hit him, step away, and watch him hurt. I want his heart."*

Smyrna Smyrna *trans. myrrh*
Mythical Greek mortal princess, the mother of Adonis.

Snacks Hoyt "Snacks" Wilhelm *(1923–)*
American baseball pitcher for the White Sox, a member of the Hall of Fame. While still in high school, he read about the knuckleball in an article, then practised it at home. He pitched a no-hitter in his first game as a starting pitcher.

Snake Jacques "The Snake" Plante *(1929–)*
Canadian hockey goaltender, the first goaltender to wear a face mask. He became known as "the Snake" for sneaking away from the goal long enough to pass the puck to a teammate.
> *"Goaltending a normal job? Sure! How would you like it in your job if every time you made a mistake, a red light went on over your desk and fifteen thousand people stood up and yelled at you?"*

Sneezy Sneezy Waters *(originally Peter Hodgson) (1945–)*
Canadian musician and actor. He played Hank Williams in the musical *The Show He Never Gave*.

Snoop Snoop Doggy Dogg *(originally Calvin Broadus) (1972–)*
American rapper.

Snoopy Snoopy
Eccentric canine companion of Charlie Brown in the American cartoon strip *Peanuts* (1950–) by Charles Schultz.

Snorri Snorri Sturluson *(1179–1241)*
Icelandic historian and poet.

Snow *Snow White and the Seven Dwarfs (1937)*
American animated film by Walt Disney. It was the first feature-length animated movie.

Snowy Snowy Baker *(Reginald Leslie Baker) (1884–1953)*
Australian athlete and silent-film star.

Soames Soames Forsyte
British hero of the *Forsyte Saga*, played by Eric Porter in the 1967 BBC series.

Soapy Soapy Sam *(Samuel Wilberforce, Bishop of Oxford) (1805–1873)*
Unctuous English preacher.

Socarris Socarris Ramirez *(active 1969)*
Cuban stowaway. He survived a flight to Spain in the unpressurized wheel-well of a Douglas DC-8.

Socks Socks Seybold *(Harry Seybold) (played 1900–1908)*
American baseball player for the As. He set a 1902 home-run record in the American League broken only by Babe Ruth.

Socrates Socrates *(469–399 B.C.)*
Influential Greek philosopher. He did not write anything, but his thoughts were documented in Plato's dialogues. He was condemned to death for impiety.
> *"I think that I had better bathe before I drink the poison, and not give the women the trouble of washing my dead body."*

Sod Sod Voccaro *(20th century)*
American barber-shop singer with the Four Aces.

Soender Soender Jylland *(active 1978)*
Danish farmer. His bull Jens set a Guinness record for progeny by fathering 220,000 live calves (through artificial insemination).

Sofya Sofya Kovalevskaya *(1850–1891)*
Russian mathematician, the first woman to earn a PhD in math. She had to invent a ficticious husband to write a letter granting her permission to study abroad.

Soichiro Soichiro Honda *(1906–1992)*
Japanese car and motorcycle manufacturer.

Sojourner Sojourner Truth *(originally Isabella Van Wagener) (1777–1883)*
American slave-born abolitionist, subject of Olive Gilbert's *The Narrative of Sojourner Truth.*

> *"That man over there says that women need to be helped into carriages and lifted over ditches, and to have the best places everywhere. Nobody ever helps me into carriages or gives me any best place! And ain't I a woman? I could work as much and eat as much as a man—when I could get it—and bear the lash as well! And aren't I a woman?"*

Sol Sol Hoopii *(1902–1953)*
Hawaiian guitar player. He performed with Bing Crosby in *Waikiki Wedding* (1937).

Solly Solly Hofman *(Arthur Frederick Hofman) (1894–1956)*
American baseball infielder for the Cubs. He was known as "Circus Solly" for his clowning moves, such as the time in 1908 when he lost a game by throwing a curveball to second base to tag a runner.

Solomon Solomon Eccles *(c. 1617–1682)*
English musician. He became a Quaker and burnt his instruments.

Solon Solon *(c. 640–559 B.C.)*
Athenian traveller, lawgiver, and poet, one of Seven Sages of Greece.

Somerset Somerset Maugham *(originally William Somerset Maugham) (1874–1965)*
French-born British writer and secret agent, author of *Of Human Bondage* (1915).

SOPHIA LOREN

> *"I forget who it was that recommended men for their soul's good to do each day two things they dislike. . . it is a precept that I have followed scrupulously, for every day I have got up and I have gone to bed."*

Son Son House *(originally Eddie James House, Jr.) (1902–1988)*
American Mississippi Delta blues guitarist, author of "Preachin' the Blues."

> *"Well I met the blues this morning*
> *Walking just like a man*
> *I said, Good morning blues,*
> *Now give me your right hand."*

Sondra Sondra Gotlieb *(1936–)*
Canadian writer and diplomatic worker.

> *"For some reason, a glaze passes over people's faces when you say 'Canada.'"*

Sonia Sonia Delaunay, *née Sonia Terk Stern (1885–1979)*
Ukrainian-born French painter and fashion designer.

Sonic Fred "Sonic" Smith *(20th century)*
American musician with the group MC5, or Motor City Five, the house band of the revolutionary White Panther Party.

Sonja Sonja Henie *(1912–1969)*
Norwegian figure skater, the "Wonder Child." She won gold medals at three consecutive Olympic competitions, then retired to become a Hollywood star.

> *"If you are not a skater you probably can't imagine what I mean. I could try to tell you by saying it's a feeling of ice miles running under your blades, the wind splitting open to let you through, the earth whirling around you at the touch of your toe, and the speed lifting you off the ice far from all things that can hold you down."*

Sonny Sonny Liston *(Charles Liston) (c. 1917–1970)*
American heavyweight champion, one of twenty-five children.

> *"In the films the good guy always wins, but this is one bad guy who ain't gonna lose."*

Soon-Yi Soon-Yi Previn *(1971–)*
American college student, step-daughter of Mia Farrow and girlfriend of Mia's boyfriend Woody Allen.

Sooz Sooz Glazebrook *(20th century)*
New Zealand potter.

Sophia Sophia Loren *(originally Sofia Scicolone) (1934–)*
Italian actress, star of *Marriage, Italian Style* (1964). She was spotted at age fifteen by her future husband, film producer Carlo Ponti, when she won a beauty contest.

> *"I'm a giraffe. I even walk like a giraffe, with a long neck and legs. It's a pretty dumb animal, too."*

Sophie Sophie Tucker *(originally Sonia Kalish) (1884–1966)*
Russian-born American vocalist, "The Last of the Red-Hot Mamas."

> *"Life begins at forty."*

Sophocles Sophocles *(496–406 B.C.)*
Handsome athletic Greek dramatist. He developed the new theory of tragedy in which fate combines with a small character defect, the "tragic flaw."

Sophonisba *The Wonder of Women, or the Tragedy of Sophonisba (c. 1605)*
English tragedy by John Marston, about Carthaginian-born Queen Sophonisba of Numidia.

Soren Soren Georg Jensen *(1917–)*
Danish designer, founder of the chain of Jensen shops.

Sosigenes Sosigenes *(active 50 B.C.)*
Greek astronomer. He helped Julius Caesar to reform the calendar into the 365¼ day Julian year we use today.

Souphanouvong Prince Souphanouvong *(1909–1995)*
Laotian aristocrat and politician, known as the "Red Prince" for his role in abolishing the hereditary nobility to make Laos a communist state.

Spa'am Spa'am
Wild Boar high priest in the film *Muppet Treasure Island* (1995). The Hormel Food Corporation lost a legal bid to ban this name as an insult to the reputation of its famed luncheon meat, SPAM.

Spade Spade Cooley *(originally Donnell Clyde Cooley) (1910–1969)*
American fiddle player, the original "King of Western Swing" before Bob Wills and the Texas Playboys popularized the genre.

Spanky Spanky McFarland *(originally George McFarland) (1929–1993)*
American child actor, one of the Little Rascals depicted in the television series *Our Gang*. In later life he said, "I've gone from 'Spanky' to 'Cranky.'"

Sparky Sparky Anderson *(George Lee Anderson) (1934–)*
American baseball player for the Phillies, manager of the Cincinnati Reds, author of *Sparky* (1990).

> *"I didn't have a lot of talent, so I tried to make up for it with spit and vinegar. I spent more time arguing with umpires than I spent on the bases. . . . Finally [the announcer] got to saying, 'And here comes Sparky racing towards the umpire again.'"*

Spartacus Spartacus *(d. 71 B.C.)*
Roman gladiator and rebel.

Spec Spec Shea *(Frank Joseph O'Shea) (1920–)*
American baseball pitcher for the Yankees, an All-Star. He was hired after he led an amateur team to a win over the Yankees in an exhibition game.

Speedo Earl "Speedo" Carroll *(1937–)*
American pop performer with the Coasters. They sang "Yakety Yak" (1958).

Spencer Spencer Tracy *(1900–1967)*
American actor. His 1937 Academy Award for *Captains Courageous* was accidentally engraved with the name "Dick Tracy."

Speranza Speranza *(pen-name of Lady Jane Francesca Wilde, née Elgee) (1826–1896)*
Inflammatory Irish poet and society hostess. When her son Oscar Wilde toured America in the 1880s, he was advertised as "son of Speranza."

Speusippus Speusippus *(c. 407–339)*
Greek philosopher. He was Plato's nephew.

Sphinx Sphinx *trans. throttler*
Mythical Greek monster with the head of a woman, the body of dog, tail of a serpent, wings of bird, and paws of a lion. She asked visitors to answer the following riddle:

> *"What creature walks on four legs in the morning, two legs at noon, and three in the evening?" Anyone who couldn't answer was devoured. Oedipus was the first to answer correctly, "man," whereupon the Sphinx killed herself in chagrin.*

Spike Spike Lee *(originally Shelton Jackson Lee) (1957–)*
American filmmaker, creator of *She's Gotta Have It* (1986).

> *"I collect names for characters. Names are valuable; they can be your first source of insight into a character."*

Spinderella Spinderella *(originally Deidre "Dee Dee" Roper) (active 1990s)*
American disc jockey with the female rap group Salt-n-Pepa.

Spiro Spiro Agnew *(1918–)*
American vice-president. In 1968, while campaigning for vice-president, he said, "If you've seen one ghetto area, you've seen them all."

Sportin' Sportin' Life
Lowlife character in George and Ira Gershwin's American opera *Porgy and Bess* (1935), played by Cab Calloway in the original production.

Spot Spot Poles *(Spotswood Poles) (1887–1962)*
American baseball outfielder. He may have been the fastest runner ever in the Negro Leagues; faster even than Cool Papa Bell.

Spranger Spranger Bany *(1719–1777)*
Irish actor.

Spud Spud Chandler *(Spurgeon Ferdinand Chandler) (1907–)*
American baseball pitcher for the Yankees. His .717 winning percentage was the highest for a 100-game winner.

Spy Spy *(pen-name of Sir Leslie Ward) (1851–1922)*
English caricaturist for *Vanity Fair* magazine, author of *Forty Years of 'Spy'* (1915).

Spyros Spyros Skouras *(1893–1971)*
American film-maker, the president of 20th Century-Fox.

Squiggy Andrew "Squiggy" Squiggman
Character on the American TV series "Laverne and Shirley" (1976–83)

> *"If ever we needed a brain, now is the time."*

Srinivasa Srinivasa Aaiyangar Ramanujan *(1887–1920)*
Indian mathematician, a self-taught prodigy who became a fellow of Trinity College, Cambridge. At his death-bed, a friend commented that the licence number of a passing taxi—1729—was "dull." Ramanujan replied, "No, it is a very interesting number; it is the smallest number expressible as a sum of two cubes in two different ways." (The cube roots for the two sums are 1 and 12; 9 and 10.)

St. Clair St. Clair Lee *(Bernard St. Clair Lee Calhoun Henderson) (1944–)*
American disco vocalist with the Hues Corporation. He sang "Rock the Boat" (1974).

Stacy Stacy Keach *(1941–)*
American actor.

Stalin Stalin Hitler Fraser *(20th century)*
Sierra Leone cricket captain.

Stan Stan Getz *(originally Stanley Gayetzky) (1927–1991)*
American tenor-saxophonist, the father of "cool jazz."

Stanford Stanford White *(1853–1906)*
American architect. He was shot by jealous businessman Harry Thaw, who had married one of White's ex-girlfriends. Thaw was found innocent by reason of insanity.

Stanislav Stanislav Grof *(20th century)*
Czechoslovakian-born American psychiatrist, the creator of "holotrophic therapy."

Stanislavsky Stanislavsky *(professional name of Konstantin Sergeyivich Alexeyev) (1865–1938)*
Russian actor and acting coach.

Stanislawa Stanislawa Walasiewicz *(later Stella Walsh)* *(d. 1980)* Polish-born track-and-field star of the 1932 Olympics, winner of the 100-yard dash. Her autopsy revealed that she was genetically male.

SPIKE LEE

Stanley Stanley Baldwin, 1st Earl Baldwin of Bewdley *(1867–1947)* English politician, three times prime minister.

"My lips are sealed."

Starlite Starlite Randall *(20th century)* American celebrity child, daughter of model Marisa Berenson.

Statilia Statilia Messallina *(married c. A.D. 66)* Roman third wife of the Emperor Nero. Nero killed her first husband to free her to marry him.

Stavros Stavros Spyros Niarchos *(1909–1996)* Greek shipping magnate, the brother-in-law and competitor of Aristotle Onassis.

Steamboat Steamboat Johnson *(Harry S. Johnson)* *(d. 1951)* American baseball minor league umpire, author of *Standing the Gaff* (1935). He was noted for his loud voice.

Steffi Steffi Graf *(1969–)* German tennis player, winner of a 1989 Olympic gold medal.

"I don't particularly like losing."

Steingrímur Steingrímur Thorsteinsson *(Steingrímur Bjarnason Thorsteinsson) (1831–1913)* Icelandic patriotic poet. He translated Hans Christian Andersen's works into Icelandic.

Stella Stella Benson *(Mrs. J.C. O'Gorman Anderson)* *(1892–1933)* English-born Chinese writer.

"Family jokes, though rightly cursed by strangers, are the bonds that keep most families alive."

Stendhal Stendhal *(pen name of Marie-Henri Beyle)* *(1783–1842)* French novelist and essayist, author of *Le Rouge et le Noir* (1830).

Stentor Stentor Mythical Greek warrior at the Trojan War. The adjective "stentorian" still means "loud," because of his "voice of bronze, whose cry was as loud of the cry of fifty other men."

Stéphane Stéphane Mallarmé *(1842–1898)* French writer.

"Every old man is a confession. Old age makes us what we were meant to be."

Stephanie Princess Stephanie *(1965–)* Monaco socialite daughter of Prince Rainier III and Grace Kelly.

Stephen Stephen Hawking *(1942–)* British physicist, author of the least-readable best-seller ever, *A Brief History of Time* (1988).

Stepin Stepin Fetchit *(originally Lincoln Theodore Monroe Andrew Perry) (1892–1985)* American actor, the definitive master of the pop-eyed double-take. He became a Black Muslim.

Sterling Sterling Relyea Walter Hayden *(originally John Hamilton) (1916–1986)* American actor.

"There is not enough money in Hollywood to lure me into making another picture with Joan Crawford. And I like money."

Stesichorus Stesichorus *(630–550 B.C.)* Greek lyric poet.

"'Tis a vain and impotent thing to bewail the dead."

Steve Steve Jobs *(1955–)* American computer designer.

"Apple is going to be the most important computer company in the world, far more important than IBM."

Steven Steven Spielberg *(1947–)* American filmmaker.

"When I grow up, I still want to be a film director."

Stevie Stevie Wonder (originally Steveland Judkins or Morris) (1950–)
American rock musician, the first Motown composer to win full artistic control over his work. His song "Isn't She Lovely" (1976) has the sound of his new baby crying in the background.

Stewart Stewart Granger (originally James Stewart) (1913–1993)
British-born American actor.

Stillman Stillman Drake (1911–1993)
American-born Canadian scientific scholar. He reconstructed many of Galileo Galilei's physics experiments.

Sting Sting (originally Gordon Mathew Sumner) (1951–)
English rock singer with the band the Police. He got his stage-name from a favourite wasp-striped T-shirt.

Stirling Stirling Moss (1929–)
British racing-car driver, known as the greatest driver never to have won the World Championship. He came second four times.

Stockard Stockard Channing (originally Susan Stockard) (1944–)
American actress.

Stoddard Stoddard King (1889–1933)
American poet.
> "Of all the pestilences dire,
> Including famine, flood and fire,
> By Satan and his imps rehearsed,
> The neighbours' children are the worst."

Stokely Stokely Carmichael (now known as Kwame Ture) (1941–)
American political worker, the first person to use the "black power" slogan. He married Mirian Makeba, and ran for parliament in West African Guinea.
> "Our grandfathers had to run, run, run. My generation's out of breath. We ain't running no more."

Stompin' Stompin' Tom Connors (1936–)
Canadian folk-singer. He uses three microphones: for voice, guitar, and stomping foot.

Stone Stone Gossard (20th century)
American guitarist with the Seattle group Pearl Jam.

Stonewall Thomas Jonathan "Stonewall" Jackson (1824–1863)
American soldier, a Confederate general. He got his name from his unwillingness to retreat. As one person put it, "See, there is Jackson, standing like a stone-wall."

Storm Storm Jameson (Margaret Storm Jameson) (1891–1986)
British novelist.

Strabo Strabo trans. squint-eyed (63 B.C.– A.D. 24)
Greek geographer and Stoic philosopher. "Strabic" means "squinty."

Strangelove Dr. Strangelove (1963)
American film by Stanley Kubrick.

Stratford Stratford Canning, 1st Vicount Stratford de Redcliffe (1786–1880)
English diplomat. He may have started the Crimean War by refusing to accept a Russian "protectorate" over Orthodox Christians.

Strepsiades Strepsiades
Worried old father in Aristophanes' satiric Greek play The Clouds (423 B.C.). After his son runs up huge gambling debts, Strepsiades sends him to study philosophy with Socrates, to learn how to argue his way out of paying.

Stretch Willie "Stretch" McCovey (1938–)
American baseball first baseman with the Giants, a member of the Hall of Fame.

Strickland Strickland Gillian (b.1869)
English writer.
> "Bilin' down his report, wuz Finnigin!
> An' he writed this here: "Muster Flannigan—
> Off ag'in, on ag'in,
> Gone ag'in—FINNIGIN."

Stringer Stringer Davis (1896–1973)
English actor, the husband of Dame Margaret Rutherford.

Stroll Lem "Stroll" Barney (1945–)
American football defensive back with the Detroit Lions, a member of the Hall of Fame.

Strongbow Strongbow *(Richard de Clare, 2nd Earl of Pembroke) (c. 1130–1176)*
English soldier.

Strother Strother Martin *(1919–1980)*
American actor. In *Cool Hand Luke* (1967) he says, "What we have here is a failure to communicate."

Struwwelpeter *Struwwelpeter (Shockheaded Peter) (1844)*
German children's book by physician Heinrich Hoffman, who created drawings of his slovenly character to warn children to behave. By 1925, there had been almost 600 German editions.

Stu Stu Cook *(1945–)*
American rockabilly bass player with the band Creedence Clearwater Revival.

Stuart Stuart M. Berger *(1954–1994)*
Short-lived best-selling American author of the health book *Forever Young—20 Years Younger in 20 Weeks, How to Be Your Own Nutritionist.*

Studs Studs Terkel *(Louis Terkel) (1912–)*
American writer and interviewer; winner of Pulitzer Prize and author of the autobiography *Talking to Myself* (1977). Economist John Kenneth Galbraith called him a "national resource."

Sturmi St. Sturmi *(d. 779)*
Bavarian protégé of St. Boniface, the "Apostle to the Saxons." He was not very successful.

Styx Styx *trans. hated*
Mythical Greek river nymph, daughter of Oceanus and Tethys.

Sue Sue Rogers *(1939–)*
English architect.

Subhas Subhas W. Pandhrinath "Fergie" Gupte *(1929–)*
Indian cricket player, a fine googly bowler.

Suboro Suboro Kurusu *(active 1940)*
Japanese ambassador. He signed the Axis Alliance treaty.

Sudden "Sudden" Sam McDowell *(1942–)*
American baseball pitcher for the Indians, an All-Star. He set a 1965 American League southpaw record with 325 strike-outs.

Suds Suds Merrick *(d. 1884)*
American robber. He specialized in cargo boats on New York's East River.

Sue Sue Cowsill *(1960–)*
American singer with the squeaky-clean Cowsills, "America's first family of song."

Sugar Sugar Ray Leonard *(Ray Charles Leonard) (1956–)*
American boxing champion.
"We're all endowed with God-given talents. Mine happens to be hitting people in the head."

Suger Suger *(c. 1081–1151)*
French abbot of St. Denis. He rebuilt his church in the brand-new Gothic style.

Suha Suha Arafat, *née Tawil (1963–)*
Palestinian political worker, wife of President Yasser Arafat of the Palestinian Authority.

Suiho Suiho Tagawa *(1899–)*
Japanese cartoonist, noted for the popular wartime comic strip "Nora Kuro."

Suitcase Harry "Suitcase" Simpson *(1925–1979)*
American baseball player for the A's and seventeen other teams in eleven years. He was called "Suitcase" because he moved so often.

Süleyman Süleyman *(d. 1084)*
Turkish Seljük sultan of Anatolia.

Sulla Sulla
Pre-Celtic English goddess of hot springs, worshipped at Bath. "Sally Lunn" cakes may be the remnant of altar offerings made in her name.

Sumuel Sumuel *(ruled 1894–1866 B.C.)*
Ruler of Larsa in Mesopotamia.

Sun Rev. Sun Myung Moon *(1929–)*
South Korean founder of the Unification Church, members of which are known as "Moonies." On August 25, 1992, he married 30,000 people in the world's largest mass marriage ceremony held since Alexander the Great married his soldiers to conquered Persian brides.

Sunny Sunny von Bülow *(20th century)*
American millionaire. Her husband, Claus von Bülow, was acquitted twice on charges of having tried to kill her.

Superman Superman *(1941–)*
Canadian-born American cartoon superhero.

Surya Surya Bonaly *(1974–)*
French figure skater. She is considered a mere gymnast by some for her excessive reliance on jumps and originality.

Sus'sistinnako Sus'sistinnako
New Mexico mythical creator. He made humanity by singing and accompanying himself on a harp spun with spider-web.

Susan Susan B. Anthony *(Susan Brownell Anthony) (1820–1906)*
American pioneer suffrage worker. The 19th amendment to the American constitution, granting suffrage to women, is sometimes called the "Susan B. Anthony amendment."
"Resistance to tyranny is obedience to God."

Susanna Susanna Moodie, *née Strickland (1803–1885)*
English-born Canadian writer, author of the descriptive *Roughing It in the Bush* (1852).

Susanne Susanne Sulley *(1963–)*
British pop singer with the Human League.

Susi Susi Singer *(1885–1949)*
Austrian-born American ceramist. She worked with the Wiener Werkstätte.

Susie Susie Orbach *(20th century)*
British psychotherapist, author of *Fat Is a Feminist Issue*, therapist to Princess Diana.

Suzannah Suzannah Ibsen *(19th century)*
Norwegian wife of playwright Henrik Ibsen. They never slept together again after the birth of their son, Sigurd.

Suzanne Suzanne Lenglen *(1899–1938)*
French tennis player. Between 1919 and 1926, she lost only one match, and created a fashion sensation with her daring knee-length costume.

Suzi Suzi Quattro *(originally Suzi Quatrochio) (1950–)*
American rock bass player and singer.

Suzy Suzy Knickerbocker *(or Aileen Mehle) (active 1960s)*
American gossip columnist.
"What I do is kick them in the pants with a dia-mond-buckled shoe."

Svein Svein I Haraldsson, *"Fork-Beard" (d. 1014)*
King of Denmark, son of Harald "Blue-Tooth" Gormsson. He was King of England too for five weeks.

Svend Svend Robinson *(1952–)*
Canadian gay-activist politician. In 1994 he was jailed for anti-logging activism.

Svetlana Svetlana Stalin *(20th century)*
Russian writer, the daughter of Joseph Stalin.

Swede Swede Risberg *(Charles August Risberg) (1894–1975)*
American baseball shortstop, one of the eight "Black Sox" banned for life for fixing the 1919 World Series.

Sweeney Sweeney Todd, the Demon Barber of Fleet Street *(1979)*
American musical play by Stephen Sondheim concerning the fictional resident of No. 186 Fleet Street and his human-meat pies.

Sweetness Walter "Sweetness" Payton *(1954–)*
American football running back with the Chicago Bears, a member of the Hall of Fame.

Swellfoot "Swellfoot the Tyrant" *(1820)*
English poem by Percy Bysshe Shelley.
"Jealousy's eyes are green."

Swift Swift John Nevison *(active 1676)*
English highwayman. He once robbed a sailor at Gadshill at 4:00 a.m. and reached York by 7:45 p.m. to establish an alibi. This may be the famous ride attributed to fellow highwayman Dick Turpin.

Swifty Paul Irving "Swifty" Lazar *(20th century)*
American actors' agent. He got his nickname after signing five deals in one day for Humphrey Bogart.

Swish Bill "Swish" Nicholson *(1914–)*
American baseball outfielder with the Cubs, an All-Star. During the Second World War he led the National League two years in a row in both homers and RBI.

Swithbert St. Swithbert *(647–713)*
Northumbrian missionary to southern Holland. He is the patron saint against angina.

Swithin St. Swithin *(or Swithun) (d. 862)*
Anglo-Saxon religious worker, chaplain to King Egbert.

Swoosie Swoosie Kurtz *(1944–)*
American actress.

Sybil *Sybil (1845)*
English novel by Benjamin Disraeli.

Sybilla Sybilla Masters *(d. 1720)*
American inventor, the first woman to have an invention patented; a device for cleaning and curing Indian corn. She registered it under her husband's name.

Syd Syd Cavill *(19th century)*
Australian athlete. In 1893, he and his brother Charles invented the Australian crawl swim stroke.

Sydney Sydney Joseph (S.J.) Perelman *(1904–1979)*
American humorist of unparalleled artificial brittleness. He won an Oscar for the screenplay of *Around the World in Eighty Days* (1956).
> *"Doctor! I've got Bright's Disease and he's got mine!"*

Sye Sye Webster *(20th century)*
Scottish soccer fan banned from his local stadium for a year after kissing the referee.
> *"I ken the meaning of suffering."*

Sylvain Sylvain Sylvain *originally Syl Mizrahi (20th century)*
American punk rocker with the New York Dolls.

Sylvan Sylvan Goldman *(20th century)*
American grocery-store owner. In 1937, he invented the first shopping cart, a basket mounted to a folding chair.

Sylvester Sylvester Stallone *(originally Michael Sylvester Stallone) (1946–)*
American actor, author of the screenplay for *Rocky* (1976).

Sylvia Sylvia Plath *(1932–1963)*
American poet and suicide, author of the novel *The Bell Jar* (1963).
> *"Poetry is an evasion of the real job of writing prose."*

Syrie Syrie Bernardo Maugham, *née Wellcome (b. 1879)*
English interior designer, the ex-wife of writer Somerset Maugham. News of her death was brought to him as he was playing solitaire. He dropped his cards and began to drum on the table, singing, "Tral-la-la! No more alimony! Tra-la, tra-la."

Syrinx Syrinx *trans. reed*
Mythical Greek nymph who turned herself into a reed to escape Pan. Thwarted, he made himself the first reed pipe or Pan-flute, also called a "syrinx."

T T-Bone Walker *(originally Aaron Thibeaux Walker) (1910–1975)*
American blues guitarist.

Taamusi Taamusi Qumaq *(1914–1993)*
Canadian Inuit lexographer, author of the definitive *Inuit Uqausillaringit* (1991).

Tab Tab Hunter *(originally Arthur Gelien) (1931–)*
American actor.

Tacitus Tacitus *(Publius Tacitus, or Gaius Cornelius) (c. 55–120)*
Roman historian.
> *"He had talents equal to business, and aspired no higher."*

Tadeusz Tadeusz Reichstein *(1897–)*
Polish-born Swiss chemist, winner of a Nobel Prize for his work on adrenal hormones.

Taffy Clarence John "Taffy" Abel *(1900–)*
American hockey player. He was the first National Hockey League player to be born in the United States.

Tai Tai Otavio Missoni *(1921–)*
Italian knitwear manufacturer, of the firm Missoni.

Taikichiro Taikichiro Mori *(1904–1993)*
Japanese deca-millionaire, the "landlord of Tokyo."

Taj Taj Mahal *(originally Henry St.Clair Fredericks) (1942–)*
American Afro-folk-rocker.

Takashi Takashi Matsunaga *(20th century)*
Japanese chairman of the All Japan Women's
Professional Wrestling Association. He offered
figure-skater Tonya Harding $2 million after her
disgrace in the Nancy Kerrigan beating.
> *"Of course, she'd have to be the bad guy at first,
> but I think she can learn to be a heroine as well."*

Takla St. Takla *(3rd century)*
Christian martyr. She is buried in Ma'lulua,
Syria.

Talbot Talbot Baines Reed *(1852–1893)*
British children's writer, creator of stories such
as "The Fifth Form at St Dominic's" (1881) for
the *Boy's Own Paper*.

Talcott Talcott Parsons *(1902–1979)*
American sociologist, author of formerly influ-
ential books such as *Sociological Theory and
Modern Society* (1968).

Taliesin Taliesin *(6th century)*
Semi-legendary Welsh bard. He and Merlin were
the founders of Welsh poetry.

Talleyrand Talleyrand *(Charles Maurice de
Talleyrand-Périgord) (1754–1838)*
French politician. Asked what action would
impress the peasantry, he replied, "You might
try getting crucified and rising again on the
third day."

Tallulah Tallulah Bankhead *(1903–1968)*
American actress. She once dropped $50 into a
Salvation Army tambourine and said, "Don't
bother to thank me. I know what a perfectly
ghastly season it's been for you Spanish
dancers."

Tam "Tam O'Shanter" *(1790)*
Scottish poem by Robert Burns.

Tam-Tam *Princess Tam-Tam (1935)*
French film starring exotic American dancer
Josephine Baker.

Tamara Tamara de Lempicka *(1898–1980)*
Russian-born painter.

Tambo Tambo Tambo *(real name Wangung)
(1863–1884)*
Australian-born American circus performer
forcibly kidnapped from the Palm and
Hinchinbrook Islands. He died of pneumonia in
Cleveland, was embalmed and forgotten until

1993, when a diligent
county coroner managed
to return his body home.

Tamerlane Tamerlane *(real
name Timur-i-lane, or the
"lame Timur")
(1336–1404)*
Samarkand-born warrior.
His empire included
Persia, Turkey, and northern India. He built trademark minarets out of decapitat-
ed heads.

TAMMY FAYE BAKKER

Tamesis Tamesis
Celtic river goddess. Her name was given to the
English River Thames.

Tamia Tamia Washington *(1976–)*
Canadian funk singer. She sang "I Will Always
Love You" to reviled Prime Minister Brian
Mulroney at his retirement party.

Tamilee Tamilee Webb *(20th century)*
American fitness guru, creator and star performer of the video *Buns of Steel* (1990).

Tammi Tammi Terrell *(originally Thomasina
Montgomery) (1946–1970)*
American blues singer, a partner of Marvin
Gaye.

Tammuz Tammuz *trans. sprout, Ezekiel 8: 14*
Accadian god popular throughout Mesopotamia
and Palestine.

Tammy Tammy Faye Bakkér *(20th century)*
American theologian.
> *"You don't have to be dowdy to be a Christian."*

Tamra Tamra Jean Tobin *(20th century)*
Canadian lawyer. In 1994, she successfully sued
her golf club for restricting women's access to
the good tee times.

Tancred Tancred *(c. 1076–1112)*
Norman crusader. He is described in Tasso's
Gerusalemme liberata (1593).

Tank Paul "Tank" Younger *(1928–)*
American football running back with the Los
Angeles Rams.

Tantalus Tantalus *trans. most wretched*
Legendary Greek founder of the tragic house of
Atreus. He suffers eternal punishment in Hades

for crimes like serving the gods' ambrosia to mortals.

Tantoo Tantoo Cardinal *(1950–)*
Canadian actress.

Tanya Tanya Tucker *(Tanya Denise Tucker) (1958–)*
American country singer. She had her first hit at the age of fourteen.

Tara Tara Hallgren *(1955–)*
Canadian entrepreneur. She and her sister Gayle founded the O-Tooz health-fast-food chain featuring goodies such as Moose Jaw Muesli.

Taras *Taras Bulba (1962)*
American film, a big-budget flop starring Yul Brynner.

Tarita Tarita Brando *(20th century)*
Tahitian third wife of American actor Marlon Brando, mother of their unhappy daughter Cheyenne.

Tark Jerry "Tark the Shark" Tarkanian *(1930–)*
American basketball player and coach at the University of Nevada, Las Vegas.

Tarzan *Tarzan of the Apes (1918)*
American film, the first based on the novel by Edgar Rice Burroughs.

Taslima Taslima Nasrin *(1963–)*
Bangladeshi anaesthesiologist feminist, author of the novel *Laiia (Shame)* (1993).

> "In our country, the injustices against women are so extreme I must be extreme. Subtlety does not work in this extremely repressive society."

Tassach St. Tassach *(also known as Asicus) (d. c. 495)*
Irish disciple of St. Patrick. He was a metalsmith, and made all of the croziers, patens, crosses, and chalices for St. Patrick's churches.

Taters George "Taters" Chatham *(20th century)*
British cat burglar. In 1947, he stole two of the Duke of Wellington's swords from the Victoria and Albert Museum.

Tatiana Tatiana Troyano *(1939–1993)*
American mezzo-soprano.

Tatum Tatum O'Neal *(1963–)*
American actress, the youngest person ever to win an Academy Award, at age ten for *Paper Moon* (1973) in which she appears with her father, Ryan O'Neal.

Tatyana Tatyana Ivanova Zaslavskaya *(1927–)*
Kiev-born sociologist and economist.

Taxile Taxile Doat *(b. 1851)*
French ceramic designer for the Sèvres porcelain factory.

Teach Eleanor "Teach" Tennant *(20th century)*
American competitive tennis player. During the 1920s, she was a tennis teacher to stars like Clark Gable.

Tecumseh Tecumseh *(c. 1768–1813)*
American chief of the Shawnee tribe. He and his brother met defeat at Tippecanoe, and then joined the British for the War of 1812.

Ted Ted Nugent *(1948–)*
American rock musician. He bid $10 million to buy the Muzak company in hopes of having the pleasure of erasing its tapes.

Teddy Teddy Roosevelt *(Theodore Roosevelt) (1858–1919)*
American 26th president. Teddy bears were named for him after an incident where he refused to shoot a bear which had been tied to a tree to wait for him.

Teena *Teena (1941–1964)*
American cartoon strip by Hilda Terry. When it was cancelled, Terry retrained in computers, and became the first expert in creating cartoons for computerized sports-stadium scoreboards.

Teiresias Teiresias *trans. he who delights in signs*
Greatest of all the Greek prophets. He changed sex and lived for seven years as a woman, so Zeus and Hera asked him to settle an argument about whether men or women got more physical pleasure from sex, to determine why Zeus cheated on Hera so much. He said it was women, and Hera blinded him in a fit of rage.

Tekahionwake Tekahionwake *(pen-name of E. Pauline Johnson) (1861–1913)*
Canadian poet. In her stage appearances she wore both English and Mohawk clothing, in honour of both her parents.

Teke Kent "Teke" Tekulve *(1947–)*
American baseball pitcher for the Pirates, an All-Star. He retired with a career record number of

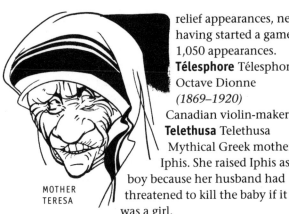

MOTHER
TERESA

relief appearances, never having started a game in 1,050 appearances.

Télesphore Télesphore-Octave Dionne *(1869–1920)*
Canadian violin-maker.

Telethusa Telethusa
Mythical Greek mother of Iphis. She raised Iphis as a boy because her husband had threatened to kill the baby if it was a girl.

Telly Telly Savalas *(Aristotle Savalas) (1924–1994)*
Bald American actor, star of the TV series "Kojak" (1973–78)

Temma Dr. Temma *(21st century)*
Japanese cartoon scientist, the creator of robot Astro Boy after his own son was killed in a traffic accident.

Temora *Temora, an Epic Poem in Eight Books (1763)*
Supposedly ancient Scottish epic poem forged by James Macpherson.

Temple Temple Grandin *(20th century)*
American autistic designer, author of *Thinking in Pictures* (1995).

Tenley Tenley Albright *(1935–)*
American figure-skater and surgeon. She recovered from childhood polio to win a 1956 Olympic gold medal. She is in the Harvard University Hall of Fame, the Ice Skating Hall of Fame, and the Olympic Hall of Fame.

Tennessee Tennessee Celeste Claflin *(1845–1923)*
American feminist reformer, stockbroker, and adventuress. She co-authored *The Human Body, the Temple of God* (1890) with her sister Victoria Woodhull, who ran for president on a free-love platform.

Tenzin Tenzin Gyatson *(1935–)*
Tibetan spiritual leader, the 14th Dalai Lama.

Tenzing Tenzing Norkay *(20th century)*
Sherpa mountaineer. In 1953, he and Sir Edmund Hillary were the first people to climb Mount Everest.

Terence Terence Hanbury (T.H.) White *(1904–1964)*
English writer, creator of the children's Arthurian classic *The Sword in the Stone* (1939), the first section of *The Once and Future King* (1958).

Teresa Mother Teresa of Calcutta *(originally Agnes Gonxha Bojaxhiu) (1910–)*
Yugoslavian-born Indian religious worker, founder of the Missionaries of Charity, winner of the 1979 Nobel Peace Prize. She owns only one sari, made of rayon so that it will dry overnight when washed. (Silk or cotton would dry more slowly, forcing her to own two garments.)

Teresia Teresia Constantia Philips *(18th century)*
English courtesan. She wrote a book of memoirs.

Teri Teri Garr *(1949–)*
American actress.

Terpsichore Terpsichore
One of the nine Greek muses of the arts. She invented dancing.

Terris Terris McDuffie *(1910–)*
American baseball pitcher with the Negro Leagues, an All-Star.

Terry Terry Fox *(Terrence Stanley Fox) (1958–1981)*
Canadian athlete. He failed to complete his one-legged cross-country charity run, but raised a record-setting amount of money for such an event: C$24.7 million.

Tertullian Tertullian *(Quintus Septimius Florens Tertullianus) (c. 160–c. 225)*
Carthaginian theologian, a father of the Latin Church.
"He who flees will fight again."

Tess *Tess of the D'Urbervilles (1891)*
English novel by Thomas Hardy.

Tessie Tessie O'Shea *(20th century)*
Plump English singer of the 1940s, "Two-Ton Tessie."

Tetsuharu Tetsuharu Kawakami *(20th century)*
Japanese baseball first baseman, the "God of Batting." In 1950, he had a .377 batting average. He spent his winters in Zen meditation, and used a red bat.

Tex Tex Avery *(originally Frederick Bean)* *(1907–1980)*
American director of animation, creator of both Bugs Bunny and Daffy Duck.

Texas Texas Guinan *(originally Mary Louise Cecilia Guinan) (1884–1993)*
American entertainer. In the 1930s, saloon-keeper Larry Fay paid her $4,000 a week to act as master of ceremonies.
"Never give a sucker an even break."

Thad Thad Jones *(Thaddens Joseph Jones)* *(1923–1986)*
American jazz trumpeter, a leader of the Count Basie Orchestra.

Thais Thais *(4th century B.C.)*
Athenian prostitute famed for her beauty and wit. She may have entertained Alexander the Great.

Thales Thales *(or Thallus) (c. 624–c. 545 B.C.)*
Greek astronomer, the founder of Greek natural philosophy, one of the Seven Sages of Greece. He is the original absent-minded professor.

Thalia Thalia *trans. festive*
Greek Muse of comedy. She carries a staff and a comic mask, and wears the thin-soled "sock" shoe of the comic actor. Her sisters are Aglaia ("Brilliance") and Euphrosyne ("Joy").

Thayendanegea Thayendanegea *(known as Joseph Brant) (1742–1807)*
Canadian Six Nations chief. He visited England, where he was entertained by James Boswell and painted by George Romney.

Thea Thea Musgrave *(1928–)*
Scottish composer.

Thebaw King Thebaw *(1858–1916)*
Burmese ruler. He was deposed by the British and sent to prison in India.

Thebe Thebe *trans. admirable*
Mythical Greek nymph. Her husband, Zethus, rebuilt the ancient city of Cadmea and named it Thebes in her honour.

TELLY SAVALAS

Theda Theda Bara *(originally Theodosia Goodman)* *(1885–1955)*
American actress, whose publicity releases coined the term "vamp" (short for "vampire") to describe her charms. She was the first person to wear modern eye makeup, invented for her by Helena Rubinstein.
"Kiss me, my fool."

Thelma Thelma *(1887)*
English popular novel by Marie Corelli.

Thelonious Thelonious Monk *(Thelonious Sphere Monk) (1920–1982)*
American bebop and jazz pianist, composer of "Round Midnight" (1947).
"Talking about music is like dancing about architecture."

Themistocles Themistocles *(c. 523–c. 458 B.C.)*
Athenian soldier. He won the battle of Salamis against Zerxes.

Theo Theo van Doesburg *(originally Christian Emil Marie Küpper) (1883–1931)*
Dutch painter, writer, architect, and designer, the central figure of the De Stijl movement.

Theobald Theobald Boehm *(or Böhm) (1794–1881)*
German flautist, the inventor of the modern flute, with levered finger-rests offset from the holes.

Theocritus Theocritus *(c. 310–250 B.C.)*
Greek pastoral poet.
"A great love goes here with a little gift."

Theodor Theodor Seuss Giesel *(known as Dr. Seuss)* *(1904–1991)*
American children's writer, author of *The Cat in the Hat* (1958).

Theodora Empress Theodora *(c. 500–548 B.C.)*
Byzantine wife of Justinian I. She was the daughter of a circus bear-tamer.

Theodore Theodore Dreiser *(Theodore Herman Albert Dreiser) (1871–1945)*
American novelist, a rival of Sinclair Lewis.

Theodoric King Theodoric the Great *(or Theoderic)* *(455–526)*
Ruler of the Ostrogoths, conqueror of Italy. He appears as heroic "Dietrich von Bern" in Richard Wagner's opera *Der Ring des Nibelungen*.

Theodorus Theodorus of Samos *(6th century B.C.)* Greek sculptor. He invented hollow casting of metal for large statues.

Theodosius Theodosius the Great *(c. 346–395)* Roman Christian Emperor. In 380, he extinguished the sacred flame of the Vestal Virgins that had burned for 1,000 years.

Theognis Theognis *(active 544–541 B.C.)* Greek poet.

> *"No one goes to Hades with all his immense wealth."*

Théophile Théophile Gautier *(1811–1872)* French poet and novelist.

> *"The work comes out more beautiful from a material that resists the process; verse, marble, onyx or enamel."*

Théophraste Théophraste Renaudot *(c. 1586–1653)* French doctor. He started a free clinic for the poor, and the world's first pawnshop.

Thérèse Thérèse Le Vasseur *(18th century)* French illiterate laundress, the long-time companion of philosopher Jean-Jacques Rousseau. They had five children, all of whom were immediately given to foundling hospitals, despite their father's lyrical writings on the beauty of childhood.

Theseus Theseus *trans. he who lays down* Legendary hero, son of Aegeus, king of Athens, conqueror of the Minotaur in the maze in Crete, and Mediterranean heart-breaker for dumping Ariadne after she helped him do it.

Thespis Thespis *(6th century B.C.)* Greek inventor of acting. He introduced a single actor to the stage to join the traditional chorus, which had developed out of dithyramb chanting in honour of Dionysus.

Thespius King Thespius of Thespia *trans. divinely sounding* Legendary ambitious Greek father. He wanted all fifty of his daughters to have children by Heracles. Heracles impregnated forty-nine of the daughters in a single night, a feat known as the thirteenth labour of Heracles. (The fiftieth daughter refused him.)

Thetis Thetis *trans. disposer* Greek Nereid. She had trouble getting dates after a seer predicted her son would be greater than his father. Finally she married King Peleus of the Myrmidons, and became the mother of the great Achilles.

Thoby Thoby Stephen *(d. 1906)* British brother of Virginia Woolf and Vanessa Bell. He shared their house at 46 Gordon Square, Bloomsbury, London, that was the centre of the "Bloomsbury Group."

Thom Thom Bell *(1941–)* American record producer, a leader in the 1970's "Philly sound."

Thomas Thomas Crapper *(b. 1837)* British inventor of the modern flush toilet, which he advertised as "Crapper's Valveless Water Waste Preventer: Certain Flush with Easy Pull."

Thomasin Thomasin Yeobright Country girl in Thomas Hardy's English novel *The Return of the Native* (1878).

Thor Thor Heyerdahl *(1914–)* Norwegian anthropologist, builder of the papyrus raft described in *Kon Tiki* (1947).

Thorbjoern Thorbjoern Berntsen *(20th century)* Norwegian politician. As minister of the environment in 1993, he was quoted in the papers saying, "the English environment minister is the biggest shitbag ["drittsekk"] I have ever met in my life."

Thorfinn Thorfinn *(or Thorfinnur Karsefni) (active 1002–1007)* Icelandic explorer. He colonized "Vinland" in North America.

Thorkelin Thorkelin *(real name Grimur Jónsson) (1752–1820)* Icelandic scholar, the first editor of the traditional epic poem *Beowulf*.

Thornton Thornton Wilder *(Thorton Niven Wilder) (1897–1975)* American playwright, winner of a Pulitzer Prize, author of *The Skin of Our Teeth* (1942).

Thorstein Thorstein Veblen *(Thorstein Bunde Veblen)* *(1857–1929)*
American economist, author of the subversive *The Theory of the Leisure Class* (1899).
  "Conspicuous consumption of valuable goods is a means of reputability to the gentleman of leisure."

Thoth Thoth
Egyptian ibis-headed god of intelligence, the scribe of the gods.

Three-Finger Three-Finger Brown *(Mordecai Peter Centennial Brown)* *(1876–1948)*
American baseball pitcher, a member of the Hall of Fame. He lost three fingers on his right hand to a corn grinder at age seven. He used his stubbed middle finger to put spin on his curve balls. To this day, the Chicago Cubs have never won a World Series without him.

Thrym Thrym
Mythical Nordic giant. He stole Thor's hammer and tried to barter it for Freya's hand in marriage. Instead, Thor arrived for the wedding feast disguised as Freya and, after eating an ox and drinking three kegs of mead, killed everyone.

Thucydides Thucydides *(c. 460–c. 400 B.C.)*
Greek historian who documented the Peloponnesian War.

Thump Thump Thomson *(20th century)*
American doo-wop revival bass player with the Darts.

Thurgood Thurgood Marshall *(1908–1993)*
American lawyer, the first black justice on the American Supreme Court, the "great dissenter."
  "We lived on a respectable street, but behind us there were back alleys where the roughnecks and the tough kids hung out. When it was time for dinner, my mother used to go to the front door and call my older brother. Then she'd go to the back door and call me."

Thurlow Thurlow Weed *(1797–1882)*
American journalist.

Thurman Thurman Munson *(1947–1979)*
American baseball catcher for the Yankees, an All-Star, winner of a Gold Glove award, 1970 American League Rookie of the Year, and 1976 Most Valuable Player. He died in his prime in a plane crash.

Tiberius Tiberius Caesar *(42 B.C.– A.D. 37)*
Roman emperor, the unpopular but efficient successor of Augustus.

Tiffany Tiffany's
New York City jewellery shop.

Tigellinus Tigellinus *(1st century)*
Italian courtier of the Emperor Nero, author of *The Satyricon.*

Tiger Don "Tiger" Hoak *(1928–1969)*
American baseball third baseman for the Pirates, an All-Star.

Tiggy Tiggy Legge-Bourke *(1963–)*
British nanny to Princes William and Harry. In 1995, her lawyers protested gossip linking her romantically with Prince Charles.

TiGrace TiGrace Atkinson *(20th century)*
American feminist, author of the article "Vaginal Orgasm as a Mass Hysterical Survival Response" in the magazine *Amazon Odyssey* (1974).

Tilda Tilda Swinton *(Matilda Swinton)* *(1961–)*
British actress.

Tilly Tilly Walker *(Clarence William Walker)* *(1887–1959)*
American baseball outfielder with the As.

Tilman Tilman Riemenschneider *(c. 1460–1531)*
German sculptor, a member of the 1525 Peasants' Revolt.

Tim Tim Horton *(originally Miles Gilbert Horton)* *(1930–1974)*
Canadian hockey defenceman with the Maple Leafs, founder of the chain of Tim Horton Donut Shops.

Timandra Timandra *trans. honoured by man*
Mythical Greek sister of Helen and Clytemnaestra. All three sisters were notorious adulteresses because their father forgot to make appropriate sacrifices to the goddess Aphrodite, and this was her revenge.

Timo Timo Sarpaneva *(1926–)*
Finnish industrial designer.

TINA
TURNER

Timon Timon, Misanthrope of Athens *(5th century)* Athenian nobleman, the inspiration for one of William Shakespeare's lesser plays.

Timothy Timothy Leary *(Timothy Francis Leary) (1920–1996)* American guru. During the 1960s he promoted psychotropic drugs.

"Turn on, tune in, drop out."

Tina Tina Turner *(originally Annie Mae Bullock) (1939–)* American rock star.

"Whatever is bringing you down, get rid of it."

Tinker Tinker Hatfield *(20th century)* American product designer for the shoe manufacturer Nike. He scouts ghettos to see how kids customize their shoes.

Tinkerbell Tinkerbell Jealous fairy friend of Peter of J.M. (James Matthew) Barrie's children's novel *Peter Pan* (1911).

Tintin Tintin *(1940s–)* Belgian cartoon boy detective, hero of Europe's most popular cartoon series.

Tintoretto Tintoretto *(real name Jacopo Robusti) (c. 1518–1594)* Venetian painter. Three of his children became painters, including his daughter Marietta.

"In judging paintings, you should consider whether the first impression pleases the eye and whether the artist has followed the rules; as for the rest, everyone makes some mistakes."

Tiny "Tiny" Rowland *(originally Rowland W. Furhop) (1917–)* British businessman. During his battle with the Fayed brothers for the purchase of Harrod's Department Store, they displayed a fake shark in the Food Halls, labelled "Tiny."

Tip Tip O'Neill *(Thomas P. O'Neill, Jr.) (1912–1994)* American politician, the Speaker of the House of Representatives.

"All politics is local."

Tipper Tipper Gore *(20th century)* American political worker, wife of Vice-President Al Gore.

Tippi Tippi Hedren *(originally Nathalie Kay Hedren) (1931–)* American actress, star of Alfred Hitchcock's movie *The Birds* (1963) and mother of actress Melanie Griffith.

Tippoo Tippoo Sahib *(or Tipú Sultán) (1749–1799)* Sultan of Mysore, India. He successfully battled the British for many years.

Tippy Tippy Martinez *(Felix Anthony Martinez) (1950–)* American baseball pitcher for the Orioles, an All-Star.

Tiran Tiran Porter *(20th century)* American pop musician with the Doobie Brothers.

Tirzah Tirzah *trans. pleasing, Numbers 26: 33, (c. 13th century B.C.)* Old Testament daughter of Zelophehad. When he died without sons, she and her four sisters managed to claim a share of their father's estate.

Tish Tish Hinojosa *(1956–)* American Tex-Mex folk-singer.

Tita Tita Frustrated Mexican heroine of Laura Esquirel's novel *Like Water for Chocolate: A Novel in Monthly Installments with Recipes, Romances and Home Remedies.*

"[Tita's cooking] was the way she entered Pedro's body, hot, voluptuous, perfumed, totally sensuous."

Titania Titania, Queen of the Fairies Fairy femme fatale of William Shakespeare's play *A Midsummer Night's Dream* (1595–96).

Tithonus Tithonus *trans. partner of the queen of day* Mythical Trojan prince. When the goddess Aurora fell in love with him, he asked her for the gift of immortal life but forgot to ask for eternal youth as well. Finally, decrepit, he shrank into a grasshopper.

Titian Titian *(Tiziano Vecellio) (c. 1488–1576)* Venetian painter.

Tito Tito (originally Josip Broz) (1892–1980)
Yugoslav Communist politician, president-for-life.

Titus Titus Oates (1649–1705)
English conspirator. He invented a tale of a Catholic conspiracy which led to thirty-five judicial murders before he was detected in perjury.

Tlaloc Tlaloc
Pre-Colombian Mexican rain god. In 1964, a 167-ton statue of him was positioned at the entrance of the new National Museum of Anthropology. Torrential rains marred the ribbon-cutting ceremony.

Tobe Tobe Hooper (1943–)
American film director of The Texas Chainsaw Massacre (1974).

Tobiah Tobiah trans. the Lord is good, Nehemiah 4: 3 (c. 5th century B.C.)
Old Testament pessimist. He ridiculed Nehemiah's plan to rebuild the walls of Jerusalem.
> "If a fox goes up on it he will break down their stone wall!"

Tobias Tobias Smollett (Tobias George Smollett) (1721–1771)
Scottish novelist.
> "Facts are stubborn things."

Toby Sir Toby Belch
Layabout uncle of Olivia in William Shakespeare's play Twelfth Night (1599–1600).

Tod Tod Browning (1882–1962)
American macabre filmmaker, creator of the original Dracula (1931), and the horrifying Freaks (1932).

Todd Todd Oldham (20th century)
American fashion designer. His mother is president of his company.

Toe Lou "The Toe" Groza (Louis Groza) (1924–)
American football defensive tackle, a member of the Hall of Fame. His specialty was kicking field goals.

Toinette Toinette
Brassy maid in Molière's play Le Malade imaginaire (1673).

Tolchard Tolchard Evans (originally Sydney Evans) (1901–1978)
British songwriter, composer of "Lady of Spain" (1931).

Toller Toller Cranston (1949–)
Canadian figure-skater and choreographer.

Tom "Colonel" Tom Parker (20th century)
American musical manager.
> "When I first knew Elvis he had a million dollars worth of talent. Now he has a million dollars."

Tomas Tomas Bata (1876–1932)
Czechoslovakian industrialist. From a small shoemaking business, he built up the largest leather factory in Europe.

Tommie Tommie Smith (1944–)
American track athlete. He gave a "black power" salute while accepting a 1968 Olympic Gold Medal in Mexico City.

Tommy Tommy Hunter (Thomas James Hunter) (1937–)
Canadian country singer, host of the TV program "Country Hoedown" (1965–91).

Tompall Tompall Glaser (originallyThomas Paul Glaser) (1933–)
American country "outlaw" musician, leader of Tompall and the Glaser Brothers.

Tomson Tomson Highway (1951–)
Canadian playwright.

Toni Toni Onley (1928–)
Canadian abstract painter. He scheduled a bonfire of his pictures for a British Columbia beach when the Canadian government decided to tax artists on their "manufacturing inventory" of unsold art. The policy was hastily changed.

Tonto Tonto (1930–)
American faithful Indian companion on the radio program The Lone Ranger. He called the Lone Ranger "Kemo Sabe," which was supposedly Indian for "trusting brave" but was actually the name of the writer's father-in-law's summer camp in Michigan.

Tony Antoinette "Tony" Perry *(1888–1946)*
American stage director. The American
Theatre Wing Institute Antoinette Perry Award
(also known as the "Tony") is named after her.

Tonya Tonya Harding *(1971–)*
American Olympic skater. In 1993, her husband
was found guilty of plotting to injure her perfect rival Nancy Kerrigan.

Toots Toots Hibbert *(originally Frederick Hibbert)*
(1946–)
Jamaican reggae musician, leader of Toots and
the Maytals.

Tootsie Tootsie Hirschfield *(19th century)*
American daughter of candymaker Leonard
Hirschfield, who in 1896 named the Tootsie
Roll after her. It was the first paper-wrapped
candy.

Tooz John "Tooz" Matiszak *(1950–1989)*
American football defensive end with the
Oakland Raiders.
> *"The Raiders aren't a team where you always
> have to straighten up your tie and wear your hair
> a certain length. As long as you put out at prac-
> tice and on Sundays, they don't care. As long as
> you stay out of jail."*

Topham Topham Beauclerk *(1739–1780)*
English dandy. Upon being told that a friend
had good moral principles, he observed, "Then
he does not wear them out in practice."

Topo Topo Gigio *(20th century)*
Italian mouse puppet, a favourite on *The Ed
Sullivan Show.*
> *"Eddy, kiss me good night."*

Tore Tore Haugen *(20th century)*
Norwegian forestry worker, creator of earrings
made from dried elk droppings as souvenirs of
the 1994 Lillehammer Olympic games.

Tori Tori Spelling *(1973–)*
American celebrity daughter of Aaron Spelling,
a star of "Beverly Hills 90210."

Torquato Torquato Tasso *(1544–1594)*
Italian poet. Lord Byron wrote a poetic "Lament
of Tasso" about his mental breakdown.

Torquemada Torquemada *(20th century)*
English cruciverbalist (crossword-puzzle maker).
In 1926, he invented the "cryptic" crossword.

Torsten Torsten Nils Wisel *(1924–)*
Swedish neurobiologist, winner of a Nobel Prize
for his work on the neurology of cat vision.

Toshiro Toshiro Mifune *(1920–)*
Japanese actor, star of *Rashomon* (1950).

Toto Toto
Canine companion of Dorothy in L. Frank
Baum's children's novel *The Wonderful Wizard of
Oz* (1900).

Touchstone Touchstone
Professional fool in William Shakespeare's play
As You Like It (1599–1600).

Toussaint Toussaint l'Ouverture *(François Dominique
Toussaint) (1746–1803)*
Haitian hairdresser and revolutionary hero.

Toxotius Toxotius *(d. 379)*
Roman husband of St. Paula. They were considered the ideal married couple; she is the
patroness of widows.

Toyah Toyah *(originally Toyah Ann Wilcox) (1958–)*
British actress and singer.

Tracey Tracey Thurman *(20th century)*
American abused wife. In 1985 she won a $2.3-
million settlement against her local police
department after her ex-husband was able to stab
her thirteen times while a police officer watched.

Tracie Tracie Ruiz *(1963–)*
American swimmer, winner of an Olympic gold
medal in synchronized swimming. Her routine
began with a 50-second underwater sequence.

Trajan Emperor Trajan *(Marcus Ulpius Trajanus)*
(c. 53–117)
Respected Roman emperor. In parts of Russia he
was worshipped as a god under the name
Trajanu.

Travis Travis Walton *(1953–)*
American logger. The tale of his abduction by a
UFO was made into the film *Fire in the Sky* (1993).
> *"When I regained consciousness . . . there were
> these little men standing over me. They were
> hairless, with chalky white-gray skin. And they
> had small features except for these huge eyes."*

Treat Treat Williams (*originally Richard Williams* (*1952–*)
American actor.

Tree William "Tree" Faison (*1939–*)
American football defensive end with the San Diego Chargers, the 1961 Rookie of the Year.

Treemonisha *Treemonisha* (*1915*)
American opera by Scott Joplin in which the heroine overthrows her male oppressors through the power of education.

Tregonwell Tregonwell Frampton (*1641–1717*)
English royal horse trainer, "father of the turf."

Trevor Trevor Howard (*Trevor Wallace Howard*) (*1916–1988*)
British actor. He played Captain Bligh in *Mutiny on the Bounty* (1962).

Tricia Tricia Nixon (*20th century*)
American political worker, daughter of Richard Nixon.

Tricky Tricky Dick (*Richard Milhous Nixon*) (*1913–1994*)
American politician; 37th president.
   "I brought myself down. I gave them a sword and they stuck it in and they twisted it with relish. And I guess if I'd been in their position I'd have done the same thing."

Trigger Trigger (*20th century*)
American horse, the long-time companion of singing cowboy Roy Rogers, who had him stuffed when he died.

Trini Trini Lopez (*originally Trinidad Lopez III*) (*1937–*)
American hit singer, known for his version of "If I Had a Hammer" (1963).

Trinian St. Trinian's
Fictional British girls' boarding-school created by cartoonist Ronald Searle. The school motto is "Get your blow in first."

Tris Tris Speaker (*Tristam E. Speaker*) (*1888–1958*)
American baseball outfielder with the Indians, a member of the Hall of Fame. In 1919, he was appointed manager while still playing on the team, and continued to do both jobs until 1926.

Tristan Tristan Tzara (*20th century*)
Romanian Dada poet.
   "The Panthéon should be cut in half vertically and the two parts set 50 cm apart."

Triton Triton *trans. being in her third day*
Greek river god, the son of Poseidon and Amphritrite, a half-man with the tail of a fish.

Trixie Trixie Norton
Wife of Ed Norton on the American TV series "The Honeymooners" (1955–71).

Trofim Trofim Denisovich Lysenko (*1898–1976*)
Russian agronomist, creator of politically correct doctrines about how heredity can be changed by proper Marxist husbandry.

Troilus *The Tragedy of Troilus and Cressida* (*1598–1601*)
English play by William Shakespeare.

Troy Troy Donahue (*real name Merle Johnson, Jr.*) (*1936–*)
American actor.

Trudy *Trudy* (*1963–*)
American cartoon panel by Jerry Marcus.
   "What wine goes best with a husband who hates fish?"

Truman Truman Capote (*pseudonym of Truman Streckfus Persons*) (*1924–1984*)
American writer, author of *Breakfast at Tiffany's* (1958). He was signing an autograph for a woman when her husband became jealous, unzipped his trousers, and said, "Since you're autographing things, why don't you autograph this?" Capote replied, "I don't know if I can autograph it, but perhaps I can *initial* it."

Trungpa Trungpa Rinpoche (*20th century*)
Tibetan guru, a favourite of poet Allen Ginsberg.

Trygaeus Trygaeus
Athenian citizen in Aristophanes' comic play *Peace* (421 B.C.). As the play opens, he is feeding dung to a large beetle, hoping it will grow large enough to fly to Zeus in the heavens and beg for an end to the Peloponnesian War.

Trygve Trygve (Halvdan) Lie (*1896–1968*)
Norwegian lawyer. He introduced the phrase "cold war," saying, "Now we are in a period

which I can characterize as a period of cold peace."

Tryphena Tryphena Sparks *(d. 1890)*
English cousin of novelist Thomas Hardy. They had a brief romantic understanding.

Tsuneo Tsuneo Horiuchi *(1948–)*
Japanese baseball pitcher for the Yomiuri Giants, known as "Bad Boy Taro" for antics like spitting on television and letting his hat fall off while batting.

TWIGGY

Tubby King Tubby *(originally Osborne Lawrence)* *(1941–1989)*
Jamaican reggae dub artist.

Tuesday Tuesday Weld *(originally Susan Kerr Weld)* *(1943–)*
American actress.

Tug Tug McGraw *(Frank Edwin McGraw)* *(1944–)*
American baseball pitcher with the Mets and the Phillies, an All-Star. He gained his nickname as a breast-feeding baby, because he tugged so hard. Asked once whether he preferred grass or artificial turf, he replied, "I don't know, I never smoked Astro Turf."

Tuki Tuki Brando *(1991–)*
Tahitian grandson of American actor Marlon Brando, born after his father, Dag Drollet, was killed by his uncle Christian Brando.

Tuli Tuli Kupferberg *(1938–)*
American poet, founder of the band the Fugs, which has been described as "a perfect mixture of sacrilege, scatology, politics and rock."
"Those who will not dance will have to be shot."

Tullio Tullio Levi-Civitta *(1873–1941)*
Italian mathematician, a pioneer of the tensor calculus later used by Albert Einstein.

Turgut Turgut Özal *(1927–1993)*
Turkish politician. In 1984 he was the first civilian president elected in thirty years.

Turkey Turkey Stearnes *(Norman Stearnes)* *(1901–1979)*
American baseball outfielder for the Detroit Stars, an All-Star. His career batting average was .350.

Turpin Turpin *(or Tilpinus)* *(d. c. 794)*
French archbishop of Reims.

Tut'ankhamun Tut'ankhamun *(ruled 1333–1323 B.C.)*
Egyptian pharaoh of the 18th dynasty. His small tomb survived to modern times unrobbed.

Tuzo Tuzo Wilson *(John Tuzo Wilson)* *(1908–1993)*
Canadian geophysicist, an expert in continental drift and plate tectonics.
"The earth is my lab."

Twanyrika Twanyrika
Mythical Australian spirit. His voice can be heard in the bull-roarer.

Tweety Tweety Bird *(20th century)*
American cartoon celebrity.
"Once a bad ol' puddy tat, always a bad ol' puddy tat."

Twiggy Twiggy *(originally Leslie Hornby)* *(1946–)*
British model. Her nickname at school was "Sticks."

Twinkletoes George "Twinkletoes" Selkirk *(1908–1987)*
Canadian-born American baseball outfielder for the Yankees, an All-Star, later the general manager of the Senators.

Twyla Twyla Tharp *(1942–)*
American choreographer.
"Art is the only way to run away without leaving home."

Ty Ty Cobb *(originally Tyrus Raymond Cobb)* *(1866–1961)*
American baseball outfielder with the Braves, the "Georgia Peach." His lifetime batting average is .367.

Tycho Tycho Brahe *(1546–1601)*
Danish astronomer.

Tyne Tyne Daly *(1947–)*
American actress.

Typhoid Typhoid Mary Mallon *(cooked 1906–1925)*
American chef diagnosed as a typhoid carrier by sanitation engineer George Soper. Warned never

to handle food again, she changed her name and got two more jobs cooking (infecting more people) before being placed in permanent quarantine for the rest of her life.

Tyrannus Tyrannus *trans. tyrant, Acts 19: 9* *(1st century)*
Ephesian teacher. He let St. Paul use his classroom over the lunch hour. (The room was empty because noon was a very hot time of day.)

Tyrel Tyrel "Tye" Sackett
Hero of Louis L'Amour's Western novel *The Daybreakers* (1960).

Tyrone Tyrone Power *(Tyrone Edmund Power, Jr.)* *(1913–1958)*
American actor.

Tyson Tyson *(weighed 1989)*
British turkey. He set two Guinness records, by weighing 86 pounds when alive, and selling for £4,400. Turkeys of this size are too heavy to have sex; they reproduce only by artificial insemination.

U U Thant *(1909–1974)*
Burmese diplomat, the third secretary general of the United Nations.

U B U B Iwerks *(originally Ubbe Iwwerks)* *(1901–1971)*
American animator, co-creator with Walt Disney of Mickey Mouse.

U-Roy U-Roy *(originally Ewart Beckford) (1942–)*
Jamaican talk-over disc jockey.

Uday Uday Hussein *(20th century)*
Iraqi son of Saddam Hussein. In 1995, his father burnt down the garage containing his collection of 100 luxury imported cars.

Udolpho *Mysteries of Udolpho (1794)*
English gothic novel by Ann Radcliffe, the very first Gothic romance. It started a great fad interrupted only by the arrival of Jane Austen.

Uffe Uffe Petersen *(20th century)*
Danish geographer. In 1978, he discovered the world's most northern island, Odaaq 0. It measures 100 feet across.

Uhura Lt. Uhura
Communications officer on the Starship *Enterprise* on the American science fiction TV series "Star Trek" (1966–69). In November 1968, she and Captain Kirk shared American television's first inter-racial kiss.

Ulf Ulf von Euler *(1905–)*
Swedish physiologist, winner of a Nobel Prize for his work isolating noradrenaline.

Ulisse Ulisse Cantagalli *(d. 1902)*
Florentine pottery manufacturer.

Ulric Ulric Richard Gustav Neisser *(1928–)*
German-born American psychologist, the inventor of cognitive psychology.

Ulrike Ulrike Meinhof *(1934–1976)*
West German anarchist terrorist, a co-founder with Andreas Baader of the Red Army Faction or Baader-Meinhof Group.

Ulysse Ulysse Comtois *(1931–)*
Canadian sculptor and abstract painter.

Ulysses Ulysses S. Grant *(Ulysses Simpson Grant)* *(1822–1885)*
American soldier and 18th president, a great foe of slavery.
    "I know no method to secure the repeal of bad or obnoxious laws so effective as their stringent execution."

Uma Uma Thurman *(1970–)*
American actress, star of the film *Even Cowgirls Get the Blues* (1993).
    "Even the air is dishonest in L.A."

Umberto Umberto Eco *(1929–)*
Italian semiotician, author of the novel *The Name of the Rose* (1980).

Umm Umm Kulthum *(7th century)*
Daughter of the prophet Muhammad, wife of the caliph Uthman.

Unca Unca Eliza Winfield *(18th century)*
American novelist, author of *The Female American* (1767), inspired by the life of Pocahontas.

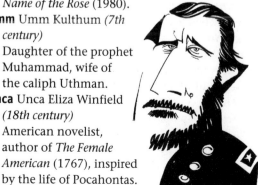

ULYSSES S. GRANT

Uncas Uncas
Noble-savage hero of James Fenimore Cooper's American novel *The Last of the Mohicans* (1826).

Unity Unity Valkyrie Mitford *(1914–1948)*
British socialite, a close friend of Adolf Hitler's.

Upton Upton Sinclair *(Upton Beall Sinclair)* *(1878–1968)*
American novelist and social reformer, author of *The Jungle* (1906).
"It is difficult to get a man to understand something when his salary depends on not understanding it."

Ur-Nammu Ur-Nammu *(ruled 2112–2095 B.C.)*
Sumerian king of Ur. He built the ziggurat mistaken by early European travellers for the tower of Babel, in Muqayyar, Iraq.

Urania Urania *trans. heavenly*
Greek Muse of Astrology. Her symbol is a globe and a pair of compasses.

Urban Urban II *(c. 1035–1099)*
French pope. His eloquence inspired the First Crusade.

Urbane Urbane Pickering *(1899–1970)*
American third baseman for the Red Sox. His only regular season was 1932, when he led American League for most errors.

Uriah Uriah Heep *(1970–)*
British rock band, named after the obsequious character in Charles Dickens' novel *David Copperfield* (1849–50).

Ursula Ursula K. Le Guin, *née Kroeber (1929–)*
American science-fiction writer, author of *The Left Hand of Darkness* (1969). She describes science fiction as "thought experiments."

Uthman Uthman *(d. 565)*
Fourth Muslim caliph. His scholars assembled the definitive Qur'an.

Uwe Uwe Beyer *(1945–1993)*
German Olympic hammer thrower. He died of a heart attack playing tennis on vacation.

Vachel Vachel Lindsay *(Nicholas Vachel Lindsay)* *(1879–1931)*
American troubadour poet.

Vaclav Vaclav Havel *(1936–)*
Czech playwright and president.

Vada Vada Prinson *(1938–1995)*
American all-star centrefielder for the Cincinnati Reds, winner of the Gold Glove.

Vagn Vagn Walfrid Ekman *(1874–1954)*
Swedish oceanographer, discoverer of the "Ekman spiral" velocity effect in deep water.

Vahan Vahan Shirvanian *(1925–)*
American cartoonist, the 1962 Best Magazine Cartoonist of the National Cartoonists Society.
"Come to bed, Ridgely. If your boomerang were going to return, it would have come back hours ago."

Val Val Logsdon Fitch *(1923–)*
American physicist, winner of a Nobel Prize.

Valdemar Valdemar Poulsen *(1869–1942)*
Danish electrical engineer, inventor of the first magnetic sound-recording device, the wire telegraphone.

Valentina Valentina Vladimirovna Tereshkova *(1937–)*
Russian astronaut, in 1963 the first woman in space.

Valentine St. Valentine *(d. c. 269)*
Roman physician beheaded during the rule of Claudius the Goth. "Valentine" love-letters are sent on his feast day, February 14, because of a mediaeval belief that birds begin to mate on that day. The saint is not associated with love.

Valeria Valeria Messalina *(c. 25–c. 48)*
Roman third wife of the Emperor Claudius. He lost patience with her many love affairs and had her executed.

Valerie Valerie Perrine *(1944–)*
American actress.

Valerio Valerio Belli *(1468–1546)*
Italian Renaissance gem-carver.

Valéry Valéry Giscard d'Estaing *(1926–)*
Conservative French president.

Vally Vally Wieselthier *(1895–1945)*
Austrian-born American ceramist. She worked with the Wiener Werkstätte.

Valmiki Valmiki *(4th century)*
Indian poet, author of the epic *Ramayama*. In the last book the lost sons of Rama are taught to read by a yogi named Valmiki. When they meet their father, the sons recite an earlier passage from the *Ramayama*, which is how he recognizes them.

Van Van Morrison *(George Van Morrison) (1945–)*
Irish singer and songwriter, creator of "Brown-eyed Girl."

Vance Vance Packard *(20th century)*
American writer, author of *The Status Seekers*.

Vanessa Vanessa Bell, *née Stephen (1879–1961)*
English painter and designer. Leonard Woolf described her attending his wedding to her sister, Virginia Stephen:

> *"In the middle of the proceeding, Vanessa interrupted the Registrar, saying: 'Excuse me interrupting; I have just remembered: we registered my son—he is two years old—in the name of Clement, and we now want to change his name to Quentin—can you tell me what I have to do?' There was a moment of astonished silence in the room. . . the Registrar stared at her with his mouth open. Then he said severely: 'One thing at a time, please, Madam.'"*

Vangelis Vangelis *(originally Odyssey Evangalos Papathanoussiou) (1943–)*
Greek synthesizer player, composer of the score for the film *Chariots of Fire* (1981).

Vanna Vanna White *(1957–)*
American TV personality.

Vannevar Vannevar Bush *(1890–1974)*
American scientist, the government administrator for the development of the first atomic bomb.

Varla Varla
Buxom American go-go dancer, one of the three main characters in *Faster Pussycat! Kill! Kill!* (1966) by Russ Meyer, who said, "It's become a woman's picture. I never thought I'd make a woman's picture, but I did."

Vasco Vasco da Gama *(c. 1469–1525)*
Portuguese navigator, the first European to sail around the Cape of Good Hope.

Vashti Vashti *trans. beautiful, Esther 1: 9 (5th century B.C.)*
Old Testament wife of King Ahasuerus. He divorced her when she refused to display herself at a banquet to impress his guests with her beauty.

Vaslav Vaslav Fomich Nijinski *(1890–1950)*
Ukrainian-born dancer and choreographer, the greatest male dancer of the 20th century. Asked if it was difficult to stay in the air as he did while jumping, Nijinski answered, "No! No! Not difficult. You have to just go up and then pause a little up there."

Vaughan Vaughan DeLeath *(1900–1943)*
American radio crooner, the first woman to work on a regular radio broadcast. Crooning was necessary because sudden loud noises broke the fragile early microphones.

Vaughn Vaughn Monroe *(1911–1973)*
American singer.

Ved Ved Parkash Mehta *(1934–)*
Indian writer, author of *Daddyji* (1972) and *Mamaji* (1979).

Vegtam "The Lay of Vegtam the Wanderer, or Edda Vegtamskvida"
Extremely old Nordic tale, sometimes called "Balder's Dream."

Veira Dr. Veira Scheibner *(20th century)*
Australian researcher who first linked Sudden Infant Death Syndrome (SIDS) with childhood immunizations.

Velvet Velvet Brown
English girl jockey, heroine of the children's novel *National Velvet* (1945) by Enid Bagnold.

Venita Venita Walker Van Caspel *(1922–)*
American stockbroker. In 1968 she became the first female member of the American Pacific Stock Exchange.

Venus Venus
Roman goddess of love and beauty.

Vera Vera Mary Brittain *(1893–1970)*
English nurse and writer, author of *Testament of Youth* (1933).

"I know one husband and wife, who whatever the official reasons given to the court for the breakup of their marriage, were really divorced because the husband believed that nobody ought to read while he was talking, and the wife that nobody ought to talk while she was reading."

Verdell Verdell Mathis *(1913–)*
American pitcher with the Memphis Red Sox, an All-Star.

Verden Verden Allen *(1944–)*
British rock musician with the band Mott the Hoople.

Verdine Verdine White *(1951–)*
American pop-soul musician with the group Earth, Wind and Fire.

Vere Vere Gordon Childe *(1892–1957)*
Australian archaeologist, author of the best-selling *What Happened in History* (1942).

Vern Vern Allison *(20th century)*
American R&B musician with the Dells.

Verner Verner von Heidenstam *(Karl Gustav Verner von Heidenstam) (1859–1940)*
Swedish writer, winner of the 1916 Nobel Prize for literature.

Vernon Vernon Castle *(1887–1918)*
American ballroom dancer, the inventor of the "Turkey Trot."

Veronica Veronica Lake *(originally Constance Francis Marie Ockelman) (1919–1973)*
American actress, known as the "Peekaboo Girl" for her hairdo, which covered one eye. She cut her hair in the interests of war safety for female machine operators, and her career vanished.

"I am a Hollywood creation. Hollywood is good at doing that sort of thing."

Verplaca Verplaca *(or Virplaca)*
Roman goddess of family harmony.

Vespasian Vespasian *(Titus Flavius Vespasianus) (9–79)*
Roman emperor. He opened the first state-sponsored school.

Vesta Vesta Tilley *(professional name of Lady de Frece, née Matilda Alice Powles) (1864–1952)*
English actress, author of *The Recollections of Vesta Tilley* (1934). She first appeared on stage at age four as the Great Little Tilley, but is most famous for her male impersonations.

Vicary Sir Vicary Gibbs *(1751–1820)*
Unsympathetic English judge, widely known as "Vinegar Gibbs."

Vicente Vicente de Espinel *(1551–1624)*
Spanish writer. He added the fifth string to the guitar.

Vicesimus Vicesimus Knox *(1752–1821)*
English essayist.

Vicki Vicki Van Meter *(1982–)*
American aviator. At age twelve, she flew across the Atlantic in a Cessna 210, accompanied by a flight instructor because she was too young to fly legally.

Vico Vico Magistretti *(20th century)*
Italian furniture designer.

Victor Victor Hugo *(Victor-Marie Hugo) (1802–1885)*
French poet, novelist, and dramatist. When he died, the prostitutes of Paris were given special government protection to join the funeral procession.

Victoria Queen Victoria *(born Alexandrina Victoria, nicknamed "Drina" as a child) (1819–1901)*
Queen of England. After seeing an imitation of herself by Alexander Grantham Yorke, a groom-in-waiting, she said,"We are not amused."

Victorien Victorien Sardou *(1831–1908)*
French dramatist. He wrote the play *Fédora* (1883) for actress Sarah Bernhardt.

Vida Vida Blue *(Vida Rochelle Blue) (1949–)*
American baseball pitcher with the As, the first black winner of a Cy Young pitching award, and the first All-Star Game winning pitcher in both leagues.

"I think I have already signed some scrap of paper for every man, woman and child in the United States. What do they do with all those scraps of paper with my signature on it?"

Vidal Vidal Sassoon *(20th century)*
International hairdressing entrepreneur.

Vidiadhar Vidiadhar Surajprasad (V.S.) Naipaul *(1932–)*
Trinidadian writer, author of *A House for Mr. Biswas* (1961).

Vidkun Vidkun Quisling *(Vidkun Abraham Lauritz Jonsson Quisling) (1887–1945)*
Norwegian politician executed after the war for his enthusiastic support for the Germans during the invasion. "Quisling" has become a generic terms for any traitor.

Vietta Vietta M. Bates *(served 1945–1949)*
American soldier. When the Women's Auxiliary Army Corps (WAAC) joined the regular army in 1949, she became the first woman sworn into the U.S. military.

Vigdís Vigdís Finnbogadóttir *(1930–)*
President of Iceland, the first woman in history elected head of state.

Viktor Viktor Meyer *(1848–1897)*
German chemist. He discovered the element thiopene, but ruined his health doing it.

Vilhelm Vilhelm Friman Koren Bjerknes *(1862–1951)*
Norwegian meteorologist, the creator of modern weather forecasting.

Vilhjalmur Vilhjalmur Stefánsson *(1879–1962)*
Canadian arctic explorer, author of *My Life with the Eskimo* (1913).

Villard Villard de Honnecourt *(worked 1225–1235)*
French Gothic mason and master craftsman.

Vilma Vilma Banky *(originally Vilma Lonchit) (c. 1930–1991)*
Hungarian silent-film actress, the "Hungarian Rhapsody." Her career was ruined by sound, which revealed her thick accent.

Vince Vince Lombardi *(Vincent Thomas Lombardi) (1913–1970)*
American football coach. His teams always won.
   "Winning isn't everything; it's the only thing."

Vincent Vincent Van Gogh *Vincent Willem Van Gogh (1853–1890)*
Dutch Post Impressionist artist, the painter of *Sunflowers* (1888).

Vincente Vincente Minnelli *(1910–1986)*
Italian-born film director, father of entertainer Liza Minnelli.

Vincenzo Vincenzo Bellini *(1801–1835)*
Italian composer of the opera *Norma* (1832).

Vinnie Vinnie Ream *(1847–1914)*
American sculptor of the Lincoln Memorial. She had previously created a much-admired portrait bust of Lincoln during five months of daily hour-long sittings.

Viola Viola MacMillan, *née Huggard (1903–1993)*
Canadian gold-rush prospector and miner. Her 1967 criminal conviction for fraudulent stock-exchange manipulation was pardoned, and she was awarded the Order of Canada.

Violet Violet Martin *(Violet Florence Martin, pseudonym Martin Ross) (1862–1915)*
Irish writer. She and her cousin Edith Somerville wrote a series of novels by "Somerville and Ross," including *An Irish Cousin* (1889).

Violeta Violeta Barrios de Chamorro *(20th century)*
Nicaraguan politician. In 1990, she defeated Daniel Ortega Saavedra.

Violette Violette Verdy *(originally Nelly Guillerm) (1933–)*
French dancer and director.

VIP Virgil Franklin "VIP" Partch II *(1916–)*
American cartoonist, winner of a first prize at the 1964 Brussels Cartoon Exhibition.

Virgil Virgil *(or Vergil, Publius Vergilius Maro) (70–19 B.C.)*
Roman poet, composer of the *Aeneid*, which describes the wanderings of Aeneas after the fall of Troy. At least one edition of this poem has been published every year for the past 500 years.
   "Love conquers all."

Virgilia Virgilia
Persuasive wife in William Shakespeare's play *Coriolanus* (1607–1608).

Virginia Virginia Woolf, *née Adeline Virginia Stephen (1882–1941)*
British novelist, author of the essay "A Room of One's Own" (1929).
   "A woman must have money and a room of her own if she is to write fiction."

VIRGINIA WOOLF

Virginie *Paul et Virginie (1788)*
Popular French tale of innocent love by Jacques Henri Berardin de Saint-Pierre.

Vita Vita Sackville-West *(Victoria Mary Sackville-West) (1892–1962)*
English aristocratic poet, novelist, and gardener. She was the model for the title character of Virginia Woolf's *Orlando.*
"I know I was cruel to other children, because I remember stuffing their nostrils with putty, and beating a little boy with stinging nettles."

Vitruvius Vitruvius *Marcus (Vitruvius Pollio) (1st century)*
Roman architect. He wrote a book on architecture which is the only Roman reference on the subject surviving.

Vitus St. Vitus *(d. c. 300)*
Sicilian-born religious worker. He was imprisoned after curing the Emperor Diocletian's son of an evil spirit, on suspicion of using sorcery, then freed when a huge storm destroyed temples. He is the patron of epileptics, dancers, and actors.

Viv Viv Richards *(20th century)*
West Indian cricket player. In 1994, he forgot an appointment to go to Buckingham Palace to collect his OBE from Prince Charles.

Viva Viva King *(1893–1979)*
English literary hostess.

Vive Vive Lindaman *(Vivian Alexander Lindaman) (1877–1927)*
American baseball pitcher for the Braves. He kept in shape by working as a mailman.

Viveca Viveca Lindfors *(Elsa Viveca Torstendotter Lindfors) (1920–1995)*
Swedish actress, voted Best Actress at the Berlin Film Festival for *No Exit* (1962).

Vivian Vivian Vance *(20th century)*
American actress, next-door neighbour Ethel on the "I Love Lucy" (1951–61) television series. Off camera, Lucy proved difficult, but Vivian resolved, "I will learn to love that bitch."

Vivien Vivien Leigh *(originally Vivien Mary Hartley) (1913–1967)*
Indian-born English actress. She played Scarlett O'Hara in *Gone With the Wind* (1939),

Vivienne Vivienne Haigh-Smith *(20th century)*
British wife of poet T.S. (Thomas Stearns) Eliot, and co-author of his early work. When she developed depression, he had her committed, and removed all references to her from his biography.

Vlad Vlad Tepes *(Vlad the Impaler) (d. 1462)*
Wallachian tyrant, son of Vlad Dracul ("Vlad the Dragon"), who was the inspiration for the fictional Count Dracula.

Vladek Vladek Spiegelman *(20th century)*
American father of Art Spiegelman, who won the Pulitzer Prize for his cartoon book *Maus: A Survivor's Tale* (1986) based in part on his father's memories of the Nazi death camps.

Vladimir Vladimir Nabokov *(1899–1977)*
Russian-born American novelist, author of the scandalous success *Lolita* (1958).

Vo Vo Nguyen Giap *(1912–)*
Vietnamese revolutionary soldier. He commanded the North Vietnamese army through the latter part of the Vietnam War.

Volpone *Volpone the Alchemist (1606)*
Elizabethan English play by Ben Jonson.

Voltumna Voltumna
Etruscan mother goddess.

Von Von Hayes *(Von Francis Hayes) (1958–)*
American baseball outfielder for the Phillies.

Von Münch Von Münch Bellinghausen *(1806–1871)*
German playwright, author of *Ingomar the Barbarian* (1851).

Vonni Vonni Ribisi *(20th century)*
American child actor on the TV series "My Two Dads" (1987–90).

Vortigern King Vortigern *(5th century)*
British ruler. He invited the Saxons into England to help him fight the Picts, which proved to be a mistake.

Vyacheslav Vyacheslav Molotov *(originally Vyacheslav Mikhaylovich Skryabin) (1890–1986)*
Long-serving Russian politician, the person assigned to vote "No" at the United Nations. Josef Stalin called him the "stone backside" for his ability to sit through endless meetings. The "Molotov cocktail" was named in his honour. (Fill small bottle with gasoline and soap; stuff with a protruding rag; light rag; throw bottle.)

Vyvyan Vyvyan Holland *(originally Vyvyan Oscar Wilde) (1886–1967)*
English son of Oscar Wilde. The family changed their name after the scandal, and he never again saw his father, though he discovered that the conviction was for homosexuality only in later life; as a child, he thought Oscar was an embezzler.
> *"When they discovered who we were, we had to leave the hotel. I was seven at the time and it has made a terrible impression on me ever since. I can't even bear to see my name in print: it gives me the horrors."*

W.C. W.C. Fields *(originally William Claude Dukenfield) (1879–1946)*
American comedian, star of the film *My Little Chickadee* (1940). During his last illness, he said, "I have spent a lot of time searching through the Bible for loopholes."

Wabash George "Wabash" Mullin *(1880–1944)*
American baseball pitcher for the Tigers. He threw a no-hitter on his birthday, July 4, 1912.

Wade Wade Hemsworth *(Albert Wade Hemsworth) (1916–)*
Canadian draftsman and folk-icon. He composed the "Blackfly Song" and many others.
> *"'Twas early in the spring, when I decide to go, to the Little Abitibi up in North Ontar-I-O . . ."*

Wahoo Wahoo Sam Crawford *(Samuel Earl Crawford) (1880–1968)*
American baseball right fielder with the Tigers, a member of the Hall of Fame. He is the only player to lead in home runs in both the National League and the American League.

Waino Waino and Plutano, the wild men of Borneo *(real names Hiram and Barney David) (performed 1850–1910)*
Developmentally disabled American circus performers.

Waite Waite Hoyt *(Waite Charles "Schoolboy" Hoyt) (1899–1984)*
American baseball pitcher with the Yankees. He had an ERA of 0.00 in 27 innings in 1921.
> *"The secret of success as a pitcher lies in getting a job with the Yankees."*

Waldo Waldo *(1940)*
American novella by Robert Heinlein. The central character, Waldo Farthingwaite-Jones, suffers from myasthenia gravis, so he develops mechanical hands, or "waldos," to do his work.

Walker Walker Evans *(1903–1975)*
American photographer. His photographs of victims of the Depression were published as *Let Us Now Praise Famous Men* (1941).

Wallace Wallace Beery *(1886–1949)*
American actor. He won an Oscar for *The Champ* (1931), the same year that Frederic March also won for *Dr. Jekyll and Mr. Hyde* (1931). After this confusion, the firm of Price Waterhouse was hired to count the votes more carefully.

Wallis Wallis Warfield, Duchess of Windsor *(previously Mrs. Earl Spencer and Mrs. Ernest Simpson) (1896–1986)*
American-born threat to the throne of England, the wife of ex-king Edward VIII.
> *"A woman's life can really be a succession of lives, each revolving around some emotionally compelling situation or challenge, and each marked off by some intense experience."*

Wally Wally Pipp *(20th century)*
American first baseman for the New York Yankees. On June 2, 1925, he pretended to have a headache, to get the day off to go the racetrack. He was replaced by Lou Gehrig, playing the first of what proved to be 2,130 consecutive games.

Walpurga St. Walpurga *(or Walburga, or Walpurgis)* *(c. 710–c. 779)*
English religious worker. The witches' feast night of April 30 is called "Walpurgis Night" because her relics were transferred from one church to another on that evening about A.D. 870.

Walt Walt Disney *(Walter Elias Disney) (1901–1966)*
American amusement entrepreneur. In 1938, he was awarded a special Academy Award for *Snow White*, with one large statue and seven smaller ones.

Walter Sir Walter Scott *(1771–1832)*
Scottish novelist. He caught polio as a child and was sent to a farm to recover, his first exposure to the Scottish Border country so important to his later work.

Walther Walther Flemming *(1843–1915)*
German biologist, inventor of the term "mitosis."

Wanda Wanda Landowska *(1879–1959)*
Polish pianist, harpsichordist and scholar.

Warner Warner Baxter *(1891–1951)*
American actor. He won an Academy Award playing the Cisco Kid in *In Old Arizona* (1929).

Warren Warren Gamaliel Harding *(1865–1923)*
American 29th president, noted for the scandalous corruption of his supporters. His father, Dr. George T. Harding, once said, "If you were a girl, Warren, you'd be in the family way all the time. You can't say no."

Warrior Bob "Warrior" Friend *(1930–)*
American baseball pitcher for the Pirates, an All-Star. His career-win percentage of .461 is the lowest of any pitcher involved in 400 or more decisions.

Warwick Warwick Windridge Armstrong *(1879–1947)*
Australian cricket player, a giant in the sport: he weighed 308 pounds at retirement.

Washington Washington Irving *(1783–1859)*
American short-story writer, author of "Rip Van Winkle" (1820).
> *"A sharp tongue is the only edged tool that grows keener with constant use."*

Washoe Washoe *(20th century)*
American chimpanzee, a pioneer of chimp sign-language.

Wassily Wassily Kandinsky *(1866–1944)*
Russian-born painter. He became a teacher at the Bauhaus, then moved to France when the Bauhaus was closed by the Nazis.

Wat Wat Tyler *(Walter Tyler) (d. 1381)*
English rebel, leader of the Peasants' Revolt of 1381. He was injured in the struggle and taken to hospital, then hauled out of his bed by the Mayor of London and beheaded.

Wati Wati *(c. 2400 B.C.)*
Egyptian court musician. His mummy, the oldest complete one known, was discovered in 1944.

Waylon Waylon Jennings *(1937–)*
American country singer.

Wayne Wayne Gretzky *(1961–)*
Canadian hockey player, the "Great One." He is the winner of twenty-three trophies, including nine for leading scorer, nine for Most Valuable Player, and two for gentlemanly conduct.

Weasel Weasel Spagnola *(20th century)*
American rocker, member of the 1960s psychedelic band the Electric Prunes.

Webster Webster Thayer *(20th century)*
American judge. In 1927, he found Nicola Sacco and Bartolomeo Vanzetti guity of murder, and refused a motion to consider new evidence, boasting in private, "Did you see what I did to those anarchist bastards?"

Weedon Weedon Grossmith *(1854–1919)*
English humorist, co-author of "Diary of a Nobody" (1892) in *Punch* magazine.
> *"I left the room with silent dignity, but caught my foot in the mat."*

Weegee Weegee *(real name Arthur Fellig) (20th century)*
American news photographer.

Wells Wells Windemut Coates *(1895–1958)*
Japanese-born English Modernist architect.

Wenceslas St. Wenceslas *(or Wenceslaus, or Vaclav)* *(c. 907–929)*
Prince Duke of Bohemia, the "Good King Wenceslas" mentioned in the Christmas carol.

Wendell Wendell Phillips *(1811–1884)*
American orator, abolitionist, and feminist.
> *"You can always get the truth from an American statesman after he has turned seventy, or given up all hope of the Presidency."*

Wendy Wendy Darling
English Mother of Lost Boys in *Peter Pan* (1904). J.M. (James Matthew) Barrie invented her name from his own childhood nickname of "fwendy-wendy."

Wep William Edwin "Wep" Pidgeon *(1909–)*
Australian cartoonist.

Werner Werner Forssmann *(1904–1979)*
German surgeon, inventor of the technique for sliding a catheter up a vein to reach the heart. Unable to get permission to test the concept on a patient, he tried it out on himself. Thirty years later, he was awarded a Nobel Prize.

Wernher Wernher von Braun *(1912–1977)*
German-born engineer, designer of the V-2 ballistic missile.

Wes Wes Farrell *(1940–)*
American songwriter and producer. His song "Boys" was covered on the first Beatles album.

Wesley Wesley Snipes *(1963–)*
American actor.

Westbrook Westbrook Pegler *(James Westbrook Pegler) (1894–1969)*
American sportswriter, winner of a Pulitzer Prize.
> *"For the fifth year in succession I have pored over the catalogue of dogs in the show at Madison Square Garden without finding a dog named Rover, Towser, Sport, Spot or Fido. Who is the man who can call from his back door at night: 'Here Champion Alexander of Clane o' Wind-Holme! Here Champion Alexander of Clane o' Wind-Holme!'?"*

Wheeler Wheeler B. Lippes *(20th century)*
American navy Pharmacist's Mate. In 1942, he removed an inflamed appendix from fellow-sailor Darrell Rector in mid-Pacific, inspiring the film *Destination Tokyo* (1943).

Whipple Mr. Whipple
American TV ad spokesperson for Charmin brand toilet paper, played for years by actor Dick Wilson.
> *"I said to my mother, 'I'm going to be an actor.' She said, 'You'll wind up in the toilet.'"*

Whitcomb Whitcomb L. Judson *(1836–1909)*
American inventor of the zipper. It was twenty years after his first patent in 1893 before the zipper worked properly. During that time there was never, ever, a repeat customer.

Whitey Whitey Ford *(Charles Edward "Slick" Ford) (1926–)*
American baseball pitcher for the New York Yankees. In 1953, he topped the Yankees in wins (18) and innings pitched (207), and in 1961 broke Babe Ruth's record for consecutive scoreless innings in World Series play. Mickey Mantle wrote *Whitey and Mickey* (1977) about their friendship.

Whitney Whitney Houston *(1963–)*
American singer.

Whittaker Whittaker Chambers *(originally Jay Vivian Chambers) (1910–1965)*
American editor of *Time* magazine. He helped to convict civil servant Alger Hiss by claiming to have found microfilm, inside a pumpkin, of a document describing State Department secrets, typed on Hiss's typewriter.

Whittle K. Whittle Martin *(20th century)*
British surgeon. In 1987, he removed a world's record 23,530 gallstones from an eighty-five-year-old woman.

Whizzer Whizzer White *(Byron Raymond White) (1917–)*
American football running back. He is the only American professional football player to have later become a Supreme Court justice.

Wilbert Wilbert Hart *(1947–)*
American soul singer with the Delfonics.

Wilbur Wilbur Wright *(1867–1912)*
American aviation pioneer. He and his brother Orville were the first to fly a heavier-than-air vehicle, in 1903 at Kitty Hawk, North Carolina.

Wild Wild Bill Hickok *(James Butler Hickok) (1837–1876)*
U.S. marshal. He did not return Calamity Jane Burke's romantic passion for him, and when she arranged for herself to be buried beside his grave, a bystander was heard to remark, "It's a good thing Bill is dead. He'd never 'a stood for this."

Wilder Wilder Graves Penfield *(1891–1976)*
American-born Canadian neurosurgeon. He accepted American CIA funding for brainwashing experiments on unwitting civilian patients at the Montreal Neurological Institute.

Wildfire Wildfire Schulte *(Frank M. Schulte) (1882–1949)*
American baseball outfielder with the Cubs, winner of the first National League Most Valuable Player award.

Wiley Wiley Post *(1899–1935)*
American aviator. He set an air record by flying around the world in 8 days, 15 hours, and 51 minutes, beating the previous record of 21 days set by the Graf Zeppelin. He died in an air crash.

Wilf Wilf Carter *(Wilfred Arthur Charles Carter) (1904–)*
Canadian folk-singer in the Jimmie Rodgers yodelling style.

Wilfred Wilfred Thesiger *(Wilfred Patrick Thesiger) (1910–)*
Ethiopian-born British writer and explorer of Arabia, author of *The Life of My Choice* (1987).

Wilfrid St. Wilfrid *(or Wilfith) (634–709)*
English religious worker. He believed in the tonsure haircut.

Wilhelm Wilhelm Reich *(1897–1957)*
Austrian-born American psychoanalyst, inventor of the "orgone accumulator" machine to improve the sex life of patients.
"The few bad poems which occasionally are created during abstinence are of no great interest."

Wilhelmina Queen Wilhelmina *(Helena Pauline Maria Wilhelmina of Orange-Nassau) (1880–1962)*
Queen of the Netherlands, author of the autobiography *Lonely But Not Alone* (1960). When Kaiser Wilhelm II boasted that his guardsmen were seven feet tall, she replied, "And when we open our dykes, the waters are ten feet deep."

Wilkie Wilkie Collins *(William Wilkie Collins) (1824–1889)*
British novelist, author of *The Moonstone* (1868) and *The Woman in White* (1860). The real "woman in white" was Caroline Greaves, with whom Wilkie lived for nine years after they met as described in the novel.

Wilkins Wilkins Micawber
Feckless optimist in Charles Dickens's novel *David Copperfield* (1849–50).
"Annual income twenty pounds, annual expenditures 19 six, result happiness. Annual income 20 pounds, annual expenditures 20 pounds ought and six, result misery."

Wilko Wilko Johnson *(originally John Wilkinson) (1947–)*
British R&B guitarist with the band Dr. Feelgood.

Will Will Rogers *(William Penn Adair Rogers) (1879–1935)*
American actor-philosopher. His first book was called *The Cowboy Philosopher at the Peace Conference* (1919).
"I never met a man I didn't like."

Willa Willa Cather *(Willa Sibert Cather) (1876–1947)*
American novelist. She describes her theories about fiction in *Not Under Forty* (1936).

Willard Willard Frank Libby *(1908–1980)*
American chemist, winner of the 1940 Nobel Prize. He discovered how to date archaeological remains using Carbon-14.

225 / **Willebrod–Winsor**

Willebrod Willebrod van Roijen Snell *(or Willebrod van Roijen Snellius) (1580–1626)*
Dutch mathematician and optician. He discovered Snell's Law of refraction.

Willem Willem Corneliszoon Schouten *(c. 1580–1625)*
Dutch mariner, the first man to sail round Cape Horn.

William William S. Burroughs *(William Seward Burroughs) (1914–)*
American writer and heroin addict, author of *Naked Lunch* (1959).
　　"I love life, but not the one I have."

Williamina Williamina Paton Fleming, *née Stevens (1857–1911)*
Scottish-born American astronomer. She discovered "white dwarf" stars.

Willie Willie Mays *(Willie Howard Mays) (1931–)*
American baseball all-round genius, the "Say Hey Kid," a member of the Hall of Fame.
After a play in which he caught the ball, spun 360 degrees counter-clockwise, and threw it in time to catch a runner out, his manager said, "I won't believe that play until I see him do it again."

Willis Willis Haviland Carrier *(1876–1950)*
American engineer, a pioneer of air-conditioning.

Wills Wills *(His Royal Highness Prince William Arthur Louis of Wales) (1982–)*
British heir.

Willy Willy Messerschmitt *(Wilhelm Messerschmitt) (1898–1978)*
German aeronautical engineer, the principal supplier of airplanes to the Luftwaffe. He created the BF109 Messerschmitt fighter.

Wilma Wilma Rudolph *(1940–1994)*
American athlete, winner of three gold medals in running at the 1960 Olympics. At age four she survived double pneumonia followed by scarlet fever and then polio. At age nine, she removed her leg brace and became an athlete.

Wilson Wilson Pickett *(1941–)*
American blues musician, "Wicked Pickett."

Wilt Wilt Chamberlain *(Wilton Norman Chamberlain) (1936–)*
American basketball player, "Wilt the Stilt." He once described himself as being "just like any other seven-foot black millionaire who lives next door."

Wilver Wilver Dornell Stargell *(known as Willie "Pops" Stargell) (1940–)*
American baseball outfielder with the Pirates, winner of six Gold Glove awards, a member of the Hall of Fame. He is the only player to have hit a ball completely out of Dodger Stadium, which he's done twice.

Wim Wim Wenders *(1945–)*
West German filmmaker, creator of *Paris, Texas* (1984).

Winfield General Winfield Scott *(1786–1866)*
American soldier. He put Santa Ana to flight in Mexico but lost a presidential election because under the electoral college system, his 44 percent of the popular vote translated into wins in only four of thirty-one states.

Winifred Winifred Goldring *(1888–1971)*
American paleontologist, the first female president of the American Paleontological Society.

Winnie Winnie *(short for Winnipeg) (d. 1932)*
Canadian–born British black bear. As a resident of the London Zoo, he was often admired by young Christopher Milne. A statue of him stands in his home town of White River, Ontario.

Winona Winona Ryder *(originally Winona Laura Horowitz) (1971–)*
American actress. She was born in Winona, Minnesota.

Winslow Winslow Homer *(1836–1910)*
American painter.
　　"Never put more than two waves in a picture. It's fussy."

Winsor Winsor McCay *(1871–1934)*
American animator, creator of the first animated short feature film, *The Sinking of the Lusitania* (1918).

Winston Sir Winston Churchill *(Winston Leonard Spencer Churchill) (1874–1965)*
British prime minister. He was the first commoner whose funeral was attended by a reigning monarch.
> *"There is no finer investment for any community that putting milk into babies."*

Winthrop Winthrop Mackworth Praed *(1802–1839)*
English poet.
> *"His talk was like a stream which runs*
> *With rapid change from rocks to roses,*
> *It slipped from politics to puns;*
> *it passed from Mahomet to Moses."*

Witold Witold Rybczynski *(1943–)*
Canadian architect, author of *Waiting for the Weekend* (1991).

Wittner Wittner Bynner *(b. 1881)*
American poet.
> *"The look in your eyes*
> *Was as soft as the underside of soap in a soap-dish."*

Wolcott Wolcott Gibbs *(1902–)*
American writer.
> *"He wasn't exactly hostile to facts, but he was apathetic about them."*

Wole Wole Soyinka *(pen-name of Akinwande Oluwole Soyinka) (1934–)*
Nigerian Ibo poet and novelist, winner of the 1986 Nobel Prize for literature.

Wolf Wolf Rössler *(c. 1650–1717)*
German goldsmith.

Wolfgang Wolfgang Amadeus Mozart *(full name Johannes Chrysostomus Wolfgangus Theophilus Mozart (1756–1791)*
Austrian composer, a genius from boyhood.

Wolfhart Wolfhart Pannenberg *(1928–)*
German Lutheran theologian.

Wolfman Wolfman Jack *(20th century)*
American rock disc jockey.

Wolfram Wolfram von Eschenbach *(13th century)*
German poet. He wrote the poem *Parsifal* used by Richard Wagner as the libretto to his opera.

Woodes Woodes Rogers *(d. 1732)*
English navigator, author of *Voyage Round the World* (1712).

Woodrow Woodrow Wilson *(Thomas Woodrow Wilson) (1856–1924)*
American 28th president, inventor of income tax.
> *"No one can worship God or love his nieghbour on an empty stomach."*

Woody Woody Allen *(originally Allen Stewart Konisberg) (1935–)*
American film auteur, of *Bananas* (1971).
> *"I don't want to achieve immortality through my work. . . . I want to achieve it through not dying."*

Wooley Stewart "Wooley" Wolstenholme *(1947–)*
English progressive-rock mellotron player.

Worf Lt. Worf
Klingon security officer on board the USS *Enterprise* on the American TV series "Star Trek: The Next Generation" (d. 1994).

Woroka Woroka *(19th century)*
Plute Indian utopian visionary, inspirer of the Ghost Dancer movement.

Worthy Frederic Franklin "Worthy" Worthington *(1890–1967)*
Scottish-born Canadian military worker, designer of the prototype for the Sherman Tank. In 1917, he was court-martialled for tampering with a machine-gun, until it was discovered that his tampering had improved it.

Wratislaw Duke Wratislaw *(or Ratislav) (d. c. 920)*
Bohemian father of St. Wenceslas.

Wray Wray Carlton *(1937–)*
American football running back with the Buffalo Bills.

Wrong Way Douglas "Wrong Way" Corrigan *(1907–1995)*
American pilot. Refused for a trans-atlantic flight permit in 1938, by authorities concerned about the safety of his $310 airplane, he took off to return to California, then flew to Ireland instead, claiming his compass froze.

Wulfstan St. Wulfstan *(or Wulstan) (c. 1008–1095)*
Anglo-Saxon religious worker, the only bishop to keep his job after the Norman Conquest of England. He helped compile the *Domesday Book*.

Wurzel Wurzel *(originally Michael Burston) (1949–)*
British rocker with the band Motörhead.

Wyatt Wyatt Earp *(Wyatt Berry Stapp Earp)* *(1848–1929)*
American lawman of Tombstone, Arizona. He won the shoot-out at the O.K. Corral accompanied by his brothers Morgan and Virgil, and Doc Holliday. The outlaws staged a later ambush, but Wyatt hunted them down, retiring only after getting the last one. Doc Holliday died in bed of consumption.

Wyndham Wyndham Lewis *(Percy Wyndham Lewis)* *(1884–1957)*
British novelist and artist.

Wynonna Wynonna Judd *(originally Christina Claire Ciminella) (1964–)*
American country singer, half of a duo with her mother, Naomi Judd.

Wynton Wynton Marsalis *(1961–)*
American jazz trumpeter. At age fourteen he appeared with the New Orleans Philharmonic Orchestra, playing music by Franz Joseph Haydn.

Wystan Wystan Hugh (W.H.) Auden *(1907–1973)*
British poet.
> *"Only those in the last stage of disease could believe that children are true judges of character."*

Xanthippe Xanthippe *(active 4th century B.C.)*
Semi-legendary shrewish wife of Greek philosopher Socrates.

Xanthus Xanthus *trans. yellow*
Greek horse, the twin of Balius. Hera gave these horses the power of speech, which they used to warn Achilles of his coming death at Troy.

Xavier Xavier Cugat *(originally Francisco de Asis Javier Cugat Mingall de Bru y Deulofeo)* *(1900–1990)*
Spanish Latin-dance-band leader.

Xaviera Xaviera Hollander *(originally Vera de Vries)* *(1944–)*
Dutch-born writer, the "Happy Hooker."
> *"I'm Vera de Vries, the Homely Homemaker, during the day. . . . Xaviera Hollander only comes out at night. . ."*

Xenophon Xenophon *(c. 435–354 B.C.)*
Greek military historian. He became overenthusiastic about his subject matter and was banned from Athens for fighting for Sparta.

Xenu Xenu
Extraterrestial tyrant. Some authorities claim that he is the source of the troubles solvable by the Church of Scientology, because, in destroying other aliens 75 million years ago, he freed their spirits, called "thetans," to attack humans. Luckily, thetans can be purged through courses in Scientology.

Xerxes Xerxes I *(ruled 486–465 B.C.)*
King of Persia, son of Darius I. He sacked Athens, but it was abandoned at the time. He may be the biblical Ahasuerus (Ezra 4: 6).

Xochiquetzal Xochiquetzal
Aztec goddess of flowers and craftsmen, the patron of prostitutes.

Xuxa Xuxa *(originally Maria da Graca Meneghal)* *(active 1990s)*
Brazilian soft-core porno actress and children's entertainer, "one of the few authentic blondes in Latin America."

XAVIER CUGAT

Yakima Yakima Canutt *(originally Enos Edward Canutt) (1895–1986)*
American rodeo rider and film stunt man. He directed the chariot race in *Ben-Hur* (1959).

Yanni Yanni *(originally Chryossomallis) (1955–)*
Greek-born New Age singer/composer.

Yao Yao Wenyuan *(20th century)*
Chinese journalist, one of the Gang of Four.

Yaphet Yaphet Kotto *(1937–)*
American-born movie actor.

Yasmin Yasmin Aga Khan *(20th century)*
Princess daughter of Rita Hayworth.

YOKO ONO

Yasser Yasser Arafat *(Mohammed Abed Ar'ouf Arafat) (1929–)* Palestinian politician. In 1988, he renounced terrorism, and in 1996 was elected the first president of Palestinian Authority.

Yasuo Yasuo Kuroki *(20th century)*
Japanese industrial designer, stylist of the first Sony Walkman.

Yat Yat Tittle *(Yelverton Abraham Tittle) (1926–)*
American football quarterback with the San Francisco 49ers.

Yaz Carl "Yaz" Yastrzemski *(1939–)*
American baseball outfielder with the Red Sox, winner of five Gold Gloves, a member of the Hall of Fame. During the 1960s he collected the most hits of any American League player, in 1967 winning a Triple Crown (.326 BA, 44 homers, 121 RBI).

Yazid Yazid *(d. 683)*
Second Umayyad caliph of Egypt.

Ycu Ycu *(1972–)*
Thai crocodile, the largest in captivity, a hydrid estuarine/Siamese 19'8" long.

Yehudi Sir Yehudi Menuhin *(1916–)*
American-born British violinist and conductor. He made his début at age seven.

Yelenna Yelenna Bonner *(1923–)*
Soviet civil-rights activist, the wife of Andrei Sakharov.

Yellow Yellow Kid *(Joseph Weil) (b. 1877)*
American swindler. He specialized in renting recently vacated banks for just an hour or two.
"I never cheated an honest man, only rascals."

Yemelyan Yemelyan Ivanovich Pugachov *(1726–1775)*
Russian Cossack soldier. After fighting in the Seven Years' War, he began a career as an imposter, pretending to be Catherine the Great's dead husband, Peter III. She had him transported to Moscow in an iron cage and executed.

Yevgeny Yevgeny Ivanovich Zamyatin *(1884–1937)*
Russian writer. His novel *We* (1920) helped to inspire Aldous Huxley's *Brave New World* and George Orwell's *Nineteen Eighty-Four*.

Yggdrasil Yggdrasil
Nordic world tree. The wicked squirrel Ratatösk ran up and down its trunk trying to cause trouble between the eagle at the top and the dragon at the bottom.

Yip Yip Harburg *(originally Isidore Hochberg) (1898–1981)*
American librettist. He wrote the song lyrics for "Buddy, Can You Spare a Dime?" (1932) and "Lydia the Tattooed Lady" (1939).

Yitzhak Yitzhak Shamir *(originally Yitzhak Jazernicki) (1915–)*
Polish-born Israeli prime minister. He emigrated to Israel at the age of twenty.

Yma Yma Sumac *(originally Emperatiz Chavarri) (1922–)*
Peruvian singer.
"I am a very simple person. Sometimes I forget I am a descendant of an Incan king. I am a human being—like you."

Yo-Yo Yo-Yo Ma *(1955–)*
French cellist.

Yoda Yoda
Prescient alien guru in the American film *Star Wars* (1977).

Yogi Yogi Berra *(originally Lawrence Peter Berra) (1925–)*
American baseball catcher with the Yankees, a record-setting member of the Hall of Fame. He got his nickname because his childhood friends thought he looked like a Hindu yogi they saw in a film travelogue.
"It's déjà vu all over again."

Yoko Yoko Ono *(1933–)*
Japanese-born artist and widow. Joan Rivers said, "If I found her floating in my pool, I'd punish my dog."

Yorick Yorick
Dead jester of William Shakespeare's play *Hamlet* (1600–1601).
"Alas, poor Yorick, I knew him well."

Yoshihito Yoshihito *(posthumous title Taisho Tenno)* *(1879–1926)*
Emperor of Japan. His son Hirohito served as regent during his last years.

Yousuf Yousuf Karsh *(1908–)*
Armenian-born Canadian portrait photographer. His subjects speak of being "Karshed."

Yukiko Yukiko Sugihara *(20th century)*
Japanese wife of consul Chiune Sugihara. During the Second World War, she massaged his hands at night to sooth the cramps created by spending all day writing transit visas to save Jewish refugees.

Yukio Yukio Mishima *(pen name of Hiraoka Kimitake) (1925–1970)*
Japanese author, icon and ritual suicide, author of *Confessions of a Mask* (1949).

Yul Yul Brynner *(originally Taidje Kahn, Jr.)* *(1915–1985)*
Japanese-born American actor. He won an Oscar for *The King and I* (1956).

Yuri Yuri Gagarin *(Yuri Alexeyevich Gagarin)* *(1934–1968)*
Soviet cosmonaut. On April 12, 1961, he became the first man in space.

Yvan Yvan Cournoyer *(1943–)*
Canadian hockey player with the Montreal Canadiens.

Yves Yves Klein *(1928–1962)*
French painter. He invented the colour "Klein blue."

Yvette Yvette Guilbert *(c. 1869–1944)*
French music-hall star. She is remembered chiefly for the poster created for her in 1894 by Henri de Toulouse-Lautrec.

Yvonne Yvonne Printemps *(20th century)*
French actress. Her ex-husband, playwright Sacha Guitry, suggested as the epitaph for her tomb, "Here lies Yvonne Printemps—for the first time cold."

Zacchaeus Zacchaeus *trans. pure, Luke 19: 1* *(1st century)*
Wealthy tax collector of Jericho, who had to climb a tree to see Jesus because he was so short. When Jesus chose to stay in his house, his followers muttered unhappily about "tax collectors and sinners."

Zachary General Zachary Taylor *(1784–1850)*
American 12th president, "Old Rough and Ready." His daughter became Jefferson Davis's first wife.

Zack Zack "Buck" Wheat *(1888–1972)*
American baseball outfielder for the Dodgers, a member of the Hall of Fame. In the last season of his nineteen-year career, playing with an injured leg, he hit a home run out of the field, then got such bad leg cramps that it took him five minutes to creep from second base to home.

Zadig "Zadig" *(1749)*
French short story by Voltaire (François-Marie Arouet) written while he was hiding out from political foes at the house of the Duchess de Maine.

Zadkiel Zadkiel *(real name Richard James Morrison)* *(1794–1874)*
English astrologer, author of *Zadkiel's Almanac*.

Zal Zal Yanovsky *(1944–)*
Canadian-born pop guitarist with the group the Lovin' Spoonful.

Zandra Zandra Rhodes *(1940–)*
British textile and dress designer.

Zane Zane Grey *(pseudonym of Pearl Grey)* *(1875–1939)*
American dentist. He assumed his mother's maiden name of Zane when he started writing cowboy fiction such as *Riders of the Purple Sage*.

Zani Zani *(16th century)*
Italian *commedia dell'arte* stock buffoon character. He inspired the English adjective "zany."

Zappafrank Zappafrank *(named 1994)*
Asteroid orbiting between Mars and Jupiter. It is named, of course, in honour of Frank Zappa.

Zara Zara Anne Elizabeth *(1981–)*
British daughter of Princess Anne.

Zarathustra *Also Sprach Zarathustra (1883–1892)*
German book by Friedrich Nietzsche.

ZaSu ZaSu Pitts *(1898–1963)*
American actress named after her two aunts, Eliza and Susan. She hit W.C. Fields on the head with a rolling pin in the film *Mrs. Wiggs of the Cabbage Patch* (1934).

Zayed Zayed ibn Sultan al-Shaykh Nahayan *(1918–)*
President of the United Arab Emirates.

Zaza Zaza *trans. moving, I Chronicles 2: 33*
Old Testament member of the tribe of Judah.

Zdenko Zdenko Fibich *(1850–1900)*
Czech composer.

Zeb Zeb Terry *(Zebulon Alexander Terry) (b. 1891)*
American baseball shortstop for the Cubs.

Zebedee Zebedee *trans. my gift, Mark 1: 19*
(1st century)
Palestian fisherman, father of the disciples James and John. The traditional site of the "fish shop of Zebedee" in Jerusalem is now occupied by a small Crusader church converted into a coffee-house.

Zebulon General Zebulon M. Pike *(1779–1813)*
American military man. Pike's Peak is named after him.

Zee Zee James, *née Zerelda Mimms (married 1874)*
American cousin and wife of the outlaw Jesse James.

Zeke Zeke O'Connor *(1926–)*
American-born footbal player with the Toronto Argonauts. In 1995, he invented a stuffed Yeti toy to raise money for the Sherpa people of Nepal.

Zelda Zelda Fitzgerald, *née Sayre (1899–1948)*
American aspiring dancer, the wife of writer F. Scott Fitzgerald. He observed, "Sometimes I don't know whether Zelda and I are real or whether we are characters in one of my novels."

ZERO MOSTEL

Zelman Sir Zelman Cowen *(1919–)*
Australian lawyer and TV personality.

Zenko Zenko Suzuki *(1911–)*
Japanese politician.

Zeno Zeno of Citium *(334–262 B.C.)*
Greek philosopher, the founder of Stoicism. His movement got its name from his school's location in the Stoa Poikile ("Painted Colonnade").

Zénobe Zénobe Théophile Gramme *(1876–1901)*
Belgian electrical engineer, inventor of the "Gramme Ring" armature for direct current dynamos.

Zenobia Zenobia *(3rd century)*
Queen of Palmyra. After her husband's death, she conquered much of Asia Minor before being captured herself by the Romans and paraded through the streets of Rome in golden chains.

Zeppo Zeppo Marx *(originally Herbert Marx)*
(1901–1979)
American comic, the straight man of the Marx Brothers.

Zerelda Zerelda Cole James *(19th century)*
American mother of robbers Frank and Jesse James.

Zero Zero Mostel *(Samuel Joel Mostel) (1915–1977)*
American character actor. His nickname was inspired by his marks in grade school.

Zerubbabel Zerubbabel *trans. seed of Babylon, I Chronicles 3: 19 (c. 6th century B.C.)*
Old Testament Judean prince. Carried into captivity in Babylon in 598 B.C., he later led the return to Jerusalem, organized the rebuilding of the Temple, and then either vanished or changed his name.

Zeus Zeus *trans. bright sky*
Greek god, sixth child of Rhea and Cronus. Cronus swallowed all his children at birth until Rhea hid Zeus by giving Cronus a rock to swallow instead. Grown up, Zeus gave Cronus an emetic drug, making him vomit up all the other children. Then they overthrew him.

Zeuxis Zeuxis *(5th century B.C.)*
Greek painter. He painted a bunch of grapes so realistic that birds tried to peck it.
"Criticism comes easier than craftsmanship."

Zhisui Li Zhisui *(1920–1995)*
Chinese doctor, the physician of Mao Zedong about whom he wrote an unflattering memoir in old age.

Zia Zia Mahmood *(20th century)*
Pakistani bridge player.

Ziggy Ziggy Stardust *(b. 1972)*
Glitter alter ego of David Bowie.

Zimmy A.A. "Zimmy" Zimmerman *(1869–1936)*
American bicycle racer. At the peak of his popularity in the 1890s, he marketed a line of Zimmy brand clothing.

Zindzi Zindzi Mandela *(20th century)*
South African daughter of Nelson and Winnie Mandela, sister of Zenani.

Zipporah Zipporah *Exodus 2: 21 (c. 13th century B.C.)*
Old Testament daughter of priest Jethro. He married her to Moses as a reward for Moses helping to water his flocks one day. She circumcized her second son herself, using a sharp flint.

Ziraldo Ziraldo Alves Pinto *(1932–)*
Brazilian cartoonist, creator of the character Supermae ("Supermom").

Zita St. Zita *(1218–1278)*
Tuscan housemaid. Disliked at first by her fellow servants for her excessive diligence, she won them over, and is now the patroness of servants.

Ziva Ziva Buganim *(20th century)*
Israeli prostitute, the mistress of ill-fated heir David Reichmann.

Zoë Zoë Akins *(1858–1886)*
American playwright.
> *"Nothing seems so tragic to one who is old as the death of one who is young, and this alone proves that life is a good thing."*

Zog Zog I *(originally Ahmed Bey Zogu) (1895–1961)*
King of the Albanians.

Zoilo Zoilo "Zorro" Versalles *(1939–)*
Cuban-born American baseball shortstop with the Senators, winner of a Gold Glove Award, the 1965 American League Most Valuable Player.

Zoltán Zoltán Kodály *(1882–1967)*
Hungarian composer, and inventor of the Kodály method for teaching music to children.

Zona Zona Gale *(1874–1938)*
American writer, author of the novel *Miss Lulu Bett* (c. 1920).
> *"The private kitchen must go the way of the spinning wheel, of which it is the contemporary."*

Zooey *Franny and Zooey (1961)*
American novel by J.D. (Jerome David) Salinger.

Zoot Zoot Sims *(John Haley Sims) (1925–1985)*
American jazz saxophone player.

Zophar Zophar *Job 11: 5*
Old Testament friend of Job, one of three friends who tried to persuade Job that he must be guilty of something for God to punish him with such misfortunes. However, God was punishing Job to prove a point to the devil and, after, demanded that Zophar and the others apologize.

Zora Zora Neale Thurston *(1891–1960)*
American writer.
> *"It is one of the blessings of this world that few people see visions and dream dreams."*

Zorba *Zorba the Greek (1964)*
American movie starring Anthony Quinn based on the novel by Nikos Kazantzakis. *Time Out* magazine called it "the dreadful movie that launched a thousand package tours."

Zoroaster Zoroaster *(also called Zarathustra or Zaradusht Spitama) (c. 630–c. 553 BC)*
Iranian Parsee prophet.

Zou *Zou-Zou (1934)*
French movie starring the immortal Josephine Baker.

Zowie Zowie Bowie *(known as Joey Bowie) (1972–)*
Celebrity son of David Bowie.

Zsa Zsa Zsa Zsa Gabor *(originally Sari Gabor) (1918–)*
Hungarian-born character actress. In 1936, she had to give up the Miss Hungary title when it was discovered she was not yet sixteen.
> *"Never despise what it says in women's magazines: it may not be subtle, but neither are men."*

Zubin Zubin Mehta *(1936–)*
Israeli conductor.

Zuleika *Zuleika Dobson (1912)*
Ironic British novel by Sir Max Beerbohm.
"Beauty and the lust for learning have yet to be allied."

Zulema Zulema Menem *(20th century)*
Argentinian first lady, a devotee of plastic surgery.
"One wants to look well for one's husband."

Zulemita Zulemita Menem *(20th century)*
Argentinian daughter of first lady Zulema Menem. Describing her mother's penchant for plastic surgery, she said, "Soon, she'll look like the daughter and I the mother."

Zulfikar Zulfikar Ali Bhutto *(1928–1979)*
Pakistani politician, the father of Benazir Bhutto. In 1977, his party won the elections but he was overthrown by a military coup and executed.

Zura Janusz "Zura" Zurakowski *(c. 1934–)*
Canadian test-pilot who took the legendary Avro Arrow on its maiden flight.

Zuri Zuri Forgie *(1987–)*
Canadian quintuplet.

Zygmunt Zygmunt Florenty von Wróblewski *(1845–1888)*
Polish physicist. He could liquify gaseous air.